Religious Perspectives on Business Ethics

RELIGION AND BUSINESS ETHICS

Series Editors: Thomas O'Brien and Scott Paeth, both of DePaul University

Rowman & Littlefield's *Religion and Business Ethics Series* bridges the gap between the field of business ethics and the study of religion. Business ethics is perennially an important field in applied ethics, yet despite the many texts produced each year in the field, little attention centers on the many contributions of religious ethics to the practice of business throughout the globe. It is the aim of this new series to fill this void and to publish books that will appeal to scholars in the field of applied ethics as well as be useful as undergraduate textbooks in introductory business ethics courses.

Religious Perspectives on Business Ethics

An Anthology

Edited by
Thomas O'Brien and Scott Paeth

With a Foreword by
Patricia Werhane

ROWMAN & LITTLEFIELD PUBLISHERS, INC.
Lanham • Boulder • New York • Toronto • Plymouth, UK

ROWMAN & LITTLEFIELD PUBLISHERS, INC.

Published in the United States of America
by Rowman & Littlefield Publishers, Inc.
A wholly owned subsidary of The Rowman & Littlefield Publishing Group, Inc.
4501 Forbes Boulevard, Suite 200, Lanham, Maryland 20706
www.rowmanlittlefield.com

Estover Road
Plymouth PL6 7PY
United Kingdom

British Library Cataloguing in Publication Information Available

Library of Congress Cataloging-in-Publication Data

Religious perspectives on business ethics / edited by Thomas O'Brien and Scott Paeth.
    p. cm. — (Religion and business ethics)
  Includes bibliographical references and index.
  ISBN-13: 978-0-7425-5010-0 (cloth : alk. paper)
  ISBN-10: 0-7425-5010-9 (cloth : alk. paper)
  ISBN-13: 978-0-7425-5011-7 (pbk : alk. paper)
  ISBN-10: 0-7425-5011-7 (pbk : alk. paper)
1. Religious ethics. 2. Business ethics. 3. Business—Religious aspects. I. O'Brien,
Thomas, 1961– II. Paeth, Scott. III. Series.
BJ1188.R43 2006
205'.64—dc22
                                                  2006017737

Printed in the United States of America

♾™ The paper used in this publication meets the minimum requirements of American
National Standard for Information Sciences—Permanence of Paper for Printed Library
Materials, ANSI/NISO Z39.48-1992.

Contents

v

Foreword

Patricia Werhane

I am honored and excited to write the foreword for this long-anticipated new anthology, *Religious Perspectives on Business Ethics*, edited by two distinguished professors in religious studies, Thomas O'Brien and Scott Paeth.

Applied ethics, broadly conceived, developed originally after the Second World War primarily at Catholic universities who saw their mission not merely to educate their students in theology, religion, and theoretical philosophy, but also to help students develop practical applications to their learning experiences.

When the field of business ethics formally began in the 1970s, it, like its precursor bioethics, was taught primarily at Catholic universities. At its inception there were almost no textbooks, and the only decent ones were written by Jesuits for use in their universities. Since that time the field of business ethics has grown enormously. Business ethics is taught in approximately three-quarters of all public, secular, and parochial colleges and universities in the United States, and it is a growing field internationally. Today there are over fifty textbooks in business ethics.

Interestingly, however, despite its philosophical and pedagogical roots, there are almost no textbooks in business ethics written from the perspective of religious ethics. Indeed, according to an informal survey we conducted at DePaul University two years ago, although business ethics is taught in philosophy, theology, religious studies, and management departments, almost all of the textbooks that are adapted for those courses come out of secular philosophical traditions. Even courses titled "Business Ethics and Religion" will usually use a philosophical textbook or one written by a professor in management, because there is almost no other choice. There are almost no textbooks framed to be used in teaching business ethics from a religious perspective. The available texts seldom consider notions of spirituality, casuistry, stewardship, or religiously based values orientations. The reason for this is not because philosophers and management professors are antireligious, but because, like all academics, they teach to their own expertise.

However, this paucity of texts for those in theology and religious studies departments teaching business ethics is now being remedied with this new and exciting anthology, *Religious Perspectives on Business Ethics*. This collection of essays is written from a broad variety of perspectives ranging from virtue theory to Confucianism. Its authors are well-known in the field of business ethics, and in this collection these thinkers are able to express themselves in spiritual as well as economic terms. Part I begins, like many texts, with normative theories. But these essays, unlike traditional philosophical thinking, link to the practice of business on terms that are closer to our spiritual dimension than essays ordinarily presented in other texts. Part II, on religious approaches to economic life, will be of special interest to managers and students of management, since this dimension of business is seldom touched upon in the business school classroom. Applying that learning to contemporary issues in business, Part III allows the student consciously to apply religious perspectives to concerns with which he or she will be wrestling in everyday personal and business life.

Our lives are not and should not be compartmentalized into work versus worship. Our spiritual self is part of what we bring to the workplace. This text helps us to think through how that is possible without promoting one particular religious point of view. It is timely because it fills a void both in academia and in how we live and apply our learning experience.

Preface

Thomas O'Brien

Textbooks dealing well with the relationship of religion to business ethics are hard to find. The volume that you are currently holding has its genesis in the struggle of professors at DePaul University to find suitable textbooks that bridge the divide between the fields of religious studies and business ethics. It offers, under one cover, many of the leading articles dealing with the intersection of religion and business ethics currently available. The editors, as well as a number of other faculty at DePaul, have made frequent use of these essays in their own classes and have found them to be tremendous resources for engaging our students around the meaning and significance of ethics, its origins, and its application to contemporary business life.

A recurrent complaint leveled by many religious studies professors teaching business ethics is the lack of appropriate texts and other instructional resources geared specifically toward teaching undergraduates business ethics from a religious perspective. While their counterparts in philosophy departments have literally dozens of voluminous textbooks offering comprehensive pedagogical tools for undergraduate instruction, religious studies faculty are faced with a far more formidable task when searching for appropriate texts for their business ethics courses. The most frequently used textbooks are often viewed as basically flawed—even by the faculty who repeatedly use them. The best of the philosophical business ethics textbooks ignore religion, even when the theories being presented have obvious religious origins. Some of the textbooks are explicitly dismissive, or even hostile to religion. Using these kinds of texts adds a further layer of explanation for religious studies professors, since they need to "correct" or "explain" the bias of the text.

Many professors we have consulted have become disillusioned by the idea of using the standard philosophical texts and have attempted to cobble together a variety of texts that approach business ethics from a religious orientation. Some use readings from the extensive and comprehensive volume, *On Moral Business*, by Max Stackhouse, Dennis McCann, and Shirley Roels.[1] However, those who use this resource frequently note that it presents too much material for a single undergraduate course, and the material is often too sophisticated for undergraduate readers, requiring too much background in business, ethics, or religion for an audience that is usually being introduced to each of these disciplines for the very first time. Therefore, this volume seems best suited for graduate-level courses in business ethics.

A number of texts dealing with business ethics from a religious perspective do so by dedicating one chapter to the business ethics of a major religious tradition. Examples of books that fall into this category are *Making an Honest Living*, by Jacob Neusner, and *Faith, Morals, and Money*, by Edward D. Zinbarg.[2] These volumes suffer from a number of significant shortcomings. First of all, the criteria of selection for the traditions represented is often not discussed, which can leave the reader with the false impression that either these are the only traditions that have ethical resources relating to business activity or that these are somehow the traditions with the most compelling ethical principles concerning business and economic issues.

Another criticism of these volumes has to do with their treatment of each tradition and their ethical beliefs. Due to the limited space afforded by the medium, the presentations are limited, superficial, and in some cases misleading. Also, many significant issues in business ethics are ignored; therefore, these books are normally not appropriate candidates for main textbooks. These texts, in addition, do not include stand-alone case studies, which again alienates them from the generally accepted modus operandi in business ethics pedagogy. Finally, the wide sampling of sometimes vague and complex ethical presentations found in these books often leaves students confused and lacking ethical direction in comparison to their counterparts who are reading secular philosophical texts.

A third category of business ethics textbooks written from religious perspectives is a group that approaches the topic from the standpoint of a single tradition. For instance, in a Catholic institution like DePaul University, where the editors teach, it is not uncommon to find one or more texts in a syllabus using Catholic social teaching or the Catholic moral tradition as its ethical foundation. Catholic reflections on ethical behavior in the marketplace are rich and well established in a long and sophisticated tradition. However, notwithstanding the natural law claims from parts of this tradition, it remains a parochial position in an otherwise religiously diverse landscape. Also, Catholic social teaching is adept at evaluating the ethical dimensions of economic structures and policy, but its principles are generally too broad to give particular guidance in regard to specific business cases. Like the other sources described above, such texts from a single religious perspective often function as supplementary material.

In addition to the difficulty of finding appropriate texts, religious studies professors are also faced with the problems associated with introducing three distinct fields of study in a single class to a student population that often has no background in any of the three fields. By its nature, business ethics is an amalgamated discipline. Like other areas of practical ethics, such as medical ethics or computer ethics, it marries the theories of ethics with the issues of a professional field. Students must become familiar with basic ethical theories and the practical fundamentals of major issues in these professions. Adding religion into this already cluttered mix can, and often does, encourage faculty to overload courses with information, truncate important discussions, and rush through explanations in order to cram in the necessary background instruction needed to properly engage in case study analysis.

Overall, we have found no texts viewing business ethics from a religious standpoint that can supplant the stand-alone business ethics textbooks that apply modern philosophical ethical theories to the full panoply of issues in the discipline. There are many reasons for this textual vacuum. The discipline of religious studies incorporates the traditions of a multitude of often mutually exclusive ethical perspectives. The attempt to bring even a representative sample of these traditions into a meaningful conversation about ethics is a monumental task in and of itself. Then one must add to this volatile mix the perspective from capitalist enterprise with its secular modernist biases. The end product promises to be long, complex, incomplete, and potentially incoherent. No wonder there is much talk about such a volume in publishing circles, but little action!

The purpose of the present volume, the first in a series on the topic of business ethics from a religious perspective, is to bring together in one book a number of excellent, recently published articles that incorporate religious perspectives into their discussion of business ethics. This reader was developed in order to simplify the process of supplementing secularized business ethics textbooks with appropriate religiously oriented resources. Although we have tried to incorporate the perspectives of as many different traditions as we could, this collection of previously published articles is predominantly Christian. This apparent Christian bias is simply the result of the vast number of articles on business ethics published from this tradition, in relation to the relative dearth of materials from most other traditions. In future editions, we look forward to publishing more resources from a greater variety of traditions as these appear in the literature.

NOTES

1. Max L. Stackhouse, et al. *On Moral Business: Classical and Contemporary Resources on Ethics in Economic Life* (Grand Rapids, MI: Wm. B. Eerdmans, 1995).

2. Jacob Neusner, *Making an Honest Living: What Do We Owe the Community?* (Belmont, CA: Wadsworth, 2001); Edward D. Zinbarg, *Faith, Morals and Money* (New York: Continuum, 2001).

Acknowledgments

This volume would not have been possible were it not for the help of a great number of people, each of whom has given to us of their valuable time and energy in order to see this project through.

Jeremy Langford, formerly editorial director at Sheed & Ward, was instrumental in bringing this project to fruition. It was his enthusiasm and support that drove us throughout this project. Additionally, we have been extraordinarily grateful for his recognition of the need for a volume such as this and his willingness to exert himself on our behalf.

Nancy Zawayta put in many hours of work securing permissions from authors and publishers to reprint these essays. This volume literally could not have been completed without her help. Additionally, Holly Grieves and Loren Kallen gave generously of their time in helping with the layout and formatting of the documents in order to put them in their present form.

James Halstead, the chair of DePaul University's Department of Religious Studies, has given us his unwavering and enthusiastic support for this project.

Particular thanks must go to our many colleagues at DePaul who teach Business, Ethics, and Society every quarter. This volume is for all of them. We hope that the suggestions and recommendations that they have offered us are reflected in the final product of our work. We would like to single out Paul Camenisch and John Leahy for special recognition. The path that we walk today was blazed by them over many decades of work at DePaul. They were the first to teach the courses that we have inherited, and though we could never fill their shoes, we hope at least to carry on the tradition that they began.

Finally, we thank our friends and families for their patience and love throughout the preparation of this book. The hours taken from them cannot be replaced, but we hope that we honor them through our work, and we are grateful for their understanding and support.

Thomas O'Brien
Scott R. Paeth
August 2005

Using This Book in a Classroom Setting

*T*his book was originally conceived as a way of collecting into one volume the articles that the editors were already using as supplementary readings in our business ethics classes. Since most textbooks on business ethics tend to ignore, dismiss, or even strip out religious content, we needed to supplement those sources with others that highlighted the ways religion could contribute constructively to the ethical conversation. The chapters in this book were chosen as the result of a rather extensive process of in-class trial and error. Those readings that seemed to be helpful tools, deepening and broadening student knowledge of religious ethics, eventually made the cut in this four-year culling process.

Therefore, the editors envision this first volume in the business ethics series as one best suited to serve the purpose of supplementing other basic introductory texts on business ethics. Most of the chapters in the book were not written with the purpose of introducing students to an ethical principle for the first time, so most of the discussions assume some prior knowledge of moral theory. Furthermore, without some basic instruction in ethical language and theory, many of the chapters in this volume would be difficult to decipher, and some could even lend themselves to misinterpretation. Nevertheless, these chapters have served us very well as companion pieces to topics students are learning from other more pedagogically oriented sources.

In order to help business ethics instructors take better advantage of this excellent collection of readings on religious voices in business ethics, the editors have created two tables that organize the readings according to the topics covered. The first table lists the articles in the first column followed by a second column that lists the main themes found therein. The second table lists some of the main topics found in the book followed by a column listing the chapters where a discussion of those topics can be found. It is our hope that these tables will make the selection of chapters easier for those who already have an established way of approaching business ethics and who might not be able to utilize the simple organizational rubric of this volume of readings. In fact, the editors themselves organize their courses in ways that do not correspond perfectly to this rubric.

Table 1: Ideas and Issues by Chapter

Chapters	Major Ideas and Issues
Introduction: Paeth	Introduction to basics of business ethics, typology of religious ethics, Masao Abe, sacred texts, *Economic Justice for All,* Paul Camenisch, Adam Smith, Dietrich Bonhoeffer, Immanuel Kant
Chapter 1: Camenisch	Introduction to basics of business ethics, the role of religion in business ethics, comparison philosophical and religious ethics, endorsement of rich diversity of ethical voices, communal/embodied nature of morality
Chapter 2: Duska	Introduction to basics of business ethics, is there such a thing as business ethics? Egoism, self-interest, the bottom line, *Endoxa*—commonly held wisdom, Adam Smith, Milton Friedman, utilitarianism, morality as rational adjudication, justice, the soulless corporation, refurbishing business ethics
Chapter 3: Borowski	Aaron Feuerstein case—Malden Mills, Kant, Categorical Imperative, management–employee relations, Scott Adams, Dilbert, Pope John Paul II, *Laborem Exercens,* Alfred North Whitehead, common good, Charles Hartshorne, the *other* as a moral category
Chapter 4: James and Rassekh	Adam Smith, Milton Friedman, the *invisible hand,* self-interest, free enterprise, market economy, *The Wealth of Nations, The Theory of Moral Sentiments,* social responsibility, "external effect," teleology, "society's interests," stockholder value
Chapter 5: Solomon	Virtue ethics, determinism, character, market forces, Aristotle, the psychology of ethics, Kant
Chapter 6: Goodpaster	Conscience, incentives for destructive behavior, Judeo-Christian ethics, awareness, personal reflection, Anthony DeMello, humility, attentiveness, community involvement
Chapter 7: Calkins	Casuistry, case method, law and legal practice, paradigm cases, inductive reasoning, maxims, probability, cumulative arguments, practicality, reasoning by analogy, moral taxonomy, pragmatism

Chapter 8: Nash	Christianity, information technology, Christian faith informing business practice, Christian values
Chapter 9: McCann and Brownsberger	Alisdair MacIntyre, virtue ethics, business as social practice, teleology, justice, the practice of management, Peter Drucker, integrity, *Pleonexia*—acquisitiveness, common good, social responsibility, Aristotle, stewardship
Chapter 10: Klay and Gryzen	Christian ethics, competition, the poor, property rights, the wealthy, cooperation, profit motive, exploitation, individual freedom
Chapter 11: Shishin Wick Sensei	Zen Buddhism, bodhisattva, Buddha, virtue ethics, teleology, giving (*fuse*), loving words (*aigo*), beneficial actions (*rigyo*) identification with others (*doji*), *dharma*, deontology, *nirvana*
Chapter 12: Koehn	Confucianism, trustworthiness, virtue ethics, China, business contracts, teleology, *jen*—exemplary human being, *guanxi*—personal relationships, relational/responsibility ethics
Chapter 13: Herman	Covenants, contracts, influence strategies, bureaucracy, management, relational/responsibility, vulnerability and contingency, mutuality
Chapter 14: Vogel	Judaism, ecological issues, Hebrew Scriptures, anthropocentrism, ecocentrism, nature, humanity, sustainability
Chapter 15: Burton-Christie	Columbia River Watershed, community, ecological issues, significance of the local vs. abstractions, consultative processes, moral-spiritual vision, prophecy, Roman Catholicism, sustainability
Chapter 16: Firer-Hinze	Just war, affirmative action, feminism, Roman Catholicism, John A. Ryan, family living wage, Catholic social thought, sexual division of labor
Chapter 17: Schilling	Sweatshops, corporate responsibility, globalization, *maquiladoras*, transnational corporations
Chapter 18: Litonjua	Globalization, Christianity, John Paul II, Roman Catholicism, transnational corporations, inequality, deracination of the corporation, predatory practices, threats to democracy, cultural homogenization, sustainability, *Centesimus Annus*, Catholic social thought

Table 2: Chapters Covering Selected Topics

Business Ethics Topics	Chapters
Introduction to business ethics	Introduction: Paeth Chapter 1: Camenisch Chapter 2: Duska
Relational/responsibility	Chapter 1: Camenisch Chapter 12: Koehn Chapter 13: Herman Chapter 15: Burton-Christie
Utilitarianism	Chapter 2: Duska
Kant—categorical imperative	Introduction: Paeth Chapter 3: Borowski Chapter 5: Solomon
Teleology	Chapter 4: James and Rassekh Chapter 9: McCann and Brownsberger Chapter 11: Shishin Wick Sensei Chapter 12: Koehn
Deontology	Chapter 11: Shishin Wick Sensei
Practical moral reasoning	Chapter 7: Calkins
Case method—casuistry	Chapter 7: Calkins
Virtue ethics—character	Chapter 5: Solomon Chapter 9: McCann and Brownsberger Chapter 11: Shishin Wick Sensei Chapter 12: Koehn
Judeo-Christian ethics	Chapter 6: Goodpaster Chapter 10: Klay and Gryzen
Conscience	Chapter 6: Goodpaster
Justice	Chapter 2: Duska Chapter 9: McCann and Brownsberger
Aristotle	Chapter 5: Solomon Chapter 9: McCann and Brownsberger
The common good	Chapter 3: Borowski Chapter 9: McCann and Brownsberger
Corporate social responsibility	Chapter 4: James-Rassekh Chapter 9: McCann and Brownsberger Chapter 17: Schilling
Management practices	Chapter 3: Borowski Chapter 9: McCann and Brownsberger Chapter 13: Herman

Stockholder vs. stakeholder value	Chapter 4: James and Rassekh
Self-interest	Chapter 2: Duska
	Chapter 4: James and Rassekh
	Chapter 10: Klay and Gryzen
Adam Smith	Introduction: Paeth
	Chapter 2: Duska
	Chapter 4: James and Rassekh
Milton Friedman	Chapter 2: Duska
	Chapter 4: James and Rassekh
Invisible hand	Chapter 4: James and Rassekh
Sustainability	Chapter 9: McCann and Brownsberger
	Chapter 14: Vogel
	Chapter 15: Burton-Christie
	Chapter 18: Litonjua
Ecological issues	Chapter 14: Vogel
	Chapter 15: Burton-Christie
Globalization	Introduction: Paeth
	Chapter 17: Schilling
	Chapter 18: Litonjua
Transnational corporations	Chapter 17: Schilling
	Chapter 18: Litonjua
Christianity	Chapter 8: Nash
	Chapter 18: Litonjua
Judaism	Chapter 14: Vogel
Buddhism	Introduction: Paeth
	Chapter 11: Shishin Wick Sensei
Confucianism	Chapter 12: Koehn
Roman Catholicism	Chapter 15: Burton-Christie
	Chapter 16: Firer-Hinze
	Chapter 18: Litonjua
Catholic social thought	Chapter 16: Firer-Hinze
	Chapter 18: Litonjua
Pope John Paul II	Chapter 3: Borowski
Just wage	Chapter 16: Firer-Hinze
Affirmative action	Chapter 16: Firer-Hinze
Feminism	Chapter 16: Firer-Hinze

A Brief Introduction to Ethical Theory

Scott R. Paeth

$\mathscr{T}$he purpose of this chapter is not to provide a comprehensive overview of ethical theory. There are many excellent books that are able to do that. This section is intended to provide a basic overview of key ethical concepts in order to aid readers who may have relatively little background in ethics.

This overview will examine several of the key ideas in the history of ethics and provide a background for the kinds of ethical claims that are examined by the chapters in this volume. Given the fact that ethical theory is a complex discipline, this will be a broadly based overview, which, of necessity, must ignore many of the nuances that are at the heart of debates about morality in general, and particularly as they relate to business. When appropriate, we will also note the role of religion in these theories, in order to make the religious dimensions of many of these theories clearer than they often are in introductory ethics textbooks. This is not intended to be a comprehensive examination of ethical theory and should be used in conjunction with other primary and secondary ethics texts.

NORMATIVE AND DESCRIPTIVE ETHICS

It is important at the outset to distinguish between normative and descriptive approaches to ethics. This distinction is particularly useful in evaluating moral arguments in the realm of business, given the frequency with which business practices are described in naturalistic terms.

In brief, descriptive ethics involves the analysis and accounting of actual ethical beliefs, behaviors, norms, and practices in which people engage. Descriptive ethics does not attempt to offer an evaluative assessment of whether a particular set of beliefs are right or wrong, mistaken or apt. It only seeks to offer a picture of actual moral behavior and its justification. Thus, for example, Adam Smith's observations that most people engage in productive economic activity out of self-interest is a *descriptive* rather than a *normative* statement of the ethical motivations that drive the engine of capitalism. It should not, however, be taken as a commendation of self-interest in general.

Normative ethics, by contract, *is* concerned with assessing the rightness or wrongness of a particular set of ideas or actions. Normative ethics has to do with the evaluation of moral claims about the rightness or wrongness of a given set of actions, or beliefs about actions, or motives for actions, on the basis of a set of criteria designed to assess better and worse moral outcomes. Normative ethics is concerned with establishing a set of standards based upon which one can come to a reliable conclusion with regard to the morality of an intended act. In other words, it is concerned with the *norms* on the basis of which we act as moral agents. This could entail, depending on the theory in question, assessing the outcome of one's action (producing greater good or greater harm), the motives for one's action (self-interest or a larger sense of moral obligation), or the sources of moral truth (God or gods, reason, passion).

The purpose of this volume is to provide a set of *normative* perspectives on the field of business ethics. However, in offering that perspective, we do not intend to neglect the descriptive ethical task. On the contrary, we recognize that description is an important element in offering an adequate normative assessment of any course of action, including the actions of businesses and businessmen and women.

THE RIGHT, THE GOOD, AND THE FITTING

Questions of normative ethics are generally related to at least one of three categories—the Right, the Good, or the Fitting.[1]

In very broad terms, the Right has to do with questions of overarching moral principles and their sources. It is connected to what is referred to in ethical theory as *deontology*, having to do with issues of duty and obligation. These overarching principles are generally understood to be prior to any considerations of particular circumstances or objectives, but in some way represent a binding set of criteria according to which human behavior should conform, at least initially. Depending on the theory in question, there may be conditions under which a particular circumstance or outcome supercedes one's obligations, but such considerations can only be taken into account when the obligations themselves have been articulated and acknowledged.

The Good, also broadly conceived, pertains to questions of the goals, ends, or outcomes of human activity, in other words, that which is good for human beings to do, or to be, or to achieve. The Good has to do with what is usually referred to as *teleological* ethics. Different teleological theories of morality emphasize different conceptions of what constitutes a relevant *telos*, or end. Some theories are thoroughly consequentialist, considering only the effects of particular actions in determining their morality, while others develop an anthropological perspective, according to which human beings are predisposed to develop in a particular way or achieve particular goals, and morality is based upon whether one's actions would hinder or promote those goals. These theories often overlap substantially with virtue theory and other contextually oriented approaches to ethics.

The Fitting has to do with questions of what the appropriate course of action under a given set of circumstances ought to be. As a category, it may be considered to cast the widest net over the variables of human behavior, since it deals not only with matters that are usually considered within the tradition of *virtue* ethics, but also relates to questions of prudential reasoning, social custom, and contextual or role-based behavioral norms. That which is "fitting" for any individual must of necessity vary depending on where and when one is asking the question. This is of particular importance to matters of business ethics, given the role-specific character of many business decisions. The ongoing debate about business social responsibility is particularly germane to considerations of "fittingness," given the argument that corporate executives are not permitted to allow personal ethical principles to affect business decisions.

APPROACHES TO NORMATIVE ETHICAL THEORY: RELIGIOUS AND PHILOSOPHICAL

Divine Command and Deontology

Deontological moral theories, having to do with adherence to duties and overarching principles, have taken myriad forms, both religious and secular. The predominant religious conception of deontology is usually referred to as "divine command" theory, while philosophical theories range from the work of Immanuel Kant and W. D. Ross to the divergent justice theories of John Rawls and Robert Nozick.

Divine command, broadly construed, is a way of speaking about the idea that moral obligations come from a God, or many gods, in the form of laws or rules. Morality, under this theory, is thus rooted in the nature, will, and righteousness of God. Such presuppositions can be found in a great deal of Christian ethical reflection. It can be seen, for example, in John Calvin's exposition on the Ten Commandments in his *Institutes of the Christian Religion* and in Karl Barth's *Church Dogmatics*.[2] In each case, the presumption is that knowledge of God's will is equivalent to knowledge of the proper moral course of action. Morality is defined in terms of divinity, which leaves open the question of whether divinity is accountable to any overarching moral claims. Such an argument is at the heart of the debate in Plato's dialogue *Euthyphro*.[3] If God is the source of morality, are the actions of God subject to moral scrutiny? This question haunts divine command theory and has produced diverse answers. Plato certainly seemed to believe that the gods were accountable to a larger moral law, while John Calvin confidently declared that God was not subject to moral judgment because God was the source of all moral judgment.

Although there are precursors to Kant's moral theory in the history of philosophy, most notably in Platonic and Stoic conceptions of moral law, most contemporary treatments of deontological ethics are based primarily on Kant's theory, as laid out in his *Groundwork for the Metaphysics of Morals* and *Critique of Practical Reason*.[4] In these two works, he describes morality in terms of what he refers to as the "Categorical Imperative." The term Categorical Imperative refers to a threefold conception of moral duty that Kant argues is rooted in the rational action of a purely good will.

The first formulation of the Categorical Imperative states that one should "act always according to that maxim whereby one can at the same time will it to be a universal law." The key to understanding Kant's approach to ethics is the idea that the Categorical Imperative is not a moral law imposed from outside of ourselves, by God or society, but is a self-imposed rule demanded by the force of reason itself. One may choose not to act rationally, but if one desires to be rational, argues Kant, one must recognize oneself as bound by the Categorical Imperative.

The second formulation of the Categorical Imperative states, "[A]ct according to that maxim whereby you treat all rational beings as ends in themselves, and not as mere means to an end." Here, Kant interprets moral responsibility not solely in terms of the demands of reason per se, but also in light of the innate dignity of all rational creatures. We owe moral obligation to one another, in other words, simply because we are all rational. This is a development and articulation, as Kant sees it, of the first formulation of the Categorical Imperative. An important qualification to this formulation is Kant's insistence that we refuse to treat one another as *merely* a means to an end, that is, as a mere object in our world without any more inherent dignity than a mop or broom. Kant is not implying here that there are no circumstances under which we may not make use of one another's skills, but that we must always do so while at the same time recognizing one another's innate worth and dignity. Thus, exploitative labor and slavery, the abuse of workers and contractors, and the failure to give full regard to the interests and aims of all those with whom we come into contact is explicitly excluded under this formulation. From the perspective of business ethics, this way of approaching this issue has enormous implications if taken seriously.

Kant's third formulation of the Categorical Imperative states that we should "always act according to that maxim that we would will as autonomous legislators in a universal kingdom of ends." This is in some ways the most perplexing of the formulations, in that it seems initially to restate the first formulation. But its actual purpose is to bring the first and second formulations of the Categorical Imperative together under the idea of a *legislating* will. Implied in this formulation is that we ought to live as though we were already living in a society in which all persons were treated as ends in themselves (as subjects) and not merely as a means to an end (as objects). Again, the implications for business ethics are significant.

While Kant's Categorical Imperative dominates the discussion of deontological ethics, it is not unassailable. The most important critique of Kant's ethical theory is that, because all moral laws are equally binding, it allows for no means by which to adjudicate among competing claims. Kant seems to have refused to acknowledge that genuine conflicts of duty were possible, but others have been far less sanguine.

British philosopher W. D. Ross sought to formulate an approach to deontological ethics that took account of the potential for conflicts among duties by articulating what he referred to as a theory of prima facie moral duties.[5] Certain moral duties, Ross argues, are properly basic, in the sense that one cannot justify them on the basis of another, prior, moral commitment. These duties include (but are not limited to) such duties as fidelity, beneficence, nonmaleficence, fidelity, gratitude, and justice. Moral agents are responsible for upholding these moral duties, and yet, these duties are prima facie (that is to say, they are duties "on their face") precisely because Ross recognizes that there are circumstances where conflicts among duties require us to make choices about which duties we will and will not uphold. "On the face of it," I have a duty not to lie; but is that duty binding on me if I must lie to preserve an innocent life? Ross doesn't provide a categorical or irrefutable argument in favor of any one position as Kant did, but rather argues that it is only by a careful examination of one's duties in a particular set of circumstances that one can determine which duties must take priority over others.

Yet another approach to deontological ethics turns its focus, not to the idea of "duty," but to the idea of "justice." Theories of justice ask questions about what our rights are vis-à-vis others, and under what circumstances those rights can be violated. Rights theory has a venerable history in modern political philosophy. For our purposes, however, we want to focus on two recent approaches to the theory—those of John Rawls and Robert Nozick.

John Rawls's theory of justice focuses on the idea of "justice-as-fairness."[6] As articulated in his classic text *A Theory of Justice*, justice-as-fairness is rooted in the idea that, as people view one another as people of equal dignity and worth, society should be set up in such a way as to offer maximal opportunities for achievement to all participants, regardless of race, gender, or condition of birth, while allowing inequalities in wealth and status only insofar as those inequalities benefit society as a whole. He advances this theory most famously in a thought experiment in which participants are asked to imagine the kind of society that they would create, as rational and self-interested actors, if they knew nothing about what their own position in that society would be. They would, Rawls argues, choose a society much like the one that he is advocating.

Robert Nozick's approach to justice is a direct response to Rawls's conception of justice-as-fairness.[7] Nozick argues for what he calls a "theory of entitlement," which roots justice in the inviolability of contracts and property rights. Each person is entitled, argues Nozick, to those things he or she has acquired justly on his or her own merits, or has gotten from another person under a legal contract. Government's role in creating equal social circumstances should be limited, Nozick argues, to the enforcement of legitimate contracts and the protection of society from violence and lawlessness. It is not to engage in the kind of broad social reform that is implied in Rawls's theory, which could only work, argues Nozick, by depriving individuals of goods to which they are properly entitled.

Deontological moral theories are compelling precisely because they understand morality as not subject to whim or social change, but in some sense as permanent and stable universal obligations. Whether the Right has to do with "rights" or whether it is rooted in duties, it is concerned with holding us up to a high standard of moral conduct. Deontological theories are often explicitly nonconsequentialist, concerning themselves with principles more than with outcomes. However, we now turn to a consideration of those moral theories that are concerned with questions of the Good, and which, in various ways, take consequences into account.

Natural Law, Teleology, and Consequentialism

As a category, teleology is broader and more unwieldy than the category of deontology. Although there is a great deal of diversity among deontological theories, they could be related back to a set of common concepts. Teleology, however, is complicated by the diversity of understandings about just what the *telos*, or "end," in question in ethics is.

Although there are strongly deontological dimensions to natural law theory, at its heart it is a teleological, or ends-based, conception of morality, having to do with the proper, or "natural," aims of human life and society. This can be seen most clearly in the approach to natural law taken by Thomas Aquinas, the architect of much of the most profound Catholic moral theology of the Middle Ages, and whose influence can still be felt in much of Catholic thought today.[8]

Aquinas adapted and synthesized his conception of natural law from a mixture of Stoic natural law theory, Aristotelian ethics, and Christian teachings. He conceives of human beings as created naturally with an inclination toward particular human and divine ends. Individuals, institutions, and society as a whole are created to achieve certain goals. For example, the goal of society is the creation of justice, much like the goal of human sexuality is the creation of human life. When these natural goals are thwarted by egoism, self-interest, or distortion, the result is a distortion of natural ends—injustice on the one hand, or perversion on the other. It is necessary to understand the naturally ordered and created orientation of life in order to live a moral life.

This form of teleology is considerably different from consequentialism, which concerns itself not with the naturally created end of human life, but with the consequences of a particular course of action. Natural law theory asks, "Who or what am I intended to be?" In contrast, consequentialism asks, "What results will my actions produce?" The objective in consequentialist ethics is to act in such a way as to maximize the good for a relevant portion of the human race, depending on the version of consequentialism under consideration.

Two key questions are important in determining the proper course of action under consequentialist theories: First, what is the nature of the good that one is seeking to maximize? And, second, whose good should we be maximizing?

Most consequentialist ethical theories consider the good in terms of happiness. Those actions that produce happiness are considered to be good, while those that produce unhappiness are deemed evil. This conception of happiness leads to the further issue of how we evaluate happiness. Jeremy Bentham, one of the founders of utilitarianism, argued in favor of a "hedonistic" conception of happiness, in which happiness is understood in terms of pleasure and unhappiness is understood in terms of pain.[9] Thus, painful actions produce unhappiness and are meant to be avoided, while pleasurable actions produce happiness and are therefore good.

Bentham developed a method of determining the relative degree of happiness versus unhappiness through what he termed a "hedonic calculus," in which one could measure one's pleasure versus displeasure on a scale that included such categories as "intensity" (does this action produce a great deal of pleasure or pain?), "duration" (how long will this pleasure or pain last?), "certainty" (is the promised pleasure or threatened pain likely to actually occur?), "propinquity" (is the promised pleasure or threatened pain remote or close at hand?), "fecundity" or "purity" (is this pleasure or pain likely to be followed by further, similar experiences?), as well as how many people are affected. Bentham believed that the proper course of action could be determined by assigning a numerical value to pleasure and pain and then choosing the actions that would maximize overall pleasure and minimize overall pain.

Although Bentham's hedonistic definition of happiness has tended to predominate utilitarian ethics, it should be noted that pleasure is not the only possible way of determining happiness. Other utilitarians have used other measures, and some have sought to define utility in ways that make no reference to happiness per se but seek other measurements on the basis of which to determine the nature of the Good.

Assuming that we can come to an agreement on the nature of the Good, however, we still have to answer the question of *whose* good is considered morally relevant.

Ethical egoism, for example, defines morality in such a way that the relevant good is that which is done for oneself, regardless of its effects on others.[10] This is not to imply that harm to others is not a factor in determining the morally proper course of action from an egoistic standpoint, but the relevant question to be asked is what the effects of harming others would be on oneself, not on the one harmed. For example, an action that would be likely to lead to prison might be morally imprudent from an egoistic standpoint, even if the action might benefit oneself in the short term.

By contrast, utilitarianism, as formulated by Bentham and John Stuart Mill, is not concerned only for the good of one or of a few, but rather is concerned, in the classical statement of utilitarianism, with "the greatest good for the greatest number."[11] This "greatest good principle" requires that the evaluation of a moral course of action take account of the results of our actions for all affected parties. Yet, many interpreters of utilitarianism understand the principle of the greatest good to allow the majority to harm the minority as long as the overall good produced is sufficient to justify it.

For example, if polluting the water table will allow you to create more jobs at a good rate of pay for the nearby village, while resulting in a small number of cases of operable cancer, this interpretation of utilitarianism would deem the good produced for the many to outweigh the potential harm done to the few. This kind of calculation is quite common in the cost-benefit analysis used in many industries (and, notoriously, used by Ford in the Pinto case), but it is unclear if Mill and other early utilitarians would accept this interpretation, particularly given Mill's stirring defense of individual rights in his seminal work, *On Liberty*.[12]

A further variation on the theme of teleological ethics has to do with the use of casuistry in ethics. Until recently, the word "casuistry" had a negative connotation in much of ethical theory, being seen as an exercise in morally justifying any course of action one desires to take by twisting moral principles beyond their intended meaning. Yet, casuistry has a long and honorable history in ethical theory, a history that has been rediscovered in contemporary ethics.

Casuistry is a method of moral reasoning based upon the analysis of cases.[13] Paradigm cases are used as a foundation upon which to analyze similar sets of circumstances, using the already solved paradigm cases as moral guides. As developed by Catholic theologians in the Middle Ages, it provided a useful tool for determining the relationship of moral norms to particular sets of circumstances. In other words, it is one thing to know that theft and murder are immoral. It is quite another, however, to know whether a particular course of action constitutes theft or murder. Casuistry originally emerged out of the practice of sacramental moral discernment in response to precisely these types of questions. Casuists believe that by comparing a given set of circumstances to analogous paradigm cases, it is possible to determine the morality or immorality of a given course of action.

Teleological theories, whether based on a conception of human beings as goal-oriented, or on an analysis of the consequences of a given course of action, or on an analysis of cases, have an enormous appeal, given their interests in the real-life circumstances of moral actors. There are multiple conceptions of the Good that fit into this framework, but the various "goods" that these theories pursue each have to do with some objective toward which morality is oriented. While deontological theories can often seem unconcerned with the human cost of adherence to moral principles, teleological theories are explicitly interested in the relationship of morality to human life. Our third category, that of the Fitting, leads us further into the human and circumstantial elements of moral decisions, by seeking to determine the proper course of action on the basis of the context in which one must act.

Act-Based and Rule-Based Ethical Theories

Before we address this third category, we need to turn and consider an important distinction. Ethical theories are often divided into two types: act-based theories and rule-based theories. Act-based ethical theories understand ethics to be about the morality of particular *acts* performed by moral agents, while rule-based theories understand it to be about conformity to general sets of moral *rules*. In other words, in an act-based system, acts are moral or immoral, independently of whether they correspond to a rule. In rule-based theories, however, once one has established the validity of a moral rule, it is binding under most circumstances. Both deontological and teleological ethical theories have act- and rule-based variants.

Rule-based deontological moral theories are best exemplified through Kant's Categorical Imperative, which, in addition to being quintessentially deontological, is also quintessentially rule-based. What is central to Kant's theory is the adherence to the moral rule established by the use of reason in conformity with the Categorical Imperative. Morality is determined by obedience to the rule, not by considerations of other matters such as the effects of the rule in a particular instance.

Act-based deontology is somewhat more complicated. It can perhaps be best understood in the context of Karl Barth's conception of ethics. According to Barth, morality is understood as obedience to the command of God. However, unlike many other Christian ethicists, Barth does not understand the command of God to be established and contained solely within the Bible or the teachings of the church. Rather, the command of God is encountered by human beings at every moment of their lives. Barth recognizes that most of the time obedience to God conforms to the "rules" established in these other sources, but he also argues that there are "exceptional cases" in which God will command us in a particular set of circumstances to do something contrary to those established rules. Yet, insofar as one acts in those particular circumstances in obedience to the command of God, one is still acting morally.

Rule-based utilitarianism bears a certain resemblance to rule-based deontology. Like rule-deontology, it views moral principles as generally binding once they are established. But it differs from the Kantian form of rule-deontology in at least two crucial respects. First, unlike Kantian ethics, which emphasizes adherence to duty in light of reason, rule-utilitarianism is concerned with establishing rules that produce the greatest degree of happiness over unhappiness. In other words, rule-utilitarianism is interested in discovering which rules, when consistently followed, create the greatest amount of good for the greatest number. Second, whereas Kant's version of rule-deontology asserts that moral rules, once known, are inviolable, rule-utilitarianism regards these rules to be *generally*, but not *inflexibly* binding. There may be narrow circumstances where the rules may be violated, if doing so will create a greater degree of good over harm. But these circumstances should be few and far between. John Stuart Mill's utilitarianism is arguably of the rule-utilitarian variant.

Act-utilitarianism, by contrast, concerns itself with whether particular acts in particular circumstances will create more good than harm. It is less interested in the binding character of general rules than in the responsibilities of individuals. When faced with a set of alternatives, under this theory, one should choose the act that will produce the greatest happiness, even if it runs contrary to what one might ordinarily think of as moral. An example of this can be seen in the work of Australian ethicist Peter Singer. Singer has advocated euthanizing severely disabled newborn infants, on the grounds that doing so will create a greater amount of good by minimizing unhappiness for both the parents and the infant. Singer recognizes that under most circumstances killing newborn infants would be immoral—precisely because doing so would create more unhappiness than happiness. However, in these circumstances, he argues that the act of euthanasia follows the greatest happiness principle and should be allowed.

There are other examples that one could give of these variants and their application. The important issue for our purposes is simply to identify them and to be aware of the distinctions among them. In the context of business ethics, among the most important decisions that one may be asked to make will involve questions of whether the moral path lies in following a particular rule or committing to a particular act, the results of which will have an impact on oneself, one's company, as well as on many outside of the company.

Contextual and Virtue Ethics

Contextual ethics are particularly concerned with questions of the appropriateness of one's actions to a particular standard of behavior, given one's context. Ethical behavior, according to this model, involves, in Aristotle's words, "doing the right thing, at the right time, and in the right way." Of course, determining what the right thing, time, or way is distinguishes various contextual ethical theories from one another. In some cases, fittingness is rooted in a conception of human excellence, or virtue, in other cases, it is dependent on the free choice of the moral agent in determining what he or she will be, while in other cases it is pragmatically rooted in the situation as it arises in particular cases.

Joseph Fletcher in his book *Situation Ethics* famously and controversially articulated a brand of contextual Christian ethics based upon the idea that one's actions, as long as they are rooted in love, should adapt themselves to one's circumstances.[14] There are no other universal overriding principles to determine the morality of one's actions. One must base one's decisions on the situation in which one finds oneself. Another, significantly different, example can be found in the approach of Paul Lehmann, who argued that a Christian contextual ethic must be based first and foremost on a recognition of the meaning of Christ as the Son of God, as well as on the context of the church as the community dedicated to following Christ.[15] In light of these two principles, he argued, one may then respond to the particular situation in which one finds oneself, with the goal, he argued, of "making and keeping human life human."[16]

Virtue theory represents the most influential strand of contextual ethics. As articulated by Aristotle and subsequently adapted by Thomas Aquinas, the theory of the virtues describes a virtuous act as one that is fitting or appropriate in a given setting.[17] However, knowledge of what constitutes an appropriate action is only possible to one who has cultivated good character and human excellence. Virtue is the mean between two extremes, one of excess and one of deficiency. Courage, for example, is not the absence of fear; rather, it is the virtue that describes the mean between excessive fear (cowardice) and deficiency of fear (foolhardiness). The foolhardy soldier will rush headlong into battle with no heed for consequences, while the coward will cringe from battle. Wisdom consists in knowing when to act and when to refrain from action, and the virtuous person is one who has developed that wisdom to a high degree.

Recently, philosophers such as Alasdair MacIntyre have sought to reorient the study of virtue theory, understanding virtue not simply as human excellence, but as an excellence in a skill that is defined by the practices of a particular community.[18] Virtue, therefore, is community-dependent and not rooted in a singular conception of human nature. MacIntyre argues that modern ethical theory, as exemplified by Kant and Mill, has become fragmented and has lost track of its own origins. As a result, modern ethical theory can only lead to moral nihilism. Only through a tradition of the virtues that is similar in content to that of Aristotle and his successors can moral theory be saved from nihilism.

Existentialist ethics, by contrast, grounds morality not in the traditions of a community, but in the individual choice of the moral actor. We are "condemned to be free," according to the classic statement of the human condition by Jean-Paul Sartre.[19] Sartre argues that human beings are not subject to an independent force called "human nature" that directs us toward goals or moral norms. Rather, first we exist, and only subsequently do we acquire through our choices a set of characteristics that define who we are. Our actions determine our character, but rather than character being defined by a universal or even communal conception of humanity, we define it for ourselves.

There is, therefore, in this conception of morality, no independent source of meaning. We create our own meaning as we create our own morality. We can give assent to particular principles or movements, but, in doing so, we exercise our choice and our freedom, rather than acknowledging some independent authority that these principles or movements possess.

Contextual ethical theories tend to be "nonfoundational." That is to say, they do not see morality as a matter of discerning a set of moral principles that are accessible to human knowledge. Whatever moral absolutes there may be, they are not infallibly knowable by human beings. Morality is about determining the best course of action on the basis of what we *can* know—our own communities, traditions, or individual circumstances.

ETHICAL THEORY AND THE PRACTICE OF BUSINESS

Ethical theory, taken by itself, cannot provide a great deal of guidance in the practice of business. Any business is a complex enterprise with many facets that need to work in harmony with one another in order to achieve success. Ethical theory can aid in the practice of business only if (1) the practitioners of business choose to value ethics as a part of the essence of business, and (2) ethical theory can be made concrete enough to aid businesspeople who want to act ethically. Unfortunately, neither of these conditions can be taken for granted.

The practice of business today is beset by ethical controversies, not least of which is the very real question of whether it is proper for businesses to even *try* to be moral in any broad sense of the term. The crises created by companies like Enron, WorldCom, and Global Crossing have established in the public mind a degree of cynicism about the practice of business that will be difficult to overcome if businesspeople themselves refuse to take seriously the moral demands of their livelihoods. As easy as it can be to compromise one's deepest values in the context of promises of easy money and small risks, only when the commitment to ethical action is deeply embedded in both the principles of business and the consciences of individual businesspeople can questions of ethical theory even find entry into the practice of business.

At the same time, if ethical theory is understood only in terms of abstruse theories or intellectual gamesmanship, it can provide no help in aiding businesspeople who are striving to act morally in the marketplace. The most important contribution that ethical theory can make to the actual moral decision-making practices of businesspeople is in giving them resources through which they can begin to consider the ethical dimension of their work. It is not necessary, in other words, to make a decision from among Kant, Mill, and Sartre, or to decide whether or not one wishes to embrace a particular religious or philosophical theory of morality. What is important in utilizing the material in this chapter is to understand it as a way of focusing one's attention on the morally significant issues that affect the lives of all those engaged in the practice of business.

In the search for moral guidance, many of us rely on our intuition to guide us to the right conclusions. We trust intuition as a guide because of a faith that we already know, on a deep level, what the right thing to do is. Yet, history, as well as today's news, reminds us how easy it is to trick ourselves into believing that what is to our economic advantage is automatically the morally right thing to do. This self-deceit is made more difficult (though by no means impossible) if we have focused our moral imagination on the larger ethical universe of which the business decisions we make are but a small part.

Ethical theory reminds us that rights and duties are morally significant categories to those who wish to live in civil, as well as civilized, society. It also reminds us that the consequences of our actions matter, whether we are university students or CEOs. It forces us to ask questions about the purposes or goals toward which we are, and toward which we should be, striving. And it reminds us that the decisions that we make define us as moral persons. Ethics takes place in a context, and how we respond to that context forms us and shapes the lives we live.

Many people (perhaps most) are capable of living well and doing right without a deep knowledge of ethical theory. The material in this chapter is not essential to the living of a moral life. Yet a sincere struggle with the questions raised in the study of ethical theory can help to create a bulwark against the kinds of pressures to compromise that can lead even good men and women into ethically untenable situations. The most important lesson that ethical theory can teach the world of business, therefore, is to take ethics seriously.

NOTES

1. The categorization of these moral theories into the Right, the Good, and the Fitting features prominently in the work of Max Stackhouse. See Max Stackhouse, "Introduction" in Max Stackhouse, Dennis McCann, and Shirley Roels, *On Moral Business* (Grand Rapids, MI: Eerdmans Publishing Co., 1995), 19ff.

2. John Calvin, *Institutes of the Christian Religion* (Philadelphia: Westminster Press, 1960) and Karl Barth, *Church Dogmatics*, 14 vols. (Edinburgh: T&T Clark, 1936–1952).

3. Plato, *Euthyphro* (Chico, CA: Scholar's Press, 1984).

4. Immanuel Kant, *Groundwork for the Metaphysics of Morals* (Oxford: Oxford University Press, 2002) and *Critique of Practical Reason* (New York: Macmillan, 1993).

5. W. D. Ross, *The Right and the Good* (Oxford: Clarendon Press, 2002).

6. John Rawls, *A Theory of Justice* (Cambridge MA: Harvard University Press, 1999).

7. Robert Nozick, *Anarchy, State, and Utopia* (Oxford: Blackwell, 1975).

8. See Thomas Aquinas, *Saint Thomas Aquinas on Politics and Ethics* (New York: W. W. Norton, 1987).

9. Jeremy Bentham, *The Principles of Morals and Legislation* (New York: Prometheus Books, 1988).

10. See, for example Ayn Rand, *The Virtue of Selfishness: A New Concept of Egoism* (New York: New American Library, 1964).

11. John Stuart Mill, *Utilitarianism* (Indianapolis IN: Hackett, 2002).

12. John Stuart Mill, *On Liberty and Other Writings* (Cambridge: Cambridge University Press, 1989).

13. See Albert Jonsen and Stephen Toulmin, *The Abuse of Casuistry: A History of Moral Reasoning* (Berkeley: University of California Press, 1990).

14. Joseph Fletcher, *Situation Ethics* (Louisville, KY: Westminster/John Knox Press, 1997).

15. Paul Lehman, *Ethics in a Christian Context* (New York: Harper San Francisco, 1976).

16. Lehmann, Paul Louis. *The Decalogue and a Human Future: The Meaning of the Commandments for Making and Keeping Human Life Human.* Grand Rapids, Mich.: W. B. Eerdmans Pub. Co., 1995.

17. Aristotle, *Nicomachean Ethics* (Cambridge: Cambridge University Press, 2000).

18. Alasdair MacIntyre, *After Virtue* (Notre Dame, IN: University of Notre Dame Press, 1984).

19. Jean-Paul Sartre, *Existentialism and Human Emotions* (New York: Citadel Press, 1984).

Introduction

Religious Ethics and the Practice of Business

Scott R. Paeth

*I*n their book, *The Smartest Guys in the Room: The Amazing Rise and Scandal-ous Fall of Enron*, Bethany McLean and Peter Elkind detail the lives and careers of many of the main figures in Enron's disastrous 2001 collapse.[1] In a cast of colorful characters, perhaps the most complex and troubling is Kenneth Lay. On the one hand, Lay is portrayed as either failing to prevent, or as actively enabling, the most corrupt practices of his employees, particularly Jeff Skilling and Andrew Fastow. On the other hand, he is portrayed as a devout Christian and frequent lecturer on business ethics.

It certainly does no favors to the field of business ethics when one of the most prominent businessmen of his time is caught in an act of massive fraud while offering the pretense of insight on matters of business morality. It also does no favors to religion when those who publicly declaim their religious worldview seem to have learned the lessons of their faith so poorly. Kenneth Lay would seem to lend credence to the canard that there really is no such thing as "business ethics," while at the same time demonstrating that religious faith is no guarantee of morality. At best, one might say that it serves the interest of a dishonest executive to appear to be a model of probity. At worst, however, it calls into question the very idea that morality and religion have any genuine ability to ensure right conduct in the field of business.

The present volume is intended to be a contribution to the defense of business ethics. Rather than succumb to the cynicism to which cases like that of Kenneth Lay tempt us, it is our belief that the practice of business can benefit from ethical analysis and reflection, and that the practitioners of business can benefit from the resources offered by the field of ethics.

Furthermore, it is our belief that the field of business ethics can benefit from a greater reliance on the materials offered by religious ethics. Much ap-

17

plied ethics relies on philosophical categories to the virtual exclusion of any reference to the relationship of religion to morality. We offer this reader as a resource to guide the thinking of both teachers and students of business ethics in regard to the contributions being made by religious ethicists in the field of business ethics.

ON RELIGION AND ETHICS

The subject of religious ethics is usually passed over lightly in business ethics textbooks. Moral theory is generally done without much concern for whether a religious perspective has anything to add to the subject, much less whether it might offer a compelling ethical option for the practice of business ethics. On the contrary, when religion is mentioned at all, it is often assigned to the topic of "divine command" ethics and then summarily dismissed as either ethically unimportant or, at a minimum, unhelpful.

In part, the reluctance to deal in a serious way with religious ethics is rooted in the modern philosophical "flight from authority," which sought to replace the dogmas of religious absolutism with the cool dispassion of human reason.[2] There were many reasons for this, not least because the religious authorities of the early modern period often seemed bent on preserving the social and intellectual status quo at any cost. This led many modern philosophers, beginning with René Descartes, to seek to find a firm and certain source of knowledge that could be relied upon apart from religious doctrines.[3] In ethics, this movement reached its apex in the work of Immanuel Kant, whose moral theory was explicitly grounded in the pure use of human reason.[4]

The result of this movement has been the marginalization of religion in ethical discourse. This is not to say that religious ethics has disappeared, but, particularly in discussions of applied ethics, it is often treated as a slightly embarrassing appendage to *real* ethics, which is described as rigorously rational and tightly bound to modern philosophical categories.

Several points should be made with regard to this approach. First, by seeking to root moral discourse in the realm of reason, apart from religious authority, modern philosophy aided in the development of modern economic and political systems that were based on the assumption of human autonomy. Insofar as the world created by the rise of capitalism has benefited human life, modern philosophy can take a great deal of the credit for that. However, there were precursors to these developments, which were in turn rooted in the ebb and flow of a social life that revolved around religious devotion. Capitalism did not spring like Athena fully grown from the brow of Adam Smith, but was in a process of development for literally centuries before Smith described its effects.

Nevertheless, the religious world out of which modern philosophy emerged did not offer a great deal to inspire confidence. The Catholic Church of the late Middle Ages was known to act in a heavy-handed and repressive manner with regard to philosophers who deviated from official church teachings, as the case of Galileo Galilei demonstrated. The Protestant churches were seldom much better. Furthermore, the religious wars of the sixteenth century gave rise to a widespread skepticism about the relationship between religion and morality, as religion was much in evidence but morality was often nowhere to be found. One can hardly fault philosophers such as Descartes, Kant, John Locke, and David Hume for seeking another way to speak about the moral life.

However, this having been said, the marginalization of religion in moral discourse has led to the assumption that a religious perspective has little to add to ethical conversation. This we strenuously dispute. If religion *were* actually reducible to irrational authoritarianism, or if its moral contribution could be reduced to bland generalities that could be known apart from religion, perhaps it would be true that religion has little to add. However, religion is a far more intricate reality than this picture would lead one to believe. The relationship between religion and ethics requires a more complex analysis than is usually offered in philosophical texts on ethics.

The situation is further complicated by the difficulty in defining the idea of "religious ethics." As William Schweiker has noted, the very idea of religious ethics can be problematic.[5] What counts as a "religion" in the first place? Given the disputed terrain of ethical thinking, what really *is* ethics? Schweiker refers to the ideas of both "religion" and "ethics" as "scholarly invention."[6] "They are," he writes, "tools for inquiry and reflection."[7] There are certainly moral practices that are associated with particular religious doctrines and practices, but attempts to collect all such practices under a single heading or set of categories have frequently proved futile.

A TYPOLOGY OF RELIGION AND ETHICS

When the relationship between religion and ethics is discussed, it is frequently assumed that religiously oriented morality is solely based upon obedience to the command of God. The ethical responsibility of the religious believer is simply to respond dutifully to the divine authority, but never to question or challenge it. Undoubtedly, much religious ethics corresponds to this characterization, particularly in the Christian and Islamic traditions, but if one takes the broad sweep of human religious experience into account, it becomes quickly apparent that the situation is more complicated.

Buddhist scholar Masao Abe, in comparing the religious traditions of Judaism, Christianity, and Buddhism, has noted that there is not simply one way of relating religion to ethical life.[8] He identifies three approaches that are distinctive to each of the three traditions he considers.[9] Christianity may be characterized by the obedient acceptance of divine commands from God, but neither Judaism nor Buddhism can be understood in this way. In Buddhism, there is no relation between religion and ethics, but instead a mutual negation, while in Judaism the path runs in both directions: Jews are commanded by God to be righteous and holy, and yet Jews may also "audaciously" demand that God act justly and righteously in return.[10] Thus, argues Abe, the relationship between religion and ethics should be understood pluralistically, rather than monolithically. Ethics doesn't necessarily run in a single direction from God to the believer, but may run in multiple directions, or none at all. (It should be said that this is but one among many possible approaches to the relation of religion and ethics. We offer it here as an example of the often-overlooked nuances in understanding their relationship.)

Even in light of Abe's typology, unresolved problems remain. Although Abe interprets Christian ethics as responsiveness to God's command, for example, it is precisely the discernment and interpretation of that command that prove exceedingly difficult. Consider the story of the German theologian and pastor Dietrich Bonhoeffer. Bonhoeffer had to struggle with the question of whether his Christian faith permitted him to take part in a plot to assassinate Adolph Hitler. The question was not whether Nazism was a great evil or Hitler a tyrant, but whether a follower of Jesus Christ was permitted to use violence in a good cause. This is not an easy question, even in retrospect, and the tradition to which Bonhoeffer belonged gave conflicting and seemingly incompatible answers. It fell to Bonhoeffer to make sense of his moral obligation in this situation through his own interpretation of his responsibility to God. By the same token there are schools of interpretation in each of these religious traditions that cut against Abe's analysis.[11] Indeed, William Schweiker argues that it is the interpretive task that is at the heart of a proper understanding of religious ethics.[12]

When religious ethics are criticized, it is often for embodying principles that are far too broad or vague to be of use in the actual practice of real-world decision making.[13] No doubt this same criticism could be made of the central principles of a utilitarian or Kantian ethic as well, although it seldom is. It is in the act of interpreting any ethical system in light of one's concrete circumstances that the system shows its metal. Neither the Categorical Imperative nor the Principle of Utility are of much use apart from concrete cases, and indeed it is in reflecting upon them concretely that they reveal their limitations. In this regard, they are no different from a religiously motivated ethic. Religious ethics do reflect, however, in a way that philosophical systems do not, a way of life and a conception of transcendent moral truth that provide an aid to the interpretation of one's obligation within concrete circumstances. It is the commitment of the believer to be true to that tradition that offers the incentive for a faithful interpretation of one's obligations.

To sum up what we have been arguing: First, as we discussed above, religious ethics are far too complex to be reduced to simply one thing. Second, religious ethics are not simply about taking divinely mandated principles and applying them. In some cases the faithful believer is permitted to ask questions *back* to the God who commands, and in other cases ethics aren't understood as subordinate to a religious source. Third, in any case, religious ethics aren't simply about mapping a broad principle onto a particular case, but about engaging in an act of *interpretation* in which the religious believer attempts to understand the situation in light of his or her religious faith. This involves engaging with a tradition of interpretation, but often it also involves an understanding of just how *religious texts* should be read, and also about how a religious worldview creates a particular *form of life*.

ETHICS AND SACRED TEXTS

Discussions of religion and morality often focus on the idea of a sacred text as the locus of divine revelation and/or moral instruction. Whether it be the Hebrew Scriptures (or TANAK), the Christian Bible, the Muslim Quran, or Hindu Vedic texts, sacred scripture is an element in many, though by no means all, religious traditions. In these texts one can frequently find moral teachings, as well as descriptions of ritual practices, oracles and prophecies, and narratives of the acts of heroes and gods. For many of those who follow these religious traditions, these texts serve as a normative foundation for ethical life, including economic life. The proper conduct of business for a Muslim, for example, is rooted in teachings of the Quran. Insofar as religion draws the believer into a particular way of living and a particular way of looking at the world, these sacred texts can offer guideposts for proper living.

However, as we noted above, this is not to say that sacred texts are always understood to provide surefire answers to moral problems. Sacred texts often provide conflicting accounts of proper action and about the place of God or the gods within human experience. Often there are what one might call "minority reports" in sacred scriptures that offer an alternative way of understanding the importance of religion in the life of the believer.

Take, for example, the book of Job from the Hebrew Scriptures. It tells the story of a righteous man, named Job, who has always done what was proper in the eyes of God. We might say that he demonstrated himself to be a thoroughly moral individual, giving God what God was due, and even atoning for the sins of his children on their behalf. According to the predominant moral worldview of ancient Israel, one who kept faith with God was rewarded with a good life, while those who broke faith with God were punished. One might expect that Job's upstanding behavior would have merited him a reward, but according to the story, God allows Satan to strike him down. In the long poem that follows, Job insists on justice before God and calls into question the ideology that assumes that human suffering must be a punishment from God. In doing this, the text calls into question a particular view of God and of morality, and indeed holds *God* responsible to the very standards of morality that God had laid down.[14] By placing this story among the many other stories in the Bible that proclaim the opposite message, the ancient editors of these sacred texts provided a counterpoint to the dominant ideology of their time. However, by doing this, they neither affirmed nor denied that dominant ideology. Instead, they added another voice, another texture to the moral and religious conversation in which they were participants. They therefore made it more difficult to confidently affirm God's justice (and to lay claim to righteousness before God on the basis of one's own prosperity!). Furthermore, by insisting that God answer his charges, Job makes the point that human obligations to God entail that God fulfill the divine obligation to human beings.

Thus, returning to Abe's typology of religion and ethics, in Judaism ethics is a two-way street between God and humanity. Ethical discourse in Judaism is dialogical, not monological; it cannot be reduced to a version of divine command ethics. Other religious traditions have their own complex relationships with their own sacred texts. To be sure, there are many followers in these traditions who hold to very strict interpretations of the meaning of these sacred texts, but in almost no case is the believer simply a passive vessel for carrying out divine commands. Religious texts often serve within a tradition as a guide, or as an authority, and often as an infallible authority when it comes to morality. But the moral life of the believer involves more than mere obedience, but rather involves embracing a way or form of life that encompasses every facet of their existence, including the practice of business.

RELIGION AS A FORM OF LIFE

In saying that religion is a form of life, what we mean is that religion does not function in the life of the believer as simply a set of disconnected intellectual affirmations that exist apart from their deepest cares and aspirations. On the contrary, what it means to adhere to a religion is that one's entire existence is shaped by the affirmations that this religious form of life entails. This is not to say that one subordinates one's decision making to a religious authority or set of authorities, although in some religious traditions that may well be a component of religious practice. Rather, what we mean here is that religion shapes the whole of the believer's life. To adhere to religious faith is to hold a view of the nature of reality that requires a response in terms of our action in the world. In this sense, there are always ethical implications to religious belief (although, again referring to Abe, it wouldn't be accurate to say that a religion *entails* a particular ethic).

As forms of life, our religious beliefs hold us accountable to their implications, but how we choose to respond to that accountability may take several different forms. For some believers, responsibility to a religious tradition may entail a vigorous defense of that tradition in the face of attempts to criticize or modify it. In every religious tradition, there are adherents for whom the form of life described by their belief system demands a rigorous observance and validation. We may dub this a "rigorist" perspective on religious tradition. It recognizes a religious form of life as requiring an uncompromising commitment of oneself to a set of mandatory core doctrines.

A second way to responding to the implications of religious traditions may be dubbed the "critical" perspective. This perspective operates from an opposite set of assumptions to the rigorist perspective. Rather than seeing the religious form of life as being one of uncompromising commitment to core doctrines, this perspective sees a religious tradition as open to comprehensive criticism. This position sees a religious tradition at least partially as the product of human action, and therefore subject to all of the flaws that creep into any human activity. Thus, a religion can endorse immoral practices and policies, support racism or sexism, and even express its deepest commitments in ways that are incorrect or improper.[15] According to this point of view, even core doctrines may not be above criticism.

Between these two positions there are any number of places where one may stand. The critical perspective can exist within the same religious institution as the rigorist perspective, and the depth of criticism can range from fairly mild to comprehensive. By the same token, one can be relatively rigorist in one's application of a religious tradition while at the same time recognizing that not every element of one's religious tradition counts as a "core doctrine."

Wherever one stands between these two poles, one is accountable for how one's life is a response to the conditions set forth in one's religious tradition. Thus, in adhering to a religious worldview, one finds oneself intrinsically entwined in questions of morality and obligation. This can be particularly true in the practice of business in the context of our modern, globalized world. What our religious lives tell us is necessary, and what our business lives tell us is expedient, may often conflict at seemingly deep and intractable levels. How we negotiate these conflicts in a way that is both true to our religious values and economically viable is the central problem to be addressed in any consideration of the relationship of religion to business ethics. As actors in the modern world, we are not only governed by one form of life, but participate in several simultaneously. Moral life involves carving a single integral identity from out of the multiple influences that impinge upon us.

RELIGION, COMMERCE, AND ECONOMICS

Given the way that economics has been studied for the better part of the last century, the idea that religion (or ethics for that matter) might have something to say to our economic lives may sound somewhat strange. Yet for this reason it is important to return to the origins of modern economics and consider briefly what Adam Smith, as the founder of modern economics, was attempting.

Adam Smith is best known as the author of *The Wealth of Nations*, the great treatise in which he laid out the philosophical and economic basis for capitalism, advocating free trade and the division of labor as essential elements of a healthy and productive economy.[16] Yet, for all of the renown that this book has brought him, Smith considered his earlier *The Theory of Moral Sentiments* to have been his magnum opus.[17] In this book, Smith articulates the moral theory that founds his later work, a moral theory rooted in the natural sympathy that humans have for one another, which was granted to them by God.[18]

Adam Smith is famous for his description of the way the self-interest of each actor in the marketplace serves to benefit the whole. He writes:

> In almost every other race of animals each individual, when it is grown up to maturity, is entirely independent, and in its natural state has occasion for the assistance of no other living creature. But man has almost constant occasion for the help of his brethren, and it is in vain for him to expect it from their benevolence only. He will be more likely to prevail if he can interest their self-love in his favour, and show them that it is for their own advantage to do for him what he requires of them. Whoever offers to another a bargain of any kind, proposes to do this. Give me that which I want, and you shall have this which you want, is the meaning of every such offer; and it is in this manner that we obtain from one another the far greater part of those good offices which we stand in need of. It is not from the benevolence of the butcher, the brewer, or the baker, that we expect our dinner, but from their regard to their own interest. We address ourselves, not to their humanity but to their self-love, and never talk to them of our own necessities but of their advantages. Nobody but a beggar chooses to depend chiefly upon the benevolence of his fellow-citizens. Even a beggar does not depend upon it entirely.[19]

Many read this quote as a summary of the ethical position often termed "egoism," that is, the belief that human beings should (or, at a minimum, inevitably do) act solely or chiefly out of self-interest. This passage is crucially important in understanding what Smith saw as the chief fact of human moral existence: that human beings for the most part act out of *self-love*. Yet, in order to put this passage into context, it is important to consider what he meant by the central term *benevolence*.

Smith's moral philosophy was based on the idea that human beings have a natural capacity to feel sympathy for one another. Whereas Immanuel Kant based his whole moral philosophy around the exercise of reason, for Smith, it was the proper formation of our *emotions* that was of central importance. Human beings, by being habituated into society, undergo a process of moral development in which they become more and more capable of imaginatively extending their sympathies to a wider and wider portion of humanity, even to humanity as a whole. The benevolence of which he writes in the above passage refers to that capacity for imaginative sympathy that morally upright human beings display. Yet, this benevolence was not, for Smith, wholly self-sacrificing. We have responsibilities to ourselves and to our families as well as to society. Smith recognizes that the benevolence that motivates us to do good for another human being can only accomplish so much good. For the sake of the economy, another emotion must be appealed to, and that is our self-love.

But even this self-love should not be understood to be sheer egoism. On the contrary, Smith's understanding of self-love is the foundation of our capacity to love others. The benevolence of which Smith writes is the philosophical translation of the Christian ethic of love for one's neighbors. Thus does Smith write: "As to love our neighbor as we love ourselves is the great law of Christianity, so it is the great precept of nature to love ourselves only as we love our neighbour, or what comes to the same thing, as our neighbour is capable of loving us."[20] Rather than egoism, the appeal that Smith makes to self-love is an appeal to the natural self-regard that actually makes benevolence possible.

It is also worth noting in this regard, Smith is not arguing that the only two options available to society are benevolence and self-love. Rather, Smith argues, society has an interest in establishing justice where benevolence fails to act:

> Though Nature, therefore, exhorts mankind to acts of beneficence, by the pleasing consciousness of deserved reward, she has not thought it necessary to guard and enforce the practice of it by the terrors of merited punishment in case it should be neglected. It is the ornament which embellishes, not the foundation which supports the building, and which it was, therefore, sufficient to recommend, but by no means necessary to impose. Justice, on the contrary, is the main pillar that upholds the whole edifice. If it is removed,

the great, the immense fabric of human society, that fabric which to raise and support seems in this world, if I may say so, to have been the peculiar and darling care of Nature, must in a moment crumble into atoms.[21]

Thus, far from promoting a society that, as the philosopher Thomas Hobbes put it, is a "war of all against all," Smith argues that human society is founded in justice, which tempers our self-love, and which in turn forms us into creatures that, at the very least, are *capable* of acts of love for our neighbors.

Given the complexities of Smith's thought, it would be difficult to pin him down as a "Christian" ethicist in the mold of some of his contemporaries. Yet, what is clear from a reading of both *The Wealth of Nations* and *The Theory of Moral Sentiments* is that Smith intended his analysis of capitalism to render both a *moral* and a *religious* economic theory. While the discipline of economics seldom seeks to understand itself as primarily an ethical discipline, its founder clearly understood it that way.

What implications does this have for business ethics? Particularly in light of the popular idea that business is solely about profit making rather than morality, a recovery of Smith's moral thought may go some way toward recovering a place for morality and religion at the table of economic discourse.[22] At the same time, Smith's thinking ought to turn the attention of businessmen and businesswomen, as they consider the social implications of their business practices, toward the questions of justice and benevolence that were so central to Smith's thinking. Furthermore, the directly religious sources of Smith's arguments offer a model for religious thinking in business ethics that can be emulated by those interested, as we are, in recovering a religious voice in the broader field of business ethics.

"ECONOMIC JUSTICE FOR ALL"?

Perhaps the most influential statement on the relationship of religion to business ethics in the past twenty-five years has been the U.S. Catholic bishops' pastoral letter, *Economic Justice for All.*[23] In this document, the bishops laid the groundwork for a religious critique of capitalist economic systems. Arguing that societies and economies are morally responsible to those who are affected by their policies, the bishops articulate several principles that they viewed as foundational for a moral economy. These principles include an emphasis on human rights and dignity, participation, and an obligation to the poorest members of society. According to the bishops, the overall wealth of a nation is secondary to what they call the "option for the poor":

> As followers of Christ, we are challenged to make a fundamental "option for the poor"—to speak for the voiceless, to defend the defenseless, to assess life styles, policies, and social institutions in terms of their impact on the poor. This "option for the poor" does not mean pitting one group against another, but rather, strengthening the whole community by assisting those who are most vulnerable. As Christians, we are called to respond to the needs of *all* our brothers and sisters, but those with the greatest needs require the greatest response.[24]

By insisting that the needs of the poor must be given priority in economic decision making, the bishops throw down the gauntlet in challenge to presumptions such as those we noted above, which insist that profit is the only proper concern of a business. Rather, the bishops argue, profit is only valuable insofar as it is of value to those who are most in need. In order to preserve basic human dignity, it is necessary to ensure that those who are naked be given clothes, those who are hungry be given food, those who are thirsty be given drink, and those who are homeless be given shelter. These are nonnegotiable moral responsibilities, but they are responsibilities that are incumbent upon the whole society—not just the church, or the state, or private charity, but business enterprises as well. Justice demands that these responsibilities be met.

A number of points bear further consideration. First, it is important to note that the bishops have a complex view of social relationships. Their arguments are rooted in a long tradition of Catholic social teaching, which extends back to Leo XIII's encyclical *Rerum Novarum: The Condition of the Working Classes.*[25] This text laid the foundations for Catholic moral engagement with the economic questions of society by offering a forceful critique of communism and socialism while at the same time calling capitalist economic systems to a higher moral standard.

According to Catholic social teaching, the various institutions of society have different roles in securing social justice. It is not up to businesses to be social welfare agencies, nor is it up to states to run the day-to-day economic activities of society. But both businesses and states have obligations to act justly to those who are under their power. Businesses have an obligation to treat employees fairly, pay them a decent wage, and allow them to organize for collective bargaining, while states have an obligation to enforce laws fairly and redistribute wealth to those who are in need through just policies of taxation and welfare. Thus, it is not up to businesses alone to secure social justice, but it is incumbent upon business to work with other social institutions to see to it that social justice is achieved.

Second, although this is a pastoral letter written by Catholic bishops and addressed to Christians, it is not intended to apply only to those who share the bishops' faith. Rather, the bishops intend their argument to be heard and responded to by all members of society. Although they make reference to a number of biblical passages in order to justify their stand, they do not *base* their arguments on those passages. Rather, their arguments are based upon an appeal to a universal morality that can be accessed by anyone of goodwill.

Third, the bishops are not making an anticapitalist argument. Rather, their argument assumes capitalism as the framework for the economic organization of society but seeks to temper the worst tendencies of capitalism by appealing to the idea that all citizens have an interest in securing social justice and the common good. The policies that the bishops recommend—working toward full employment, providing job-training programs for the unemployed, securing the rights of workers and families—are all formulated in light of the economic fact of capitalism. As such, it is not an "antibusiness" document. Businesses, like all other institutions of society, are called upon to work toward the improvement of the whole society rather than concerning themselves solely with matters of profit.

Needless to say, *Economic Justice for All* did not capture the hearts and minds of all Americans, nor even all Roman Catholics. It did, however, create a great deal of controversy and discussion about the proper role of religious institutions in formulating economic policies. There were certainly no shortage of critics who claimed that the bishops had exceeded their mandate as well as their competence by presuming to speak on economic matters. Rather, the argument went, it was for religious leaders to speak on "spiritual matters" and to leave questions of economics and politics to those who were best suited to those vocations.

Yet, from the perspective of religious ethics, it is simply not possible to concentrate on the spiritual dimension of human existence without attending to the material conditions in which human beings exist. In saying this, we are not claiming to break any new ground. Nor were the bishops breaking new ground. Rather, this principle is at the heart of the Catholic moral tradition, the Protestant social gospel movement, and the religious teachings of numerous other religious traditions. While religion is concerned with more than simply our physical well-being or modes of social organization, these matters fall well within its realm of concern, insofar as that realm is always focused on human good.

What the bishops' letter offers is one model of a religious ethic that self-consciously appraises the practice of businesses and their effects on society. Just as Adam Smith's economic theory was rooted in a religious morality that encompassed a far larger set of concerns than simple "self-interest," so the religious morality of the Catholic bishops brings the question of moral responsibility right into the realm of business practices. The controversy that this letter raised was due in no small part to the fact that it directly challenged the prevailing view that larger moral considerations have no part in the world of business. The bishops insisted that we are all—pastors, professors, politicians, entrepreneurs, along with all the members of society—responsible for bringing about conditions of human flourishing.

"THE HEART OF THE MATTER"

We would like to conclude this essay by referring to another one. Paul Camenisch, our colleague at DePaul University, once wrote a now-classic essay, "Business Ethics: On Getting to the Heart of the Matter."[26] In this essay (not reproduced in this volume) Camenisch asks his reader to imagine a company that met all of the standard definitions of a "moral" business—it gave to charity, it paid its employees a fair wage, it was ecologically responsible and civic-minded. Yet, the only possible use for its products was human torture. Could such a business be considered moral? Camenisch argues not. Rather, the "heart" of business was not to be found in its productivity, nor in its profits, but in the *kinds* of products that it makes. It is in making products that authentically contribute to human well-being that the question of morality in business really hits bedrock. It is the *product* of an enterprise that finally makes it moral. It is the decision that we make as owners and managers to produce goods that aid others or harm others, or the decision that we make as employees to participate in making such products, that in large measure defines our morality.

But, in this case, the question that we must end with is this: How do we become the kinds of people who choose properly which kinds of enterprise in which to engage? From whence comes the wisdom that leads us to say no, as Dietrich Bonhoeffer did, when asked to participate in work that harms another? And from whence comes the knowledge that enables us to identify which work is helpful and which is harmful? And, finally, from whence comes the strength to say yes to those possibilities that genuinely correspond to our moral calling as human beings?

What religious ethics offer is not one single, simple answer to these questions, but rather a way of confronting the world, of internalizing a set of values rooted in a religious tradition that corresponds to our deepest human aspirations. The moral life cannot be found in any book, but must be discovered through our lived choices as responsible agents. Religion can give us models and guides, and offer us some connection to a larger reality than ourselves. But it rarely, if ever, provides us with an answer that we ourselves don't have to go to the hard work of discovering. Like all things, morality takes practice. But, at least in part, it is in the intention to act morally that we may discover the kernel of genuine moral action, because in that intension rests the consciousness that we are accountable to something outside of ourselves. If the heart of business ethics lies in the choice we make to strive for human flourishing, then the heart of that choice must lie in our willingness to think carefully about what morality consists of, and what is required of us in the quest to live a genuinely moral life.

NOTES

1. Bethany McLean and Peter Elkind, *The Smartest Guys in the Room: The Amazing Rise and Scandalous Fall of Enron* (New York: Portfolio, 2003).

2. Jeffery Stout, *Flight from Authority: Religion, Morality, and the Quest for Autonomy* (Notre Dame, IN: University of Notre Dame Press, 1987).

3. Rene Descartes, *Meditations on First Philosophy* (Indianapolis, IN: Hackett Publishing, 1979).

4. Immanuel Kant, *The Critique of Practical Reason* (New York: Macmillan, 1956).

5. William Schweiker, "On Religious Ethics," in *The Blackwell Companion to Religious Ethics*, ed. William Schweiker (Oxford: Blackwell Publishers, 2004), 1.

6. Schweiker, "On Religious Ethics," 2.

7. Schweiker, "On Religious Ethics," 2.

8. Masao Abe, "A Rejoinder," in *The Emptying God,* ed. John B. Cobb and Christopher Ives (Maryknoll, NY: Orbis Books, 1990), 157ff.

9. Abe, "A Rejoinder," 185.

10. See Darrell J. Fasching and Dell DeChant, *Comparative Religious Ethics: A Narrative Approach* (Oxford: Blackwell Publishers, 2001), 174ff.

11. Fasching and Dechant, *Comparative Religious Ethics*, 311.

12. Schweiker, "On Religious Ethics," 3.

13. See William H. Shaw, *Business Ethics*, 5th ed. (Belmont, CA: Thompson Wadsworth, 2005), 10–12.

14. See Fasching and DeChant, *Comparative Religious Ethics*, 174ff.

15. See, for an example of this approach, the chapter "Feminist Audacity and the Ethics of Interdependence," in *Comparative Religious Ethics*, ed. Fasching and DeChant, 267ff.

16. Adam Smith, *An Inquiry into the Nature and Causes of the Wealth of Nations* (New York: Oxford University Press, 1976).

17. Adam Smith, *The Theory of Moral Sentiments*, ed. D. D. Raphel and A. L. MacFie (Oxford: Clarendon Press, 1976).

18. For an intriguing interpretation of how Adam Smith's moral theory would translate into the contemporary economic world, see Jonathan B. Wight, *Saving Adam Smith* (Upper Saddle River, NJ: Prentice-Hall, 2002).

19. Smith, *Wealth of Nations* I.2.2.

20. Smith, *Theory of Moral Sentiments*, I.i.5.5.

21. Smith, *Theory of Moral Sentiments*, II.ii.3.3.

22. This viewpoint is rooted in the work of Milton Friedman, whose classic declaration that the only moral responsibility of a business is to make a profit and play by the rules has set the stage for much thinking about the role of ethics in economics. An important counterpoint to this attitude is Amartya Sen, whose books *On Economics and Ethics* (Oxford: Basil Blackwell, 1987) and *Development as Freedom* (New York: Random House, 1999) attempt to recover a place for moral language in the field of economics. For the original context of Friedman's statement, see "The Social Responsibility of Business Is to Increase Its Profits," in *New York Times Magazine* (September 13, 1970). For further analysis of the relationship between morality and economics in the work of Adam Smith and Milton Friedman, see Harvey S. James and Farhad Rassekh, "Smith, Friedman, and Self-Interest in Ethical Society," in this volume.

23. United States Conference of Catholic Bishops, *Economic Justice for All* (Washington, DC: U.S. Catholic Conference, 1986).

24. United States Conference of Catholic Bishops, *Economic Justice for All*.

25. Pope Leo XIII, *Rerum Novarum: On the Condition of the Working Classes* (Boston: Pauline Books & Media, 2000)

26. Paul Camenisch, "Business Ethics: On Getting to the Heart of the Matter," in *Business, Religion, and Ethics* (Cambridge, MA: Oelgeschlager, Gunn & Hain, 1982).

Part I

RELIGIOUS ETHICS AND NORMATIVE THEORIES

On Monopoly in Business Ethics: Can Philosophy Do It All?

Paul F. Camenisch

In a post-9/11 world there are many who have a hard time imagining a positive role for religion in our public life. From the aggressively antireligious views of humorist Bill Maher to the growing anti-Muslim sentiment in Western Europe, religious participation in public life is looked upon with increasing suspicion. In this chapter, Paul Camenisch addresses a very similar sentiment that was expressed by some philosophers about the supposed inadequacy of religious studies to take up the task of constructing an appropriate business ethic. Camenisch addresses his philosophical critics by first demonstrating the weakness of the claim concerning religion's so-called unique handicaps, which, as our author shows, also appear to be shortcomings shared equally by philosophy. The chapter concludes by pointing out some of the positive distinctive contributions that a religious studies approach brings to the discipline of business ethics.

The position maintained below, along with several of the supporting arguments, was previously articulated in an article in the *Journal of Business Ethics* in 1986,[1] largely in response to the thought of Richard T. DeGeorge concerning the role, or, more accurately, the lack of a role for religious/theological thought in business ethics.[2] While the following discussion is still significantly shaped by DeGeorge's position as then articulated, the argument has been reorganized and is no longer tailored to his position. A number of new, related issues have also been introduced.

As I hope will be clear very early, my goal here is not to displace philosophy and other disciplines and their contributions to business ethics with religious materials and methods, but rather simply to defend a legitimate role for religious contributions and to argue that even if one does not accept the tools, methods, analyses, conclusions, or recommendations of any given religious tradition, the business ethics done with an openness to those elements and an understanding of what they aim at and how they proceed will be a more adequate business ethics. The reverse, of course, is also true, that a religious/theological business ethics well informed about and open to, even appropriating, the contributions of philosophy and the social sciences will also be a more adequate business ethics.

To forestall the need for repeated disclaimers, I will state here what should be obvious: Nothing here should be taken to suggest that the author endorses any and all influence that any religion has ever had on the conduct of individuals and groups. Religious persons in general are no more obliged to answer for the suicide/murders of the followers of Jim Jones in Guyana, or the strange presence/influence of religious leaders and beliefs in the recent acquittal of HealthSouth's Richard Scrushy, or—to provide a more parallel comparison—they no more have to answer for the theology and theologians who gave rise to the Spanish Inquisition than do philosophers in general have to answer for the philosophers who undergirded the Nazi enterprise. Having entered this general disclaimer, I will attempt here to focus on the best that religion/theology and philosophy have to offer business ethics. Readers, I hope, will do the same as they consider the following treatment of those contributions.

Similarly, I hope it is clear that I argue here not for the role of any specific religious tradition in business ethics but for the legitimacy of religious participation as such, although such participation will almost always—and, to my mind, must, if it is to be meaningful—come from a specific tradition. This disclaimer is not meant to obscure the fact that I think and speak largely out of my own Protestant Christian background and training even as I attempt to speak about or for "religion in general."

THE TASK OF BUSINESS ETHICS

Before we can consider what any discipline can contribute to business ethics, we need at least a tentative statement of the goal or purpose of business ethics. That task or goal can be stated somewhat generally as being to assist persons in understanding and then appropriately responding to ethical or moral issues arising in business. Most, I believe, would be willing tentatively to accept this as a working definition, while rightly insisting that we must go further and discuss what forms such assistance is to take, the grounds on which it rests, and so forth, knowing full well that the devil here, as usual, is in the details. But before we pursue this question of the forms such assistance rightly takes, we should briefly consider another possible response to the above definition.

Virtually all can be expected to see the increase in complexity as we move from the "understanding" part of the above task, much, if not all of the assistance for which can be seen as an analytical and descriptive enterprise, to the "appropriately responding" part, which introduces, even if ever so gently, a normative element, assistance for which, of course is a much more complex undertaking. However, a small minority of philosophers may not only see the greater complexity of this second element, but may go even further and maintain that philosophy should stop with the analytical/descriptive elements of the first part of the task, that the normative task, especially with regard to specific cases and dilemmas, is not a proper undertaking for academic philosophy.

Philosophers, of course, are free to define the task of philosophy as they wish, as long as any such definition does not claim exclusive rights to functions properly shared by other disciplines, nor in any other way inappropriately limit how other disciplines define their tasks. But we need not here enter into an extended discussion of the place of the making and supporting of normative judgments in the task of academic philosophy, for a brief perusal of the numerous business ethics texts, articles, and monographs produced in recent decades by philosophers clearly shows that persons generally recognized as philosophers, in writings generally recognized as philosophical, do indeed make normative judgments about the moral issues arising in business. This claim of some philosophers concerning a "value-free," entirely descriptive/analytical business ethics would also seem to be undercut by the simple fact that even to present some "cases" as of interest in the context of ethics implies the recognition of some norms according to which those situations but not others are morally interesting and even problematic.

The philosopher determined to maintain the value-free stance might argue that in presenting such cases she is simply describing what others seem to see as problematic given the norms those others, or perhaps the society in general, claim to accept. But any such argument would have to be accompanied by an explanation of why such an activity or discipline as that should not be seen as a sociology, or anthropology, or ethnography of business, with a focus on what some see as ethical issues, rather than being presented as business ethics.

While such philosophical activities including the making and defending of normative judgments, along with parallel activities in medical, professional, and similar areas, are sometimes set off from the rest of academic philosophy under the label of "applied ethics," seldom has this labeling contained or even implied an argument that this was not really philosophy. Thus, I will assume in the following that however these various internal issues are settled by philosophers, in business ethics as currently being done in universities across the country, both philosophically and religiously/theologically trained scholars are engaging in the making and supporting of normative judgments. At least brief treatment of this issue is essential here because the grounds for criticizing or even denying the role of religious thought in business ethics are generally of two sorts—the one being that religious/theological business ethics contain normative judgments at all, and the second being about how those normative judgments are arrived at and defended. If I am correct that most if not all philosophers engaged in business ethics also end by making normative judgments, then the grounds for that first criticism are undermined or, at the very least, religious ethicists are under no darker cloud for offering normative judgments than are their philosophical counterparts. Thus, we can here focus on the second sort of criticism—those having to do with *how* religious/theological normative judgments are arrived at and defended and whether they are somehow inherently weaker or less defensible than their philosophical counterparts.

But first, a few brief comments on religious approaches and the first part of the above task—the descriptive/analytical part—are called for. It has sometimes been suggested that the descriptive/analytical part of business ethics is essentially a philosophical function; thus, persons from other disciplines or fields engaging in such activities are there doing philosophy. The analytical and descriptive contributions of philosophers, such as clarifying, analyzing, and teasing out the presuppositions of moral judgments, have helped all of us who want to think more clearly about business ethics. But it is not at all clear how one would ground the claim that this is a uniquely, even an exclusively philosophical task. Responsible practitioners in all disciplines seek to be clear, critical, and analytical. Of course, philosophers may claim that anyone engaged in these tasks thereby functions as a philosopher. But until persuasive grounds for such disciplinary imperialism are offered, I believe that such claims are best and rightly set aside.

REPLIES TO SPECIFIC OBJECTIONS TO RELIGIOUS/ THEOLOGICAL CONTRIBUTIONS TO BUSINESS ETHICS

The Multiplicity of Religious Voices

One frequent and entirely appropriate response to the introduction of religious considerations into business ethics or, in fact, into the discussion of almost any issue of public importance has to do with the multiplicity of religions and the fact that they see the world in quite different ways and urge quite different responses to it. "So," says the critic, "if we are to talk religion, just whose religion should it be?" Justified though this question is, as a criticism intended to turn us to philosophy as a better guide, it is a telling criticism only if the philosophy to which we turn speaks with a single voice itself. But we can almost as readily respond with, "Whose philosophy?" Do we start with the basic assumptions about the world and existence of existentialism, or those of one of the more traditional "essentialisms"? Or in ethics do we start with those almost omnipresent options of applied ethics, Kant or utilitarianism, or with some of the other emergent, but less historically established options? Or, to be even more specific, on a particular ethical issue such as justice, do we start with Rawls, or Nozick, or Walzer, or Aristotle, or . . . ?

If a multiplicity of voices from a single discipline or field is a serious obstacle to that discipline or field's participation in the public square, then while religion will have to find a way to deal with that problem, philosophy is far from being exempt from this same challenge.

The Clear, Single Voice of Reason

To use a language perhaps now somewhat dated, in the past the full participation of religion and of persons speaking out of their religious traditions in discussions of public issues was often challenged on the basis of the assertion, or often just the assumption, that religious teachings rested on revelation, while philosophy spoke on the basis of reason, or, to be more precise and more informative for our current concern, on the basis of *human* reason. While a number of issues spring from this apparent dichotomy, the key one, at least for our current concern, was that revelation—generally taken to mean some process or channel by which the divine spoke through and/or to religious literature, religious leaders, and their communities in ways that did not depend on, in fact, in ways that largely bypassed, human capacities of reasoning and understanding—and its content were known to and certainly were persuasive only for members of that particular religious tradition, that is, those persons who had subscribed to the worldview, the basic beliefs about the divine, the nature of the universe, and of the human, of that tradition. Thus, those outside that tradition were at least figuratively "in the dark" about the truth of such matters addressed by that revelation.

Philosophy, on the other hand, at least in the "Western" tradition has generally claimed to speak only out of the human capacities for understanding and reasoning that we all presumably possess. Thus, the ethical recommendations of religious traditions were surds for nonmembers, for they did not fit into any framework of knowledge and understanding available to the public at large, while the ethical recommendations of the philosophers, rooted only in human capacities, could presumably be understood and endorsed by all carefully thinking persons. Therefore, the conclusion easily followed, that in public matters concerning the society at large, specific religious traditions should remain silent. Although this debate, at least in these specific terms, seems to surface less and less frequently, its assumptions and implications still appear to exert considerable influence.

Once again, a brief response to this challenge is all that is possible here. First, except for those who attempt to take the teachings of their sacred literature literally, and perhaps even for them, virtually all the capacities of the human mind are enlisted to understand, to apply, and, in some contexts and to some extent, to test what is thought to have been revealed—perhaps not to test the revelation itself, for that might be a blow to the very conception of revelation and its authority as many understand it, but at least to test whether our understanding or interpretation of the meaning of that revelation seems to be authentic or valid. For example, one way this is frequently done is to see if the content of one revealed doctrine seems to be consistent with the larger body of revealed teachings already accepted by that community.

Thus, while the original nugget of revealed teaching with which a community begins, and its justification, may be inaccessible to some significant degree to those outside the faith, most subsequent discourse about it should be largely accessible to those who honestly try to understand the conversation. Furthermore, as I shall show below, while the terminology varies, it seems to me that the dynamics of the beginning of philosophical discourse suffer, if that is the proper term, under many of these same limitations.

Secondly, those traditions that see the divine as responsible for the creation of the entire universe have sound grounds for maintaining that the will of the creator can be detected in multiple loci in the universe: from human reason, to the historical consensus of societies concerning what is required for a viable community, to the very structure of the physical universe. This conviction can be seen in some Christian traditions' distinction between special revelation, which was the sort coming in the extra- or suprarational manner noted above, and general revelation, which was the sort embedded in various ways in the universe and was therefore at least potentially accessible to any who would seek it. This latter sort of "revelation" should be much less problematic, for a number of obvious reasons, in discussions of public matters.

The Multiple, Richer Voices of Reason

Nevertheless, many seem still automatically to assume that reason—and often in academic circles dealing with ethics, philosophical reason—has a clear advantage, even a legitimate hegemony over all other ways of knowing and proceeding. There are at least three kinds of questions to be put to this elevation of reason in most of Western philosophy. (It should be clear to the reader by now that we are here using "reason" in a "narrow" rather than a "broad" sense covering all "natural" human capacities, a distinction that will be clarified below.)

The first kind of question has to do with the inadequacy of such reason, or of such a conception of reason, even if, for the sake of the discussion, we accept most of its major supporting assumptions. The second has to do with the emergence—even in the "West," the cultural home of this idea of a univocal reason—of multiple other ways of knowing, understanding, and judging that seem to fall outside the traditional view of reason we have in mind here. The third has to do with the insularity, the parochialism of any such single, culturally based conception of reason in light of our growing awareness of the great diversity of cultures, both past and present, and their varied ways of understanding, ordering, and responding to their worlds. Each of these calls for at least brief comment.

First, we turn to weaknesses of philosophical reason even on its own terms. It is not at all clear that reason is any more capable of establishing its own authority, especially its authority as the one reliable way of perceiving, understanding, and responding to the world, than is the sacred book or doctrine of any religious tradition. The process of such self-authenticating authorization would seem to be equally circular in both cases. The conclusions of both processes would seem, by their very nature, to be dependent on our first having accepted some fundamental beliefs about the nature of the tool or source being used, beliefs that the tool or source itself could not get behind, under, or prior to in order to authenticate. While many agree that this argument poses a basic problem for religious sources and methods, they are less ready to see it as being equally a problem for reason.

Part of the difference in these two reactions arises, I believe, from the mistaken belief that the reason of the philosophers, if it is not identical to, is at least significantly continuous with the reason of mathematics and formal logic, on the one hand, and the reason of the natural sciences, on the other. The identification with the reason of math and formal logic is the most easily discredited. The various elements and dynamics of humanly created symbol systems such as math and formal logic are connected in much tighter, more consistent, and more evident ways than are the elements and dynamics of the natural world, of human experience and activity, and of the other subject matter studied by philosophy. Thus, the "rules" by which the former operate are much more susceptible to being understood by the human mind and navigated by human reason than are the latter, in no small part because the former are, to a considerable degree, the products of that same human mind or reason that now seeks to understand and apply them.

The question with regard to the reasoning processes on which modern sciences rest is not whether they have largely legitimated themselves by their impressive success in understanding and manipulating the natural world to bring about the effects the scientists sought. The question, rather, is whether philosophy's reason has had or conceivably could have similar success, given the very different nature of the enterprise in which philosophy is engaged, the subject matter with which it deals, and the goals it pursues. What would such success in terms of generating predicted and desired outcomes look like in areas such as philosophical cosmology, anthropology, aesthetics, or ethics? Thus we should resist privileging philosophical reason over religious or theological reason by uncritically ascribing to it traits and capacities of the reason employed by math and the natural sciences.

The second sort of challenge to be put to some of philosophical reason's claims arises from the growing awareness in this same "Western" context that we perceive and understand ourselves and the world, and that we advance our store of knowledge and determine how to apply it to the world, in ways other than the more or less abstract, analytical, discursive, philosophical reason we have been discussing. Here I must make explicit what many readers may already have detected, that I have been using "reason" in a narrow sense to refer to the sort of tool just described, rather than in a broader sense that would include the multiple and varied capacities with which humans understand and interact with the world. The typical tendency of the narrower view of reason to set analytical, discursive reason off from other human ways of knowing and being in the world is exemplified, for example, in the frequent admonition, "Now let's think (be reasonable) about this, and not get emotional."

But many are increasingly convinced that the emotions and other capacities and sensibilities we possess are also important means of enlarging our understanding of the self, others, and the world at large, and of charting our responses to them. Many of these processes and their fruit do indeed seem to be more private and personal and less susceptible to some sort of public verification than we believe most of our more "reasoned" knowings are, but this does not automatically mean that they are somehow inferior to or less valid than the narrower form of reason and its conclusions, unless, of course, we begin our assessment of them by taking the protocols of this narrower sense of reason as our standard for all human knowing. But of course, that would clearly be to beg the question, to predetermine the answer to the very question we are asking, which is whether this narrow sort of reason is our best, or even our only, way of knowing the world in all its aspects.

Such a broader understanding of reason would include ways of knowing such as that presented by Carol Gilligan and further developed by many feminists, which would seem to maintain, among other things, that we know or learn how we should respond to problematic situations not (only?) by the abstract principles purportedly established by the philosophical reason we have been examining, but (also) by our sense of what is appropriate arising from our actual relationships with and what we know about the relationships among the various parties involved in the situation.[3] The appropriate response learned in such a manner is often presented as a mode of caring appropriate to the persons involved and the relations among them. While the convictions about proper conduct arising from this source can, no doubt, be approximately translated into the language of obligations, rights, justice, benefits, and harms of more traditionally reasoned positions, the proponents of these "other" ways of knowing would surely argue that such translations and their frequently more abstract concepts are secondary attempts to help others understand what they see as appropriate and are not the means by which such insight was initially gained. This knowledge, they would say, came through the complex chemistry of being part of and/or trying to understand the relations among persons that constitute the problematic situation being addressed.

Or to cite another example—while many of us disagree with the conclusions he drew from it concerning human cloning, I believe that there is at least an initial persuasiveness in Leon Kass's basic thesis that there is a kind of wisdom or knowing in our repugnance at certain situations or certain proposed actions.[4] Of course we cannot ignore here the risk of ending in a subjectivism in which we not only disagree with each other but in which we have little or no access to the grounds of the position we wish to contest. I cannot experience your repugnance unless I truly share it. And while some of the significance and possibly even some of the grounds of your repugnance can perhaps be translated into more public language and concepts that I can understand, it is clear that the fundamental experience of your repugnance as a way of knowing will be distorted and/or greatly simplified in any such translation. In other words, these alternative ways of knowing are not just new disguises for the same old reason. They are, at least arguably, different and even independent cognitively helpful ways of learning about and relating to the world and to each other.

Not only is the narrower reason of the philosophers offered as the best way to increase our knowledge, but it is also offered as the best way to convey it to others. The best means of such communication will, of course, vary with the content of what is being conveyed. But here too, the hegemony of analytical, discursive reason is also being challenged. One alternative means for conveying what we know, sense, or feel about the world and ourselves is the arts. Picasso's *Guernica* could, to some extent, be reduced to a more "rational," literal form or even to a verbal argument against war. But for most of us that would also be a reduction in the pejorative sense, reducing a richer, more complex phenomenon to elements that are simpler, and perhaps in some ways more precise, at the cost of losing the richer complexity and more powerful statement of the original work.

I may seem to have wandered far afield from the issue of the role of religion and religious studies in business ethics, especially in comparison to the role of philosophy and what I have been calling philosophical reason. But the larger issue here is how we decide, discover, or discern what is the morally most appropriate way to conduct our lives and whether what I am calling the philosophers' reason is the only tool adequate to that task. It may therefore be useful to cite some examples where nondiscursive forms of reason seem to play a significant role in how we direct our moral lives even though they may initially seem remote from our immediate concerns. The intention here, of course, is to establish that the range of tools or methods we employ is larger and more varied than a focus on reason in any narrow sense would lead us to believe. And that, it is hoped, will make room for other methods, including religious ones, to be taken more seriously.

When most of us think about the most significant relationships in our lives, the connections to others that make us who we are and play a major role in revealing who we are and in determining who we will be as persons in general and as moral agents, we find that discursive reason has played a very small role in founding, grounding, or sustaining those relations. How do we know whom to trust, or whether our best friend or spouse or partner is trustworthy, or is to be watched at every turn? How do we choose a friend, a career, a life-changing commitment, whether to a person or to a cause? There may be elements of discursive reasoning involved here, a listing of plusses and minuses, a gathering of evidence about who this person is and how she has handled previous commitments. But finally, none of us is relieved in these matters of the need to make a decision, to exercise our judgment, to commit ourselves. And that is not the same thing as adding up the numbers of a sum, drawing a conclusion from a classical syllogism—"Socrates is mortal"—or following empirical evidence to the only possible conclusion about right or wrong in this situation.

In most of the important matters of our lives, certainly including difficult moral decisions, we finally have to step beyond what has felt like the firm ground of reason, with its careful, orderly, deliberate, analytical methods, into a realm where the importance of the matter is exceeded by a complexity that refuses to be boiled down to simple formulas and where, on the basis of knowings we cannot adequately explain even to ourselves, we know we must do "x" and not "y." Are we sometimes wrong (by whatever standards we and/or others later judge our performance)? Almost certainly. But doesn't reason also sometimes mislead us? But whatever our methods of moral knowing or discerning, there is no guarantee that they will not sometimes mislead us. And would it not be even more misleading for us to assume that in these matters there is only one way of knowing.

One situation in which we must step beyond where reason can with certainty take us, is when incompatible duties that seem equally incumbent upon us will not yield to a single common denominator, to a neat ordering according to some principle that transcends them both. In Tracy Kidder's account of Dr. Paul Farmer's service to the Haitians he came to identify with so fiercely, he writes:

> [O]ther voices . . . would praise a trip like this for its good intentions, and yet describe it as an example of what is wrong with Farmer's approach. Here's an influential anthropologist, medical diplomat, public health administrator, epidemiologist, who has helped to bring new resolve and hope to some of the world's most dreadful problems and he's just spent seven hours making house calls. How many desperate families live in Haiti? He's made this trip to visit two.

Kidder then goes on to say that Farmer would "insist [that] if you say that seven hours is too long to walk for two families of patients, you're saying that their lives matter less than some others', and the idea that some lives matter less is the root of all that's wrong with the world."[5]

Was Farmer's choice reasonable? He certainly had his reasons. Was it more reasonable than the alternative more pragmatic, efficiency-oriented critics would have supported? Who can say? Both positions have their seemingly unassailable reasons, and the way we choose between them, the way we know what is right for us at that time and place, exceeds reason's ability to explain and to verify. There seems to be no reason that can get beyond these two quite different sets of reasons to adjudicate their competing claims. And so unless we are willing to say that Farmer simply flipped a coin or chose whimsically, and it seems highly unlikely that a man of Farmer's character and history would keep himself on track that way, then we must acknowledge that there is some other way of knowing, some other way of arriving at an answer to this dilemma.

A final challenge to the hegemony in business ethics of Western philosophical reason surfaces when we note that in most current discussions of business ethics, unless the range is intentionally and explicitly enlarged, the discussion is almost always about the contributions of "Western" religions and "Western" philosophy to business ethics. I say this with regret for this increasingly inexcusable parochialism, and with a sense of realism about the major locus, at least the original major locus of both the current form of business that is most frequently the subject of business ethics, and of the current incarnation of business ethics. Once we acknowledge the growing global dominance, for good or ill, of this form of business, we must also see that the questions of "whose religion?" and "whose philosophy?" or, perhaps more to the current point, "whose reason?" go far beyond the family quarrels among Western religions and philosophies.

Such an enlargement of our understanding of and even sympathy with a much larger and more diverse set of ways of understanding and responding to this form of economic activity becomes all the more urgent as the mode of business in view ("Western" mixed capitalism) moves into more diverse cultures, unless it is the case, as I desperately hope it is not, that just as other economic forms succumb to the onslaught of this capitalist one, so too the cultures of those countries are also displaced by the culture—the consumer capitalism—to which this new form of economic activity has given clear dominance. If this latter is the case, then we no longer need to consider the values and the ways of knowing of those now dying or already dead cultures by which these newly "capitalized" peoples historically structured their world and their lives. But if this is the shape of our global future, then we face problems and tragic losses far larger than any business ethic can deal with.

RESPONDING TO CHALLENGES TO THE ETHICAL CONTRIBUTIONS OF RELIGION/THEOLOGY

Of course, pointing out the weaknesses of another discipline's position or methodology does not necessarily strengthen the case for one's own. Thus we must respond to some of the other challenges that have been mounted against most religious positions/methodologies, and then finally, and perhaps most importantly, present the positive points that can be made about what religious approaches can contribute to our understanding of and responding to the world in general and, here of course, specifically to ethical issues arising in the conduct of modern business.

One charge frequently made against religious approaches is that they bring with them too much "baggage," too many doctrines or beliefs on which they claim all else rests, but which are not generally open to examination—or are simply impossible to examine each time a specific issue arises. While not all religious persons would agree with the tightness and precision ascribed to religious worldviews in Hale's statement to Proctor in Arthur Miller's *The Crucible*, that "[t]heology, sir, is a fortress; no crack in a fortress may be accounted small," many, at least in doctrinally defined or oriented traditions would agree that their beliefs do in general aim at constituting a view of the world, an attempt to see the world and its meaning as a whole, and that their various practices and teachings, including moral ones, are rooted in that understanding of the world. While constructing such a comprehensive picture of the world and its significance is a huge undertaking that quite predictably exposes its proponents to a number of possible charges, unless one simply decides to go entirely with instinct, intuition, emotion, or just spontaneity and serendipity, some such view of the larger context in which we exist and act—whether explicitly religious or not—would seem to be the only possible ground for our concluding that some sorts of actions, persons, relations, and communities are admirable and desirable, and others are not.

Otherwise it is not clear on what sort of foundation our ethical convictions and recommendations could rest. Those who pretend such "baggage" is not needed seem to be trying to move the world ethically or morally while having no place on which to stand and no fulcrum on which to rest the lever of their normative judgments. "Come, let us speak of justice," says the philosopher. But how do we begin such a conversation without first considering what the participants understand about the nature of the human species and our potential for taking seriously the needs and claims of others, for getting beyond our own self interest—if that is part of our "anthropology"—and our potential for building relationships and living in community, and about the nature and foundation of the good, and of any ties or obligations we have to each other, Without some such foundation, any talk of justice would seem to be building castles in the air, or simply a statement of personal preferences or inclinations. And I would maintain that we lay such a foundation as the starting point of our moral discourse, whether it be explicitly religious or not, without benefit of tightly reasoned and verifiable supporting arguments.

Lest all this seem to be jousting with straw philosophers, let me offer as an example John Rawls, whose importance in contemporary philosophy and the frequency with which he is invoked in discussions of economic justice in business ethics would seem to make this an appropriate choice. Behind Rawls's[6] careful construction of the original position and the veil of ignorance lie at least two assumptions, which, to my knowledge, he never directly explains or defends: first is an assumption of fact, that is to say, that left to our own devices most of us would try to construct a society more favorable to ourselves than to its other members. (It is striking that this rightly influential philosopher can make this assumption that crucially underlies, in fact requires, the remedy of his much invoked veil of ignorance, and evoke little resistance, while few seem to have noticed its striking resemblance to important elements of the Christian doctrine of original sin, or to Martin Luther's teaching that fallen humans are "curved in upon themselves," which religious positions would doubtless receive a much different reception from most philosophers.) It is probably not irrelevant to note in this context that decades ago Protestant theologian Reinhold Niebuhr suggested that original sin is the only empirically verifiable Christian doctrine.

Much more important for my current point is Rawls's second assumption, the normative one that such a self-serving shaping of society would be morally inappropriate. My question is whether reason alone, at least in our usual understanding of it, or even in the most frequently offered philosophical understandings of it, can establish this latter assumption, that such a society would be morally inferior to the one Rawls envisions. Or, as I believe is the case, does that assumption represent a truly fundamental conviction of Rawls—and perhaps of one major strand of Western liberal moral thought. If I am correct here, this important philosopher appears also to begin with some essential unreasoned (although not necessarily unreasonable) starting points. Another way to test the universal rationality of Rawls's procedures and conclusions would be to ask if his two principles of justice, especially the first one concerning maximal liberty, would be as self-evident, as rationally persuasive to starving, disease-ridden, brutalized, illiterate peasants of the developing world as they have been to middle-class, Western, tenured professors of philosophy. Might not the peasant *reasonably* trade some of Rawls's liberty for a measure of physical and economic security?

One possible implication of the above is that while religion does bring considerable "baggage" to ethical discussions, that fact is so openly acknowledged by religious persons and is so obvious to most others that there is little chance that the influence of those prior beliefs will go unnoticed or unchallenged. If, on the other hand, philosophy is presumed to bring only its method of rational reflection but is in fact also working out of substantive prior convictions, then the influence of those convictions is much more likely to go unnoticed and thus unexamined. It would seem obvious that philosophers' own criteria for reasonable and reasoned conversation would require the exposition and examination of such prior beliefs, whatever their origin and nature.

My suggestion is that both philosophy and religion use reason, but also go beyond or behind reason in doing ethics. Thus the question becomes not who uses reason and who does not, but how and where they use it, how they understand or define the "reason" they appeal to, and, most important here, whether they will openly acknowledge when they go beyond or behind reason as it is usually understood. I believe that philosophical and religious ethics exhibit more parallel dynamics and problems than the usual portrayal of their differences allows for, that while their procedures and their conclusions may vary, the functionally equivalent elements in the two need more careful examination than they normally receive. This means not that the philosopher-king has no clothes, but only that he is no better attired than are the rest of us pilgrims stumbling together toward the celestial city of Moral Truth.

RELIGION AND THE COMMUNAL/
LIVED NATURE OF MORALITY

It is time to say as clearly as I can what I believe religion and religious studies offers ethics in general and business ethics in particular that is distinctive, and that philosophy seems for the most part not to offer. I should note that here I speak with most confidence concerning my own Christian tradition. With regard to the following discussion other traditions will have to answer for themselves. The major strength of religious ethics with regard to the matters we have been discussing is that for religion, ethics and morality are always *embodied realities,* and reflection upon them is always aimed at effecting a more faithful embodiment of a tradition's teachings in individuals and in communities, or, perhaps more accurately, in *individuals in community.*[7] In seeking to articulate, understand, and apply the moral teachings of a religious tradition, the goal is not to identify the duties that come to bear upon humans because of some abstract understanding of what the "essence" of being human is, or to follow out the logic of some universal Moral Reason. It is rather to determine what sorts of actions, character traits, institutional patterns, and policies are most likely to make possible, to sustain, and to enhance a form of community consistent with the worldview of that tradition, a form of living together that faithfully reflects what the community claims to believe.

All of the remaining points I wish to make, both in support of religious ethics and in challenging the dominant modes of philosophical ethics, can be derived from or traced back to this fact about religious ethics. One advantage of coming to ethics with at least an understanding of how religious belief and life work, especially in their communal dimensions, even if one does not endorse them, is that we thereby have better access to what I believe history tells us most often motivates moral agents. Again, not all the influence of religion on conduct has been positive. But where we do see the courageous undertaking of challenging moral tasks, whether those facing individuals or those facing a society, we are much more likely to find actions, or even entire lives, motivated by religious beliefs and commitments than by reasoned philosophical arguments. Any list of contemporary moral heroes, it seems to me, would be heavily populated by persons in whom religious beliefs played a much larger role than did philosophical analysis and arguments. Most such lists could reasonably be expected to include persons such as Mahatma Gandhi, Bishop Tutu, Dr. Martin Luther King, and Mother Teresa very near the top. And while most of the moral life, and the moral lives of most of us, are lived on the plain of daily routine, rather than on the mountain tops scaled by these persons, there is no reason to believe that the motivating forces are radically different at those different elevations.

Religious ethics is also sometimes criticized for being too idealistic and individualistic, challenging the believer to unrealistic heights, while most of life gets on, and may even get on better, with the more realistic, the more modest aspirations of ordinary morality. And yet understanding morality as embodied or lived should help explain the interest of religious persons and communities in the lives of exemplary persons—the saints and moral heroes. In a morality so understood, why should not the lives of a Gandhi or of a Martin Luther King, for example, count for more than philosopher Jan Narveson's supposedly rational proof that "the pacifist's central position is untenable"?[8] Whether rationally defensible or not, we see in historical instances and exemplary lives that pacifists—like bumble bees, not knowing that they cannot fly, simply fly anyway—will sometimes succeed in the only way moral agents and communities care about, by resolving human conflicts with less damage and injury than any available alternative would have, even if their "central position is [rationally] untenable."

Seeing the community as the true locus of the moral life and even of moral reflection, as I am maintaining most religious traditions do, also enables religious ethics to fulfill another task seldom considered in applied ethics but absolutely essential to the survival of a moral society, and that is the task of passing the moral tradition of the community on to the next generation. Again, not all that has been done in this regard is praiseworthy. The differences between education and moral formation on the one hand and indoctrination and manipulation on the other have not always been respected or even recognized by religious communities. But if societies are to avoid having to reinvent the moral wheel in every generation, this task must be taken on. And as theologian John Howard Yoder has written, "Moral obligation is learned, after all, by growing up in historic communities. Our 'knowing' it is prior, in the orders both of knowing and being, to the 'reason' with which we question and clarify it, as well as to the awe and affectivity with which it grasps us."[9] Or, as philosopher Annette Baier has argued: "The philosopher's theoretical versions of morality have not passed the practical test of having been transmitted from parents to children, when moral conscience is formed. Thus they are in one important way less thoroughly tested than the non-intellectual, 'uncritical' tenets of morality that philosophers usually despise as unreflective."[10]

In fact, not only has philosophy largely ignored this task and what I would argue is its inescapably communal nature, but following what they saw as the strictures of "rational" moral discourse about rights, some philosophers, even according to one of their own, have done a significant disservice in the matter of our obligations to future generations that here go beyond our introducing them to the moral life. Joel Feinberg writes:

For several centuries now human beings have run roughshod over the lands of our planet, just as if the animals who do live there and the generations of humans who will live there had no claims on them whatever. Philosophers have not helped matters by arguing that animals and future generations are not the kinds of beings who can have rights now, that they don't presently qualify for membership, even "auxiliary membership" in our moral community.[11]

This elevation by some philosophers of the seeming requirements of consistent, rational discourse over the needs of the community have also led to positions in business ethics that I would suggest have been a significant disservice to the larger community. Several years ago a significant episode in the discussion of corporate responsibility was centered on an examination of agents generally agreed to be accountable or capable of loyalty to discover the necessary prerequisites of being such. The conversation then turned to the question of whether business corporations exhibited those characteristics. If so, then they could be held accountable as moral agents;[12] if not, they are not be expected to act like moral agents.[13]

But from a more community-based perspective, whether religiously articulated or not, there would seem to be a much more direct and I believe a more valid way into this question. Corporations wield considerable economic, political, and social influence. They have tremendous potential for doing good or ill in the society. Given what many of us see as the rapidly growing power of for-profit business corporations over virtually all aspects of our common life, life in community is unlikely to become better, in fact is likely to become considerably worse for most of us, if we understand those corporations as being accountable to no one beyond themselves and their stockholders. On this ground alone I would argue that they must be held accountable to the larger society, whatever results the philosophers' reason yields. On this view, it would in fact be immoral not to hold them accountable.

"But" responds the philosopher, "that is simply a blatant appeal to what society needs and not to what is rational." True enough, in one very limited sense of "rational," although surely we must challenge any concept of rationality that ranks human needs in such matters below the requirements of rational discourse. On the interpretation of morality being offered here it is not at all clear that reason's arguments should weigh more heavily in the scales of moral decision making than do the legitimate needs of the persons and communities affected by those corporations' policies and actions. Just how would one show that Kant's Categorical Imperative, or Mill's Principle of Utility, or Rawls's two principles of justice, or Nozick's entitlement theory of justice ought to weigh more heavily in a decision about a corporation's polluting emissions than does the health of the children in the nearby low-income neighborhood. Of course there are complexities here that limits of space require me to ignore. But I would despair of having a serious conversation about the morality of such a decision with anyone for whom the claims of the children's health did not at least prima facie carry major, and probably even decisive weight. A clear sense of the embodied, community nature of morality and/or of the appropriate roles of business and other economic activities in making community life possible, sustainable, and humane would remove any doubt about the accountability of corporations, even in the absence of "rationally" persuasive arguments.

CONCLUSION

In summary, I am arguing that religious ethics begins with a community's perspective on or interpretation of reality itself, an interpretation that finds in or assigns to all of reality value and human significance, and on the basis of which the community and its members address the fundamental questions of human existence: Who are we? Why are we here? What is the meaning of existence, of the universe, of nature, and of history? Seen in this light the moral life of individuals and communities emerges out of a comprehensive interpretation of reality. The articulation of such a worldview is the central task of every major religious tradition that comes to us with a proposal, "See the world this way." And from seeing the world in a certain way—a way supported and/or challenged by facts, evidence and data, and our own experience, but not finally proven or disproved by them—we can see that certain moral choices, certain actions, policies, and kinds of institutions are appropriate in a world thus envisioned and that certain others are not. Only with the help of such a worldview, whether traditionally religious or not, can specific moral and ethical issues be put in a larger context of meaning, and only in this way do we have a starting point from which to address them

QUESTIONS FOR DISCUSSION

1. Does religion have a legitimate role to play in the discipline of business ethics that is different from the one played by philosophy? What sorts of intellectual tasks does religion utilize that mirror tasks done by philosophers?
2. How does Camenisch address the criticism that religion confronts us with multiple traditions that are frequently framing their ethical worlds in very different ways?

3. What are some of the distinctions that our author draws between a narrow, analytical notion of reason and a broader grasp of how we come to know what is right or wrong in a given situation? What examples does he cite in order to challenge what he sees as the hegemony of analytical, discursive reason?

4. How does Camenisch respond to the criticism that religious approaches to business ethics bring too much "baggage" consisting of doctrines, beliefs, and worldviews that are not sufficiently open to critical examination?

5. What are the distinctive contributions that religious studies has to offer the discipline of business ethics, according to Camenisch? After reflecting on your own religious or cultural tradition, would you add anything to Camenisch's list of contributions?

NOTES

1. Paul F. Camenisch, "On Monopoly in Business Ethics? Can Philosophy Do It All?" *Journal of Business Ethics* 5, no. 6 (1986): 433–43.

2. Richard T. DeGeorge, *Business Ethics* (New York: Macmillan, 1982).

3. Carol Gilligan, *In a Different Voice: Psychological Theory and Women's Development* (Cambridge, MA: Harvard University Press, 1982).

4. Leon R. Kass, "The Wisdom of Repugnance," in *The Ethics of Human Cloning,* ed. Leon R. Kass and James Q. Wilson (Washington, DC: AEI Press, 1998).

5. Tracey Kidder, *Mountains beyond Mountains* (New York: Random House, 2003): 293-94.

6. John Rawls, *A Theory of Justice* (Cambridge, MA: Harvard University Press, 1971).

7. John Leahy, "Embodied Ethics," *Journal of Business Ethics* 5, no. 6 (1986): 465–72.

8. Jan Narveson, "Pacifism: A Philosophical Analysis," *Ethics* 75, no. 4 (1965): 259–71.

9. John Howard Yoder, "The Hermeneutics of Peoplehood: A Protestant Perspective on Practical Moral Reasoning," *Journal of Religious Ethics* 10 (1982): 59–60.

10. Annette Baier, "Dialogue on Applied Ethics," *Humanities* 2 (1981): 15.

11. Joel Feinberg, "The Right of Animals and Unborn Generations," in *Ethical Theory and Business*, ed. Tom L. Beauchamp and Norman E. Bowie (Englewood Cliffs, NJ: Prentice-Hall, 1979), 576.

12. Peter A. French, "The Corporation as a Moral Person," *American Philosophical Quarterly* 3 (1979): 207–15.

13. John Ladd, "Morality and Ideal of Rationality in Formal Organizations," *Monist* 54 (1970): 488–517.

Business Ethics:
Oxymoron or Good Business?

Ronald Duska

In this article, Ronald Duska addresses the common conception that business ethics is an "oxymoron"—a contradiction in terms. Beginning by taking this response in all seriousness, he looks at some of the reasons why people might consider ethics incompatible with the practice of business. Examining the idea of self-interest as the central motive for business, he then contrasts this with several common arguments in favor of ethical practice in business. Finally, he ends by proposing a way of "refurbishing" business ethics through a re-understanding of the relationship of ethics to business.

To live happily is the desire of all men . . . first therefore, we must seek what it is that we are aiming at; then we must look about for the road by which we can reach it most quickly.

—Seneca, *Moral Essays*

The good is that at which all things aim.

—Aristotle, *Nichomachean Ethics*

Capitalists have been living on their (ethical) inheritance and it is running out. . . . Free enterprise has degenerated into greed and rapacious capitalism. . . . But the current view is the result of refusing to recognize that economic systems of whatever type are like engines: They provide motive power but do not determine the direction of travel.[1]

"*B*usiness ethics! That's an oxymoron." More often than not, that is the reaction when I tell people I teach business ethics. "There is no such thing," they bark. The responses are so uniform they make one think that the only purpose of business ethics is to give currency to the word "oxymoron."

My usual answers to such a dismissal of business ethics has been to point out that without ethics, business could not function, since it requires a great deal of trust and integrity. Or I have pointed out that even though there is unethical business behavior, that is the exception. On the whole, most people in business act ethically most of the time.

Recently, though, I listened as a former CEO reflected on why he left business. He recounted the incredible pressures on him to get return on equity and meet fourth-quarter earnings goals, tasks he viewed as his overriding responsibility. He related his struggle to avoid doing something unethical to meet the demands of his shareholders.

His story made me wonder whether those who think there is no such thing as business ethics might not have a point. Is there some truth to what they say? It occurred to me that some of us in the field ought to ask some hard questions. What if business ethics is a contradiction in terms? What if those of us concerned about its legitimacy were like the cuckold—the last to know? Were those of us touting the possibility of business ethics so blind that, like the emperor and his sycophants, we didn't listen to the children saying we had no clothes? Have we become mere apologists for a corrupt system? Have we become co-opted by the institution we are responsible for examining?

In the face of such doubts, it certainly wouldn't hurt to be a bit critical about our enterprise and recognize, as Aristotle pointed out, there is usually at least partial truth in commonly held beliefs. In fact, Aristotle began most inquiries by examining commonly held opinions, what in Greek were called *endoxa*, to see what truth could be gleaned from them. Given that so many people think business ethics is oxymoronic, it might be prudent to investigate why and to determine what if any truth or partial truth they see.

Thus, as a hueristic device, I propose to seriously examine the claim that business ethics is a contradiction in terms, and see what follows if business ethics is oxymoronic.

BUSINESS ETHICS AS OXYMORON

If one looks at the purpose of ethics/morality[2] and the common conception of the purpose of business one can make a fairly good case that business ethics is an oxymoron. The argument would run along the following lines. To the extent that business and the market in which it flourishes is driven by an unconstrained pursuit of self-interest, an attitude consistent with egoism,[3] and since egoism is manifestly unethical, business must inevitably run afoul of ethics, which furnishes rules of justice constraining self-interested behavior to avoid the egoism. Business pushes one way, ethics the other. If achieving ever-increasing profit is the basic purpose and principle of business, and economic profitability is the primary and overriding factor in strategic business decisions, ethical behavior and business behavior eventually must conflict. Of course, to make such an argument persuasive we must first show that the nature of business is as we construed it and then specify what we take as the nature of ethics or morality, showing its incompatibility with business.

Business as Pursuit of Self-Interest: The Bottom-Line Perspective

Morality or ethics is incompatible with business if following the rules of business practices *inevitably* leads to the *exclusive* pursuit of self-interest—that is, if the practices are *selfish* and thereby violate the demands of justice. As we shall see, business is a social construct, so it can be what society determines it to be and prevailing opinion will be a major factor in determining what it is, that is, the received descriptions will turn into prescriptions. Hence the justification, "That's just business."

My impression is that while most business ethicists would not agree with this, the general consensus, *endoxa*, is that there are no responsibilities for business other than the self-interested pursuit of profit. I arrive at that conclusion from my experience in a number of areas. It is apparent in the words of corporate apologists when they claim, "Business must do whatever it takes to survive." There is no shortage of defenders of this view, from Albert Carr[4] to Milton Friedman[5] who states, without qualification, "*There is one and only one* social responsibility of business . . . to use resources designed to increase its profits."[6]

If business is such that its one and only responsibility is to increase profits, it is quite sensible to claim there is no such thing as business ethics. Given the competitive pressures of the marketplace, any business will reach a situation where the only way to increase its profits will be at the expense of another. Be it downsizing or firing or just producing, with its attendant externalities, the well-being of a company will demand that action, which will be harmful to some person or persons, be taken. Such an attitude has become ingrained in the leading practitioners and analysts of business today. Consider the following examples.

> A (recent) award of 120.5 million dollars to Teresa Goodrich, who lost her husband because Aetna Health Care delayed approving an experimental treatment that might have saved his life, provoked Aetna's chief executive to declare that the jury had been swayed by a "skillful ambulance-chasing lawyer, a politically motivated judge and a weeping widow." (He later apologized to the widow.)[7]

What would lead a CEO, assuming he is a decent person, to be so concerned about his fiduciary obligations to defend the interests of his company, that he abandon all sympathy for the widow and make such a comment? Such callous behavior only can be explained if the CEO believes he is doing right by fulfilling his responsibility to enhance company profits, and if that view has become ingrained in his outlook.

How did the CEO develop such an attitude? The answer is that continual concern over one's responsibility to the bottom line builds up a habitual single-minded view that has no room for justice when it conflicts with strategic profit making. One could call it bottom-line myopia. It is the mark of the rift between ethics and business and the embeddedness of the belief that business is first and foremost about increasing profit.

The behavior of the Aetna CEO is reminiscent of a story allegedly told by Phil Jackson, the former coach of the Chicago Bulls. It was a story about a frog and a tarantula. The tarantula could not get across a stream and the frog in a friendly gesture suggested that he could give the tarantula a ride on his back. But fearing the tarantula's deadly sting, the frog elicited a promise from the tarantula not to bite him. Having agreed, the tarantula hopped on the frog's back and they began to cross the stream. All was going well until halfway across when the tarantula bit the frog. Knowing the worst, the frog (in true utilitarian fashion) said, "Why did you do that? Now we'll both die." To which the tarantula replied, "I know, but that's what I do." Business makes profits. That's what it does. If people get hurt in the process, that's too bad.

But CEOs are not monsters. They are simply pieces in an inescapable game of profit making. Consider a hypothetical case which shows how an environment, where concern for return on equity is paramount, coupled with a fiduciary responsibility to maximize profit, leads to a bottom-line fixation incompatible with ethics.[8]

The president and CEO, John Edgerton, must release the third-quarter financial results for High Performance Life to the investment community within the next ten days. The High Performance Life Insurance Company, a stock life insurer traded on the New York Stock Exchange, has completed three quarters of its current fiscal year. Sales for the year and for the quarter are significantly behind its financial plan and are disappointing. Consequently, its revenues are lower than projected and causing pressure on earnings projections for the future. The last quarter of the fiscal year, however, is typically the strongest sales quarter of any year. In order to meet the revenue plan and the earnings goals it will need to be by far the largest sales quarter in company history. High Performance Life is a career agency company offering a full portfolio of life insurance and health products. During the third quarter it released to its sales force a new interest-sensitive life product that it expects will stimulate an increase in sales in the future. The company has had a steady and continuous growth in sales, revenue, and earnings over the past five years. Its revenue growth and stock price have outpaced industry averages.

He must decide whether or not to raise serious doubts about the achievement of the previous revenue and earnings plan for the fourth quarter, or he must indicate that he expects sales to rebound very strongly in the fourth quarter and meet both revenue and earnings projections. He knows that the analysts are very sensitive to the company's sales expectations, and if he sends a signal that he expects to miss his plan, then it will affect the stock price. In addition, he has a meeting with Standard and Poors rating agency personnel, and the last time he met with them they expressed concern about the aggressive sales plan being achievable.

He called in his senior vice president of sales and emphasized to him the urgency of the disappointing sales results. He stressed in no uncertain terms that the five-year consistent earnings growth and the stock price were in jeopardy unless the sales plan was met. It was clear that the senior vice president of sales had significant reservations as to whether or not the sales level necessary could be realistically met in the fourth quarter. After some pushing and prodding, however, he admitted that there was a chance of meeting the plan with a company-wide all-out effort. The senior vice president of sales stressed that it would require the coordination and cooperation of not only everyone in the sales organization, but he also really needed the full cooperation of the operations and support departments in the home office to make certain that the new business is processed efficiently.

The president is acutely sensitive to the importance of continuing the positive growth and performance that his company has shown over the past five years. The shareholders and board of directors are expecting continued growth in revenue and earnings, and indeed his own stock options and incentive bonus are closely tied to both the sales growth and earnings target. He is somewhat encouraged by the fact that in the past five years his staff have had to respond to other challenges and problems, and in each instance they came through for him. He believes that his "just get it done" management style has had a positive impact on the company's performance and has caused his key personnel to stretch beyond their normal performance levels to achieve these results.

When faced with this scenario, most business practitioners to whom I have introduced it will remark on how much it reminds them of their own company. Further, they think that given the pressures of such a situation, most CEOs—including those from companies with high ethical aspirations—not only will opt to push as hard as possible for the sales but also are forced to do so by the pressure of their position. The truth, no matter how we would like to deny it, seems to be that in business, the pressure from competition and stockholders is such that self-interested pursuit of more and more profit rules the day. The bottom line rules all.

As a final piece of evidence that the bottom-line perspective is not only the common opinion, but the driving opinion about business, consider this account of the career of Jack Welch.

> More than 300,000 people have lost their jobs in Jack Welch's 17-year tenure as CEO at GE, earning him the nickname "Neutron Jack"—for the bomb that destroys people but leaves buildings intact.
>
> For most business people, such moves have made Welch America's premier corporate changemaster, the wunderkind of Big Business. His methods are extolled in business schools, praised by the media and copied by others.[9]

In short, in the real world, business practitioners are admired not for concerns about justice but for bottom-line performance. There are numerous other examples of the pursuit of ever-increasing profits or return on equity at the expense of ethical concerns in business today. How, for example, to defend an executive in an advertising company who helps persuade people (pace Von Hayek) to buy products they really don't need, products that may be harmful? What are we to make of the entertainment industry, whose violence-filled products are cited as causes for similar violence in the streets? What of the tobacco industry, which produces a deadly product? Each of these industries, identified by their critics as socially irresponsible (i.e., unethical), is judged on the stock market by its success in generating profit.

Given the pressures of the marketplace and the stock market, and the notion, supported by law, that executives have a fiduciary responsibility to increase profits, is it any wonder that business leaders seem almost exclusively bottom-line oriented, so there appears to be no room for justice or ethics, *when and if it interferes* with increased profit?

The Development of the Current Endoxa: Adam Smith's Views

How did the current view of the nature and purpose of business arise? How did this attitude develop, and how did it become so ingrained in ordinary thinking? It was not always the predominant view. The primary rationale in legitimating the current view is found in *The Wealth of Nations*, the work of Adam Smith, the famous eighteenth-century philosopher, ethicist, and economist. In that work Smith develops his notion of the system of natural liberty where the pursuit of self-interest is the major force of the market, driving both production and exchange.

Smith indicated that what motivates a great deal of activity is self-interest. He maintained—correctly it seems—that the free pursuit of self-interest without the intent to benefit society will, as if directed by an invisible hand, bring about more social benefit than if visible hands (government intervention) try to intervene and bring about just results. We are all familiar with the following passage.

> It is not from the benevolence of the butcher, the brewer or the baker, that we expect our dinner, but from their regard to their own interest. . . . We address ourselves not to their humanity but to their self-love, and never talk to them of our own necessities but of their advantages. He generally indeed, neither intends to promote the public interest, nor knows how much he is promoting it . . . and by directing that industry in such a manner as its produce may be of the greatest value, he intends only his own gain, and he is in this, as in many other cases, led by an invisible hand to promote an end which was no part of his intention. Nor is it always the worse for society that it was no part of it. By pursuing his own interest he frequently promotes that of the society more effectually than when he really intends to promote it.[10]

But Smith, as well as being an economist, was an ethicist who did not see the market as incompatible with morality. Smith cautioned that the free pursuit of self-interest must be limited by considerations of justice and fairness. "Every man, *as long as he does not violate the laws of justice* [italics mine], is left perfectly free to pursue his own interest his own way, and to bring both his industry and capital into competition with those of any other man, or order of men."[11] Further, Smith noted that there were two great motivators of humans—self-interest, and a concern for others, which he called "sympathy." He thought this sympathy and concern for the benefit of others would motivate people to check their self-interest when it was at the expense of others and justice or fairness demanded it. I assume he thought this sympathy would keep a rein on business.

While Smith helped bring about the modern notion of business, as an enterprise involved in the pursuit of self-interest, a careful look at his work shows that he would never envision the unconstrained pursuit of self-interest that is legitimated today. Smith always qualifies his observations about self-interested behavior. For example, while he says, "One who intends only his own gain is led to promote an end (the public good) no part of his intention," he recognizes that this result doesn't always occur. It happens "*in many other cases.*" Further, Smith qualifies the self-interested pursuit with the following words: "*Nor* is it *always* the worse for society" that one pursues one's self-interest, implying that the pursuit of self-interest is sometimes worse for society. Finally, Smith notes that, "In pursuing his own interest he *frequently* promotes that of society." Since frequently does not mean always, it is clear that Smith does not assert that society will *always* be served by individuals promoting their own interest. Rather, he insists that there are cases where society is not served, and in those cases the constraints of justice override self-interested pursuits.

Be that as it may, Smith's cautions against egoism in favor of justice, for very legitimate reasons, are only a minor part of his work, a part of his work that has been largely ignored by subsequent thinkers. His greatest influence on contemporary notions of business is his powerful view legitimating the pursuit of self-interest. The fact that his concerns for justice are so small a part of Smith's work, and consequently have so little influence on today's views, can be explained in the light of the outlook of the people of his day. Smith needed to argue against his own day's *endoxa*, which frowned on the pursuit of self-interest. The burden of proof for Smith was to show the acceptability of pursuing self-interest. To hit his mark of legitimating a system of natural liberty and the pursuit of self-interest, he needed to counter the beliefs of a society largely influenced by the Christian insistence on altruism and self-sacrifice, and argue against a background where notions of fair price and fair wages were paramount. To put his view in focus we need to remind ourselves that his society's concern for justice and its demands was the background out of which he made his recommendations. Whereas in his day, a concern for the laws of justice over against the self-interested attitude of business would have been part of the form of life, today such a concern has been lost and needs to be reintroduced.

Today's defenders of business's pursuit of self-interest do not have to overcome scruples about a self-interested perspective. Contemporary society does not operate out of a background where one must overcome scruples about being self-interested. On the contrary, it operates from a decidedly self-interested perspective.[12] Thus, business exclusively pursuing profit is like the tarantula. It does what it does. Hence the phrase usually uttered in resignation to justify a business activity that one is ethically uncomfortable with: "That's just business."

COUNTERING THE SMITH AND FRIEDMAN APPROACH TO ETHICAL BUSINESS

Still, society is not about to accept a practice that is patently harmful and unjust. Such practices need justification. Defenders of Friedman will not agree that business ethics is oxymoronic. Rather they will point out that tough-minded profit making leaves the society better off as a whole—the modern adaptation of Adam Smith's invisible hand argument and a utilitarian justification of its practices. They will claim that business's self-interested pursuit of profits has led to better things and a better world.

But the argument is more a priori than empirical. In theory, allowing owners to get maximum profit will enhance investment and entrepreneurship by rewarding it. In that way the entire society will be better off, because a rising tide will lift all boats. Justification of business's pursuit of self-interest leads to the greatest good for the greatest number of people. This is an extremely important point, for if it is true, the frustration of self-interested pursuits in the name of justice might cause more harm than help in the long run by dampening productivity.

However, since the argument is a utilitarian justification of self-interested pursuits, it faces two difficulties found in any utilitarian approach: the problem of identifying appropriate ends as well as the problem of fair distribution.

Unless one specifies what the consequences of capitalism are and judges these as good, the position that capitalism leads to the greatest good for the greatest number of people cannot be defended empirically. It is unquestionable that this capitalist free-market system that promotes the self-interested pursuit of profit has produced a higher material standard of living (meaning more material goods) than any other system in history.[13] But it is questionable whether the increase in overall wealth is an adequate goal for a flourishing life. At most it is an instrumental goal. Wealth for what? Goods for what? To encourage the goal of increased material goods at the expense of all other goals is to engage in a debilitating materialism.

Hence it can be claimed that business, viewed as primarily a profit-making enterprise, is incompatible with ethics because it promotes a good that is ethically inappropriate as a final goal. For business to be ethical it needs to subordinate its profit-making goal to other more appropriate goals, a necessity that Friedman recognizes by appealing to the utilitarian invisible hand argument. But then that newer goal, be it more productivity or wealth, must be judged by an adequate view of what counts as a worthy goal. Those ethicists who criticize business because of the tawdry products it supplies utilize this approach. Those who criticize it for creating a fetish for goods use this approach. Those who critique it for its concern with having rather than being use this approach. It is an approach that says not all economic goods are ethical goods.

It would be refreshing to see a serious discussion of what counts as goods for human beings. Those goods and services need to be, pace Mill and Bentham, not merely pleasures, but real quality-of-life goods, and they cannot be instrumental goals functioning as final goals. Which goals are appropriate is partially determined by what human beings and their societies are, as well as by which of their potentials are worthy of pursuit. But such goods need to be discovered by analysis, investigation, and experimentation.

There is a second problem that arises from the utilitarian approach of Friedman. Even if one concedes that business promotes good, there is the distribution problem. How are the goods to be distributed fairly? Did capitalist society achieve this material wealth by unfair distribution of goods or exploitation of some segments of society? To promote the maximization of goods at times requires inequitable distribution. It also requires as much freedom to pursue self-interest as possible. The appropriate ends of activities that affect a society *must*, to be fully ethical, be distributed according to some rules of *fair distribution*—rules utilitarianism does not provide. Any system that appeals to self-interest to maximize goods needs to adopt constraints against selfishness—determinations of who gets how much. For example, if we ask who should get the profits, the notion that the owners get all the profits seems unfair to those who think work should also be one of the chief determinants of how much property one deserves to get. Thus, ethics has to address both the appropriateness of the goods produced and fair distribution of those goods—aspects not adequately covered in the utilitarian justifications. Thus, the invisible hand defense of business ethics is inadequate.

However, there are two other attempts to establish ethics in business, even business that is wholly profit oriented. The first shows that business needs ethics as a prerequisite for social stability.[14] The second shows that business needs ethics as a strategic advantage—the view that maintains that good ethics is good business. We need to examine them briefly.

Ethics as a Prerequisite for Social Stability

As we have mentioned, a facile response to "business ethics is an oxymoron" is to show that businesses could not operate without a requisite amount of honesty, trust, and respect for others' freedom (lack of coercion). Being ethical, then, gets equated with being honest and trustworthy.[15] It is rightly claimed that business would be nearly impossible if most people did not practice some ethical constraint—keeping promises and not deceiving. It is also shown that coercion is incompatible with ideal market transactions that require free choice. Further it is agreed that when honesty, trust, and lack of coercion are employed in business transactions, monitoring costs are lowered, business is generally more efficient, and ideal conditions for market interchange are provided.

However, the need for trust, honesty, and some respect for freedom is true of any well-run organization, even a recognizably immoral one. There must be honor even among thieves. To take two common examples, organized crime and the Nazis, it is clear that even in those organizations there has to be a modicum of honesty and trust among members, and their leaders have to be given enough latitude to do their jobs. So if ethics is reduced to showing that organizations need trust, honesty, and the encouragement of creative individual initiatives, then all well-run organizations are ethical. But that is just false. The ultimate goals of the leaders of organized crime and the Nazis are immoral and misguided, not their dedication, leadership ability, loyalty, and trustworthiness. Hence, it is not enough to keep promises and tell the truth to be ethical. As we have seen before, in the difficulty with utilitarian justification, to have an adequate ethics a company's goals must be appropriate.

Ethics as a Strategy for Good (i.e., Profitable) Business

A second approach among defenders of ethics in business is the approach of those who want to claim that good ethics is good business, usually called the "strategy approach" to business ethics. Most of the time, being ethical (where that means being trustworthy and not deceiving) does lead to good business, in the sense of more productivity and profit. For example, it is argued that being honest with customers and looking out for their interests will establish long-term relationships that create customer satisfaction and lead to more sales in the long run. Or treating one's employees fairly or generously will improve employee morale, thereby enhancing productivity. So if being ethical in business means treating customers with care and employees kindly, then that kind of approach is ethical business.

But there is a serious difficulty with this approach. It warrants ethical behavior because it produces good bottom-line results. It subordinates all of the ethical goals into instruments for the final goal, profit maximization. Hence it suffers the very bottom-line myopia or fixation it attempts to overcome. Strategic reasoning appreciates the claims of stakeholders other than stockholders, but not as legitimate claims in themselves—attended to by the corporation because it owes those stakeholders something, as an ethical perspective would—but only as instruments for fulfilling fiduciary obligations to stockholders.

Strategic reasoning looks at ethics as an instrument for serving the bottom line—which, by the way, is the chief way to market any ethics program. (We would do well to consider the impact that the sentencing guidelines have had on the popularity of ethics training sessions.) There are those who claim that one can look at a proposed action from both a strategic and ethical point of view, and find a win–win solution to an issue. But not all issues have win–win solutions. In win–lose cases, to view business from other than a bottom-line, strategic point of view puts one at odds with the view of the responsible businessperson presented by such luminaries as Albert Carr, Milton Friedman, Andrew Stark,[16] and any number of the "Good Ethics Is Good Business" people, including the new strategic-oriented stakeholder theorists.[17]

The overall problem of such an approach is that if and when good ethics is not good business, so much the worse for good ethics. Make no mistake about it. Sometimes good ethics will be bad business, if good business is defined as bottom-line success. At times to act ethically will be hard and will cost.

After all, as Aristotle pointed out almost twenty-five hundred years ago, if being virtuous was always easy, we wouldn't praise it.

Thus, there needs to be more to ethics than the trust and honesty that are requisites of any well-run organization and the ethical strategies such as care for customers, clients, employees, and others that pay off in increased profit. What is it? We propose to look at the purpose of ethics and morality to see what is missing in the views examined thus far.

The Purpose of Ethics

Morality has been aptly described as a social system of rules created to allow human beings (1) to adjudicate disputes rationally, without resorting to physical force, so that (2) the relationships affected by the dispute can endure, and allow the individuals in those relationships to flourish.[18] Since most ethical disputes arise over who is entitled to certain goods, two questions are crucial in ethics: What goods help humans to flourish? And how are they to be distributed fairly?

Morality's goal of adjudicating disputes to allow relationships to flourish requires a *rational* adjudication. We can adjudicate disputes by force, but in that case we abandon ethics and might makes right. Rational adjudication of ethics must put fairness in the forefront. The rationality of the principle of fairness can be elucidated simply. Fair treatment requires that "the same should be treated the same," and difference in treatment is justified only when there are relevant differences that justify the different treatment. Determining what counts as relevant is at the heart of ethical inquiry.

To demonstrate the irrationality of unfairness, consider what occurs if we treat two identical things differently. If there were two identical paintings, and we thought one had superb composition, it would be illogical to think that the other painting did not also have superb composition. Similarly, if two people are identical in all *relevant ways*, it is irrational to think that one can be entitled to something while the other is not. At an early age, children recognize quite clearly the basic principle of fairness, "the same should be treated the same." They know it is unfair if one of their siblings, who they see as essentially the same, is given a bigger piece of cake. Of course if it is the sibling's birthday, the sibling is entitled to more cake, for having a birthday constitutes a relevant difference for cake distribution. So justice and fairness demand that if we believe most human beings are alike in most morally relevant respects, they should be treated the same in those respects.[19]

Reflecting on the principle of fairness helps us see the unethical nature of selfishness. The defense of selfish behavior rests on the false belief that we are not the same as others, but somehow more deserving. It is important to note that selfishness is not the same as self-interest. The pursuit of self-interest is a perfectly natural and acceptable activity. However, if one puts one's own interest first in a situation where pursuing that interest is unfair to another, one is being selfish. Selfishness occurs when the pursuit of self-interest is *at the expense of another.*

The phrase "at the expense of another" is ambiguous. It can mean a situation where the other is hurt or harmed, or it can mean a situation where the other is harmed by being denied a good to which one is entitled. The selfish approach ignores the entitlement claim. Because I want cake, after eating the piece my mother saved for me (a self-interested action), I also eat the piece she saved for my brother (a selfish action). That's selfish, not simply because I hurt my brother by depriving him of a good, but because I deprived him of a good to which he was entitled. My brother is deprived of the cake to which he was entitled, which is quite different from simply being deprived of the cake, as might happen if the rule for distribution was "first-come, first-served." It is impossible in this situation to have one person's self-interest satisfied without it being at another's expense. Thus, selfishness cannot be understood simply as pursuit of one's interest when it hurts another. The hurt must occur over the deprivation of a good to which the other was entitled.

The additional notion of the entitlement claim to selfishness is crucial, particularly in laying out claims of stakeholders, because not all harming is selfish. For example, one may be forced to close down a plant, for the survival of the company, thereby hurting the people in the community. Is that selfish behavior on the part of the company or just self-interested survival behavior? In such a case one could argue the latter. But that is quite different from a case where a plant was closed, obviously hurting people, but where there was some entitlement—because of implied promises or such—to support from the company. One of the main tasks of ethics is to spell out the basis for entitlements and examine situations to see if the grounds of entitlement exist.

Because of situations of scarcity of goods, society lays down rules of what in a society will count as fair distribution. The distribution rules become part of that society's operative rules of morality. They spell out what is considered fair and/or just in that society. The demand for justice and enhanced quality of life results in a set of rules for appropriate behavior found in any society—the ethical rules of that society. Ideally these rules would be established by a process of trial and error, and through assigning responsibilities, all of which aim for social stability that will allow the needs of the individuals of the society to be fulfilled.

Capitalism's fairness rules governing how property gets distributed are a basis for the charge that business is unethical. Ask most everyone in our society, "Who is entitled to the profits of a company?" and they will say, "The shareholders." That principle of distribution is so ingrained, so second nature, we don't even think about it. If we ask why, which we rarely do, the answer will be that the owner took the risks or had the idea.

As we have seen, what makes capitalism successful in increasing wealth and productivity is that the rules for distribution tie entitlement to the pursuit of self-interest. If the pursuit of self-interest (survival or profit making) leads a company to act in its own behalf while harming others (workers, community, future generations) it is entitled to act in ways that are harmful by a system that legitimizes that harmful behavior. When we justify harmful behavior with the phrase, "That's just business," we are avoiding the charge of injustice since we appeal to the self-interest within the rules. Hence the primary principle that the owner or shareholder is entitled to the profits, and that profits are to be maximized in any way possible short of deceit, fraud, or coercion, leaves no room for other stakeholders to claim entitlement.

But is this system (form of life) ethical? Is it just?

Two Notions of Justice

Cicero points out that justice can have two meanings, the first of which is giving everyone their due.[20] The second has to do with not inflicting harm on others and shielding them from harm. With respect to the first meaning of justice, where everyone gets their due, we have seen that our society through its rules, generally favoring business, determines who is due what and on what basis. Since we determine what is due by utilizing the current morality, we need an outside set of evaluations with respect to the fairness of the system. Thus we have questions of fairness within the system, where the rule is that the owner is entitled to the profits, and fairness of the system, where one can ask whether the distribution that follows from those internal rules is fair.

Cicero, in referring to the second notion of justice, which we can use to evaluate the fairness of the system, claims that an injustice is done, "On the part of those who inflict wrong, and on the part of those who, when they can, do not shield from wrong those upon whom it is being inflicted." This second notion, of shielding from wrong, seems to fit a number of classic cases in the business ethics literature—the Ford Pinto case, the Nestle infant formula controversy, and any number of plant closings. Thus, when getting one's due (the profits) is at the expense of not shielding employees or clients from harm, the claim of the justice within the system conflicts with the justice of the system. Of course, currently, the wrongs done in the pursuit of profit are euphemized as externalities or simply seen as unavoidable and the price of the overall benefits of the system. They are not seen as unjust.

But what would constitute a wrong? A wrong would occur when one has more goods than enough to meet one's needs and keeps them away from those who need them. Here we return to a precapitalist notion of justice, found in the work of John Locke, that rests on the principle put forth by Thomas Aquinas, the thirteenth-century philosopher/theologian. Recognizing scarcity, Aquinas constrains property acquisition in the following consideration: "Therefore the division and appropriation of property, which proceeds from human law, must not hinder the satisfaction of man's necessity for such goods. Whatever is held in superabundance is owed, by natural right, to those in need."[21] To the extent that business's notion of what's due to the owners keeps necessary goods out of the hands of others, it is unethical in Cicero's second sense of justice.

Free-market capitalist society has determined that business is a bottom-line profit machine. Like the tarantula, that's what it does. That's its telos, or purpose. However, since the telos of a specific social institution is not predetermined by nature but is determined by society, it can change its direction. If it is to get in concert with ethics, it must reexamine its goals and the fairness of its mode of distribution. So, in common opinion, business is viewed as unethical because it commits avoidable harm in the name of its distribution rules and in the name of giving freedom of choice to purchasers of goods: "We're only giving the customers what they want." Business at times creates harmful products in the name of profit and overlooks people in need in the name of allowing others to acquire more than they need. These are the common beliefs about business that conflict with the common beliefs about ethics.

A Moral Schizophrenia

When ethics has one goal and business a different, incompatible goal, we can expect a number of consequences. One is the development of a moral schizophrenia within individuals arising from the conflict between bottom-line myopia and ethical concerns for justice as meeting people's needs. This bottom-line myopia results from a misguided sense of fiduciary responsibility, the responsibility arising from playing one's role. The schizophrenia develops because of the tension between corporate responsibility and personal morality that occurs when business goals are in conflict with ethical ones and are not subsumed under the ethical, but ranged alongside them. They do not coalesce but conflict.

This is what Albert Carr, in his much-maligned but perceptive and realistic article, sees. For Carr one must choose between the two spheres, business and ethics, and cannot expect to develop the integrity necessary for being a whole person. Unless it was a crass public relations strategy, the fact that the CEO of AETNA apologized for his remark about the "weeping widow" shows that he recognized his view as seriously flawed from an ethical perspective. Assuming he is a decent person, he is torn between his personal ethical viewpoint and his feeling that he has a fiduciary obligation to defend the interests of the company, no matter what the implications for the widow.

If the system is instrumentally valuable and we have freely chosen our role in the system, then we have an obligation because of our commitment to carry out that role. In a well-functioning corporation that division of labor serves the ends of the corporation. If those ends of the corporation are morally acceptable, then my role gains legitimacy from its instrumentality. If those ends are not morally acceptable, then though the requirements of my role are set, the immorality of the enterprise makes my fulfilling that role morally questionable. Thus the Nuremberg rule. A soldier's duty is clear as a soldier, but he has a higher duty to morality if he is engaged in fighting for an unjust cause. Similarly a doctor's need to care for his patient is clear, but not if the care involves what some consider life-terminating activities, such as abortion or assisted suicide.

Thus, role morality is insufficient if the role is instrumental in contributing to an unjust system. On a more mundane level, if one is encouraged by one's superiors to cheat one's customers to maximize bottom-line productivity, one is forced to abandon the obligations consequent upon the role.

But the schizophrenia of the individual is also seen on an institutional level in the conflict between what is good for the corporation and what is good for society. The invisible hand is supposed to guarantee that what's good for business is good for society. But it doesn't always. In the meantime, though, the belief that it does and the consequent adoption of profit maximization as the only purpose of the corporation leads to what I choose to call the "soulless corporation."

The Soulless Corporation

The modern corporation has lost its soul.[22] The soulless corporation is a one that has lost its purpose and survives simply for the sake of survival. But surviving is an instrumental good. Survival for what? Purposes give reason for existence. A well-founded purpose legitimates an institution. If the primary goal of corporations is profit and survival, there will be a bad fit between the public's needs (consumers and others) and those corporations' goals. A purpose such as maximizing profit, which is merely instrumental, cannot sustain itself as an identifiable enterprise. It perverts or loses its meaning.

Modern corporations with their emphasis on profitability necessarily lose their focus. Consider GE as an example.

The layoffs were part of Welch's transformation of a once-great research and manufacturing company, which he through gut-wrenching upheaval turned into a financial services firm. He closed or sold 98 plants in the U.S., 43 percent of the 228 it operated in 1980. Rather than reinvesting heavily to exploit the company's historic skills, he chose to quit business after business because the money to be made lending money or producing television shows was greater than the Edisonian mission of making things. In the process a great research institution was diminished. The company Thomas Edison began today generates more revenue from selling insurance, lending money, servicing residential mortgages, managing credit cards, and other financial activities than it does from its five largest manufacturing businesses combined. Financial services, 8 percent of corporate earnings in 1980, generates about 40 percent today.[23]

As long as the main purpose of a corporation is maximizing profit in the competitive marketplace, it is impossible to subordinate profit making to providing quality goods and services—which is the reason society let business develop in the first place. Looked upon simply as investment opportunities, corporations have been turned into things to be bought and/or sold, not centers of production. Given the ethical maxim, *nemo dat quod non habet* (no one gives what he does not have), it is impossible to expect corporations of that sort to think about ethics, except as instrumental strategy.[24]

ON REFURBISHING BUSINESS ETHICS

From an economic point of view, one can afford to be ethical only as long as one remains competitive and that is only as long as there are inefficiencies in competitors' operations, or as long as doing the ethical thing leads to efficiencies. After that one will lose the competitive game. To guarantee ethical behavior, then, one must recognize what it consists in, and promote legislation or regulation that makes it economically desirable. The law must serve the ethical point of view.

Beyond legislation and regulation, for any substantial change to occur in business ethics, for it to be even possible, a new view of the purpose of the corporation—one that breaks the spell of the view that its purpose is maximizing profits—is required, as well as a strong identification of ethics with just distribution and appropriate goals.

The function and purpose of the corporation must be viewed from a societal perspective. From society's point of view, the function and purpose of a corporation is not maximization of profits for individuals, but the creation of goods and services to make the members of the society more fulfilled, and not at the expense of those in need. Society invented business to serve its needs, to help its members to flourish. Business, from a societal perspective, was not invented to allow some individuals to prosper at the expense of others. As I have argued elsewhere, the maximization of profits cannot be the primary purpose of business. Identifying profit maximization with business's purpose confuses purposes and motives. That is like confusing the purpose of the train, to get me to London, with what gets me there, the engine. Profits are the engines. The goods and services are the purpose and direction.[25]

Of course, such a call for reenvisioning the purpose of business seems quaint in the high-power world of mergers and acquisitions, but it also seems the only way for businesses to recapture their souls, to remember what they should be about.

IS BUSINESS ETHICS IMPOSSIBLE?

Let's return to our original problem. Business ethics seems to be a contradiction in terms if we see the sole purpose of business as the pursuit of profit and believe that ethics, being concerned with appropriate ends and distributive justice, eschews those exclusive self-interested pursuits. To establish ethics in business, we need to refocus on the purpose of business. It can't be about being a tarantula. But aside from more regulation, reflecting the public's will on how business activity should be constrained, what can be done? The pessimist in me says, not much. But the optimistic fool, rushing in where angels fear to tread, lets me offer a suggestion for a change of mind.

What I propose, partially as a lark, but partially in a serious mode, is a conversion of the statement, "Good ethics is good business," into the statement, "Good business is ethical." This conversion subsumes good business behavior into the class of good ethical behavior.

Our society has determined that the production of cocaine is not (a) good business. It is a business that does harm. For a time society determined that gambling was not a good business for it likewise did harm. There is talk of tobacco production and sales being a bad business, because it does harm. Society itself declares that some products (goods in the economic sense, for which there is a market) are not good (in an ethical sense). Violence in entertainment is the latest product to be targeted for control. For better or worse, society, or rather its members, make decisions about what is good or not, and put constraints on its production. Thus, while the production and distribution of cocaine is successful for its owners from an economic point of view, it is bad business from an ethical point of view. The current debates on gun manufacture, pollution, sustainability, and other topics all show that ethics is attempting to constrain business because it is not productive of acceptable and appropriate goods.

All of our goals or ends and those of our society are not laudable. The goal of accumulating wealth, if it becomes a final goal and not a merely instrumental goal, will come up short. So will the goal of pleasure. A person fixated with pleasure seeking, or a person fixated with the mere accumulation of wealth, are to morally healthy humans what a shriveled tomato is to a red, juicy, robust, vine-ripened tomato one picks in the middle of August. To understand what appropriate goods are we need to turn to something like Aristotle's notion of the good life, which he equated with activity in accord with virtues, especially the virtues of prudence, justice, temperance, and fortitude.

In conclusion, we would point out that business cannot serve only itself. It is thoroughly intertwined in almost every aspect of contemporary life. It operates within an economic system that takes over huge portions of our time, interests, and lives. It has become a form of life, with fairness rules, that govern the distribution of assets and liabilities, rules that have become second nature to most of us and which we rarely question. It can be viewed as a game that has its rewards, and the successful businessperson knows how to play the game well. But such playing, without concern for the wrong it does, allows ethics to be subsumed under business. We must reverse that.

The thrust of a business ethic, which would be possible and not oxymoronic, would begin with a vision of the good life, individually and institutionally. It would be aspirational. Johnson and Johnson's credo is an example of what they take a virtuous company to be. Portraits of ethical business leaders and statements of business leaders who aspire to be ethical such as James Autry's read this way.

> I take seriously the role of business and its impact on society. I shudder when I hear some businessperson say, "It's just business," because that usually means something is being done in the name of business that would not be done if that person were doing it in the name of himself or herself. Always remember this: If we can commit an injustice in the name of business, we can commit an injustice in the name of anything.[26]

To the challenge that the statement, "Good business is good ethics," when construed this way is tautological, one can only reply, "Of course." It cannot be empirically true if by good business we mean good bottom line, and by good ethics we mean the right thing. Sometimes doing the right thing will negatively affect the bottom line. To the claim that it is idealistic, one can only reply, once more, "Of course." But paradoxically, what moves people are aspirations and views of the possible. The thrust of business ethics must be to hold out a model of the most desirable that is possible, an aspiration to bring the system of business into accord with the aspirations of justice, a justice defined in terms of quality of life. That is why recent books such as Solomon's *Ethics and Excellence*,

Hartman's *Organizational Ethics and the Good Life*, Freeman's *Strategic Management*, and the work of Laura Nash and Lynne Sharp Paine, such as "Managing with Organizational Integrity," are on the mark. Stories and hagiography will be the business ethics of the new millennium. Ideals will impact on the law and the culture, to make it easier for individuals and organizations to achieve integrity.

QUESTIONS FOR DISCUSSION

1. Why do some argue that business ethics is an oxymoron? How does the idea of egoism factor into this argument?

2. What is "bottom-line myopia"? How does it affect our ability to act with justice or compassion toward others, according to Duska? Explain how the story of the frog and the tarantula illustrates the attitude of bottom-line myopia?

3. How does Duska portray the role of ethics in the philosophy of Adam Smith? What role does the idea of sympathy play in his outlook? How does this contrast with the interpretation of the invisible hand usually advanced in business?

4. What are some arguments the author offers in favor of business ethics? Are they persuasive? Why or why not?

5. Why does Duska argue that unfairness is irrational? How does this refute selfishness?

6. Explain the two conceptions of justice described by Cicero. How do we determine what people are due? How does this relate to matters of fairness? What does the second conception of justice add to this?

7. What does Duska mean by "moral schizophrenia"?

8. What is the author's proposal for "refurbishing" business ethics? Is this proposal workable? Why or why not?

NOTES

1. David C. Stolinsky, "Capitalism Is Squandering Its Inheritance," *New Oxford Review*, April 1999, 43.

2. I propose to use the words interchangeably in this paper, since I see no significant difference between them.

3. I take egoism to be the ethical theory that maintains one ought always to pursue one's own self-interest. Anything short of demanding the "always" adopts an overriding

principle that is not egoistic in some cases. For example, a theory such that everyone ought to pursue their own interest unless it hurts someone else qualifies the egoism and utilizes some other ethical theoretical principle as a basis for its decision making.

4. Albert Carr, "Is Business Bluffing Ethical?" *Harvard Business Review*, January/February 1968.

5. Milton Friedman, "The Social Responsibility of Business Is to Increase Its Profits," *New York Times Magazine*, September 13, 1970.

6. Even if Friedman did not mean the strong phrase "one and only one" (which is a highly dubious assumption since he quotes it in an infamous article from his earlier book *Capitalism and Freedom*), most defenders of this neoclassical view of corporate responsibility seem to agree with the "one and only" qualification.

7. Editors, *Journal of Commerce*, April 22, 1999, 10A.

8. This scenario is part of a case written by Chuck Soule, former CEO of Paul Revere Insurance Co., and is used with his permission.

9. Thomas F. O'Boyle, "Profit at Any Cost," *Business Ethics*, March/April 1999, 14.

10. Adam Smith, *The Wealth of Nations*, ed. R. H. Campbell and A. S. Skinner (Oxford: Oxford University Press, 1976; reprinted Indianapolis, IN: Liberty Classics, 1981), I, ii, 2.

11. Smith, *Wealth of Nations*, IV, ix, 51.

12. Cf. Ayn Rand, *The Virtue of Selfishness* (New York: New American Library, 1989).

13. How much the invisible hand depends on the social stability of an ethics-driven society remains a largely unexplored question, but analysis of the introduction of free-market economics in Russia seems to show that it does not work well absent some basic ethical cohesion of the society.

14. There are similarities here to Kant's ethics, which rests on the necessity of consistent behavior. Compare his use of the first Categorical Imperative, which shows that if dishonesty were universalized, trust would disappear. Cf. Norman Bowie and Ronald Duska, *Business Ethics*, 2nd ed. (New York: Prentice-Hall, 1990), 45ff.

15. Note the recent spate of articles on integrity, honesty, and trust in the literature.

16. Andrew Stark, "What's the Matter with Business Ethics?" *Harvard Business Review*, April 1993.

17. See the April 1999 edition of the *Academy of Management Review*.

18. Stanley Cavell, *The Claims of Reason* (New York: Oxford University Press, 1980), 245.

19. Such a notion of fairness and rational thinking is what underlies a principle like the Golden Rule, "Do unto others as you would have others do unto you," or Kant's principle of respect for persons, "Act so as never to treat another rational being merely as a means." These principles reinforce the notion that others are the same as you or me in most relevant respects.

20. Cicero, *De Officiis*, Bk. I, sec. 7, "Justice," Loeb translation (Cambridge, MA: Harvard University Press, 1930).

21. Thomas Aquinas, *Summa Theologica*, II-II, Q. 66, art. 7.

22. I mean by soul a notion equivalent to form, in an Aristotelian sense, where the formal cause, the "what" the thing is, is determined by the final cause, its "for what"

(raison d'etre). The purpose of anything (its final cause) defines what it is (its form), as well as the rules that tell us whether it is good or not.

23. O'Boyle, "Profit at Any Cost."

24. Sadly, this even applies to nonprofits, which use the same bottom-line techniques. They just have larger margins for expenses. For example, in the competition for students, colleges have catered to students' wants instead of to the primary purpose of colleges—the pursuit and transmission of truth. Birthrights are sold for a mess of porridge.

25. See my "The Why's of Business Revisited," *Journal of Business Ethics* 16 (1997): 1401–9.

26. James A. Autry, *Life and Work: A Manager's Search for Meaning* (New York: Avon Books, 1995).

Manager-Employee Relationships: Guided by Kant's Categorical Imperative or by Dilbert's Business Principle

Paul J. Borowski

In this chapter, the author reflects on the relationship between management and employees, which is frequently adversarial, asking if there are ways to improve these relationships by focusing on the human dignity of the "other." Familiar business ethics resources such as Kant's Categorical Imperative, utilitarianism, and Milton Friedman are combined with other ethical sources like Alfred North Whitehead and the papal encyclical *Laborem Exercens* in order to enrich our understanding of the dignity and worth of human persons. The chapter challenges us to view the humanity of our fellow workers first, rather than reducing them to the role they play in the corporate structure.

The relationship between employer and employees is a central one in the world of business, and it is one that is often the source of tension for the workplace. Employers are seemingly in constant mistrust of workers, while workers often look upon their bosses as "less than competent." Paul Borowski attempts to offer ethical analysis of the question of whether this "adversarial" relationship should continue unabated or whether the employer-employee relationship should be governed by different rules.

THE CASE OF AARON FEUERSTEIN[1]

On December 11, 1995, a catastrophic fire nearly destroyed all of the Malden Mills textile manufacturing plant in Lawrence, Massachusetts, and seemed certain to put its three thousand employees out of work. The likely response of the CEO of Malden Mills, Aaron Feuerstein, might have been one where he would collect the insurance money and go elsewhere with his business.

However, the response of Feuerstein was unlike what has become expected from the stereotypical idea we have of management in today's society. Instead of being "heartless" and "uncaring" about his employees, Feuerstein announced during the week following the fire that he would keep all of his three thousand employees on the payroll for a month while he started rebuilding the ninety-year-old family business. In January 1996, he announced he would pay his employees for a second month, and then in February announced he would pay them for a third month. By March, most of the employees had returned to work full-time and those who had not were offered help in making other arrangements.

In an atmosphere where at-will employment, monitoring employees on the job, drug testing, polygraph testing, and incidents that seemingly invade an employee's private life are common occurrences, the question becomes why an owner of a company would show care and concern for his workers. The relationship between management and employee appears to fall behind the primary promissory relationship between management and stockholders.[2] The example of Feuerstein shows another way to look at things. Feuerstein believes that what sets him apart from other CEOs is that he considers his workers an asset, not an expense. His role as CEO at Malden Mills goes beyond that primary promissory relationship with his stockholders to increase their profits; he also sees his responsibility to the workers, and even extends this responsibility to the community where his factory is found. During his years as CEO, Feuerstein has arranged for heart-bypass operations for several workers and offers of free soft drinks and breaks to workers on the manufacturing lines during the days of summer heat.

Is this an isolated case of sentimentalism and foolish compassion in the American business scene or is it a model of the relationship that needs to exist between workers and management? Most critics of Feuerstein see his actions as a "poor business decision." His decision to pay workers while he was rebuilding the factory cost his company several million dollars; many would look at the bottom line of financial loss and say: "Is this any way to run a business?" Business is not meant to be a charitable organization. When profits are down, it is the job of management to find a way to turn things around. Managers cannot "needlessly" take money away from their stockholders to help employees or even society—if so they fail in their primary responsibility.

Back in 1962, Milton Friedman wrote:

> The view has been gaining widespread acceptance that corporate officials and labor leaders have a social responsibility that goes beyond serving the interest of their stockholders or their members. This view shows a fundamental misconception of the character and nature of a free economy. In such an economy, there is one and only one social responsibility of business—to use its resources and engage in activities designed to increase its

profits so long as it stays within the rules of the game, which is to say, engages in open and free competition, without deception or fraud.[3]

This idea of responsibility deals with the stockholders, but what about the workers? Did Feuerstein go against his duties as CEO by helping workers in their moment of need? The world of business today is full of discussions about certain issues in the relationship between management and employees; issues such as whistle blowing, safe working conditions, and a proposed bill of rights for employees.[4] Beyond specific issues a somewhat general question needs to be asked: What principles should govern the normal (day-to-day) relationship between management and employees? This relationship seems to be an adversarial one—almost as if management and workers were on two different competing teams. Is not a business organization geared toward a final goal with all the members—stockholders, management, and employees—working together? Many companies work at building a team notion to promote the unity of the company—can the idea of a team be fostered in an atmosphere of mistrust, back-biting, and constant criticism? Feuerstein's example as CEO at Malden Mills suggests that the relationship between management and employee should be a civil one, not a warring one. If the relationship between the two were based on civil ideas rather than an attitude of suspicion, the life of the business may likely prosper. Feuerstein treated his employees with human respect, partly because he is a religious man, but also because of his firm belief that "happy employees" make "productive employees." At Malden Mills, Feuerstein believes the quality of the product is paramount and it is the employee who makes the quality; if the quality slips, the employee can destroy the company's profit.

There are a variety of principles that can govern the relationship between management and employees. If Friedman's view of social responsibility is used, then the relationship with the workers is placed second behind making a profit for the stockholders. However, this relationship between management and employees is basically a human relationship and as such should be governed by guidelines that would govern any human relationship. Does the relationship continue to go along with profit as the sole guide, the sole motivating factor, thus allowing feelings of tension and animosity to continue to flourish? Why do most employees try to deceive their bosses and why do most bosses try to exert extreme power over their laborers? Is this a healthy, moral foundation for a human relationship and will it help business increase its revenue? Or do we introduce guidelines where management and employees treat each other as human beings and members of the same team? There are a variety of guidelines that need to be introduced to see where this relationship is heading. Many principles have been set up to guide human relationships, and since business is made up of humans in relationship with one another, perhaps we can see what they have to offer us in dealing with this issue.

THE DILBERT PRINCIPLE OF BUSINESS[5]

- A major technology company simultaneously rolled out two new programs: (1) a random drug testing program, and (2) an "individual dignity enhancement" program.
- A company once purchased laptop computers for employees to use while traveling. Fearing that they might be stolen, the managers came up with a clever solution: permanently attach the laptop computers to the employees' desk.
- A freight company reorganized to define roles and clarify goals. Management decided to communicate changes by ordering each department to build floats for a "quality parade."
- A manager at a telecommunication company wanted to reinforce the "team" concept in his department. He held a meeting to tell the assembled "team" that henceforth he will carry a baseball bat with him at all times and each team member will carry a baseball while at work. Some team members found a way to hang the baseball around their necks so they do not have to carry it. Others fantasized about wrestling the bat away from the manager and using it.
- A company decided that instead of raises it will give bonuses if five of seven company goals are met. At the end of the year the employees are informed that they have met only four of seven goals, so no bonuses. One of the goals they missed was "employee morale."

Scott Adams is the creator of the *Dilbert* cartoon strip featured in thousands of daily newspapers throughout the country. The basic theme that runs throughout his work is a theme of the "bad boss." Some may contend that Adams's creation is merely a figment of his imagination, an exaggeration of the way life is in the business world, or is a reflection on his own painful experience in the corporate world; however, he receives hundreds of e-mails daily from people describing life in their own little corner of the business world and how the "bad boss" theme is on target. The above examples are real-life examples and help to illustrate the increasing tension between management and employees. Neither party seems to want to trust the other. Employees feel management makes "clueless" decisions and management feels that employees are trying to avoid work or "get something for doing nothing." An atmosphere of distrust is prevalent and the results can become absurd.

From the five examples above, we may now ask the question: Is this any way to run a business? In 1995, Adams wrote an article that originally appeared in the *Wall Street Journal* from which comes his concept of the Dilbert Principle. The basic tenet of the Dilbert Principle is *that the most ineffective workers*

are systematically moved to the place where they can do the least damage: management.
Adams has created a career out of satirizing the workplace and many might say
he is overstepping the lines of decency. However, does not his principle and his
daily cartoon strip represent a common attitude in the workplace? An attitude
that managers do not know what they are doing and are to be avoided at all
costs? An attitude that workers are simply devising new ways to escape their
duties while taking advantage of everything the company offers them? This attitude places the managers in a dangerous position; they feel they are outsiders
in the firm, that they have no connection with the employees and thus will
act in ways to show their "power" in the workplace. It fosters a belief among
employees that discussing anything with management will be a waste of time
since it would be basically "over their heads."

For Adams, the workplace is an area of life that is full of tension and
constant battling between those in charge and those who are found down
the ladder of corporate life. In a description of the business world where one
seems to toss their hands in the air and say that the situation is worthless, Adams writes:

> I find great humor in the fact that we can never take ourselves seriously.
> We rarely recognize our own idiocies, yet we clearly identify the idiocies of
> others. That's the central tenet of business. We expect others to act rationally
> even though we are irrational. It's useless to expect rational behavior from
> the people you work with, or anybody else for that matter. If you come to
> peace with the fact that you are surrounded by idiots, you'll realize resis-
> tance is futile, your tension will dissipate and you can sit back and have a
> good laugh at the expense of others.[6]

In a sense it seems as if the Dilbert Principle paints a picture of the workplace where the prevailing attitude is "us vs. them." One reads each new strip
daily and it seems as if the workplace is not a place where we go to be productive but simply a place that we have to endure. We speak of work as "pure
agony," as something to "be endured," as something that we come home from
feeling "physically and mentally exhausted." We all try to avoid situations of
stress and conflict; we as humans have the desire for a safe, known place. If the
relationship between management and employees is one of tension and strife, it
will then produce an unhealthy and unproductive work place. It will produce
an environment that both parties will seek to avoid at all costs.

Why mention Scott Adams and his "fictional" creation of Dilbert in his
own little "fictional" business world? Is the office life of Dilbert far from reality? Why are so many people drawn to it and why can numerous comments,
such as, "that's the way it is at my job," be heard. Adams is not offering any
moral guidelines or delving into the philosophy that should govern the work-

place; he is stating what he perceives business to be all about, and it seems as if his perception is echoed by many people. What can lead us out of this seemingly vicious circle where mistrust rules the roost of the business world? Is the future of the American business life condemned to be defined by the Dilbert Principle where workers feel their bosses are incompetent? Can we restore the concept of humanity to a relationship that is seemingly broken on all counts across the board? In the relationship between management and employees, one should look at the implications to the moral life—besides how it affects profit. In this light, we now turn to examine some moral philosophical guidelines to help us discuss this relationship.

IMMANUEL KANT'S CATEGORICAL IMPERATIVE: AN ATTEMPT TO INTRODUCE HUMANITY

Numerous ethical theories exist and have existed throughout history. They have all been formulated in an attempt to answer the ultimate questions of moral philosophy. Back in the days of Socrates, Plato, and Aristotle the questions that challenged their minds included "Why be ethical?" and "What does being ethical really mean?"—and the same questions challenge our minds today. To the first query the Greeks responded with the idea that happiness stems from being moral, that there is a close relationship between moral virtue and the healthy human personality. It is the second inquiry that has led to the development of ethical theories. The theories of consequentialism (e.g., egoism, utilitarianism) focus on the result of actions. If the end result is a good one then the action, no matter what the act is, is morally acceptable. For Immanuel Kant, these theories of consequentialism relied too much on empirical evidence. They were theories that could never say that such an action is definitively right or wrong—the circumstances could change the result. Kant was a man who placed emphasis on reason; he firmly believed that reason alone could yield a moral law. The moral truths that we arrive at need to be reasonable, they must be logically consistent and free from internal contradiction.

Kant believed that one command is categorical—that is, necessarily binding on all rational agents, despite any other considerations. From this one categorical imperative, this universal command, we can derive all commands of duty. Kant's *Categorical Imperative* says that we should act in such a way that we can will the maxim of our action to become a universal law.[7] Can we logically make the maxim of our actions into universal law? His theory of ethics offers us a clear-cut way to realize how we should act; it is neither hypothetical nor based on the end results, the consequences.

While Kant's Categorical Imperative has been debated as a valid principle for determining what is morally correct, it offers some interesting insights concerning the relationship between management and employees. Behind the Categorical Imperative lies a basic belief for Kant: Every human person has an inherent worth from the very fact that they are rational creatures. As rational creatures, we should treat every person with respect and, in philosophical language, we should treat every person as an end and never merely as a means. Looking at the values behind the Categorical Imperative, perhaps we begin to reach a guideline for the way relationships within the business world should be handled. Taking Kant to heart, the seemingly adversarial relationship between management and employees has no place. Both groups within the organization are first and foremost human individuals and need to be treated as such. While the debate continues to go on dealing with specific issues of management–employee relationships, Kant goes to the heart of the issue: In order for business to be morally acceptable, all parties must be treated with mutual respect because we as people deserve it.

In *Groundwork of the Metaphysic of Morals*, Kant writes: *"Act in such a way that you always treat humanity, whether in your own person or in the person of any other, never simply as a means, but always at the same time as an end."*[8] People are not objects that we simply have for use at our disposal. The manager who is above us, the employee who works under us, each must never be treated as anything less than a human person in the thought of Kant. A principle that governs business by saying the most ineffective people reach management positions goes against the heart of Kant's theory. Treating people simply as a means is to regard them as something that we use for our own purposes without their full and free consent. Such actions are inherently wrong. Being used against one's will simply as a means to someone else's end violates individual freedom.

In an age where technology continues to run nearly every aspect of our lives, there may be a tendency to treat one another as simply objects that are programmed to perform a task. Managers are more than *computers* who have been programmed to increase the company's profits; employees are more than mere *robots* who have been given the job to complete their assigned tasks. Businesses are made up of human beings who work together for a common goal. Businesses are people who work together to supply other humans with goods and services. Business is primarily an activity for and by human beings. The philosophy of Kant reflects an essential element of business: It is made up of rational beings. With that in mind, those who make up business (managers and employees) should begin to act as rational beings.

This thinking is echoed in the writings of Pope Paul II in his encyclical, *Laborem Exercens* (On Human Work). The belief of Kant in the value of the human person is paralleled by Pope John Paul II as we read:

[T]he primary basis of the value of work is man himself, who is its subject. This leads immediately to a very important conclusion of an ethical nature: however true it may be that man is destined for work and called to it, in the first place work is "for man" and not man "for work." . . . Given this way of understanding things, and presupposing that different sorts of work that people do can have greater or lesser objective value, let us try nevertheless to show that each sort is judged above all by the measure of the dignity of the subject of work, that is to say the person, the individual who carries it out.[9]

What does being ethical entail? To Kant it entails treating others as rational human beings. Where does work receive its value? To Pope John Paul II it is rooted in the very person of the individual worker. The basic work relationship between management and employee needs to reflect these values. It is in a relationship between two people that businesses are founded.

While Kant's Categorical Imperative offers us insights into what should guide the relationship between management and employees, there is another philosopher whose insights may also be helpful. Kant emphasizes the role that reason must play in our moral thinking; other philosophers have done the same. While he never wrote a work specifically dealing with moral philosophy or the business world, Alfred North Whitehead's works reflect an interest in the good. His interest in man's life and *how* one is to live are of importance to our continuing discussion. The following section reflects the ethical implications of Whitehead's writings with a primary focus on the ethical implications that arise in the forming of any human relationship.

MOVING TOWARD A GOOD FOR ALL OF SOCIETY: REFLECTIONS ON THE "OTHER"

The selectiveness of individual experience is moral so far as it conforms to the balance of importance disclosed in the rational vision; and conversely the conversion of the intellectual insight into an emotional force corrects the sensitive experience in the direction of morality. The correction is in proportion to the rationality of the insight.

Morality of outlook is inseparably conjoined with generality of outlook. The antithesis between the general good and the individual interest can be abolished only when the individual is such that its interest is the general good, thus exemplifying the loss of the minor intensities in order to find them again with finer composition in a wider sweep of interest.[10]

One's actions, to be considered in the light of moral thinking, must be rational actions. When a person is mentally disturbed, we say that he is not responsible for his actions. In the American legal system a person who is found guilty of a crime because of insanity is placed in a mental hospital for treatment instead of a prison for punishment. The human acts that we consider as right or wrong need to be performed by a person who knows what he is doing. The ability to act rationally is regarded as an important part of moral acting. When one is unable to act in a rational manner, whether because of cognitive or emotional defects, one's free choice is also diminished."[11] The action needs to have been thought out and thought through.

Another important point is brought out in the quotation from Whitehead, and that is the balance between the good of the individual and the good of the whole. The tension that can exist between the two needs to be done away with by the individual acting for the good of all. A person living out his life may be faced with a decision to enhance his personal concerns that may hinder the advancement of society. An individual should postpone the fulfillment of one's own desires to promote the good of the society. It is a morality that places *the other* before oneself.[12] It is a moral way of living that realizes that in placing the needs of the society first, my own needs, now postponed, may be met later. Whitehead is saying that each individual should have as his main concern the interest of *the other.*

A Whiteheadian ethic would emphasize that we act for the common good. It is not just a matter of foregoing my own interest, but it is a recognition that I am part of a larger society and my actions should benefit that society. One may relinquish one's own interest but does so to benefit oneself eventually since one is also a member of the society. All our actions should be directed to help the greatest good.[13]

> In our relatively high grade of human existence, this doctrine of feelings and their subject is best illustrated by our notion of moral responsibility. The subject is responsible for being what it is in virtue of its feelings. It is also derivatively responsible for the consequences of its existence because they flow from its feelings.[14]

A person as subject is responsible for his actions. Our feelings, our inner convictions, our moral faculties are what will cause us to act and they are precisely ours. These feelings are within us and cause us to act. In Whitehead's view we have an effect on *the other* since we are social by our very nature, but we are still free to make our own decisions. The environment around us will affect us, but our own inner feelings make us responsible for our own actions.

Moral responsibility is connected with the idea of personal identity. A person freely decides to act in a certain way, and even later on down the line one is still held accountable for the action. Perhaps one has progressed in one's moral growth. A person may have broken a law, and now many years later, when they catch that person, he realizes that what he did was wrong. A person has matured in a moral sense, but we still hold him responsible for his actions. One freely chooses to act in such a way, and years do not exempt him from accepting the consequences of previous actions. Our civil laws reflect this very sensitivity. The one who is in prison for robbery is the same person who committed the crime; personal identity is shown "when the change in the details of fact exhibits an identity of primary character amid secondary changes of value."[15] A person cannot escape responsibility for the actions he has committed. Our actions flow from our inner convictions and they are a representation of ourselves. Whitehead holds firmly to the idea of holding a person accountable for his own actions. "In a communal religion you study the will of God in order that he may preserve you; in a purified religion, rationalized under the influence of the world-concept, you study his goodness in order to be like him. It is the difference between the enemy you conciliate and the companion you follow."[16]

For Whitehead those who embraced a communal religion seem to follow the regulations of their religion to avoid the wrath of an angry God. It is the way little children obey their parents to escape punishment from them. A rational, purified religion begins to have us acting under the influence of the world-concept. Again we are faced with the fact that moral acting deals more with *the other* than just ourselves. In effect there is no action that we perform that does not touch the lives of people around us. We decide to act morally to bring value to the surroundings in which we are. We begin to picture that our actions play a role in the world as a whole. There are no individual acts of morality; our moral lives affect the lives of countless others. It is when we adopt this world-concept that we try to do what is good for those with whom we live. We wish to make the society a peaceful, tranquil location. Our moral lives wish to bring us into contact with *the other* instead of driving others away.

In a sense, those who love their moral life in this way are not acting based on principles. A desire guides them to live in harmony with the world. It is not a pie-in-the-sky morality but it is a very deep one that recognizes the value that is intrinsic in each and every individual. A moral way of living—which must include the way we conduct business—based on process thought moves us beyond ourselves into a realm of constant care and concern for people around us. Similarly, Charles Hartshorne says that "ethics is the generalization of instinctive concern, which in principle transcends the immediate state of the self and even the long-run career of the self, and embraces the ongoing communal process of life as such."[17] A morally mature person has the life and livelihood of *the other* before himself. It is a way of moral living that places the needs of society before one's own needs.

As we conclude our look at the thought of Whitehead regarding the moral life, a few final points need to be made. First, he appears to have an attitude against moral codes that have been established throughout the years. We can see these codes as an attempt to lead one toward being a moral person but can never be the final end. Whitehead did not hold to the existence of universal moral principles that were true in every time, place, and situation. We read: "But no heroic deed, and no unworthy act, depends for its heroism or disgust, upon the exact second of time at which it occurs, unless such change of time places it in a different sequence of values. The value-judgment points beyond the immediacy of historical fact."[18]

There is something indeed beyond time and space that gives value or lack of value to any action we may perform. Whitehead held that one is to live out one's life to attain the ideals that will have as their aim the perfection of society. While holding to this, one will also hold to the fact that absolute perfection is not attainable in this world. For Whitehead the idea of moral living was also progressive. One aims at living a moral life to promote peace and harmony, within oneself and within the society. Any discussion of moral living must be one that is based on a rational perspective.[19] The moral life that one leads is to be a continuous adventure, not a static existence. Living as morally as is possible will entail more than a passive acceptance of rules and regulations. It will be going beyond the law.

Justice demands that we follow all the rules and regulations of the society of which we are part. Rights need to be respected. Fairness guides all people. In Whitehead's view there has to be more, and ethics turns into one of love for *the other*. In our moral life we are trying to keep the interests of *the other* before our eyes. We aim at trying to promote peace and harmony within our society. We strive to avoid being interested only in ourselves and what is in it for us. An ethics of love can bridge the gap between harmony and self-concern. Justice itself is not enough to make a person morally mature.

What makes a person morally mature lies with the self—a self that in reflecting sees the need to leap beyond its own existence. It is the self that is not tuned in on its own cares and concerns but a self that can recognize the needs of *the other* and act accordingly. Most of the time we will obey the law for fear of being caught. Very often we will act in such a way because we feel it will win the approval of our peers. Perhaps, one day we may even begin to act because we feel an urge to live out the universal principle of justice. Within the self is the lure to go even beyond justice and fairness. Within the self there is the conviction to aim toward the perfection of society. A morally mature person lives to bring about peace and harmony.

This is what civilization—which includes the world of business—should be about: striving toward harmony. It is a striving that finds its origination within the self to go out of the self. Disorder and chaos rule our world now as we attempt to live out a moral life. Disorder emerges when justice is done, but love fails to emerge. We strive to live an ethics of love that goes out of self; it is an ethics that goes beyond the rules that are established. "How much can I do?" is the question of a morally mature person instead of "How much ought I to do?" Principles limit us but the self is lured beyond its limits and creates a world of harmony.

A morally mature person will go beyond his own little world and encompass the view of the larger world. It is an ethics of moving beyond to strive and live out aims that seem unattainable. Trying to live for the good of *the other* becomes the primary concern and that gives us reward, knowing that we tried to live for *the other*. It is an ethics that strives to bring about unity and harmony in the midst of conflict and division; it is an ethics that aims at peace and tranquility instead of conflict and war. It is an ethics that no longer asks the question "Is this right?" but the question "Is this aimed at bringing peace?"

One transcends one's own self. Personal interests are secondary and society's concerns are primary. Selfishness gives way to giving of oneself. This is how one begins to see if he or she is morally mature: answering questions about bringing harmony instead of saying one followed the rules.

Everyone will not attain the notion of moral living for *the other*. It is placed before us as the ideal to be striven after. There will always be those who strive to meet their own personal interests before helping the society in which they live.

BUSINESS: COMPOSED OF INEFFECTIVE PEOPLE OR MADE UP OF "THE OTHER"

Immanuel Kant places emphasis on treating other people as rational creatures. Our dealing with the rest of the world should have us realize we are dealing with people. Can this attitude exist in the world of business between managers and employees while still allowing a company to follow its goal in making a profit? Why is it that, when we walk into the workplace, we are supposed to stop acting like human persons and instead act as machines driven with but a single-mindedness of making money? We enter the workplace precisely because of our humanity, and if the workplace is to be a place of morality we must allow our humanity to exist. Managers and employees are not two different species, and the dealings that each has with the other should reflect this fact. We allow the fact that one has power and the other feels powerless to change the way we would expect normally to act with our fellow human beings. We expect civilness in our dealings with people outside the workplace; is it wrong to expect anything less while on the job?

Alfred North Whitehead was not primarily interested in ethics and was less interested in the world of business. Still, his thought on life and our striving to bring about peace and harmony in society can be applied to the world of business. His thoughts on our relations and dealings with *the other* can be applied to the world of business and our relationships there. Perhaps it seems like an idealistic notion to live an "ethics of love" as he writes, but is there anything in such a notion that goes against any business principle or any tenet of capitalism? We have seemingly given into the Dilbert Principle proposed by Scott Adams: Management is made up of ineffective people; this is a reality and the sooner we admit this the sooner we can move on with our lives. This may be a defeatist attitude. Simply because that is the way things are does not necessarily mean that it is morally correct or will never change. Management and employees must both be open to change, both must be accepting of the fact that the one on the other side of the relationship is truly a person and not a "monster" (as Scott Adams frequently refers to managers).

Perhaps Kant's idea of *humanity* being part of ethics and Whitehead's idea of *the other* being part of living is asking too much of the business world. I think Aaron Feuerstein would disagree. To conclude, I would like to return to the opening case involving Feuerstein. His actions of rebuilding the plant after the fire illustrated concretely some beliefs contained in both Kant's and Whitehead's writings. As a manager, he treated his employees as the human beings they actually are. It was not a warring relationship but one based on a desire to respect *the other*. Perhaps there will always be those who feel that the relationship between managers and their employees will always have people at odds. It is my opinion that this need not be. An ethical relationship between management and employees is due to the fact respect should govern all human relationships—be they in the workplace, the church, the neighborhood, the university (including the professor/student relationship), or wherever. Finally, there is nothing in a "morally correct" relationship between managers and employees that goes against the company's desire to make a profit; on the contrary, such a peaceable relationship can help to meet this desire. Before the fire at the Malden Mills factory, the plant was producing 130,000 yards a week; after the fire production was up to 230,000 yards. A group of inefficient managers or disgruntled employees could not meet these figures. Feuerstein feels the relationship between management and employees is a vital one—one that mistrust need not ruin, but one that we should foster and in turn will foster the growth of the company.

QUESTIONS FOR DISCUSSION

1. Can the idea of a team working toward a final goal be fostered in an atmosphere of mistrust, back-biting, and constant criticism? Why do some employees try to deceive their bosses and why do some bosses try to exert

extreme power over their laborers? Is this a healthy moral foundation for a human relationship and will it help a business increase its revenue?

2. According to Scott Adams, the most ineffective workers are systematically moved to the place where they can do the least damage: management. Is this true?

3. The ethicists cited by the author affirm that the meaning and purpose of work and production have their root in the dignity of the human person. Is this true, and if so, how might this insight change the way workers and managers relate to one another?

4. For Whitehead, the recognition of the dignity of other human beings leads us, by necessity, to act in ways that promote the common good. How might this insight change the manager–employee relationship?

5. The chapter claims that within every self there is a lure to go beyond justice and fairness, aiming toward the more exalted goal of the perfection of society. How might this inner motivation toward social perfection aid in realigning warped relations in a business setting?

NOTES

1. Information dealing with the Malden Mills manufacturing plant fire and the subsequent response by the CEO, Aaron Feuerstein, appears in Michael Ryan, "They Call Their Boss a Hero," *Baltimore Sunday Sun, Parade Magazine*, September 8, 1996.

2. This argument in effect states that management agrees (promises) to maximize stockholder wealth in return for specific compensation. Following from this is the argument that such relationship imposes an obligation on management that is inconsistent with any other responsibility other than maximization of the company's profit.

3. Milton Friedman, *Capitalism and Freedom* (Chicago: University of Chicago Press, 1962), 133.

4. For a discussion of a proposed bill of right for employees see David E. Ewing, "A Proposed Bill of Rights," in *Freedom inside the Organization* (New York: E. P. Dutton, 1977), 144–51.

5. The following section is a brief look at Scott Adams, *The Dilbert Principle* (New York: HarperCollins, 1996). While primarily the author of a comic strip that appears throughout the country, Mr. Adams has appeared to touch a common belief that exists in the "Corporate World" about the prevailing attitudes concerning management and workers.

6. Adams, *Dilbert Principle*, 7.

7. Immanuel Kant, *Groundwork of the Metaphysic of Morals*, trans. H. J. Paton (New York: Harper & Row, 1956), 22.

8. Kant, *Groundwork of the Metaphysic of Morals*, 96.

9. Pope John Paul II, *Laborem Exercens* (On Human Work) (Boston: Daughters of St. Paul, 1991), 17.

10. Alfred North Whitehead, *Process and Reality*, corrected ed., ed. David Ray Griffin and Donald W. Sherburne (London: Macmillan; reprinted New York: Free Press, 1979), 15.

11. R. Campbell, "Moral Justification and Freedom," *Journal of Philosophy* 85 (April 1988): 192.

12. The phrase "the other" is printed in italics throughout the text in order to connect it with the phrase as it is used in the writings of Emmanuel Levinas. "One has to respond to one's right to be, not by referring to some abstract or anonymous law, or judicial entity, but because of one's fear for the Other. . . . Responsibility for the Other, for the naked face of the first individual to come alone. A responsibility that goes beyond what I may or may not have done to the Other or whatever acts I may or may not have committed, as if I were devoted to the other man before being devoted to myself." Emmanuel Levinas, "Ethics as First Philosophy," in *The Levinas Reader*, ed. Sean Hand (Oxford: Basil Blackwell, 1989), 82–83.

13. John B. Cobb Jr., *A Christian Natural Theology: Based on the Thought of Alfred North Whitehead* (Philadelphia: Westminster Press, 1965), 124.

14. Whitehead, *Process and Reality*, 222.

15. Alfred North Whitehead, "Immortality," in *The Philosophy of Alfred North Whitehead*, ed. Paul Arthur Schilpp (New York: Tudor Publishing Company, 1951), 689–90.

16. Alfred North Whitehead, *Religion in the Making* (Cambridge: Cambridge University Press, 1927), 30.

17. Charles Hartshorne, "Beyond Enlightened Self-Interest," in *Religious Experience and Process Theology: The Pastoral Implications of a Major Modern Movement*, ed. Harry James Cargas and Bernard Lee (New York: Paulist Press, 1976), 318.

18. Whitehead, "Immortality," 684.

19. Paul Arthur Schilpp, "Whitehead's Moral Philosophy," in *The Philosophy of Alfred North Whitehead*, ed. Paul Arthur Schilpp (New York: Tudor Publishing Company, 1951), 610.

• *4* •

Smith, Friedman, and Self-Interest in Ethical Society

Harvey S. James Jr. and Farhad Rassekh

In this article, Harvey S. James and Farhad Rassekh examine the writings of Adam Smith and Milton Friedman regarding their interpretation and use of the concept of self-interest. They argue that neither Smith nor Friedman considers self-interest to be synonymous with selfishness and thus devoid of ethical considerations. Rather, for both writers self-interest embodies an other-regarding aspect that requires individuals to moderate their actions when others are adversely affected. The overriding virtue for Smith in governing individual actions is justice; for Friedman it is noncoercion.

*S*uppose a company president comes to the realization that the firm's manufacturing operations, and those of competitors, discharge a harmful pollutant, and the pollutant is not subject to the country's environmental regulations. What should the company president do? Suppose the company president wanted to make the decision in accordance with the doctrines of Adam Smith and Milton Friedman as presented in a typical business ethics textbook. What would the action be? The most likely answer is that the doctrines of self-interest and profit seeking would advise the president to conceal the information and continue with business as usual. Is this an accurate assessment of Smith and Friedman?

Adam Smith maintains that market participants, in pursuit of their self-interests, are guided by an "invisible hand" and thus unknowingly benefit society. Closely related to Smith's doctrine is a thesis put forth by Milton Friedman that the "social responsibility of business is to increase its profits."[1] Implicit in Friedman's thesis is the Smithian doctrine that the pursuit of profit is beneficial to society. It is common in many business ethics textbooks to find Smith and Friedman interpreted as follows: People *should* pursue their self-interests; businesses should do whatever improves their financial position, even if others are harmed; and in some way the "invisible hand" ultimately makes the effects of such actions right for society. Is this interpretation correct?

In this chapter we examine both Smith's doctrine and Friedman's thesis, particularly as they relate to the role of self-interest and to the modern notion of business ethics. We are motivated by the fact that virtually every textbook in business ethics devotes at least a section to Smith in connection with the role of self-interest in capitalism and a section to Friedman in relation to the social responsibility of corporations. However, many of these presentations are often a confusing explanation of self-interest and how Smith and Friedman interpret and use that concept. Many textbooks at best make an incomplete presentation of Smith and Friedman; at worst, they misrepresent them. We find this curious. Modern scholarship on Smith acknowledges his belief that self-interest must be tempered by virtues such as justice. And Friedman at least on one occasion has expressed his unhappiness regarding the interpretation of his position on social responsibility.[2]

We intend to present Smith and Friedman based on their writings and to show that self-interest, as expounded by Smith and Friedman, is not the same as selfishness but rather has a moral and other-regarding component. To be clear, we argue that both Smith and Friedman would agree that the company president, when faced with the environmental problem outlined above, ought to inform the public and accept the consequences. And this course of action would be consistent with both Smith's and Friedman's interpretation of self-interest and its role in a market economy.[3]

Why is an accurate interpretation of Smith and Friedman important? The Smithian analysis of the pursuit of self-interest represents one of the most influential doctrines in the history of ideas, forming the foundation of the market system. Similarly, Friedman's analysis of corporate social responsibility represents one of the most controversial ideas in modern business ethics. Consequently, it behooves all individuals—particularly textbook writers and instructors who teach and critique—to understand Smith and Friedman accurately and completely regarding their interpretation of the nature and role of self-interest in society. Only then is it fair to conduct a normative evaluation of Smith's and Friedman's arguments.

This chapter is organized as follows: It presents a textbook treatment of Smith and Friedman; examines the concept of self-interest in Smith's writings; analyzes Friedman's thesis on social responsibility, particularly as an application of Smith's advocacy of self-interested behavior; and offers a concluding note.

TEXTBOOK TREATMENT OF
ADAM SMITH AND MILTON FRIEDMAN

Consider two quotes from Smith and two from Friedman that are well known and form the basis for the popular characterizations of how they view self-interest. In *An Inquiry into the Nature and Causes of the Wealth Nations* (WN), published in 1776 [1981], Smith outlines how markets operate, particularly with respect to the role of self-interest in society. In the first quote, Smith explains why self-interest is necessary, and in the second he shows how the pursuit of self-interest, via the invisible hand, benefits society:

> It is not from the benevolence of the butcher, the brewer, or the baker, that we expect our dinner, but from their regard to their own interest. We address ourselves, not to their humanity but to their own interest.[4]

> As every individual, therefore, endeavors as much as he can to employ his capital in the support of domestick industry, and so to direct that industry that its produce may be of the greatest value; every individual necessarily labours to render the annual revenue of the society as great as he can. He generally, indeed, neither intends to promote the publick interest, nor knows how much he is promoting it. By preferring the support of domestick to that of foreign industry, he intends only his own security; and by directing that industry in such a manner as its produce may be of the greatest value, he intends only his own gain, and he is in this, as in many other cases, led by an invisible hand to promote an end which was not part of his intention. Nor is it always the worse for the society that it was no part of it. By pursuing his own interest he frequently promotes that of the society more effectually than when he really intends to promote it. I have never known much good done by those who affected to trade for the publick good. It is an affectation, indeed, not very common among merchants and very few words need be employed in dissuading them from it.[5]

What does Smith mean by regard to one's own interest? Why is the pursuit of self-interest necessary in a market economy? Does Smith place any restriction on the pursuit of self-interest? Typical answers to these questions from business ethics textbooks are as follows: "Smith believed that only through egoistic pursuits could the greatest economic good for the whole society be produced."[6] Later in their text, Shaw and Berry explain, "Smith reasoned that the greatest utility will result from *unfettered pursuit of self-interest.* . . . Government interference in private enterprise should be eliminated, free competition encouraged, and *economic self-interest made the rule of the day,*" which "results in the greatest benefit to society"[7] [emphasis added]. Similarly, Buchholz and Rosenthal state that the "pursuit of one's own *selfish ends*, without outside interference, is believed to result in the greatest good for the greatest number of people"[8] [emphasis added]. Velasquez remarks that Smith's definition of self-interest fails to recognize that "human beings regularly show a concern for the good of others and constrain their self-interest for the sake of the rights of others."[9] The idea is that nothing more than the pursuit of one's self-interest, with self-interest defined in narrowly egoistic terms, is necessary for a market economy to function well, since an invisible hand will guide such actions so as to produce positive effects for society.[10]

Now consider Friedman's application of Smith's principle of self-interest to the issue of corporate social responsibility. In the first quote, which comes from *Capitalism and Freedom*, Friedman defines the social responsibility of business. In the second, from an article entitled "The Social Responsibility of Business Is to Increase Its Profits," he gives his reason.

> There is one and only one social responsibility of business—to use its re- sources and engage in activities designed to increase its profits so long as it stays within the rules of the game, which is to say, engages in open and free competition, without deception or fraud.[11]

> In a free-enterprise, private property system, a corporate executive is an employee of the owners of the business. He has a direct responsibility to his employers. That responsibility is to conduct the business in accordance with their desires, which generally will be to make as much money as possible while conforming to the basic rules of the society, both those embodied in law and those embodied in ethical custom.[12]

Friedman also says that a social responsibility other than to generate as much profit as possible for business owners is a "fundamentally subversive doctrine."[13] What does Friedman mean when he says the pursuit of profits is the only responsibility of business? Textbook answers to this question vary, but generally reflect the idea that Friedman's argument "attempts to ground busi- ness ethics . . . in the profit element only"[14] and is a "declaration of *profits over ethics*"[15] [emphasis added]. Primeaux states that "Friedman's ethical imperative . . . is too myopic, too *focused on bottom-line accounting profits alone*"[16] [emphasis added]. And Buchholz states that

> the social and ethical responsibilities of business are exhausted in terms of marketplace performance. As long as business performs its economizing functions well, it has fulfilled its social and ethical responsibilities and noth- ing more need be said. Thus [this] view of ethics . . . *does not necessitate any conscious ethical considerations* of business's responsibilities to society or to the environment other than successful economic performance. Ethics is totally captured by the notion of economizing.[17] [emphasis added]

Similarly, Velasquez says that Friedman's position on profit and ethics "can be . . . used to justify a manager's *unethical or illegal conduct*"[18] [emphasis added].

Hay and Gray equate Friedman with the dictum "let the buyer beware," meaning managers "are not necessarily concerned with product quality or safety, or with sufficient and/or truthful information about products and services."[19] According to these authors, Friedman says that it is justifiable for businesses to pursue any actions that increase profits since businesses' only function is to generate profits for stockholders. Any consideration other than profits is against the interests of business owners.

Popular interpretations of Smith and Friedman suggest that self-interest is devoid of ethical and other-regarding considerations. As we show below, however, these interpretations reflect a widespread misconception of what Smith and Friedman actually say.[20] A careful reading of Smith and Friedman will show that their use of the principle of self-interest is consistent with ethical conduct and that they never advocated the pursuit of one's interest to the detriment of individuals and society. Below we present a brief analysis of the Smithian system, including what Smith considered to be the proper behavior in business. This analysis leads us to Friedman's thesis on corporate social responsibility.

ADAM SMITH'S ANALYSIS OF SELF-INTEREST

Smith is generally known for his economic treatise *The Wealth of Nations*. But to understand Smith's social design, one would have to begin with his earlier book, *The Theory of Moral Sentiments* (TMS), published in 1759, which he considered to be a superior work to WN.[21] Although TMS is a work on moral philosophy, it lays down the foundation for a social system to which Smith devoted his entire intellectual energy. An important element of Smith's social design is a proper political-economic system, which he analyzes in WN where he describes, inter alia, the operation of markets and the role of government. To understand Smith's political economy, one must study his moral philosophy, otherwise his overall social system will be incomplete, misinterpreted, and misunderstood.[22]

In recent years, numerous books and articles have carefully delved into all writings of Smith and, as a result, accurately present Smith's ethical and economic systems. A sample of such scholarship on Smith includes Werhane, Muller, Brown, and Young, as well as many papers by Evensky that are referenced in his 1993 article.[23] In spite of the extensive contemporary examinations of Smith's moral philosophy and economics, many of the insights these scholars provide are not yet fully incorporated into mainstream business ethics literature. Hence, we present some essential points that are indispensable in understanding Smith.[24]

Smith accepts as a matter of fact that we are endowed with many impulses, including self-love. But he maintains that we are also endowed with the capacity to exercise self-command to contain our passions when the pursuit of self-love injures other people. Self-command plays a central role in Smith's ethical system, and it is a key to understanding his interpretation of self-interest as a proper motive for individual behavior.[25] "Self-command is not only itself a great virtue, but from it all other virtues seem to derive their principal luster."[26]

While the virtue of self-command moderates one's actions, the approval of an action, according to Smith, depends on the judgment of an imaginary figure, the "impartial spectator." The following excerpt from TMS illustrates Smith's application of the impartial spectator in his ethical system.

> There can be no proper motive for hurting our neighbor. . . . To disturb his happiness merely because it stands in the way of our own, to take from him what is of real use to him merely because it may be of equal or of more use to us, is what no impartial spectator can go along with. . . . *In the race for wealth, honors, and preferments, he may run as hard as he can, and strain every nerve and every muscle, in order to outstrip all his competitors. But if he should justle, or throw down any of them, the indulgence of the spectators is entirely at an end. It is a violation of fair play, which they cannot admit of.*[27] [emphasis added]

Clearly, Smith disapproves of actions that injure other people. An individual motivated by self-love "to outstrip all his competitors" in the pursuit of "wealth, honor, and preferment" ought not to "justle, or throw down any of them." This principle permeates Smith's entire social and ethical systems, including his economics.

Smith expounds the doctrine that market transactions motivated by individual interests can benefit others. Although this doctrine figures prominently in WN, the genesis of the idea that self-interest drives market transactions is introduced in TMS.[28] The reason Smith appeals to self-interested motives in the market, according to Jacob Viner, is that Smith considers market exchanges to be mechanical and generally anonymous in comparison with social relations within families and between friends.[29] Sentiments such as sympathy and benevolence, which are prevalent in social behavior and familial relationships, are "insufficiently strong as a disciplinary force, and self-interest, moderated by an inner sense of justice as well as by politically enforced justice, would be the dominant psychological force" in market exchanges.[30]

Two crucial points about self-interest emerge in Smith's writings. The first is that the pursuit of self-interest is bound by the laws of justice:

> All systems either of preferences or restraint, therefore, being thus completely taken away, the obvious and simple system of natural liberty establishes itself of its own accord. *Every man, as long as he does not violate the laws of justice, is left perfectly free to pursue his own interest his own way,* and to bring

both his industry and capital into competition with those of any man, or order of men.[31] [emphasis added]

Viner notes that to Smith "justice is a negative virtue; it consists of refraining from injury to another person and from taking or withholding from another what belongs to him. . . . Smith considered justice, so understood, to be the necessary foundation of a viable society."[32] Advancing one's interest at the expense of others is unacceptable because to "hurt in any degree the interest of one order of citizens for no other purpose but to promote that of some other, is evidently contrary to that justice and equality of treatment which the sovereign owes to all different orders of his subjects."[33]

The second point is that in Smith's mind there is a sharp distinction between selfishness and self-interest. Raphael and Macfie point out that "Smith recognizes a variety of motives, not only for actions in general but also for virtuous action."[34] These motives include self-interest or, to use the eighteenth-century term, self-love. It is this, not "selfishness," that comes to the fore in WN. Smith distinguished the two expressions, using "selfishness" in a pejorative sense for such self-love as issues in harm or neglect of other people. In fact, Smith believes "that to feel much for others and little for ourselves, that to restrain our selfish, and to indulge our benevolent affections, constitutes the perfection of human nature; and *can alone produce among mankind that harmony of sentiments and passions* in which consists their whole grace and propriety"[35] [emphasis added]. In short, Smith believes that selfishness is a vice to be avoided and that social harmony depends upon restraining selfishness and indulging benevolence.

The application of the foregoing argument in business is that for self-regarding actions to promote society's interest, businesspeople must refrain from injuring others, in the sense that business must be conducted without deception, fraud, or political rent-seeking (i.e., lobbying the government for favors and concessions). These actions violate the laws of justice and benefit one group only at the expense of another group—society's interest will not be advanced.[36]

As an example of political rent-seeking, consider restrictions on international trade. These restrictions benefit import-competing industries at the expense of consumers and export industries. Tariffs often provoke retaliation thereby reducing exports. Even in the absence of retaliation, tariffs hurt exporters because they generally reduce import payments, causing an appreciation of domestic currency, thereby making exporters less competitive on world markets. Moreover, restrictions on international trade will lead to higher prices and fewer choices for consumers. Smith condemned political rent-seeking by businesses because of the harm it inflicts on others.[37] Political rent-seeking amounts to "justling" or "throwing down" competitors rather than trying to "outstrip" them by improving quality and lowering prices.

In business, the invisible hand leads every individual who wishes to generate the greatest value for himself to adhere to the desires of consumers, producing what society values the most. Thus businesspeople attempting to generate profit (or to avoid losses) unintentionally maximize the economic interests of society.[38] Moreover, competitive behavior, driven by self-interest, results in lower prices or higher quality, as well as the introduction of new products in the market. This process, however, often harms those who are outcompeted because consumers prefer efficient producers to the inefficient ones in the market.

Smith resolves this conflict of interest between buyers and inefficient producers by siding with "the great body of the people to buy whatever they want of those who sell it cheapest" as opposed to the interests of "merchants and manufacturers."[39] To elaborate, suppose firm A figures out a way to produce less expensively what firm B is producing. If A does not enter this market because B will be (likely) hurt, then society will be deprived of lower prices or higher-quality products. In the Smithian system, self-interest motivates A to enter the market, which advances consumers', and thus society's, interests. Smith, however, makes it clear that the competitive process must not involve unethical behavior such as deception and political rent-seeking. These actions not only redistribute benefits, they actually reduce them because time and talent that were spent on devising a scheme could have been spent on some other (beneficial) activity.

In summary, Smith presents a social paradigm whose harmony depends on benevolence (i.e., disposition to do good) and whose survival depends on justice (i.e., refraining from injuring others). He regards the pursuit of self-interest as an efficient way of organizing economic activities, which benefit the society provided that it is restrained by self-command and moderated by inner justice as well as by administratively enforced justice. Thus, "Smith's ideal economic actor is a person of goodwill, prudence, and self-restraint who operates both cooperatively and competitively in a social and economic milieu based on a foundation of morality, law, and justice."[40] Market mechanisms can effectively transform self-interested actions into socially beneficial outcomes if selfishness is avoided and justice is observed.

MILTON FRIEDMAN'S ANALYSIS OF SOCIAL RESPONSIBILITY

A careful reading of Milton Friedman regarding self-interest and the social responsibility of business shows that his philosophy is grounded in the writings of Adam Smith. In particular, Friedman's interpretation and application of self-interest to profit seeking also embodies restrictions that individuals are ethically required to observe. To understand Friedman's views on self-interest and the pursuit of profit, one must understand his philosophy as detailed in many of his writings.

Friedman believes the political-economic problem involves designing a social system that effectively coordinates the activities of people. "The basic problem of social organization," explains Friedman, "is how to co-ordinate the economic activities of large numbers of people."[41] He then explains the two fundamental approaches—central planning and market processes. He rejects central planning because it necessarily involves some degree of coercion by the state.

Friedman takes the "freedom of the individual, or perhaps the family, as [the] ultimate goal of judging social arrangements."[42] For him, social processes that increase individual freedom should be encouraged while those that are restrictive or coercive should be avoided. Thus, freedom is the fundamental criterion by which one should judge individual actions. Freedom also forms the basis for Friedman's interpretation of self-interest as a motivation for human action.[43]

Because Friedman values individual freedom so highly, he strongly advocates market mechanisms characterized by voluntary exchanges between individuals. The "key insight of Adam Smith's *Wealth of Nations*," according to Friedman, is "if an exchange between two parties is voluntary, it will not take place unless both believe they will benefit."[44] Voluntary exchange means "individuals are effectively free to enter or not to enter into any particular exchange."[45] This is important because "voluntary exchange is a necessary condition for both prosperity and freedom."[46] The result of such voluntary exchanges, however, goes far beyond the creation of economic wealth. There are many complex and sophisticated areas of human life that arise out of voluntary interactions among individuals, such as language, scientific knowledge, culture, and social conventions.[47]

Friedman makes it clear that self-interest, motivating individuals to enter into exchange relationships, should not be interpreted narrowly given the pervasiveness of the economic and social effects of voluntary exchanges. There is a

> broad meaning that must be attached to the concept of "self-interest." Narrow preoccupation with the economic market has led to a narrow interpretation of self-interest as myopic selfishness, as exclusive concern with immediate material rewards. Economics has been berated for allegedly drawing far-reaching conclusions from a wholly unrealistic "economic man" who is little more than a calculating machine, responding only to monetary stimuli. That is a great mistake. *Self-interest is not myopic selfishness.* It is whatever it is that interests the participants, whatever they value, whatever goals they pursue.[48] [emphasis added]

Because Friedman does not equate self-interest with selfishness, his interpretation is consistent with Adam Smith's on the other-regarding nature of self-interested behavior. But Friedman goes beyond the recognition that self-interest does not imply selfishness. He also recognizes the ethical and other-regarding dimension of decision making.

> [In] a society freedom has nothing to say about what an individual does with his freedom; it is not an all-embracing ethic. Indeed, a major aim . . . is to leave the ethical problem for the individual to wrestle with. The "really" important ethical problems are those that face an individual in a free society—what he should do with his freedom. There are thus two sets of values . . . the values that are relevant to relations among people, which is the context in which he assigns first priority to freedom; and the values that are relevant to the individual in the exercise of his freedom, which is the realm of individual ethics and philosophy.[49]

Friedman maintains that a balance between individual freedom and individual moral responsibility is necessary in any free society. The freedom that Friedman advocates is not "all-embracing." Rather, individuals have a moral obligation to "wrestle with" the ethical implications of their decisions and to exercise self-restraint when necessary. For this reason, Friedman states, "freedom is a tenable objective only for responsible individuals."[50] Furthermore, "absolute freedom is impossible. However attractive anarchy may be as a philosophy, it is not feasible in a world of imperfect men. Men's freedoms can conflict, and when they do, one man's freedom must be limited to preserve another's."[51] He then cites a statement by an unnamed Supreme Court Justice who said that "my freedom to move my fist must be limited by the proximity of your chin."[52] On another occasion, Friedman reiterates his belief that "freedom cannot be absolute. We do live in an interdependent society. Some restrictions on our freedom are necessary to avoid other, still worse, restrictions."[53]

Friedman believes that the ethical responsibility of individuals in the exercise of their freedoms requires that they take into consideration the involuntary costs or harms they impose on others. He calls these costs "neighborhood" or "external" effects, and he defines them as "arbitrary obstacles" that prevent others "from using [their] capacities to pursue [their] own objectives."[54] He also argues that external effects should be avoided because "it is difficult to identify the effects on third parties and to measure their magnitude."[55]

External effects can be allowed only if those adversely affected by them allow such actions, which they might under two conditions. First, they must be informed about the nature of the external effects; second, they must be adequately compensated or able to avoid the effects at relatively low cost. As an example, Friedman tells of a polluter of a stream. He explains that "the man who pollutes a stream is in effect forcing others to exchange good water for bad. These others might be willing to make the exchange at a price. But it is not feasible for them, acting individually, to avoid the exchange or to enforce appropriate compensation."[56] Friedman distinguishes between harm caused by "external effects," which he opposes, and the personal consequences of decisions individuals make when they freely enter into risky transactions, which he accepts as necessary in a free society. According to Friedman, the former reduces individual freedoms while the latter does not. Thus, "everyone [is] free to go into any business, follow any occupation, buy any property, subject only to the agreement of the other parties to the transaction. Each [has] the opportunity to reap the benefits if he succeeded, to suffer the costs if he failed. There [are] no arbitrary obstacles."[57] Therefore, in the absence of external effects, individuals voluntarily accept the risks and consequences of the decisions *they* rather than others make. Friedman says that there are "probably more losers than winners. . . . But for the most part they went in with their eyes open. They knew they were taking chances. And win or lose, society as a whole benefited from their willingness to take a chance."[58] Friedman argues that when actions involve external effects, the question is not *whether* but *how* such actions should be restrained. He believes strongly that individuals should limit their conduct with self-restraint when possible. Otherwise, it is the duty of government to intervene through "the enforcement of contracts voluntarily entered into, the definition of the meaning of property rights, [and] the interpretation and enforcement of such rights" in order "to prevent coercion of one individual by another."[59]

The foregoing analysis leads us to Friedman's discussion of the "social responsibility of business." Since actions that impose involuntary harm on others are unacceptable, business actions must be examined in the context of whether they are voluntary and compatible with the freedom of those affected by the decisions. In other words, if social responsibility means that businesses must take actions to positively affect society in some way, such actions must require the consent of all affected parties. And if some people are harmed by the actions, then they must agree to be affected (through compensation or some other process, for instance). Otherwise, "what it amounts to is an assertion that those who favor the [action] in question have failed to persuade a majority of their fellow citizens to be of like mind and that they are seeking to attain by undemocratic procedures what they cannot obtain by democratic procedures."[60]

Although Friedman argues that business executives should focus on profit maximization, he does not condone all behaviors that increase financial returns.[61] Quite explicitly, he places four restrictions on profit seeking: Businesspeople must obey the law, follow ethical customs, commit no deception or fraud, and engage in open and free competition.[62] The last restriction means political rent-seeking and anticompetitive behavior in any form must be avoided. For Friedman, social responsibility means pursuing one's interests (such as making a profit) without adversely interfering with the freedom of others, so that everyone can freely enter into agreements "with their eyes open." These individuals would be fully aware of the risks and consequences of their actions.

Indeed, Friedman has both teleological and deontological reasons for advancing the thesis that business executives should pursue only profit and stay away from actions that purport to promote society's interests. On teleological grounds, he argues that it may not be possible for businesspeople to know what constitutes society's interests. Thus he asks, "[C]an self-selected private individuals decide what the social interest is? Can they decide how great a burden they are justified in placing on themselves or their stockholders to serve that social interest?"[63] Therefore, Friedman is skeptical of the *net* social benefits resulting from businesspeople intentionally seeking to promote society's interests.

On deontological grounds, Friedman believes that business actions, justified as "socially responsible," violate specific duties of those pursuing the actions. For example, unless businesspeople obtain the consent of those affected, they violate the duty not to coerce others. Similarly, business executives have a duty to act in the interest of those who hire and pay them (the stockholders). If executives do not act in the interest of their employer, then they are coercing them into financing a project that the owners do not want. "He [the business executive] has a direct responsibility to his employers," with the duty to act in their interests.[64] This does not mean, as some have argued, "Friedman is in error when he maintains that a business can ignore its other commitments," such as obligations to employees or suppliers.[65] Rather, it means that executives must recognize to whom their "primary responsibility" is directed. Those affected by the business action should give their consent. Otherwise,

> the corporate executive would be spending someone else's money for a general social interest. Insofar as his actions in accord with his "social responsibility" reduce returns to stockholders, he is spending their money. Insofar as his actions raise the price to customers, he is spending the customer's money. Insofar as his actions lower the wages of some employees, he is spending their money.[66]

Moreover, Friedman disapproves of the motives of businesspeople who pursue actions under the "cloak of social responsibility," even though the actions may be in the corporation's interest, for example, when they "generate goodwill as a by-product of expenditures."[67] He denounces such actions as "hypocritical window-dressing" and as "approaching fraud," although he acknowledges that "the attitudes of the public [may] make it in their interest to cloak their actions in this way."[68]

Friedman makes it clear that this argument applies only to companies in which the decision makers are not the owners of the company. He distinguishes between the "social responsibilities of individuals" and the "social responsibilities of business."[69] The former requires individuals to examine and mitigate the extent to which their actions harm others, while the latter necessarily involves more explicit duties by executives to specific individuals or groups, such as stockholders. Thus, individual business owners and executives may voluntarily donate their own money to charity or other philanthropic causes. "The situation of the individual proprietor is somewhat different. If he acts to reduce the returns of his enterprise in order to exercise his 'social responsibility,' he is spending his own money, not someone else's."[70] Indeed, this is the great advantage of a free-market economy, according to Friedman, because "it forces people to be responsible for their own actions and makes it difficult for them to 'exploit' other people for either selfish or unselfish purposes. They can do good—but only at their own expense."[71]

In summary, Friedman believes that social benefits are achieved when individuals exercise their freedom without limiting the freedom of other people. Thus, individuals have an ethical obligation to conduct their actions without coercion, which requires the exercise of self-restraint. The principle of freedom implies that if business owners want profits, they are entitled to earn them, or to have employees they hire (and who agree to work for them) generate those profits. Executives who use the firm's resources to pursue any goal other than profit will necessarily coerce some people (stockholders, workers, or consumers) in the process, and it is coercion that Friedman objects to. Pursuit of profit and only profit is entirely ethical as long as business owners or their managers do not engage in illegal, deceptive, or fraudulent practices.

A FINAL NOTE

Adam Smith and Milton Friedman argue that the benefits to society are enhanced when individuals pursue their own interests. "But isn't concern for one's self-interest the very heart of behavior that conflicts with ethical behavior?" ask Bowie and Duska.[72] The answer to this question is in the affirmative when self-interest is narrowly interpreted to mean selfishness. However, a careful reading of Smith and Friedman reveal that they do not use the concept of self-interest in this narrow sense. For Smith the overriding principle governing his interpretation of self-interest is justice, while for Friedman the principle is freedom (i.e., absence of coercion). For both writers, self-interest embodies an other-regarding aspect that requires individuals to moderate their actions when others are adversely affected. It is this concept of self-interest that Smith and Friedman advocate.[73]

QUESTIONS FOR DISCUSSION

1. According to the authors, how are Adam Smith's and Milton Friedman's conceptions of self-interest ordinarily treated? What conception of self-interest does this lead to? Do the authors view this conception as adequate?

2. Is there a difference between self-interest on the one hand and selfishness on the other? What is that difference?

3. What is the relationship between self-interest and justice for Adam Smith? What is the nature of justice? In what way is it a "negative virtue"?

4. What is the relationship between self-interest and freedom for Milton Friedman? What role does social responsibility play in this? Does respect for freedom of others constrain us morally? In what ways?

5. Is there a place for external compulsion in Friedman's worldview? May freedom be restricted for the good of society? How does self-restraint factor into his analysis?

6. How does Friedman argue that profit seeking should be restricted?

7. What are the moral arguments offered by Friedman as to why business executives should pursue only profit?

NOTES

1. Milton Friedman, "The Social Responsibility of Business Is to Increase Its Profits," *New York Times Magazine,* September 13, 1970, 32.

2. Upon reading an earlier draft of this chapter, Friedman wrote to the authors (December 1, 1998): "As you recognize, I have been very unhappy about some of the interpretations that have been placed on my position."

3. In a private correspondence, one of the authors asked Friedman what his advice would be to the company president. Friedman replied (May 23, 1996) if he were the president, he "would be very unwilling to continue running that enterprise as [he] had before without that information being made available. . . . [The] appropriate course of action is to make publicly available the information." This is in contrast to the conclusion reached by T. Carson, "Friedman's Theory of Corporate Social Responsibility," *Business and Professional Ethics Journal* 12, no. 1 (1993): 3–32—that Friedman's statements on corporate social responsibility "imply that corporations have no duty to

warn the public about the hazards which they create" (18, emphasis in original). For an example of a similar conclusion from a business ethics textbook, see R. A. Buchholz and S. B. Rosenthal, *Business Ethics: The Pragmatic Path beyond Principles to Process* (Upper Saddle River, NJ: Prentice-Hall, 1998), 49.

4. Adam Smith, *An Inquiry into the Nature and Causes of the Wealth of Nations* (Indianapolis, IN: Liberty Classics, 1981), 27. Hereafter WN.

5. WN, 456.

6. W. H. Shaw and V. Barry, *Moral Issues in Business*, 7th ed. (Belmont, CA: Wadsworth, 1998), 60.

7. Shaw and Barry, *Moral Issues in Business*, 147.

8. Buchholz and Rosenthal, 106.

9. M. G. Velasquez, *Business Ethics: Concepts and Cases*, 4th ed. (Upper Saddle River, NJ: Prentice-Hall), 181.

10. Adams and Maine offer the following "economic" definition of self-interest. "Human beings . . . are motivated to do whatever it takes to satisfy their individual desires. Further, human beings are relatively indifferent about how their actions affect others. This does not imply that they are mean or spiteful, just that they tend to be disinterested about those effects." Although they do not directly attribute this definition to Adam Smith, they imply it by describing it as a basic tenant of neoclassical economics, with "a long and distinguished pedigree, going back to the philosopher Thomas Hobbes." D. M. Adams and E. W. Maine, *Business Ethics for the 21st Century* (Mountain View, CA: Mayfield, 1998), 29. However, as Werhane has argued, Smith was not a Hobbesian. See P. H. Werhane, *Adam Smith and His Legacy for Modern Capitalism* (New York: Oxford University Press, 1991).

11. Milton Friedman, *Capitalism and Freedom* (Chicago: University of Chicago Press, 1962), 133.

12. Milton Friedman, "Social Responsibility," 33.

13. Milton Friedman, *Capitalism and Freedom*, 133.

14. Paul Camenisch, "Business Ethics: On Getting to the Heart of the Matter," in *Moral Issues in Business*, ed. Shaw and Berry, 242.

15. E. E. Englehardt and D. D. Schmeltekopf, *Ethics & Life: An Interdisciplinary Approach to Moral Problems* (Dubuque, IA: Wm. C. Brown, 1992), 313.

16. P. Primeaux, "Maximizing Ethics and Profits," in *Perspectives in Business Ethics*, ed. L. P. Hartman (Chicago: Irwin-McGraw-Hill, 1998), 259.

17. R. A. Buchholz, *Principles of Environmental Management: The Greening of Business* (Upper Saddle River, NJ: Prentice-Hall, 1998), 49.

18. Velasquez, *Business Ethics: Concepts and Cases*, 36.

19. R. D. Hay and E. R. Gray, "Introduction to Social Responsibility," in *Business and Society: Cases and Text*, 2nd ed. (Cincinnati, OH: South Western Publishing, 1980), 341, 345.

20. There are some exceptions, such as A. A. Marcus, *Business and Society: Strategy, Ethics, and the Global Economy* (Chicago: Irwin, 1996), 50–57, which treats both Smith and Friedman accurately. A. A. Goldsmith, *Business, Government, Society* (Chicago: Irwin, 1996) presents Smith accurately (62–64), but the analysis of Friedman although not wrong is incomplete (70).

21. T. D. Campbell, *Adam Smith's Science of Morals* (London: George Allen & Unwin Ltd., 1971), 16. In the introduction to TMS, Smith's foremost scholars note that "the two books complement each other and that the understanding of either is helped by studying both." D. D. Raphael and A. L. Macfie, "Introduction," in Smith, *An Inquiry into the Nature and Causes of the Wealth Nations* (Indianapolis, IN: Liberty Classics, 1984), 21.

22. Sen notes the following as an example of misinterpreting Smith. "Smith was often cited by imperial administration for justification of refusing to intervene in famines in such diverse places as Ireland, India, and China." A. Sen, *On Ethics & Economics* (New York: Basil Blackwell, 1987), 27.

23. Smith has been subjected to intense scholarship for over two hundred years. During this time some scholars have debated whether Smith's writings in TMS are inconsistent or even contradictory with his writings in WN, an issue known as "the Adam Smith Problem." However, the examples of recent scholarship we cite examine Smith's collective work and generally conclude that "the so-called 'Adam Smith Problem' was a pseudo-problem based on ignorance and misunderstanding" (Raphael and Macfie, "Introduction," 20).

24. Readers who wish to grasp Smith's philosophy on a deeper level than presented in this chapter should consult our citations on Smith.

25. For an elaboration, see Raphael and Macfie, "Introduction."

26. Adam Smith, *The Theory of Moral Sentiments* (Indianapolis, IN: Liberty Classics, 1984), 241. Hereafter TMS.

27. TMS, 82–83.

28. TMS, 304.

29. Viner is generally regarded as "[t]he greatest historian of economic thought that ever lived." D. A. Irwin, *Jacob Viner, Essays on the Intellectual History of Economics* (Princeton, NJ: Princeton University Press, 1991), 3.

30. Jacob Viner, "The 'Economic Man', or the Place of Self-Interest in a 'Good Society,'" in *Jacob Viner, Essays on the Intellectual History of Economics,* ed. D. A. Irwin (Princeton, NJ: Princeton University Press, 1991), 74.

31. WN, 687.

32. Jacob Viner, "Adam Smith," in *Jacob Viner, Essays on the Intellectual History of Economics,* ed. D. A. Irwin (Princeton, NJ: Princeton University Press, 1991), 252.

33. WN, 654.

34. Raphael and Macfie, "Introduction," 22.

35. TMS, 25.

36. Cavanagh correctly notes that Smith's position is "when morally conscientious individuals follow their own self-interest, it works to the benefit of society as a whole." G. F. Cavanagh, *American Business Values with International Perspectives* (Upper Saddle River, NJ: Prentice-Hall, 1998), 120.

37. For an analysis of Smith's views on rent-seeking, see, J. Evensky, "Retrospectives: Ethics and the Invisible Hand," *Journal of Economic Perspectives* 7, no. 2 (Spring 1993): 197–205; and J. D. Bishop, "Adam Smith's Invisible Hand Argument," *Journal of Business Ethics* 14 (March 1995): 165–80.

38. Baumol comments that, to Smith, the market system is "as an instrument of Deity designed to curb the frailty of humanity. . . . It is a device adopted by a very practical

Providence to deal with the unfortunate but very weakness of human character." W. J. Baumol, "Smith versus Marx on Business Morality and the Social Interest," in *Adam Smith and the Wealth of Nations 1776–1976 Bicentennial Essay,* ed. E. Glahe (Boulder: Colorado Associated University Press, 1978), 117. For this reason, observes Baumol, Smith says that individuals in the pursuit of their self-interests are "led by an invisible hand" not "led *as though* by an invisible hand" to promote society's interest (121).

39. WN, 493–94.

40. Werhane, 180.

41. Friedman, *Capitalism and Freedom*, 12.

42. Friedman, *Capitalism and Freedom*, 12.

43. Thus, we disagree with Primeaux's conclusion that "it is evident that the values [Friedman] wants to encourage are focused exclusively on utility." Primeaux, "Maximizing Ethics and Profits," 259.

44. Milton Friedman and R. Friedman, *Free to Choose: A Personal Statement* (New York: Avon Books, 1980), 5.

45. Friedman, *Capitalism and Freedom*, 14.

46. Friedman and Friedman, *Free to Choose*, 3.

47. Friedman and Friedman, *Free to Choose*, 3.

48. Friedman and Friedman, *Free to Choose*, 18–19.

49. Friedman, *Capitalism and Freedom*, 12.

50. Friedman, *Capitalism and Freedom*, 33.

51. Friedman, *Capitalism and Freedom*, 25–26.

52. Friedman, *Capitalism and Freedom*, 26.

53. Friedman and Friedman, *Free to Choose*, 61.

54. Friedman and Friedman, *Free to Choose*, 119.

55. Friedman, *Capitalism and Freedom*, 31–32.

56. Friedman, *Capitalism and Freedom*, 30.

57. Friedman and Friedman, *Free to Choose*, 124.

58. Friedman and Friedman, *Free to Choose*, 129.

59. Friedman, *Capitalism and Freedom*, 27.

60. Friedman, "Social Responsibility," 124.

61. Hence Boatright states that Friedman's argument "does not permit corporations to act in a socially irresponsible manner." J. R. Boatright, *Ethics and the Conduct of Business*, 2nd ed. (Upper Saddle River, NJ: Prentice-Hall, 1997), 352.

62. Novak comments that these restrictions require "a high level of moral performance." Michael Novak, *Business as a Calling* (New York: Free Press, 1996), 141. Trevino and Nelson concur by noting that Friedman's statement on the social responsibility of business "tacitly embraces two of the three additional components of the corporate social responsibility pyramid: legal and ethical responsibilities." (The third additional component is philanthropic responsibilities.) L. K. Trevino and K. A. Nelson. *Managing Business Ethics: Straight Talk about How to Do It Right* (New York: John Wiley & Sons, 1995), 29.

Carson argues that the first two conditions, which he labels the "second formulation," derived from Friedman's 1970 article, are inconsistent with the final two conditions, which Carson calls the "first formulation" from Friedman's 1962 book, a criticism we can perhaps call "the Milton Friedman Problem." T. Carson, "Friedman's Theory of Corporate Social Responsibility," *Business and Professional Ethics Journal* 12, no. 1 (1993): 3–32. In a critique similar to "the Milton Friedman Problem," Mulligan states that Friedman's reference to "open and free competition without deception or fraud" in *Capitalism and Freedom* shows that he "does not recognize that even these restrained words lay open a broad range of moral obligation and social responsibility for business." T. Mulligan, "A Critique of Milton Friedman's Essay 'The Social Responsibility of Business Is to Increase Its Profits,'" *Journal of Business Ethics* 5, no. 4 (1986): 269. We see no contradiction in Friedman's writings. Rather, we suggest that his conditions of obeying the law, following ethical custom, committing no deception and fraud, and engaging in free and open competition are complementary and consistent with all of his writings.

63. Friedman, *Capitalism and Freedom*, 133–34. In an interview with *Business and Society Review*, Friedman gives the following example: "During the 1930s, German businessmen used some corporate money to support Hitler and the Nazis. Was that a proper exercise of social responsibility?" Friedman, "Social Responsibility," 6.

64. Friedman, "Social Responsibility," 33.

65. D. Stewart, *Business Ethics* (New York: McGraw-Hill, 1996), 56.

66. Friedman, "Social Responsibility," 33.

67. Friedman, "Social Responsibility," 124.

68. Friedman, "Social Responsibility," 124. L'Etang also rejects business actions promoting social good on Kantian grounds because "beneficiaries can be used as a means to the end of improving the company's image." J. L'Etang, "Ethical Corporate Social Responsibility: A Framework for Managers," *Journal of Business Ethics* 14 (February 1995): 126.

69. Friedman, "Social Responsibility," 33.

70. Friedman, "Social Responsibility," 124.

71. Friedman, "Social Responsibility," 124.

72. N. E. Bowie and R. F. Duska, *Business Ethics*, 2nd ed. (Englewood Cliffs, NJ: Prentice-Hall, 1990), 25.

73. We wish to thank William Baumol, Milton Friedman, and Glen Moots for helpful comments on an earlier draft of this chapter. The usual disclaimer applies.

• 5 •

Victims of Circumstances?
A Defense of Virtue Ethics in Business

Robert C. Solomon

Robert Solomon argues in this essay that virtue ethics makes an important contribution to the field of business ethics. A clearer conception of the requirements of character can aid in the moral evaluation of the practices of business and enable us to recognize our genuine moral responsibility when faced with pressures to conform to practices or obey commands that violate our moral sensibilities. The social sciences can shed light on the nature of character, how it is formed, and how vulnerable it can be, though they do not provide all of the answers in themselves. Character turns out to be a complex and difficult concept, and conflicts of competing virtues can sometimes create insoluble dilemmas even for people who desire to act morally. How we "choose our circumstances" can often be the first step in the formation of our character, for better or for worse.

$\mathcal{B}$usiness ethics is a child of ethics, and business ethics, like its parents, is vulnerable to the same threats and challenges visited on its elders. For many years, one such threat (or rather, a family of threats) has challenged moral philosophy, and it is time it was brought out in the open in business ethics as well. It is a threat that is sometimes identified by way of the philosophical term "determinism," and though its status in the philosophy of science and theory of knowledge is by no means settled, it has nevertheless wreaked havoc on ethics. If there is determinism, so the argument goes, there can be no agency, properly speaking, and thus no moral responsibility. But determinism admits of at least two interpretations in ethics. The first is determination by "external" circumstances, including pressure or coercion by other people. The second is determination within the person, in particular, by his or her character. In the former case, but arguably not in the latter, there is thought to be a problem ascribing moral responsibility.[1]

The argument can be readily extended to business ethics. Versions of the argument have been put forward with regard to corporations, for instance, in the now perennial arguments whether corporations can be or cannot be held responsible.[2] One familiar line of argument holds that only individuals, not corporations, can be held responsible for their actions. But then corporate executives like to excuse their actions by reference to "market forces" that render them helpless, mere victims of economic circumstances, and everyone who works in the corporation similarly excuses their bad behavior by reference to those who set their agenda and policies. They are mere "victims of circumstances." They thus betray their utter lack of leadership. Moreover, it doesn't take a whole lot of research to show that people in corporations tend to behave in conformity with the people and expectations that surround them, even when what they are told to do violates their "personal morality." What (outside of the corporation) might count as "character" tends to be more of an obstacle than a boon to corporate success for many people. What seems to count as "character" in the corporation is a disposition to please others, obey superiors, follow others, and avoid personal responsibility.

In general philosophy, Kant tried desperately to separate determinism and moral responsibility, defending determinism in the domain of science and "Nature" but preserving agency and responsibility in the domain of ethics. "I have found it necessary to limit knowledge to make room for faith," as he put in one of his most concise but rather misleading bon mots. Other philosophers were not so bold. They were willing to accept determinism (even if conjoined with skeptical doubts) and somehow fit agency and responsibility into its domain. David Hume and John Stuart Mill, the two most illustrious empiricist promoters of this strategy, suggested that an act is free (and an agent responsible) if it "flows from the person's character," where "character" stood for a reasonably stable set of established character traits that were both morally significant and served as the antecedent causal conditions demanded by determinism.[3] Adam Smith, Hume's best friend and the father of not only modern economics but of business ethics too, agreed with this thesis. It was a good solution. It saved the notions of agency and responsibility, it was very much in line with our ordinary intuitions about people's behavior, and it did not try to challenge the scientific establishment. So, too, a major movement in business ethics, of which I consider myself a card-carrying member, is "virtue ethics," which takes the concept of character (and with it the related notions of virtue and integrity) to be central to the idea of being a good person in business. Among the many virtues of virtue ethics in business, one might think, is that, as in Hume and Mill, it would seem to keep at bay the threat of situational ("external") determinism.

Such a solution seems particularly appropriate for business ethics because the concept of character fills the void between institutional behaviorism ("organizational behavior") and an overblown emphasis on free will and personal autonomy that remains oblivious to context, the reality of office work, and the force of peer and corporate pressures. It provides a locus for responsibility without sacrificing the findings of "management science." But I have mixed feelings about the empiricist solution. On the one hand, it seems to me too weak. It does not account (or try to account) for actions "out of character," heroic or saintly or vicious and shockingly greedy behavior, which could not have been predicted of (or even by) the subject. And it does not (as Aristotle does) rigorously hold a person responsible for the formation of his or her character. Aristotle makes it quite clear that a wicked person is responsible for his or her character not because he or she could now alter it but because he or she could have and should have acted differently early on and established very different habits and states of character. The corporate bully, the greedy entrepreneur, and the office snitch all would seem to be responsible for not only what they do but who they are, according to Aristotle's tough criterion.

On the other hand, however, the empiricist solution overstates the case for character. (This is what some psychologists, and Gilbert Harman, refer to as the "attribution error.") The empiricists make it sound as if character is something both settled and "robust" (the target of much of the recent psychological literature). Character consists of such traits as honesty and trustworthiness that are more or less resistant to social or interpersonal pressures. But character is never fully formed and settled. It is always vulnerable to circumstances and trauma. People change, and they are malleable. They respond in interesting and sometimes immediate ways to their environment, their peers, and pressures from above. Put into an unusual, pressured, or troubled environment, many people will act "out of character," sometimes in heroic but more often in disappointing and sometimes shocking ways. In the corporate setting, in particular, people joke about "leaving their integrity at the office door" and act with sometimes shocking obedience to orders and policies that they personally find unethical and even downright revolting.

These worries can be taken care of with an adequate retooling of the notion of character and its place in ethics, and this is what I will try to do here. But my real worry is that in the effort to correct the excesses of the empiricist emphasis on character, the baby is being thrown out with the bath toys. In recent work by Gilbert Harman and John Doris, in particular, the very notion of character is being thrown into question.[4] Indeed, Harman suggests that "there may be no such thing." Doris entitles his book, tellingly, *Lack of Character*. Both Harman and Doris argue at considerable length that a great deal of what we take as "character" is in fact (and demonstrably) due to specific social settings that reinforce virtuous conduct. To mention two often-used examples, clergy act like clergy not because of character but because they surround themselves with other clergy who expect them to act like clergy. So, too, criminals act like criminals not because of character but because they hang out with other criminals who expect them to act like criminals. Harman argues vehemently against what he calls the illusion of "a robust sense of character." Doris argues, at book length, a very detailed and remarkably nuanced account of virtue and responsibility without character. The conclusion of both authors is that virtue ethics, construed in terms of character, is at best a mistake, and at worst a vicious political maneuver.

It is worth saying a word about this "vicious political maneuver" that is the political target of Harman's and Doris's arguments. I share in their concern, and I, too, would want to argue against those who, on the basis of an absurd notion of character, expect people to "pick themselves up by their own boot-straps," blaming the poor, for instance, for their own impoverishment and thus ignoring social and political (not to mention medical and racial) disadvantages that are certainly not their fault. I, too, reject such a notion of character, but I am not willing to dispense with the very notions of character and the virtues in order to do this.

So, too, in business ethics, there is a good reason to be suspicious of a notion of character that is supposed to stand up to overwhelming pressures without peer or institutional support. I would take Harman's and Doris's argu-ments as a good reason to insist on sound ethical policies and rigorous ethical enforcement in corporations and in the business community more generally, thus maximizing the likelihood that people will conform to the right kinds of corporate expectations. Nevertheless, something extremely important can get lost in the face of that otherwise quite reasonable and desirable demand. It is the idea that a person can, and should, resist those pressures, even at considerable cost to oneself, depending on the severity of the situation and circumstances. That is the very basis on which virtue ethics has proven to be so appealing to people in business. It is the hope that they can, and sometimes will, resist or even rise up against pressures and policies that they find to be unethical.

So whatever my worries, I find myself a staunch defender of character and the indispensability of talk about character in both ethics and business ethics.[5] To quote my friend and colleague Ed Hartman, "the difference between Peter Hempel [one of the most wonderful human beings we ever met] and Richard Nixon is not just a matter of environment." In both everyday life and in business, there are people we trust, and there are people we do not, often on the basis of a substantial history of disappointments and betrayal. And we trust or distrust those people in much the same circumstances and under much the same conditions. To be sure, character is vulnerable to environment but it is also a bulwark against environment. Character supplies that familiar and sometimes uncomfortable or even uncanny resistance to untoward pressures that violate our "principles" or morally disgust us or are damaging to our "integrity." It is character and not God or the Superego that produces that nagging inner voice called "conscience." (It has been suggested that conscience produces character rather than the other way around, but apart from religious predilections there seems to be little sound philosophical argument or empirical research to defend this.) One person refuses to obey a directive to shortchange his customers while another refuses to cheat on her expense account despite the fact that everyone around her is doing so. It is character that makes the difference, though not, to be sure, all the difference.

Some of my concern with this issue is personal. Like most conscientious people, I worry about my integrity and character, what sorts of temptations and threats I could and would withstand. I feel ashamed (or worse) when I give into those temptations and humiliated when I succumb to (at least some of) those threats. I am occasionally even proud about those temptations and threats I have withstood. Philosophically ("existentially"), I worry about how we view ourselves when the balance of accounts is shifted over to causal and statistical explanations of behavior instead of a continuing emphasis on character, agency, and responsibility. Will that give almost everyone an excuse for almost everything?[6] And professionally, I have made something of a reputation for myself as a "virtue ethicist" in business ethics, in the twisted tradition of Aristotle and Nietzsche, and virtue ethics requires a solid notion of character. But not a fixed and permanent notion of character. To be sure, many writers about the virtues, perhaps betraying their own insecurity, tend to describe good character and integrity in terms of rock and stone metaphors, suggesting that the truly virtuous person is capable of standing up against anything. (A handful of mostly legendary examples provide the paradigm.) But I for one never said that virtue ethics requires a strong sense of autonomy, the ability to cut oneself off from all influences and pressures from other people and institutions and ignore one's personal "inclinations" and make a decision on the basis of one's "practical reason" alone. On the contrary, I have argued that one's inclinations (one's emotions, in particular) form the essential core of the virtues, and I have argued that so do Aristotle and (more obviously) Nietzsche. And one's emotions are largely reactive, responsive to other people and the social situations in which one finds oneself. Virtue ethics need not, and should not, deny any of this.

THE "NEW EMPIRICISM" —VIRTUE ETHICS AND EMPIRICAL SCIENCE

Behind the attack on character and virtue lies another commendable motive. John Doris puts it well. Virtue ethics, he says, can be traced back to the momentous writings of Aristotle, 2,500 years ago. Unfortunately, however, the social psychology on which virtue ethics rests is also 2,500 years old. Even the work of Hume, Mill, and Adam Smith is pressing on 250 years, ancient times in the scope of modern psychology. As both Doris and Harman properly point out, there has been a great deal of research in the social sciences, much of it within the last 50 years, that ought to be taken into account. And this, they think, seriously undermines the claims of virtue ethics and its emphasis on character.

As so often in these discussions, there is an easy, but wholly misleading, analogy with physics. Paul Griffiths, for instance, compares our present "folk psychology" to Aristotle's obviously erroneous category of "superlunary objects," an arbitrary grouping wholly determined by ancient ignorance of astronomy.[7] So, too, Harman juxtaposes our ordinary intuitions about morality with the findings from scientific research, arguing (by analogy) that just as we are wrong in our intuitions about classical mechanics so, too, we can be wrong in our moral intuitions. But I think there are very real questions about the extent to which modern empirical studies of human behavior have in any sense replaced rather than merely supplemented or possibly deepened our age-old "folk psychology" in anything like the way that modern astronomy and physics have introduced revolutions in the way we see the world. I do not doubt that many of our moral intuitions are erroneous or archaic, left over from earlier phases of human culture and no longer practical (what Nietzsche once called "the shadows of God"). Nor do I doubt that many of our moral judgments are based on hypocrisy, self-deception, and wishful thinking. But our moral intuitions are not like our intuitions in physics. There is no "matter of fact" independent of our intuitions and attitudes. (Against the moral realists of his day, Nietzsche insisted that "there are no moral facts," and contemporary authors such as Simon Blackburn have argued for a "quasi-realism" in which our personal intuitions and attitudes are ineliminable from moral concerns.)[8] The social sciences, our ordinary intuitions, and moral philosophy are all of a piece. There is no easy separation of "facts" about personal character and evaluations of moral merit.[9] Character traits and virtues—honesty, trustworthiness, and a sense of fairness—are normative. They are not mere behavioral tendencies. *All* psychology, if it is psychology at all, is one or another version of "folk psychology" ("the only game in town," according to Jerry Fodor).

Harman and Doris attack virtue ethics in general and the concept of character in particular on the grounds that they do not survive experimental findings in the past few decades. Exhibit number one for both of them is the infamous Stanley Milgram experiment in which people with supposedly good character performed the most despicable acts when encouraged to do so by an authority (the experimenter). But though empirical research in social psychology can on occasion shock us, surprise us, annoy us, and sometimes burst our illusions, it all gets weighed and accounted for, whether well or badly, in terms of our ordinary folk psychology observations and the ordinary concepts of belief, desire, emotion, character, and interpersonal influences, interactions, and institutions. There are no Copernican revolutions and no Michelson-Morley experiments. The Milgram and other experiments such as those by Darley and Batson that play a central role in Doris's and Harman's arguments get rationalized and explained in all sorts of ways, but none of them in violation of the basic forms of psychological explanation that Aristotle would have found perfectly familiar.[10] Of course, there remains a debate about the relative influence of "external" (environmental) and "inner" factors (character), but the debate, whichever way it goes, remains within the framework of folk psychology and our ordinary psychological concepts.

We might be disturbed, for example, that so many subjects followed the instructions of an authority figure to the point of (what they thought was) the torturing of another human being, but the various explanations in terms of "obedience to authority" or the unusual circumstances of the experiment (how often are most of us told to punish anyone?) do nothing to challenge our ordinary moral intuitions. It just reminds us of something we'd rather not remember, that ordinary people sometimes act very badly in group and institutional situations. This should come as no surprise to those of us who do corporate and organizational ethics.

I would not want to rest my argument on a general and contentious claim about the social sciences, however. On the contrary, what is disturbing to me is Harman's and Doris's juxtaposition of virtue ethics against the social sciences. One of the virtues of virtue ethics, I have always thought, is its utter compatibility with the social sciences. It rests on (one or another) theory of human nature, and it is unashamedly a theory about how people are, not how they ideally ought to be. Kantian ethics is explicitly not so. Its main thrust lies in the domain of autonomy and it matters only marginally what people in fact want to do or normally do. In virtue ethics, by contrast, what people want to do and normally do makes a great deal of difference. And learning what people want to do and normally do is always relevant, even if only as a warning that our practices and institutions are offering up the wrong kind of role models and encouraging the wrong kinds of desires, ideas, and behavior. (Utilitarianism is also rigorously empirical and shares this virtue with virtue ethics, but it tends to emphasize the consequences of behavior and thus ignore the intentions and motives—and thus the character—of the agent.)

I have long been an advocate of cooperation between moral philosophy and the social sciences in business ethics. I think that the more we know about how people actually behave in corporations, the richer and more informed our moral judgments and, more important, our decisions will be. In particular, it is very instructive to learn how people will behave in extraordinary circumstances, those in which our ordinary moral intuitions do not give us a clue. All of us have asked, say, with regard to the Nazi disease in Germany in the thirties, how we would have behaved; or how we would behave, think, and feel if we worked for a tobacco company. But even in an ordinary corporation (which is not the same as a university in which there is at least the illusion of individual autonomy and "academic freedom"), the question of "obedience to authority" comes front and center.

Thus an experiment like the Milgram experiment is shocking precisely because it does not seem to presuppose any extraordinary context. Milgram's experiment, which would certainly be prohibited today, has to do with subjects inflicting potentially lethal shocks to victim-learners (in fact the experimenter's accomplices). Even when the victim-learners pleaded for them to stop, the majority of subjects continued to apply the shocks when ordered to do so by the authorities (the experimenters). One could easily imagine this "experiment" being confirmed in any corporation.[11] But I find the use of such research to undermine the notion of character not at all convincing.[12] Harman, for example, argues that

> [e]mpirical studies designed to test whether people behave differently in ways that might reflect their having different character traits have failed to find relevant differences. It is true that studies of this sort are very difficult to carry out and there have been few such studies. Nevertheless, the existing studies have had negative results. Since it is possible to explain our ordinary belief in character traits as deriving from certain illusions, we must conclude that there is no empirical basis for the existence of character traits.[13]

But in addition to leaping from "very few studies" that are "difficult to carry out" to the conclusion that there is "no empirical basis for the existence of character traits," the whole weight of the argument comes to depend on the possibility of explaining our ordinary belief in character traits as "deriving from certain illusions." But what would such an explanation consist of? What illusions are we talking about? And what is our "ordinary belief in character"? I will argue that it does not require the "robust" notion attacked by Harman.

Doris is much more cautious and painstaking in his conclusions. He admits that empirical psychological studies are deeply flawed and limited especially in the fact that the studies he employs describe only particular behavior in particular (artificial) situations and not long-term patterns of behavior—which is what character is all about. He admits that "meaningful generalization outside of the laboratory" is "questionable."[14] He even says, borrowing from Churchill on democracy, "I'll readily admit it: experimental psychology is perhaps the worst available method for understanding human life. Except, I hasten to add, for all of the other methods" (including the use of moral "intuitions" of armchair moral philosophy).[15] His main objection to those who champion virtue ethics, however, is that "they presuppose the existence of character structures that actual people do not very often possess."[16] But unless such structures are supposed to be indefensibly wooden and the "not very often" means "very rarely," this is a fairly weak claim that is perfectly compatible with what virtue ethicists require in terms of character.

WHAT IS A VIRTUE AND WHENCE CHARACTER?

Harman does a nice job of delimiting the ordinary notions of virtue and character, namely those that are most relevant to business ethics. He distinguishes character from various psychological disorders (schizophrenia, mania, depression). More dubiously, he distinguishes character from "innate aspects of temperament such as shyness or being a happy or sad person."[17] Kant, oddly enough, quite correctly insists that being happy (though an "inclination") can be a virtue, as it makes us more inclined to do our duty. But Harman is not just attacking the virtues. He is after character traits in general. Shyness, for example, is a nonmoral example of a character trait. Harman considers this a prime example of "false attribution." But I think Jean-Paul Sartre has his eye on something very important when he refers to the citing of such a character trait as "bad faith," namely, where we point to a causal syndrome where we should be talking about decisions and the cultivation (in a very strong sense) of character.[18] There is a certain element of such Sartreanism (an insistence on existential choices rather than robust character) in Harman's argument (with which I quite agree), but this is a very different set of reasons for questioning or qualifying the concepts of character and the virtues.[19]

Harman then considers such Aristotelian traits as courage, cowardice, honesty, dishonesty, benevolence, malevolence, friendliness, and unfriendliness. (Although it is not clear, contra Hume, that benevolence and malevolence are virtue and vice, respectively. Doing and not merely wishing, beneficience and maleficence, are the virtues in question.) Aristotle describes "the ordinary conception of such character traits" as relatively long-term dispositions to act in certain ways. (We might note again that Aristotle was describing the ordinary conception of his Mediterranean peers twenty-three hundred years ago.) Doris calls this long-term disposition to act in certain ways "globalism," which involves (a) consistency of character traits, (b) stability of character traits, and (c) the integration of various such traits, what in Aristotle is usually called "the unity of the virtues." It is what he ultimately claims to be "empirically inadequate."[20] Character traits involve activity, not just "possession," habits and operative desires and not just skills. Skills and knowledge may well be involved but are not sufficient for the attribution of the virtue (or vice). Furthermore, character traits must be broad-based rather than narrow dispositions. (A particular fear does not signify cowardice.)

But the attribution of virtue (or vice) and the ascription of character traits are particularly tricky notions in Harman's and especially in Doris's discussions. To deny that a particular fear or phobia entails cowardice is not yet to leap to the "global" hypothesis that a virtue or character trait must be all-pervasive in one's personality. Doris discusses "local traits" (honesty in particular) and observes that people are sometimes honest in one sort of situation but not in another. This, of course, is no surprise. (Alfred Carr, among others, has often noted the inappropriateness of the virtues in at least some business settings.)[21] But in the defense of the virtues one need not insist on global virtues (or vices) any more than one should insist that each and every bit of behavior is the reflection of a virtue (or lack thereof). Doris's dramatic postmodern conclusion, "The Fragmentation of Character," the idea that there is no single "core of character" that alone explains our social behavior, is on the one hand (like most postmodern rhetoric) enormously overblown. On the other hand, it is just a bland description of what we all recognize, when we are not being blindly moralistic or overly philosophical, that the virtues are contextual and only rarely "global" in nature.

In the ordinary conceptions of character traits and virtues, Harman and Doris tell us, people differ in their possession of such traits and virtues. People are different, and these differences explain their differences in behavior. Harman: "We ordinarily suppose that a person's character traits *help* to explain at least some of the things the person does" (italics mine). But, he says, "the fact that two people regularly behave in different ways does not establish that they have different character traits. The difference *may* be due to their different situations rather than differences in their characters" (italics mine). But notice that there is no inconsistency whatever between insisting that a person's character traits help to explain their behavior and insisting that a difference in behavior may be due to the different situations in which two people find themselves. So, too, Doris's objection to globalism is that people (in experimental situations) fail to display the consistency and stability that explanations in terms of character require. But, again, the short-term experiments that he cites do not undermine our more ordinary long-term judgments about personal propensities and dispositions. At best, they force us to face some hard truths about ourselves and consider other propensities and dispositions that may not be virtuous at all.

In our "ordinary conception" two people (one honest, one dishonest) in the same situation (discovering a lost wallet in the street, encountering a person in apparent desperate need, being ordered by an experimenter to "keep on punishing") will very probably act differently. But any philosopher worthy of his or her debating trophies will quickly point out that no two situations are sufficiently similar to make that case. It is only a very thin description of "the situation" (the experimental set-up) that makes it seem so. Subjects come from different backgrounds and different social classes. They are different genders. They may as a consequence have very different senses of the situation. I would not join Joel Feinberg in claiming that those students who do not stop for a stranger in need (in Darley and Batson's much-discussed "Good Samaritan" experiment) have a "character flaw," but neither would I conclude (with Doris) that their behavior is largely "situational."[22] The student's way of seeing and being in the situation may be very different, and this, of course, is just what Aristotle says about character. It is, first of all, a kind of perception, based on good upbringing. Thus I think Harman is being a bit disingenuous when he argues that "they must be disposed to act differently in the same circumstances (as they perceive those circumstances)." The question of character begins with how they perceive those circumstances.

In his subsequent discussion, Harman follows Nisbett and Ross in arguing that "people often choose the situations to which they are exposed."[23] "Thus clerics and criminals rarely face an identical or equivalent set of situational challenges. Rather they place themselves, or are placed by others, in situations that differ precisely in a way that induce clergy to look, feel, and act consistently like clergy and that induce criminals to look, feel, and act consistently like criminals."[24] Furthermore, in the presence of their peers, people "sometimes feel obliged even committed to act consistently."[25] True enough (and Jean-Paul Sartre could not have put it better). Corporate managers and employees feel obliged and committed to act in conformity with corporate pressures and policies even when they are questionable or unethical, and they learn to rationalize accordingly. The question is, does any of this imply that we should give up or give in on character? Or should we say that character is both cultivated and maintained through the dynamic interaction of individuals and groups in their environment and they in turn develop those virtues (and vices) that in turn motivate them to remain in the situations in which their virtues are supported, reinforced, and not threatened?

In Milgram's famous "shocking people" experiment in the early 1960s (just as America was getting more deeply involved in the morass of Vietnam), the experimental data were indeed shocking, even to Milgram and his colleagues who expected no such result. In the social context of the times, questions about obedience to authority (left over from the Nuremberg trials not so many years before) had a special poignancy, especially in the face of the soon to be challenged American "innocence" of the time. It was very upsetting to find that good, solid, ordinary middle-class people could be ordered (but not coerced) to act so brutally (whether or not they had severe misgivings about their behavior at the time—a matter of no small importance here). The facts of the experiment are beyond dispute. But what the experiment means remains highly controversial, and it does not deserve the central place in the attack on character that it is now receiving. Doris claims that "Milgram's experiments show how apparently non-coercive situational factors may induce destructive behavior despite the apparent presence of contrary evaluative and dispositional structures." Accordingly, he "gives us reason to question the robustness of dispositions implicated in compassion-relevant moral behavior."[26]

Well, no. The disposition (virtue) that is most prominent and robust in this very contrived and unusual situation, the one that virtually all of the subjects had been brought up with and practiced every day since childhood, was doing what they were told by those in authority. Compassion, by contrast, is a virtue more often praised than practiced, except on specially designated occasions (giving to the neediest at Christmas time) or stretching the term to include such common courtesies as restraining one's criticism of an unprepared student or letting the other car go first at a four-way intersection. (I would argue that such examples betray a lack of understanding of what compassion is.) Most often, people display compassion by "feeling sorry for" those much worse off than they, a very small expenditure of effort even when it is sincere. It seems to me that what the Milgram experiment shows—and what subsequent events in Vietnam made all too painfully obvious—was that despite our high moral opinions of ourselves and our conformist chorus singing about what independent individuals we all are, Americans, like Germans before them, are capable of beastly behavior in circumstances where their practiced virtues are forced to confront an unusual situation in which unpracticed efforts are required. In the Milgram experiment as in Vietnam, American subjects and soldiers were compelled by their own practiced dispositions to follow orders even in the face of consequences that were intolerable. Obedience may not always be a virtue. But that is not what is being challenged by Harman and Doris. They are denying (contrary to the empirical evidence) that people have robust dispositions. I would say, no. They are just looking at the wrong disposition.

In discussions of Vietnam, those who were not there (especially politicians) like to talk about the virtue of courage as the defining trait of the American forces. What they ignore, of course, is the very nature of the war. In several important memoirs by soldiers who served there, Bill Broyles and Tim O'Brien, it becomes clear that courage was just about the last thing on most of the soldiers' minds.[27] They were terrified of losing legs and arms. They were moved by camaraderie and a sense of mutual obligation. (The virtue-name "loyalty" misses the mark.) The only discussion of courage in O'Brien's book has to do with a single heroic figure, a Captain Johansen whom he likens to Hector in Homer's *Iliad*. But this one character is exemplary in precisely the fact that he alone talked about and exemplified true courage. But the absence of courage (which is not to imply anything like cowardice on the part of the American troops) had a great deal to do with the nature of this particular war. It lacked any sense of purpose or progress. It lacked any sense of meaning for most of the men. And so, in that moral vacuum, all that was left for most soldiers was the worry about their own physical integrity and their keen sense of responsibility for each other. The atrocities at My Lai and Thanh Phong followed as a matter of course. There was no context in which either character or courage could be exercised.

Which brings us back to the misgivings and feelings of discomfort experienced by some (not all) of the subjects and the "grunts" in Vietnam. Feelings of compassion (and other moral sentiments) may not be definitive in motivating behavior, especially if one has not faced anything like the awful situation in which the subjects and soldiers found themselves. But it does not follow that there is nothing more for virtue ethics to say about such cases. Experiments such as Milgram's are no longer allowed on college campuses, and for good reason. The feelings provoked in the subjects were too painful, and often with lasting damage.[28] And this is nothing, of course, compared to the posttraumatic experiences of many of those who served in Vietnam. The robustness of compassion must be measured not simply in terms of whether the subjects refused to continue with the experiment or not (most did) or whether the soldiers continued to do as they were ordered but by how powerful and upsetting the feelings they experienced both during and after the experiment. It is worth noting that there were a few sadists who actually enjoyed cruelty. There were others that were brutalized by the experiment and many who were brutalized by the war. That, it seems to me, should not be discounted. Bosses today are once again being forced to lay off thousands of their managers and employees. ("Market forces" is the inescapable explanation.) But there is all the difference in the world between those monsters like the infamous Al "Chainsaw" Dunlap who took such evident pride in across-the-board cuts and virtual saints such as Aaron Feuerstein who felt so badly about having to lay off workers (after a fire gutted his factory) that he kept them on the payroll until the company got back on its feet.[29]

THE MILGRAM EXPERIMENT REVISITED: A MODEL OF CORPORATE LIFE?

Is corporate life nothing but the vectors of peer pressures, leaving very little or even no room for the personal virtues? Does social psychology show that this is not the case only for corporate grinds but for all of us? Empirically minded philosophers love to find a single experiment, or perhaps two, that make this case for them, that is, which provide the basis for speculative excursions that go far beyond the (usually rather timid) findings of the social psychologists themselves. Harman's appeal to the two famous experiments by Milgram and by Darley and Batson are illustrative. Doris takes in a much wider swath of the social science literature, but even he is forced to admit, throughout his admirable book, that there are profound reasons for not generalizing from particular experiments to a good deal of "real life."

Regarding the Milgram experiment, Harman (following Ross and Nisbett) rejects as implausible any explanation in terms of a "character defect" and suggests instead the "step-wise character of the shift from relatively unobjectionable behavior to complicity in a pointless, cruel, and dangerous ordeal." I think that this is indeed part of the explanation. Milgram's subjects needed to have their callousness cultivated even as they dutifully obeyed the authorities (like the proverbial frog in slowly boiling water). The subjects could not have been expected to simply shock strangers on command. But where Harman adds that we are tempted to make the "fundamental attribution error" of blaming the subject's destructive obedience on a personal defect, I would say instead that what the Milgram experiment shows is how foolish and tragic the otherwise important virtues of conformity and obedience can be. There is no "personal defect" on display here precisely because what the experiment shows is the consistency and stability of that virtue. And the fact that it is (like all virtues) not always a virtue is no argument against its status as part of the core of the explanation of the subjects' behavior. The rest of the explanation involves not just the incremental but also the disorienting nature of the situation.

But one-third of the subjects in the Milgram experiment did quit. And those who did not were indeed confused. Is there no room for character in a complete explanation? Or do the differences between the subjects and their behavior and feelings demand such an explanation? Where are all of those studies on individual differences that would explain the differences (without necessarily taking anything away from the importance of the situation and the importance of the authority of the experimenters)? What about that voluminous literature not in social psychology but in the (artificially competing) field of personality theory, from Freud, Gordon Allport, David McClelland, and more recently, Costa and McRae? At the University of Minnesota, just a few blizzards away from Doris's previous base in Ann Arbor, the continuity and stability of character has become something of a minor industry.[30] If we want to play off moral philosophy and virtue ethics against the social sciences, let's make sure that all of the social sciences are represented and not just social psychology, which tends to define itself (artificially again, in competition with personality theory) as the study of the social dimensions of human behavior.

The other often-used case for "lack of character" is the case of the "good Samaritan," designed by Darley and Batson. Seminary students, on their way to give an assigned lecture (on "the good Samaritan") were forced to confront a person (an accomplice of the experimenter) on their way. Few of them stopped to help. It is no doubt true that the difference between subjects and their willingness to help the (supposed) victim can be partially explained on the basis of such transient variables as the fact that they were "in a hurry." And it is probably true as well (and not at all surprising to those of us who are not pushing "faith-based initiatives" these days) that people who were (or claimed to be) religious or who were about to talk on a religious topic of direct relevance to the experience did not act so differently as they would have supposed. But does it follow that character played no role? I would say that all sorts of character traits, from one's ability to think about time and priorities to one's feelings of anxiety and competence when faced with a (seemingly) suffering human being all come into play. Plus, of course, the sense of responsibility and obligation to arrive at an appointment on time, which once again slips into the background of the interpretation of the experiment and so blinds us to the obvious.

As in the Milgram experiment, how much is the most plausible explanation of the case precisely one that the experimenters simply assume but ignore, namely the character trait or virtue of promptness, the desire to arrive at the designated place on time? It is not lack of character. It is a conflict of character traits, one practiced and well-cultivated, the other more often spoken of than put in practice. Theology students have no special claims on compassion. They just tend to talk about it a lot. And as students they have had little opportunity to test and practice their compassion in ways that are not routine.

In his discussion, Harman argues that people often choose the situations to which they are exposed. But on what basis do they make such choices? Surely part of the explanation is their wanting to act as they believe they ought to, with the knowledge that they are prone to temptation and peer pressure. A more obvious aspect of their choice is their judgment that they would feel more comfortable in one situation rather than another and that their comfort depends, in part, on their virtues. Thus clerics and criminals place themselves, or are placed by others, in situations that differ precisely because they induce clergy to look, feel, and act consistently like clergy and induce criminals to look, feel, and act consistently like criminals. None of this eliminates situational factors as an explanation of behavior. On the contrary, it furthers them and explains why people "feel obliged and even committed to act consistently." None of this implies that we should give up or give in on character but rather tells us that circumstances and character cannot be pried apart and should not be used competitively as alternative explanations of virtuous or vicious behavior.

Harman notes that employers mistakenly think that they can gain useful information from interviewing potential employees. But such interviews, Harman argues, only add "noise" to the decision process. This may explain, by the way, Princeton's peculiar (and so far as I know unique) policy of hiring new professors without interviews, on the basis of the written work alone. But I doubt that it has much justification in social science. First of all, it is a falsification of the interviewing process to think that what it provides is more information. Rather it provides an opportunity for employers (or their chosen representatives in "Human Resources") to "get the feel" of a candidate, see how much "in sync" they are, in order to anticipate how they will "get along." This explains why most interviewers describe themselves as typically having made a decision for all intents and purposes within the first minute or so, which would make little sense if the purpose of the interview were to gather "more information." Second, of course, there are people who have the skill (not necessarily a virtue) to interview well and others who do not. This can indeed be misleading, and it is all the worse if the candidate is also skillful at deception, hiding his or her crasser motives and intentions in order to "make a good impression." But none of this undermines the importance or intelligibility of the interviewing process. It just means that interviewers should be on their toes and learn to ferret out insincerity and deception, skills on which most of them already pride themselves.

What is not debatable, it seems to me, is that people present themselves differently, whether or not their presentations accurately represent their virtues and vices (which longer exposure is sure to reveal). I have long argued that the subject of explanation is not just the behavior of an agent but the behavior of an agent-in-situation (or some such odd locution). In business ethics, in particular, the behavior in question is the behavior of an "individual-within-the-organization," which is not for a moment to deny that this context may not be the only one of relevance in moral evaluation. Context is essential but it isn't everything. Virtues and vices are important for our explanations of human behavior, but they make sense only in the context of particular situations and cultural surroundings. There is no such thing as courage or generosity in abstraction, but it does not follow that there is no such thing as courage or generosity.

CONCLUSION: IN DEFENSE OF BUSINESS VIRTUE ETHICS

Virtue ethics has a long pedigree, going back to Plato and Aristotle, Confucius in China, and many other cultures as well as encompassing much of medieval and modern ethics—including, especially, the ethics of Hume, Adam Smith, and the other "Moral Sentiment Theorists." But we would do well to remind ourselves just why virtue and character have become such large concerns in the world today—in business ethics and in politics in particular. The impetus comes from such disparate sources as the Nuremberg trials and American atrocities in Vietnam, teenage drug use and peer pressure, and the frequently heard rationalization in business and politics that "everyone is doing it." The renewed emphasis on character is an attempt to build a personal bulwark (call it "integrity") against such pressures and rationalizations and (though half-heartedly) to cultivate virtues other than those virtues of unquestioning obedience that proved to be so dominant in the Milgram[32] experiments and in Vietnam atrocities such as My Lai.

Nevertheless, I share with Harman and Doris a concern that virtue ethics and talk about character is being overused and abused. Too often preachers of the virtues praise (in effect) their own sterling personalities without bothering to note how little there has been in their lives to challenge their high opinion of themselves. Too often, people are blamed for behaving in ways in which, given the situation and their personal backgrounds, it is hard to see how they could have acted or chosen to act otherwise. In contemporary politics, in particular, the renewed emphasis on character is prone to bullying and even cruelty, for example, as a way of condemning the victims of poverty and racial oppression for their behavior and insisting that such people "bootstrap" their way to respectability. Thus I could not be more in agreement with Harman when he throws suspicion on the American conservative William Bennett. But Nietzsche beats him to it, a full century before *The Book of Virtues*: "Then again there are those who consider it a virtue to say, 'virtue is necessary'; but at bottom they believe only that the police are necessary."[31]

I think that Harman's and Doris's ultimate aim is to take moral philosophy away from such vicious moralism and give it back to the good old empirical social engineer. Indeed, B. F. Skinner is never far from these new empiricist accounts, although neither Harman nor Doris would accept the absurdities of strict behaviorism. But once we have downplayed character and with it responsibility and put all of the emphasis back onto the environment, the "situation," all that is left is to design circumstances conducive to desirable behavior. To be sure, such design is important and essential and almost totally ignored by too many virtue ethicists today. If we are to combat intolerance, encourage mutual forgiveness, and facilitate human flourishing in contexts plagued by ethnic hatred, for instance, there is no denying the need for mediating institutions that will create the circumstances in which the virtues can be cultivated. Closer to home, the cultivation of the virtues in much-touted moral education also requires the serious redesign of our educational institutions. And much of the crime and commercial dishonesty in the United States and in the world today is due, no doubt, to the absence of such designs and character-building contexts. (The market, said the late great "Buddhist" economist E. F. Schumaker, "is the institutionalization of non-responsibility.")[32] We need less moralizing and more beneficent social engineering.

I could not agree more with these aims. But the existentialist twist to which Harman alludes (that we choose our circumstances) and the postmodern turn encouraged by Doris (that we acknowledge that for the most part our circumstances make us) convince me not that we should eliminate talk of the virtues and character but fully acknowledge both the role of the social sciences (all of the social sciences) and stop preaching the virtues without due emphasis upon both personal responsibility and the force of circumstances. Like Doris, we should appreciate more such "out of character" heroic and saintly behavior (he mentions Oscar Schindler in particular) and the exigencies of context and circumstances. But we should insist, first and foremost, that people—at any rate, people like us—are responsible for what they do, and what they make of themselves.

QUESTIONS FOR DISCUSSION

1. How does Solomon contrast "character" in a corporate setting with character as it is more commonly understood? Is there a relationship between character and responsibility? How is responsibility treated in corporate settings according to Solomon?
2. How does Solomon define "virtue ethics"? What are some of its advantages?
3. Why might virtue ethics be construed as a "vicious political maneuver"? Is this a valid critique? What is Solomon's response? Is he persuasive? How does this apply to matters of business ethics?
4. What does Milgram's "Obedience to Authority" experiment have to tell us about moral psychology? What implications does this have for virtue ethics?
5. What does it mean to say that virutes are "contextual"?
6. Do experimental data on matters of "character" tell the whole story, according to Solomon? What do they accentuate? What do they leave out? Do the Milgram and "Good Samaritan" experiments add anything to our understanding of virtue? How do they illustrate "conflicts" of character traits?

NOTES

1. See, for example, Robert Young, "The Implications of Determinism," in *A Companion to Ethics*, ed. Peter Singer (London: Blackwell, 1991). I am not considering here the post-Freudian complications of determination by way of compulsion or personality disorder.

2. E.g., Kenneth Goodpaster and John B. Matthews Jr., "Can a Corporation Have a Conscience?" *Harvard Business Review*, January–February 1982; John Ladd, "Morality and the Ideal of Rationality in Formal Organizations," *Monist*, October 1970; Peter A. French, *Collective and Corporate Responsibility* (New York: Columbia University Press, 1984); Peter A. French, "Responsibility and the Moral Role of Corporate Entities," in *Business as a Humanity*, ed. R. Edward Freeman, Ruffin Lectures II (New York: Oxford, 1994); Peter A. French, "The Corporation as a Moral Person," *American Philosophical Quarterly* 16, no. 3 (1979); Manuel G.Velasquez , *Business Ethics* (Engelwood Cliffs, NJ: Prentice-Hall, 1982 and further editions).

3. David Hume, *An Enquiry Concerning Human Understanding*, 2nd ed., ed. L.A. Sleby-Bigee (Clarendon: Oxford University Press, 1902). John Stuart Mill, *A System of Logic*, 8th ed. (New York: Harper & Row, 1874). Adam Smith, *Theory of the Moral Sentiments* (London: George Bell, 1880).

4. Gilbert Harman, "Moral Philosophy Meets Social Psychology: Virtue Ethics and the Fundamental Attribution Error," *Proceedings of the Aristotelian Society* 99 (1998–1999): 315–31. Revised version in G. Harman, *Explaining Value and Other Essays in Moral Philosophy* (Oxford: Clarendon Press, 2000), 165–78. See also, "The Nonexistence of Character Traits," *Proceedings of the Aristotelian Society* 100 (1999–2000): 223–26. John Doris, *Lack of Character: Personality and Moral Behavior* (New York: Cambridge University Press, 2002).

5. Two philosophical defenses of character are Joel Kupperman, "The Indispensability of Character," in *Philosophy* 76, no. 2 (April 2001): 239–50, and Maria Merritt, "Virtue Ethics and Situationist Personality Psychology," *Ethical Theory and Moral Practice* 3 (2000): 365–83.

6. The fight against the pervasiveness of excuses is something I learned early from Jean-Paul Sartre and pursue in some detail in my series, *No Excuses: Existentialism and the Meaning of Life* (Chantilly,VA: Teaching Company, 2000).

7. Paul Griffiths, *What Emotions Really Are* (Chicago: University of Chicago Press, 1997).

8. Simon Blackburn, *Essays in Quasi-Realism* (New York: Oxford University Press, 1995).

9. Alasdair MacIntyre, *After Virtue* (Notre Dame, IN: Notre Dame University Press, 1984).

10. I would plead for something of an exception in the case of the fascinating flow of neuropsychiatric research of the last thirty or so years, which does indeed go beyond folk psychology, not only in its particular findings but in the very vocabulary and structure of its explanations. Nevertheless, what is so dazzling in much of this research is precisely that way in which neurological anomalies violate our ordinary "folk psychology" explanations. I will limit my references to two. The first is a wonderful series of studies published by Oliver Sachs over the years, including *The Man Who Mistook His Wife for a Hat and Other Clinical Tales* (New York: Touchstone, 1998). The second is the recent research of Antonio Damasio, especially in *Descartes' Error* (New York: Putnam, 1994).

11. Stanley Milgram, "Behavioral Study of Obedience," *Journal of Abnormal and Social Psychology* 67 (1963); and *Obedience to Authority* (New York: HarperCollins, 1983).

12. I have argued with both Harman and Doris that they have made selective use of social science research. In particular, they have restricted their appeals and references al-

most entirely to social psychology and have been correspondingly neglectful of counter-arguments in personality theory. The difference in perspective—and consequently the tension—between these two branches of empirical psychology is extremely significant to the argument at hand. See, e.g., Todd F. Heatherton and Joel Lee Weinberger, eds., *Can Personality Change?* (Washington, DC: American Psychological Association, 1994), xiv, 368; A. Caspi and B. W. Roberts, "Personality Continuity and Change across the Life Course," in *Handbook of Personality: Theory and Research*, 2nd ed., ed. L. A. Pervin and O. P. John (New York: Guilford, 1999), 300–26; and Thomas J. Bouchard Jr., "The Genetics of Personality," in *Handbook of Psychiatric Genetics*, ed. Kenneth Blum, Ernest P. Noble, et al. (Boca Raton, FL: CRC Press, 1997), 273–96.

13. Gilbert Harman, "Moral Philosophy Meets Social Psychology," available at http://www.princeton.edu/~harman/Papers/Virtue.html (accessed June 6, 2006), 1.

14. Doris, *Lack of Character*, 24, 67 (all page numbers are to the unpublished manuscript, courtesy of John Doris).

15. Doris, *Lack of Character*, 15–16.

16. Doris, *Lack of Character*, 12, 42, 68.

17. But see a similar distinction defended by Ed Hartman, "The Role of Character in Business Ethics," in *The Next Phase of Business Ethics: Integrating Psychology and Ethics*, ed. J. Dienhart, D. Moberg, and R. Duska (Amsterdam: JAI/Elsevier, 2001), 341–54.

18. Jean-Paul Sartre, *Being and Nothingness*, trans. H. Barnes (New York: Philosophical Library, 1956), see for instance 104f.

19. An essay that uses the Milgram experiment to talk about "excuses" is A. Strudler and D. Warren, "Authority, Heuristics, and the Structure of Excuses," in *The Next Phase of Business Ethics*, 355–75. My own view is that "everybody's doing it" is *no* excuse, or at best a mitigating one. See my *No Excuses: Existentialism and the Meaning of Life*. See also the now-classic essay by Ron Green, "Everybody's Doing It," *Business Ethics Quarterly* 1, no. 1 (1991): 75–94.

20. Doris, *Lack of Character*, 41–42.

21. Alfred Carr, "Is Business Bluffing Ethical?" *Harvard Business Review*, January-February 1968.

22. J. M. Darley and C. D. Batson, "From Jerusalem to Jericho: A Study of Situational and Disposition Variables in Helping Behavior," *Journal of Personality and Social Psychology* 27 (1973).

23. R. Nisbett and L. Ross, *Human Inference: Strategies and Shortcomings of Social Judgment* (Upper Saddle River, NJ: Prentice Hall, 1980).

24. Nisbett and Ross, *Human Inference*, 19.

25. Nisbett and Ross, *Human Inference*, 19 (italics in original).

26. John Doris, *Lack of Character: Personality and Moral Behavior* (New York: Cambridge University Press, 2002): 69.

27. William Broyles Jr., *Brothers in Arms* (New York: Knopf, 1986); and Tim O'Brien, *If I Die in a Combat Zone Box Me Up and Ship Me Home* (New York: Delacorte, 1973).

28. See Milgram, *Obedience to Authority*.

29. See my discussion in *A Better Way to Think about Business* (New York: Oxford University Press, 1999), 10.

30. For a good summary of the debate and the differences between the two approaches, see D. T. Kenrick and D. C. Funder, "Profiting from Controversy: Lessons from the Person-Situation Debate," *American Psychologist* 43 (1988): 23–34; and David C. Funder, "Personality," *Annual Review of Psychology* 52 (2001): 197–221.

31. *Thus Spoke Zarathustra*, Part II, "On Virtuous," trans. Kaufmann (New York: Viking, 1954), 207.

32. E. F. Schumaker, *Small Is Beautiful* (New York: Harper and Row, 1973).

· 6 ·

Conscience and Its Counterfeits in Organizational Life: A New Interpretation of the Naturalistic Fallacy

Kenneth E. Goodpaster

In this chapter, Kenneth E. Goodpaster explains and defends three basic propositions: first, that American attitudes toward organizational ethics are conflicted at a fairly deep level; second, that in response to this conflict in our attitudes, we often default to various "counterfeits" of conscience, by which he means non-moral systems that serve as surrogates for the role of conscience in organizational settings; and third, that a better response would be for leaders to foster a culture of conscience within organizations. Goodpaster concludes by proposing several practical strategies to foster such a culture, and compares this late twentieth-century response to the problem of counterfeits to the classic "naturalistic fallacy" identified in early twentieth-century ethics by British philosopher G. E. Moore.

PART 1. THE CONFLICT: SKEPTICISM BOTH WAYS

𝒯he first proposition—that our attitudes (particularly as Americans) toward promoting organizational ethics are conflicted at a fairly deep level—is what some would call a paradox. The conflict begins with the simple observation that we are skeptical about the moral credentials of both the profit-driven market system and the election-driven political system. Over the last thirty years we have seen the grounds for this skepticism from Watergate to Whitewater—and from the career crashes of inside-traders like Ivan Boesky to literal crashes, like that of NASA's space shuttle Challenger. We have seen some of the most reputable names in American business implicated in questionable behavior: General Electric, Sears, E. F. Hutton, H. J. Heinz, Prudential Insur-

ance, and the list goes on. Most recently, we have heard debates and allegations about campaign funding abuses in the political arena that call into question the integrity of our democratic processes.

An Occupational Hazard in Business

I believe that these abuses stem from an occupational hazard found in organizational life that I have elsewhere labeled teleopathy[1] or the unbalanced pursuit of purpose. I have identified its symptoms as fixation, rationalization, detachment. And I believe that this hazard needs to be avoided. Let me illustrate the problem with a story from poet David Whyte's book *The Heart Aroused*. Whyte attributes the story to a friend of his named Joel Henning:

> The idea, issuing from the boardroom, was to offer tempting prizes and outlandish financial rewards to the one department in the company that could achieve the highest level of growth over the following financial year. Before long it became evident that one particular department had it completely sewn up, and Jim Harrison, the vice president in charge of that area, was the hero of the occasion. By the end of the following financial year his department had doubled its income; no one else came even close to the seductive figures appearing on his reports to the president. Harrison was sent back and forth across the country to give speeches and talks at all the company plants. The toast of the company, by the middle of the following year he had been disgraced and fired. The success of Jim Harrison was based on the neglect of every constituent part of the system except the one order programmed from above to improve profitability. Rather than being educated into the broad needs of the business, he was manipulated to produce one result at all costs. In his turn he reflected back to upper management an almost Biblical parable of their own narrow vision. To achieve this, his department had dropped all its education and training programs, stopped all new hiring, cut its research and development to the bone, and instilled the chill atmosphere of a police state onto the office floor. In the second year Harrison's department lost money at a greater rate than any other department. His people were leaving in droves despite the glittering prizes of the previous year, he had trained no one to replace them, and there were no new products appearing on the horizon for them to sell.[2]

This story illustrates what I have called the unbalanced pursuit of purpose. It indicates how business life, like political life, can frequently suffer from an atmosphere in which destructive behavior is actually incentivized or encouraged.[3] In the same spirit, we could reflect with chagrin at the comment of a former managing director of McKinsey and Company, who remarked about the kinds of professionals his company sought to hire: "The real competition out there isn't for clients, it's for people. . . . And we look to hire people who are first, very smart; second, insecure and thus driven by their insecurity; and third, competitive."[4]

The first half of my point is that we are often skeptical about organizational decision making because of its tendency to become fixated on goals while putting ethical considerations aside. But the other half of the conflict or paradox is that we are equally skeptical about the most natural way to resolve this problem, namely to bring ethics into the decision-making structures of organizations.

Distrust of Spirituality and Religion

In a June 1993 cover story in *Training* magazine entitled "The Search for Spirit in the Workplace," authors Chris Lee and Ron Zemke mention the baby-boom generation's quest for a spiritual home.[5] But what is particularly significant for purposes of understanding the paradox to which I have been referring is the authors' acknowledgment that there is real skepticism about the new emphasis on spirituality in the workplace. The skeptics seem to see the work/spirituality linkage either as a "fad" or as a dangerous and imperious intrusion, an invitation to inefficiency and unaccountability in both private- and public-sector economic activity. Management guru Tom Peters (coauthor of *In Search of Excellence*) laments that "by getting overtly into the spiritual stuff, the pendulum is swinging too far." Peters apparently fears the loss of a safe secularity in the quest for ethical values in business. In Peters's less-than-eloquent phrasing: "When you cross the line between the secular and the spiritual you're edging up on something that bugs me."[6]

The Reel Precision Manufacturing (RPM) case series, in which a Minnesota company articulates its ethical convictions in explicitly Judeo-Christian terms, never fails to elicit suspicion from a substantial number of my students, both graduate and undergraduate. The students' first concern is about company leaders seeking to "impose their religious values" on employees.[7] It is interesting to observe, however, that when I ask students whether their apprehension about the RPM case is anchored in the Judeo-Christian language of the company's "Direction Statement" or in the ethical substance of that statement (abstracted from any faith-based source), their response is equivocal. The issue moves from "imposing religious values" to "imposing values" period, full stop. Arguments against the sacred or the spiritual often mask underlying arguments about moral substance of any kind, including the secular.[8]

Distrust of Secular Conscience as Well

Even if we do not cross the line that "bugs" Tom Peters, therefore, there are obstacles to avoiding teleopathy. For our postmodern culture identifies almost any substantive moral commitment, whether its foundation be faith or reason, as suspect.

Many arguments offered in legal and regulatory contexts[9] caution against too much "moral discretion," presumably out of a concern that fiduciary responsibility would be threatened without significant boundaries on executive discretion. Even though most states in the United States have passed "constituency statues" to protect corporate boards of directors who sought during the hostile takeovers of the 1980s to consider the interests of all stakeholders, not just the stockholders, the often-voiced counterarguments were (and still are) that directors should stick to their knitting and tend to the principal stakeholders—those who put up the capital. Even champions of corporate social responsibility like Christopher Stone are cautious about encouraging the transformation of private-sector corporations into public-sector organizations.

To reiterate, the second half of our conflicted attitude asserts itself in our reluctance to prescribe the most obvious cure for the problem of the first half: the use of moral criteria to balance managerial (and political) decision making. Beyond concerns about conflating sacred and secular, our laws and our social norms tend to pressure managers (as agents of shareholders and the corporation) to suspend their ethical judgment—to literally alienate it. Perhaps we fear that incompetence might parade as virtue, or that ethical judgment might mean moral fanaticism. In any case, we resist our most instinctive approach to a cure for the unbalanced pursuit of purpose.

An irony in all this is that we urge the importance of ethics in business and in politics, but are often intimidated by the thought that chief executives and politicians might actually practice it! For many it appears to be essential, yet somehow both dangerous and illegitimate, to guide business decision making by moral values. It appears to be essential because the requirements of business life are often so intensely goal directed that they blind both individuals and organizations to the ethical aspects of what they do. It appears to be dangerous and illegitimate because appeals by organizational leaders to ethical values, when they are not looked upon as questionably sincere, are often looked upon as outside either their zone of discretion or their competence.[10]

So much for the statement of our conflictedness (my first proposition). If we now ask what we typically do in the face of that conflictedness, the answer appears to be that nature (even organizational nature) abhors a moral vacuum. What we do in the absence of the real thing in this world of virtual this and virtual that is to try to simulate it. But the problem is that virtual conscience can easily be counterfeit.

PART 2. COUNTERFEITS OF CONSCIENCE

My second proposition is that in response to the conflictedness of our attitudes toward ethics in organizations, we default to various counterfeits of conscience.[11] Calls for integrity and responsibility in institutional life—often in the wake of scandals—seem regularly to lose energy and effect. Like pebbles in a pond, their initial splash dissipates and seldom results in very much structural or cultural change. Business-as-usual (and politics-as-usual) is reinforced by the system itself in many ways.

Our social reality seems to be that ethics is more easily invoked than institutionalized. Efforts to avoid the "occupational hazard" (in the first half of the paradox) are muffled by worries about fanaticism and fiduciaries (in the second half of the paradox). The economic and social architecture of organizational life presents more formidable challenges to ethically motivated managers than we might think.

In the contemporary business or corporate arena, surrogates for conscience are not difficult to identify:

- First, there is market approval. The secular clergy for the market ethic are Wall Street analysts, ready to receive the "sacrifices and burnt offerings" of cutbacks and downsizings in exchange for recommendations to buy a company's stock. Nielsen ratings can call the tune in a similar way for media organizations; as do political consultants for reelection campaigns in the public sector.
- Second, there is the multilayered network of laws and regulations, represented by agencies like the FDA, the FCC, the EPA, and OSHA. In this context, an organization's "conscientiousness" takes many forms, but includes complex reports, seeking out preliminary rulings, and a willingness to pay costs of lobbying, usually for industry protection. In the same vein, there are international treaties and regional trade agreements that for some governments and corporations represent the highest moral authorities.
- Other surrogates for conscience can be found in constituency threats: shareholder derivative suits from those who question whether profits are sufficient, voter recalls in the public sector, boycotts and class action plaintiffs' suits from consumers, and strikes by employees. Each of these threats represents an external sanction on executive decision making the fear of which can come to replace good judgment.
- Within organizations, employees are often invited to find surrogates for their consciences in the imperatives of career advancement, loyalty as measured by eighty-hour work weeks, quotas for sales forces and departments, and incentive and bonus systems.

- Other organizations search for conscience in ombudspersons or ethics officers, who are assigned to manage code violations.[12]

What do all these items have in common in organizational life? For one thing, they represent relatively tangible measures of success with some claim to avoiding the conflict or paradox mentioned in Part 1 above. They are "objective" and "reliable" objects of devotion (market value, legal compliance, security from external threats, organizational loyalty and excellence, etc.), accompanied by visible, public commandments (codes, rules, measurement systems, and sanctions). They seem to dodge both our skepticism about occupational hazards and our worries about incompetence, fanaticism, and fiduciaries.

They supply a sense of discipline and orderliness to organizational life without the risks of runaway private mysticism and spirituality that so "bugged" Tom Peters. What more could we want? What more should we want? Isn't this the profile of the institutional habits of a postmodern society at the end of the twentieth century?

Alas! What these counterfeits also have in common is individual and joint insufficiency. We can easily imagine and illustrate examples of decision making guided by market approval, government regulation, and safety from constituency threats that are nevertheless ethically inadequate. For markets, laws, and regulations are imperfect at best; and constituency threats often depend on the capacity of stakeholders to mobilize the influence of markets, laws, and regulations.

Déjà-vu in Modern Ethics

We have come to a point that may seem vaguely familiar to attentive philosophers. I ask other readers to be patient with a brief historical excursion that I believe is relevant to the current issue of conscience and its counterfeits in organizational ethics.

Early in twentieth-century ethical theory, a key debate centered around the definability of basic ethical concepts like "the right" and "the good." So-called naturalists offered definitions of these terms in an effort to put normative ethics on a solid, usually empirical, foundation. Without such translations of the basic predicates of ethics, naturalists argued, we would never be in a position to verify ethical claims about right and wrong, good and bad, virtue and vice. And without verifiability, we were left with nonsense or fanaticism or, at best, highly personal expressions of moral emotion.

On the opposite side of this now-classic debate were the "intuitionists" who, while they agreed that ethics had to avoid nonsense, fanaticism, and mere emotivism, insisted that the solution lay not in empirical definitions of concepts like "the right" and "the good." The solution lay instead in recognizing that the central ideas of ethics were simple and indefinable—and that ethical understanding was to be found more directly, more intuitively, than the naturalists thought. Indeed, one of the most powerful arguments in the arsenal of the intuitionists was the "open question argument" made famous by British philosopher G. E. Moore.

Confronted with a naturalistic definition of "good," such as "pleasurable," Moore would ask if the question "This is pleasurable, but is it good?" made any sense. If it did, then identifying "good" with "pleasurable" was mistaken. And intuitionists like Moore and H. A. Pritchard and others were convinced that this line of argument extended far beyond the case at hand, revealing a basic flaw in the definitional program itself—what came to be called the "naturalistic fallacy." The question would always remain open because no analysis could substitute satisfactorily for fundamental ethical insight.

Now, this old debate in ethical theory may seem both quaint and irrelevant to the challenges of organizational ethics on the threshold of a new millennium, but we should look more closely. For while applied ethics today is less preoccupied with the language of "indefinability" and "simple properties," it is very much preoccupied with how to orient, institutionalize, and sustain the ethical values of organizations.[13]

Systems So Perfect

T. S. Eliot, in one of his "Choruses from the Rock" (1934), observes that humankind spends too much time "dreaming of systems so perfect that no one will need to be good."[14] The power of this poetic phrase can be appreciated in the context of the surrogates or counterfeits for conscience identified above.

The "systems so perfect" are the external systems of the market, the law and regulatory machinery of government, the social infrastructure that supports constituency threats to executive decision makers, and the internal organizational systems of rewards and incentives and sanctions that guide the behavior of individual managers. But the "dreaming" in Eliot's phrase signals the futility of such systems relative to the need for individuals and organizations to be good.

The central challenge in applied ethics at the end of the twentieth century is a practical analogue of the central challenge in ethical theory at the century's beginning: Can we identify a system or a process to guide organizational decision making so that no one will need to be good? If we affirm the need for ethical categories to avoid teleopathy, and yet are conflicted by concerns of fanaticism, subjective judgments, and fiduciary responsibility, can we find suitable systemic substitutes for conscience—either outside the organization or inside? Can we dream up systems so perfect that they escape the open questions: Yes, this practice is warranted by the market, but is it good? Or yes, this policy is permitted by the law, but is it right?

It is my conviction that the quest for "systems so perfect" in organizational ethics is doomed to failure because there are no such systems. And the reason lies in the nature of conscience itself as a form of awareness that cannot be "outsourced" or "automated" as many organizational functions (like advertising, payroll services, employee assistance programs, etc.) can be.

PART 3. CONSCIENCE AS AWARENESS

So now we ask, is there a way out of the puzzle described in Part 1 and elaborated in Part 2? Is there a way to avoid the unbalanced pursuit of purpose on the one hand and moral fanaticism on the other—without relying solely on the insufficient counterfeits, the "systems so perfect" that we embrace "so that no one will need to be good"? My third proposition is that we can do better than trusting to counterfeits. We can try to institutionalize ethical awareness or conscience in organizational cultures.

Anthony DeMello, a Jesuit priest-psychologist who was raised in India as a Buddhist until his teen years, tells a story about an eager young disciple who went to the master and said, "Could you give me a word of wisdom? Could you tell me something that would guide me through my days?" Since it was the master's day of silence, he picked up a pad and wrote on it. It said, "Awareness." When the disciple saw it, he said, "This is too brief. Can you expand on it a bit?" So the master took back the pad and wrote, "Awareness, awareness, awareness." The disciple said, "Yes, but what does it mean?" The master took back the pad and wrote, "Awareness, awareness, awareness means—awareness."[15]

The point of DeMello's little story, and the source of its amusement, is that we sometimes look for complex solutions when much simpler ones are available. But simple does not necessarily mean easy. The significance of "awareness" is great, but so is the challenge of institutionalizing awareness in modern organizations.

DeMello's view is reminiscent of the views of the intuitionists in ethical theory at the beginning of the twentieth century. Ethical awareness is what we call conscience, and conscience is an active, engaged, perspective on decision making that resists "definition"—replacement by systems outside or inside the organization.[16]

What drove us into counterfeits in Part 2 was the worry expressed at the end of Part 1 that ethical awareness and insight were somehow too diverse and so too unstable to serve as a foundation for business judgment. But what if this impression is superficial? What if there really is something we could call a shared moral consciousness, which we can approach in a disciplined way rather than fleeing it as if it were fragile and fragmentary?[17]

What if, like a corporation's strategy, a corporation's conscience could be identified, articulated, symbolized, developed, adapted, celebrated, reinforced, and sustained by constant awareness at all levels and in all parts of the organization? If so, then our twenty-first-century challenge may be more a matter of making moral awareness pervasive than of fleeing it as somehow risky or dangerous.

To be sure, ethical disagreements will occur among and between executives, employees, consumers, suppliers, and shareholders regarding corporate policies and their implementation. And allegations of fanaticism or incompetence or fiduciary failure may sometimes be warranted. The key point to remember for the sake of avoiding counterfeits is that such allegations are not self-justifying.

"Awareness, awareness, awareness," wrote DeMello. Instead of looking away at the first sign of moral disagreement or ethical imperatives that might seem economically and legally expensive, we are encouraged to look more closely. Often looking more closely leads to more agreement than disagreement about, for instance, appropriate workplace safety or product safety practices, marketing strategies, sales incentives, financial reporting. The best response to the postmodern presumption of moral fragmentation is simply to look more closely. Similarly, looking more closely at economic and legal consequences of not following agreed-upon ethical imperatives frequently reveals unnoticed or undervalued economic costs and legal exposure.

What are the characteristics of a corporate culture that institutionalizes ethical awareness—that "looks more closely" in the ways indicated in the previous paragraphs? I would suggest (based on my own experiences in the classroom as an educator and in corporate offices as a consultant) four principal manifestations of corporate ethical awareness: reflectiveness, humility, anticipation, and community involvement.

Four Manifestations of Corporate Ethical Awareness

(1) By reflectiveness I mean a cultural disposition to encourage periodic relief from the goal-directedness and busy-ness of everyday work life.

In our individual lives, few of us would have trouble appreciating how important it is to create regular—daily, weekly, yearly—opportunities for silence, reflection, and meditation on the meaning of what we do. It is much easier to become fixated if we deny ourselves access to a larger understanding of our efforts. It is much easier to settle for counterfeits when we are impatient for results—operating out of a closed attitude of demand rather than a more open attitude of request.

Organizations, like persons, can suffer from the pathology of activism, the misplaced devotion of never stopping to reflect on their missions. An organizational culture can be too busy or too focused to think—to be aware of what it is doing. An atmosphere of reflectiveness helps organizations ensure their ethical integrity more than any preoccupation with rules, laws, and programs for policing wrongdoing.

This can take the form of daily, weekly, monthly, and/or annual periods of silence, thoughtfulness about the purpose and practices of the enterprise. Some companies, like Medtronic, Inc., actually construct special spaces (meditation rooms) and support annual retreats for executives aimed at rekindling their sense of corporate mission and values.[18] What is distinctive and powerful about this feature of an organizational culture is that it recognizes a need for balance in the pursuit of goals and objectives, and affords opportunities to cultivate that balance.

In an age of information explosion and noise, of voice mail, e-mail, and fewer people doing more work, in a culture of competitiveness and workaholism, it is relatively easy for corporations to evacuate whatever vestiges of silence and thoughtfulness there might be and to treat executive development more as "skills development" than as a chance to get in touch with the meaning of the enterprise.

(2) Humility may seem an odd virtue to attribute to a corporate culture, so it deserves some further clarification. Companies that have the courage to articulate their core values and to communicate them clearly to insiders and outsiders are inviting the charge of hypocrisy on a regular basis. None of us is immune to observations of disconnection between aspiration and action ("talk" and "walk"), one definition of hypocrisy. Some corporate cultures manifest humility in the sense that they are willing to be self-critical about gaps between their articulated core values and practice. Several companies that I have worked with do regular exercises and audits designed to elicit from managers and other employees their perceptions of such gaps and their suggestions about repairing them.

Such companies can, without much hesitation, initiate newly hired employees into the culture and symbolize and celebrate their core values in memorable ways. Awareness of falling short, together with a commitment to improving on the shortfalls, is understood and taken seriously. Humility is also reinforced by corporate communication channels (newsletters, helplines with ombudspersons) and employee development efforts aimed at confirming and clarifying the ethical values of the company in specific contexts.

It is much easier to rationalize wrongdoing when we deny ourselves access to honest and candid feedback from our peers on both our walk and our talk. We can help one another avoid the dangers of groupthink and the conventional filters that we put on our perception of the environment. Self-deception (both of the personal variety and of the group variety) is not impossible in the presence of the discipline of dialogue, but it is more difficult. Organizations that institutionalize awareness by regularly setting aside instinctive preoccupations with the material efficiencies, attending to the spiritual and interpersonal dimensions of workplace culture, are less vulnerable to counterfeits of conscience, less likely to settle for less in the constant pursuit of more.

(3) If a corporation's ethical awareness is to sustain itself over time, then the leaders in the organization need to anticipate and avoid loss of awareness through attentive recruiting, promotions, and succession planning. If there is physical entropy in our world, a tendency toward loss of order and substance, we might expect corresponding "ethical entropy" in the realm of organizational values. Anticipating this phenomenon means providing for constant vigilance and renewal. Awareness is sustained by careful selection and orientation of both new hires and new leaders.

In addition, many companies, especially in the last two decades of the twentieth century, have grown by acquisition, and the cultural implications of acquisitions can be profound, not only economically but ethically. A corporation contemplating a merger or an acquisition would be foolish to look solely at the compatibility of balance sheets and other economic synergies. Cultural compatibility—including especially shared ethical values—is at least as important in the life of the new organization, and awareness on this front is another form of anticipation.

(4) The fourth characteristic of an ethically aware corporate culture is community involvement. The essence of this characteristic is engagement with the various communities in which the company does business—through avenues like philanthropy, in-kind contributions, and employee released time. This characteristic of corporate culture is not simply "nice to have" in relation to the first three. It is an extension of ethical awareness, especially to those less advantaged in the company's relevant communities, to stakeholders who are least able to reciprocate, at least in the short term.

One of the key roles of service in the lives of each of us as individuals is to break us free from the bonds of self-centeredness and the detachment that can accompany it. And I use the term "bonds" quite deliberately, since there is a kind of imprisonment associated with being disconnected from family and community, and a paradoxical threat to one's own integrity in the process.[19] Corporate community involvement is an institutional manifestation of what for individuals is an acknowledgment of connectedness and some degree of responsibility for the well-being of the surrounding social system.[20]

Organizations that institutionalize community involvement not only through corporate financial contributions, but also through encouraging employees to contribute pro bono time and talent, are fostering an awareness of vulnerable stakeholders—those less able to demand the attention of corporate decision making, though often every bit as influenced or affected by it. They are at the same time avoiding the habit of treating government as our sole vehicle of compassion, a way of outsourcing our encounters with the less advantaged.

CONCLUSION

This chapter has sought to explain and defend three propositions: (1) that our attitudes toward organizational conscience are conflicted; (2) that as a consequence we often default to various counterfeits of conscience, reminiscent of the "naturalistic fallacy" in early twentieth-century ethical theory; and (3) that we would do better to foster a culture of ethical awareness in organizations.

The four key manifestations of such corporate ethical awareness are reflectiveness, humility, anticipation, and community involvement. While these characteristics may sound old-fashioned, they keep corporate conscience awake and alive without assuming "systems so perfect that no one will need to be good." Companies displaying these characteristics need be neither fanatical nor antifiduciary. They simply need to avoid the occupational hazards of fixation, rationalization, and self-centered detachment.

The alternative to pursuing corporate ethical awareness—pursuing its counterfeits instead—may be grim, in view of the sobering observation attributed to Winston Churchill: "First we shape our institutions, and then they shape us."

QUESTIONS FOR DISCUSSION

1. What is "teleopathy"? What are its symptoms? How does Goodpaster argue that teleopathy undermines organizational ethics?
2. Why is "conscience," whether or not it is rooted in religious values, a problem for some businesses? Is a religious set of values appropriate to a business setting? Is any value system appropriate?
3. What are some of the "counterfeits of conscience" that Goodpaster identifies? Why are they counterfeit? How do they substitute for genuine conscience?
4. What is the "naturalistic fallacy"? How does it play into the debate between ethical naturalism and ethical intuitionism?

5. What does the author mean by "conscience"? How is it connected to the idea of awareness? What does he identify as manifestations of corporate awareness?

6. Evaluate Goodpaster's arguments in favor of corporate conscience as awareness in light of your own experience of business. How might it be applied? What are some obstacles to its application? What strategies would aid in overcoming these obstacles?

NOTES

1. For a fuller definition of "teleopathy," see *Blackwell Encyclopedic Dictionary of Business Ethics* (1997), 627.

2. David Whyte, *The Heart Aroused: Poetry and the Preservation of the Soul in Corporate America* (New York: Doubleday, 1994), 270.

3. We could add scores of similar stories based on well-researched case studies of business organizations. We could also discuss the widely quoted "Parable of the Sadhu" by Bowen McCoy (*Harvard Business Review* 1997): 54, in which an executive loses his sense of humanity on a Himalayan mountain-climbing expedition and leaves a man to die on the slope. Many companies have ended up in scandal during the last quarter of this century due to goals or targets presented to management as overriding—to be met "come hell or high water."

4. Ron Daniel, former managing director, McKinsey & Co., *Fortune*, November 1, 1993, 72. We see from this example that teleopathy can afflict organizations as well as individuals!

5. Chris Lee and Ron Zemke, "The Search for Spirit in the Workplace," *Training*, June 1993, 21–28: "It seems that mid-life crises combined with economic insecurity are persuading some boomers to return to their childhood religions, some to turn to unconventional churches and some to the various 12-step programs of the 'recovery' movement. . . . Besides boomers' mid-life crises and general economic insecurities, we might add to the list of contributing trends: downsizing and 'delayering' as a result of global competition, decisional and informational overload, social disintegration through crime, broken marriages and families, and fractured urban education systems."

6. Peters quoted in Lee and Zemke, "Search for Spirit," 26.

7. RPM's "Direction Statement" opens with: "RPM is a team dedicated to the purpose of operating a business based on the practical application of Judeo-Christian values for the mutual benefit of: co-workers and their families, customers, shareholders, suppliers, and community. We are committed to provide an environment where there is no conflict between work and moral/ethical values or family responsibilities and where everyone is treated justly. The tradition of excellence at RPM has grown out of a commitment to excellence rooted in the character of our Creator. Instead of driving each other toward excellence, we strive to free each other to grow and express the desire for

excellence that is within all of us." See K. Goodpaster and L. Nash, *Policies and Persons*, 3rd ed. (New York: McGraw-Hill, 1998), 135–50.

8. "By adhering to the following principles, we are challenged to work and make decisions consistent with God's purpose for creation according to our individual understanding: DO WHAT IS RIGHT—We are committed to do what is right even when it does not seem to be profitable, expedient, or conventional; DO OUR BEST—In our understanding of excellence we embrace a commitment to continuous improvement in everything we do. It is our commitment to encourage, teach, equip, and free each other to do and become all that we were intended to be. TREAT OTHERS AS WE WOULD LIKE TO BE TREATED; SEEK INSPIRATIONAL WISDOM—by looking outside ourselves, especially with respect to decisions having far-reaching and unpredictable consequences, but we will act only when the action is confirmed unanimously by others concerned." Goodpaster and Nash, *Policies and Persons*, 145.

9. American Law Institute Proceedings, ERISA language on pension fund managers' responsibilities, etc. See my 1991 article in *Business Ethics Quarterly*, "Business Ethics and Stakeholder Analysis," 10. "For those who want to lobby for a more radical effacement or shift in the locus of the public/private boundary, there is opportunity for attack along the lines of unseating corporations from their entitlement to ordinary constitutional liberties. Some of the liberties that protect natural persons might not apply, or might apply less stringently, when corporations and other associations of various sorts are the claimants. The less heavily we weigh their liberty claims, the more we would be justified to encumber them with obligations. . . . I do not doubt that if we could see to origins, we would find what is public and what is private lying close to the heart of the human feelings that give rise to governments." From "Corporate Vices and Corporate Virtues: Do Public/Private Distinctions Matter?" *University of Pennsylvania Law Review* 130, no. 6 (June 1982).

10. This is, of course, the now-classic argument of Milton Friedman in "The Social Responsibility of Business Is to Increase Its Profits," *New York Times Magazine*, September 13, 1970.

11. *Oxford English Dictionary*: "counterfeit—adj. 1 (of a coin, writing, etc.) made in imitation; not genuine; forged. 2 (of a claimant etc.) pretended.—n. a forgery; an imitation." Counterfeits or surrogates are in some ways like autopilots, external systems that free us from the tedium of having to pay attention. They become substitutes for "guidance by awareness" or mindfulness; indeed they are tools for (temporary) thoughtlessness.

12. Mention of codes here deserves some qualification. The point is not that codes of conduct (industry codes, company codes, professional codes for engineers, accountants, and consultants to mention only a few) are in themselves objectionable, but that in the absence of a culture of dialogue surrounding them, they have the potential to become counterfeits for conscience.

13. See Goodpaster, "Ethical Imperatives and Corporate Leadership." This chapter was first presented as a Ruffin Lecture in Business Ethics at the Darden School, University of Virginia, in April 1988. It was later published in *Ethics in Practice: Managing the Moral Corporation*, ed. Kenneth R. Andrews (Boston: Harvard Business School Press, 1991).

14. "Choruses from the Rock," VI (1934).

15. Anthony DeMello, S.J., *Awareness* (New York: Doubleday, 1990), 56.

16. DeMello would have agreed wholeheartedly with philosopher Hannah Arendt's observation that "A life without thinking is quite possible—but it is not fully alive. Unthinking men are like sleepwalkers." Hannah Arendt, "Thinking," *New Yorker*, December 5, 1977, 195.

17. As we contemplate our answer to this question, we might consider the remark of political scientist Glenn Tinder, who warns us that at the end of the twentieth century "[o]ur position is precarious, for good customs and habits need a spiritual base; and if it is lacking, they will gradually—or perhaps suddenly, in some crisis—disappear. To what extent are we now living on moral savings accumulated over many centuries but no longer being replenished?" Glenn Tinder, *The Political Meaning of Christianity* (Baton Rouge: Louisiana State University Press, 1989), 51. Tinder also remarks that Jews and Christians "will be deeply suspicious of the maxim that the invisible hand of the market is always to be trusted in preference to the visible hand of government. Such a maxim has a look of idolatry. The principle that only God, and never a human institution, should be relied on absolutely suggests a far more flexible and pragmatic approach to the issue" (185).

18. For a much fuller discussion, see K. Goodpaster and T. Holloran, "Anatomy of Corporate Spiritual and Social Awareness: The Case of Medtronic, Inc.," Proceedings of the Third International Symposium on Catholic Social Thought and Management Education, Goa, India, January 1999.

19. If we ask whether the awareness that comes from conscience is self-sacrificial, the answer might surprise us. It may be different from that usually intended by those who see sacrifice as destructive. Consider the words of British philosopher Richard Norman: "The sacrificing of one's own interests need not be a sacrificing of oneself to something external. My commitment to my friends or my children, to a person whom I love or a social movement in which I believe, may be a part of my own deepest being, so that when I devote myself to them, my overriding experience is not that of sacrificing myself but of fulfilling myself" (*The Moral Philosophers* [Oxford: Oxford University Press, 1983], 249).

20. In Minnesota and nationally, Dayton Hudson Corporation is perhaps best known for institutionalizing corporate community involvement, but as this article goes to press in the summer of 1999, the Twin Cities community is quite concerned about the loss of Honeywell, Inc. (acquired by Allied Signal of New Jersey). Honeywell's record of corporate community involvement has been extraordinary in private-public partnerships for improving neighborhoods, increasing minority employment, work-family balance, and many other arenas.

· 7 ·

Casuistry and the Business Case Method

Martin Calkins

From the very beginning of the discipline in the early 1980s, business ethics has borrowed from the pedagogical methods used in business schools. One method that stands out among all the others is the case method approach. In current practice, cases are used to illustrate ethical principles or as an analysis tool, giving students an opportunity to apply ethical theories to actual business circumstances, or to cases that at least accurately simulate these realities. Normally, instructors and authors do not attempt to systematically relate cases to one another, categorizing the cases according to the issues they raise and the types of ethical resolutions that might plausibly arise from these moral deliberations. Nonetheless, the almost universal adoption of the case method approach to business ethics raises the possibility that such a systematic approach to the cases might evolve some time in the future. This systematization of the case method is known as casuistry, and in this chapter Martin Calkins discusses the rich resources that the casuistic method provides for students of business ethics.

The chapter argues for the compatibility of casuistry and the business case method. It describes the salient features of casuistry and the case method, shows how the two methods are similar yet different, and suggests how elements of casuistry contribute to the use of case method in management education. Toward these ends, it show how casuistry and case method are both inductive and practical methods of reasoning focused on single settings and real-life situations and how both methods stress that real-life decision making is not the exclusive domain of experts. It also shows how casuistry and the case method are not identical processes but have different purposes and emphasize order and problem-solving differently. In the end, the chapter suggests that, despite their differences, casuistry and the case method might be brought together to benefit business management and the field of business ethics.

*W*hen I mention the word casuistry in business circles, I usually get blank stares in return. If it is recognized at all, casuistry is thought to be an obscure and anti-quated process of moral reasoning that was discredited and put to rest in the late seventeenth century. While the lack of familiarity with casuistry would not be remarkable under most circumstances, it is striking in the context of business be-cause managers tend to use a form of casuistry in their everyday deliberations.

Business managers—not unlike doctors, lawyers, and priests—tend to resolve dilemmas through the use of cases and the so-called business case method. As we will see, this case method is similar, but not identical, to some of the earliest forms of casuistry. Not unlike casuistry, the case method is an inductive and practical way of reasoning that focuses on a single setting and a real-life situation. In both methods, decision making does not depend on ex-perts. Rather, ordinary people use it. Even so, the case method and casuistry are not identical. They have different purposes, emphasize the resolution of dilem-mas to different degrees, and stress order differently. While these are important differences, bringing the two together might benefit business management and, in particular, might enhance the field of business ethics.

CASUISTRY'S CHARACTERISTICS

A mini-revival of interest in casuistry has occurred in recent years. Just as Alasdair MacIntyre's *After Virtue* sparked an interest in virtue theory among mainstream and applied ethicists, so Albert Jonsen and Stephen Toulmin's *The Abuse of Casuistry* stimulated an interest in casuistry among moralists.[1]

What is casuistry? As Jonsen and Toulmin describe it, [Casuistry is] "the analysis of moral issues, using procedures of reasoning based on paradigms and analogies, leading to the formulation of expert opinions about the existence and stringency of particular moral obligations, framed in terms of rules or maxims that are general but not universal or invariable, since they hold good with cer-tainty only in the typical conditions of the agent and circumstances of action."[2]

In its simplest rendering, casuistry involves the use of settled cases to resolve present moral dilemmas. When exercised, casuistry has the individual compare an ambiguous present situation to a past incident or set of incidents in which judgments have already been rendered. The individual then uses these earlier judgments to determine a proper course of action in the present. Casuistry is engaged, for example, in deliberations about the fair distribution of costly drugs to treat AIDS patients when people invoke Merck's decision to distribute ivermectin freely to victims of river blindness (a case of corporate altruism) or when they refer to Plasma International's decision to charge a great deal of money for blood after a natural disaster (a case of corporate selfishness).[3]

Table 1. Casuistry's Characteristics

1.	Case usage: the chief tools of deliberation are settled cases (resolved real-life situations).
2.	Paradigm cases: deliberations turn to touchstone cases that have intrinsic and extrinsic certitude.
3.	Inductive reasoning by analogy: deliberations draw analogies between past and present situations.
4.	Maxims: deliberations invoke pithy sayings that embody a particular truth and act as shortcuts in discourse.
5.	Complexity: deliberations retain their situational messiness.
6.	Probability: deliberations de-emphasize the absolute certainty in judgments in favor of high probability.
7.	Cumulative arguments: judgments emerge from a "bottom-up" process of multiple arguments.
8.	Practicality: resolutions can be applied.
9.	Resolution: judgments are expected to be acted upon.
10.	Ordinary constituency: deliberations do not depend upon experts.

Table 1 lists the specific features of casuistry.

Casuistry's most important feature is its use of cases, which can be described as events or happenings in which there is a "confluence of persons and actions in a time and a place."[4] Casuistry's cases are simply accounts of real-life situations. As such, they are rich in detail, practical, concrete rather than abstract, and formed by the congealing or growing together of many different circumstances.[5]

Second, casuistry features the use of so-called paradigm cases—settled cases that convey intrinsic and extrinsic certitude. Paradigm cases recount unambiguous incidents of good and evil and reveal "the most manifest breaches of the general principle, taken in its most obvious meaning."[6] They are useful in moral deliberation because they demonstrate the most obviously and unarguably wrong or right course of action to be taken.

Third, casuistry features the ordering of cases under a principle by analogy. In casuistry, all cases—especially paradigm cases—are objects of comparison. Accordingly, a new situation (the present moral problem) is compared to previously settled cases through an inductive process involving analogy. In this process, similarities and differences between the present set of circumstances and previously settled cases are sought out. Because a clear principle or norm is not evident in the present situation (hence, the dilemma), the casuist must find a fit with some incident in the past where judgments have been satisfactorily rendered. Since the present situation rarely mirrors the past, a number of settled cases must be brought in to inform the present deliberation. Typically, appeal is made first to the clearest incident of right and wrong, that is, the paradigm case. Then, more ambiguous cases are brought to bear and deliberation moves away from the paradigm by the introduction of "various combinations of circumstances and motives that [make] the offense in question less apparent."[7] In this way, as Donald Klinefelter summarizes, "[The casuist] works outward from the paradigm by analogy to more or less problematic instances. . . . As the analogy weakens, the debate concerning the morality of the proposed action intensifies, and we must move to a more careful description of the particulars of the case."[8]

Fourth, casuistry is characterized by the use of maxims. While paradigm cases reflect one or more unquestioned principles, they are understood more easily through maxims or general truths expressed in sententious form. Not unlike the rhetorical device of enthymemes, maxims presume and leave as unstated at least one of the propositions of an argument. Rooted in intuition and a commonsense view of the world, maxims are pithy sayings or aphorisms of a proverbial nature that appeal to common knowledge in a formulaic manner. As Jonsen and Toulmin explain,

> [Maxims are] the kinds of phrases typically invoked by ordinary people when arguing a moral issue: "Don't kick a man when he is down" or "One good turn deserves another." These maxims are seldom further proved; their relevance is seldom explicitly demonstrated; yet they play an important role in the development of a moral argument.[9]

Businesspeople invoke maxims all the time. "A penny saved is a penny earned" and "waste not, want not" are two examples of business-related maxims that convey the need for frugality. "Nothing ventured, nothing gained" and "no risk, no reward," in contrast, convey the benefits of risk taking. In practice, a particular maxim is invoked when there is a fit between the saying and a particular circumstance. Usually, the fit works. Yet, the pithy nature of the maxim leaves as unstated certain elements of the argument put forth and this, we shall see later, can lead to error. Even so, the compact nature of the maxim helps to advance a particular position, support a certain judgment, or rebut another alternative in a powerful way.

Fifth, casuistry is noted for its ability to account for the complications posed by circumstances. Circumstances, the "who, what, when, where, why, how, and by what means" of a situation, "stand around the center of the case" which is constituted of maxims.[10] Circumstances both produce the case and help the decision maker to qualify judgments about a particular situation. Though variable, circumstances are embedded within social institutions that are, "if not immutable, at least relatively stable."[11] As Richard Miller notes, circumstances impinge upon our moral reasoning in ways that enable us to respond appropriately to a given situation.[12] In this way, variable circumstances alert us to the need for stability and moral action in complicated situations.

Sixth, casuistry is characterized by a de-emphasis on epistemic certainty. Casuistry stresses the certitude of practical conclusions rather than intrinsically convincing general rules or principles. As Klinefelter notes, "[This shift] deflect[s] the charge of moral hubris that is so frequently leveled against applied ethicists by skeptical philosophers, while at the same time it avoids the radical relativism and cynicism frequently associated with so-called market solutions to . . . practical problems."[13]

The concentration on practical judgments in moral deliberation can influence the mien and flow of moral deliberation. In their 1974 meeting with the National Commission for the Protection of Human Subjects of Biomedical and Behavioral Research, for example, Jonsen and Toulmin found that the concentration on practical conclusions helped commission members agree upon practical recommendations even though they did not necessarily agree on the reasons or principles underlying certain recommendations.[14] By concentrating on practical conclusions, commission members were able to get around the insurmountable problems associated with epistemological foundationalism. While members were not certain that their decisions fulfilled the requirements of a universal principle, they were fairly certain that their conclusions were valid. In casuistic deliberations then, just as in the commission meeting, epistemic certainty is de-emphasized in a process that ultimately seeks practical judgments about pressing moral issues.

Seventh, casuistry relies on cumulative arguments to persuade the listener of the correctness of a particular course of action. In casuistry, the justification of an opinion typically rests on relatively short arguments from a number of seemingly disparate sources. In business, for example, arguments may be derived from normative sources such as the company's mission statement, its code of conduct, or the laws that govern the business. These arguments will not strive to justify the overall merit of a particular norm. Rather, they will seek to convince (persuade) the listener of the overall merit of a particular course of action. Accordingly, argumentation will follow an inductive, almost rhetorical, sort of logic. Arguments will be stacked upon each other. They will be built up from small and varied sources. They will be layered like a pousse-café to deliver a punch more powerful than any argument used in isolation. In this way, a favored position may be established and listeners may be convinced to follow a particular course of action to resolve the dilemma at hand.[15]

Finally, casuistry is noted for its emphasis on the resolution of moral problems. Casuistry's goal is not the establishment of "formal proofs of a kind that can be judged by anyone with an eye for 'necessary connections.'"[16] Rather, casuistry's goal is to provide "advice about the moral licitness or permissibility of acting in one particular way or another."[17] Casuistry's primary objective is to lead people to practical conclusions that they can act upon—and casuistry insists that users do so.

DRAWBACKS

While casuistry has many positive attributes, it also has some important drawbacks. As others have noted, casuistry retains a stubborn reputation for advancing "[t]edious complexity, specious distinctions without difference, and rationalizing self-justification."[18] Casuistry's maxims, for example, can seem to be true, but may actually be false when applied to particular incidents. As noted earlier, casuistry's maxims can leave out important aspects of an argument and thereby mislead the user. Moreover, as John Arras points out, casuistry can suffer from ideological distortions and can lack a certain critical edge that may lead it "to ignore certain difficult but inescapable 'big questions' (e.g., 'What kind of society do we want?')."[19] Beside these tendencies toward laxity, casuistry can promote a certain conventionalism and can fail to question epistemic authority. In these and other ways, casuistry is seriously deficient.

Yet, despite these deficiencies, casuistry is a method that ordinary people can employ. It does not demand that decision makers become (or turn to) moral experts prior to making ethical judgments. In this way, by insisting that actual decision makers retain responsibility for their decisions, casuistry respects the moral deliberative capacities of those who actually must make ethical decisions. As a result, casuistry helps those who must make decisions overcome their reluctance to do so. Put simply, it encourages those who actually can make ethical decisions to do so when they otherwise might not or when they might be inclined to defer decision making to so-called moral experts.

In business, managers often resolve moral dilemmas through the use of cases. Although the cases and process of deliberation used here appear to be identical to those of other disciplines (bioethics, law, theology, and so forth), the business case and case method are fairly specific to business.

THE BUSINESS CASE

In general, the business case can be described as an open-ended construct designed "to give each individual student a practical and professional training suitable to the particular business he [or she] plans to enter."[20] While there is little agreement among case methodologists about the business case's proximity to reality, the business case has certain identifiable features.[21] Some of these features are listed in table 2.[22]

Table 2. Characteristics of a Business Case

1. A tool for deliberation
2. A vehicle for classroom discussion
3. A record of a real-life managerial dilemma
4. A clinical study of events
5. Focused on a specific time
6. Focused on particular facts
7. Emphasizes decision making
8. Short and lightly footnoted
9. Open-ended
10. Concerned with human relationships
11. Controversial and pertinent
12. A mini-drama, but "not just a story"

As is true of casuistry's cases, the business case is a tool for deliberation. Often it is a vehicle for classroom discussion. Typically, the business case is an account of a real-life situation, an in-depth exploration of an incident that is rich in detail. While it usually is based on firsthand experience, it may be derived from another's account.[23] Always, the business case is concrete rather than abstract and focused on the particular problems faced by managers.

Typically, the business case is short—usually fifteen to twenty pages in length—and lacks the heavy footnoting common in other disciplines (as in law, for example).[24] This brevity is attributable in part to the business case's "open-endedness." In general, the case is expected to be of sufficient length to describe a business problem without providing its solution.[25] At the same time, it must contain enough data to be useful. This means that certain cases will be more elaborate and lengthy than others. Due to the greater complexity of today's business situations and the tendency of publishers to demand that cases be scientifically and analytically rigorous, the trend of late has been toward lengthier cases.[26] Consequently, today's business cases vary in length with simple cases having only one issue and a sparse amount of material tending to be short and more complex cases with multiple issues (or issues that are not readily apparent) tending to be somewhat lengthy.[27]

While case length may vary, the content of the business case remains fundamentally about human relationships. This is so, as Charles Gragg pointed out years ago, because "business management is not a technical but a human matter. It turns upon an understanding of how people—producers, bankers, investors, sellers, consumers—will respond to specific business actions, and the behavior of such groups always is changing, rapidly or slowly."[28] Not unlike business management, the business case expresses a comprehension of the human responses at play in a particular situation. In essence, the business case is a mini-drama about people engaged in business management. It

Table 3. Case Types

1. Iceberg cases: those that offer a sample of a situation.
2. Predictive series of cases: those in which "the diagnosis and action recommended of the first case may be compared with the reality of the chronologically next case."
3. Multimedia cases: those that rely on audiovisual augmentation.
4. Living cases: those where "one or more executives are questioned by the class to discover the facts of the situation before analysis and action planning."
5. Focused decision cases: those where the decision to be made is fairly clear and the task is to analyze alternatives and decide the best course of action.
6. Unfocused decision cases: those where the task is to discover and define the problem and then decide the best course of action.
7. Implementation cases: those that include the question of how the favored decision is to be implemented, that is, who should say or do what to whom?
8. Appraisal cases: those where the immediate problem is not readily apparent and where one has to ask penetrating questions to uncover the assumptions, processes, and characteristics of the organization and situation that are under investigation.
9. Simple or complex cases: those that vary according to student capabilities and where they are used in a course of study.

is a narrative that synthesizes the seemingly disparate events that comprise a particular business situation. It is an action-drama and a fable. It recounts the actions of managers so others can understand how to act appropriately in similar situations. Accordingly, it can be grouped or "typed" according to the list in table 3.[29]

THE BUSINESS CASE METHOD

In the United States, business case usage typically follows the method developed at Harvard University's law and business schools in the late nineteenth and early twentieth centuries.[30] This so-called business case method, Arthur Dewing explains, involves the "class discussion of possibilities, probabilities, and expedients—the possibilities of the combinations of very intricate facts, the probabilities of human reactions, and the expedients most likely to bring about the responses in others that lead to a definite end."[31]

The purpose of the business case method is to help managers sharpen their analytical skills, enhance their ability to put order into unstructured situations, identify problems, develop conclusions, and recommend actions in complex business situations.[32] In line with these objectives, the case method encourages managers and students to develop the particular habits of discernment and other personal traits listed in table 4.[33]

Table 4. Case Method Objectives

1. Greater knowledge: helps individuals gain an understanding of a particular subject.
2. Technical expertise: provides a forum to practice and master particular analytic techniques.
3. Good habits of analysis: stimulates clear thinking, analysis, and curiosity so that these may become natural and automatic with time and practice.
4. Manager's perspective: encourages the broad, entrepreneurial, and administrative perspective essential to effective business management.
5. Problem-solving skills: helps individuals sharpen their analytical skills and ability to put order into unstructured situations and helps individuals identify problems, develop conclusions, and recommend actions in complex business situations.
6. Communication skills: facilitates communication and stresses the importance of good questioning in the analysis of business data.
7. Consensus-building: stimulates consensus in the face of individual differences.
8. Personal development: strengthens the individual's sense of internal security and facilitates leadership, assertiveness, personal responsibility, active learning, and a realistic assessment of one's own abilities and expertise.
9. Risk management: strengthens the ability to deal successfully with an unpredictable future.

In general, the case method challenges managers and students to become more curious and critical about the fine points of business. The case method helps people become more confident in handling business problems by allowing them to develop analytical skills within the context of a relatively nonthreatening environment. It assists users as they try to order unstructured situations, to identify problems, to develop conclusions, to effectively manage risk, and to recommend actions in complex business situations. In short, the business case method helps individuals learn the limits of their own assertiveness, personal responsibility, abilities, and expertise and helps them to develop specific leadership skills.

Another important aspect of the business case method is its emphasis on good communication. The case method stresses listening and verbalization. It challenges individuals to improve their interpersonal skills and helps people discover the importance of consensus-building and good questioning in the analysis of business data.[34]

Not surprisingly, most case method business schools stress student participation in class discussions. At the University of Virginia's Colgate Darden Graduate School of Business Administration, for example, students are graded on the basis of both the quantity and the quality of their input. The idea behind this grading system is to encourage students to speak and thereby enhance the students' understanding of the nuance of the narrative and the issues at hand. More important from a learning perspective, required participation encourages students to develop their interpersonal skills and to learn how to reach consensus about an acceptable course of action despite individual differences.

As Wallace Donham notes, a facility with case discussion gives students "a sense of internal security, assurance in their capacity to get on with people collaboratively and to deal successfully with the unpredictable future."[35]

THE BUSINESS CASE METHOD AND CASUISTRY

To a great extent, the business case method is not the relatively new phenomenon that business educators tend to think it is. As the history of casuistry shows, moralists have tackled business problems through the use of case-based reasoning for centuries. The issue of usury, for example, was a special problem for high-era casuists and businesspeople alike as money lending became important to the spread of mercantilism.[36] Indeed, as Keenan and Shannon and others have pointed out, many of the moral problems that we face today are not all that different from those of the past, for just as then we face

> the explosion of new data from an expanded vision of the world; a turn
> to the subject as singularly responsible to account for one's actions both
> religiously and ethically; the failure of existing principles to resolve satisfactorily urgent issues; and the inability to achieve consensus among moral
> thinkers, church and political leaders, and the general population.[37]

While certain of today's moral issues resemble those of casuistry's high-era, people today tend not to seek the counsel of confessors or itinerant casuist preachers as they did in the past. Today, people—managers, in particular—typically resolve moral problems on their own or in small groups. In doing so, they often use cases and adopt casuistic practices. The following section considers how the case method and casuistry overlap.

Similarities

As we have seen, the case method and casuistry are deliberative instruments that identify and explore the details of real situations. Both compare present circumstances to those of the past, both rely on cumulative arguments, and both strive to establish the high probability of judgments. In both, discussion and argumentation are not embraced as purely intellectual pursuits, but for their capacity to guide action. As a result, both methods emphasize practicality and stress probability over certainty. Neither attempts to establish "formal proofs of a kind that can be judged by anyone with an eye for 'necessary connections.'"[38] Rather, each strives to advise the user about the "licitness or permissibility of acting in one particular way or another."[39] The case method and casuistry are alike in other ways. Some of these similarities are listed in table 5.

Table 5. Similarities: The Case Method and Casuistry

1.	Instrumental: both are tools for deliberation.
2.	Account: both record actual events.
3.	Manifold: both are complex and consider the complications posed by situations.
4.	Facilitate: both rely on shortcuts to expedite reasoning.
5.	Comparative: both rely on objects of comparison: paradigms, analogies, and maxims.
6.	Precedence-seeking: both consider how prior dilemmas were resolved.
7.	Practical: both stress practical relevance.
8.	Cumulative: both gather arguments to support or rebut a position.
9.	Probability: both emphasize the probability rather than the certainty of judgments.
10.	Distill: both draw out the salient elements of a dilemma.
11.	Contextualize: both emphasize the social context and other environmental aspects of the dilemma.

As noted earlier, the business case method and casuistry are comparative processes. Although they do so differently, both rely on analogies, maxims, and paradigms in decision making. Typically, analogies, maxims, and paradigms are associated more with casuistry than with business, but in reality, managers rely on them just as much as casuists do.

In business meetings and disputes, for example, managers typically (often unknowingly) appeal to conventional culture-based maxims to introduce, support, or rebut their positions. A manager may use a "zinger" of a maxim, for instance, to get others' attention or to redirect a discussion. "We aim above the mark to hit the mark" or "A person who aims at nothing is sure to hit it" are two zingers that might be used to quell quibbling in a business meeting and redirect conversation to a higher plane. Similarly, Ralph Waldo Emerson's, "What you do speaks so loudly that I cannot hear what you say," or Spencer Ante's more humorous, "The road of good intentions is paved with Hell," can be effective in silencing someone holding forth in a meeting.[40] Maxims such as these effectively establish a speaker's presence and redirect discussion according to the speaker's wishes. They silence others, give the speaker time to flesh-out his or her argument, and channel the discussion according to the speaker's intentions.

The use of pithy sayings to persuade is important, too, to the advertisements, rallying cries, identifiers, and positional statements of companies, organizations, and industries. Avis's "We Try Harder" and Ford's "Quality Is Job #1" are examples of long-standing, industry-specific, code phrase–dependent advertisements that have been successfully institutionalized. Not only have they served these particular companies well, they have been adopted by the public and integrated into our regular discourse. Ford's "Quality Is Job #1," for instance, not only enlivened Ford's employees and customers about the prospect of that company's renewed commitment to customer service, it also inspired groups as widely divergent as the Association of American Medical

Colleges, Computerised Numerical Controls (India) Pvt. Ltd., and the rock band Propagandhi to consider their concerns with quality.[41]

In addition, as we saw, maxims help users distill complex notions and inspire and persuade people to act. Maxims are useful to business at a base level because they help managers save time. Managers operating under the gun, for example, typically eschew long and wordy deliberations in abstract and theoretical terms. They rely instead on maxims in the form of code phrases or brief statements to facilitate the flow of decisions as they "multitask" (talk on the phone, sign correspondence, give directions, keep mental profit ledgers, and so forth).

Similarly, managers are inclined to rely on business-specific paradigmatic cases in their decision making. Although not obvious or named as such, business-specific paradigmatic cases exist and can be located easily enough in the tables of contents of case-based texts. Business ethics texts are particularly noteworthy for their reliance on these cases.[42] There, we find Merck's experience with river blindness in Africa, Plasma International's response to the Nicaraguan disaster, Burroughs Wellcome's experience with Retrovir, Johnson and Johnson's experience with the cyanide tampering of Tylenol capsules, Ford's experience with the Pinto faulty fuel tank, and a host of other cases recounted over and over.[43] Although each rendering describes the case slightly differently, the incidents are nearly identical. In each, the situation is portrayed as complex while certain actions are portrayed as unambiguously right or wrong. Although they have not been named as such, cases such as these are, by virtue of their repeated use, longevity, and ability to represent right or wrong choices, de facto paradigmatic for business ethics. They, just as the cases of the era of high casuistry, effectively represent for business management "the most manifest breach . . . of the general principle, taken in its most obvious meaning."[44]

Differences

While the business case method and casuistry are alike in many ways, they are dissimilar in a few key areas. Some of these differences are listed in table 6.

Table 6. Differences: The Case Method and Casuistry

1. Case resolution: casuistry's cases are resolved; business's cases are typically open-ended or inconclusive.
2. Order: casuistry maintains a taxonomy of cases; business's cases float freely without order.
3. Nomination: casuistry's paradigm cases may be named such because agreement on an issue and its moral weight is possible within a particular culture; particular business cases may, in fact, be paradigmatic, but these cases are not named such because there is no naming body nor is there consensus about the specific content of cases.

First, the business case method and casuistry differ in terms of their conclusiveness. As we saw, one of the hallmarks of the business case is its "open-endedness" or lack of closure. While the business case contains all of the information necessary to make a decision, it typically does not reveal the actual decision rendered. Typically, it is written in such a way as to leave the impression that the incident is current and in need of the reader's decision. As a result, the reader is not informed about how the problem was actually resolved. Often, curious students will try to find out what happened in the end by doing their own research or by questioning knowledgeable contacts in the business world. As far as the case is concerned, however, what is important is not the resolution, but the issue(s) at hand and the elements that will enhance deliberation.

In casuistry, in contrast, touchstone cases are resolved or settled. For the casuist, settled cases—because they are settled—contain action-guiding prescriptions for fruitful deliberation about a present situation. They are sought out because they speak authoritatively and prescriptively about the moral worth (rectitude) of some past decision that bears likeness to the present. Little or no attempt is made to conflate the past case into the present. Instead, the settled case remains rooted in its earlier time frame and is drawn upon because of its ability to inform about some aspect of a current issue. Consequently, there is a back and forth interchange between the past and the present in casuistry. While there is admittedly a danger of misrepresenting the past here, casuistry's settled cases remain intact and obviously dated, but also lack the sort of conflation of the past into the present that occurs with the business case method.

Second, the business case method and casuistry differ in regard to the emphasis placed on order. Surprisingly, it is casuistry that is more ordered than business. As we have seen, casuistry insists on a taxonomy of cases where each settled case is categorized according to its ability to inform the user about right and wrong. The business case method, in contrast, has no such established taxonomy. Although some cases may be de facto paradigmatic, they are not categorized nor are they ordered according to their ability to inform about right and wrong. Lacking an established order, business cases simply float around in a cache of miscellaneous cases; that is, each case remains distinct from and unrelated to the others. This serves to diminish the overall effectiveness of business cases, for they become hard to find and difficult to use together.

Third and related to the issue of order, the business case method and casuistry differ in terms of their orientation to the naming of cases. In essence, casuistry's cases are named according to their moral content whereas business's cases are not.

Although case merchants such as Harvard Business School, Richard Ivey School of Business, Darden School of Business, INSEAD, the European Case

Clearing House, and others maintain good case databases, and while the Case On-Line Information System (COLIS) is an excellent web-based database search mechanism, cases are hard to locate in terms of their ethical content. Database search mechanisms rely on keywords, but the identifying words for cases tend to be company names, products, industries, dates, or meaningless general phrases such as "social responsibility" or "ethics." Cases are rarely coded for their specific moral content. A web-based search through COLIS, for example, reveals two cases under the topic of "stealing," four under the heading of "lying," and two under the heading of "cheating." In all instances, the words stealing, lying, and cheating were contained in the case titles, not the abstracts.[45]

Unless an author happens to entitle his or her case with an ethical code word, the case is likely to be lost in a collection of over fourteen thousand miscellaneous cases.[46] This lack of good case coding prevents the sort of casuistic deliberations described earlier. Without collation, cases cannot be arranged, paradigms cannot be named, and resemblances cannot be detected in the manner of casuistry. In short, without good coding of case content, casuistic deliberation has a difficult time getting off the ground.

The issue of case coding underscores the previously mentioned point about the ordering appropriate for business ethics cases. Whenever a case is coded, it is identified or listed according to some standard. When the author states that a case is about "stealing," for example, he or she admits to certain norms about proper claims to ownership, honesty, trustworthiness, and so forth. To ask for coding, then, is to ask authors or database maintainers to admit to some sort of order grounded in specific norms. This poses a difficulty for those who are unfamiliar with norms and those concerned with the specificity of norms.

At the very least, the suggestion of a taxonomy displeases those who view such systemization as a rigid, anti-intellectual, authoritarian thing of the past. A taxonomy, however, need not have any of these negative qualities. As the history of moral reasoning shows, the casuistries of the past were the products of changing mores and the finest minds of their ages. High-era Christian taxonomies, for example, changed enormously as the economy and population of Europe expanded during the thirteenth to eighteenth centuries. Shifts there were so profound that by the mid-sixteenth century, casuists largely abandoned manuals based on taxonomies with alphabetical arrangements for those based on the Ten Commandments or Seven Deadly Sins.[47] This shift in taxonomies continues to the present.

Today, moral taxonomies are alive and flourishing. Even the so-called old taxonomies of the Ten Commandments and Seven Deadly Sins continue to influence our thought and are, as the film *Se7en* attests, regularly updated and contextualized for contemporary consumption.[48] In this way, "modernized" old taxonomies continue to influence our private affairs and public judgments.

BRINGING CASUISTRY AND THE CASE METHOD TOGETHER

The lack of a taxonomy for business cases suggests that business management is immature in its use of cases. While it would be difficult to establish a single taxonomy for business cases (especially business ethics cases), the alternative of no taxonomy and the current miasma of discrete cases that float freely without imparting any sort of moral influence on users hardly seems preferable. If we were to adopt casuistic practices, what might we expect to achieve?

First, the adoption of casuistry's ordering mechanism might help us—and especially managers—become more efficient, productive, and confident in decision making. Casuistry's method gives clear direction to its users. It provides users with a map to cut through or accept ambiguity when making moral decisions. Adopting some form of casuistry will likely lead users to make stronger and more defensible moral decisions.

Second, the adoption of casuistry's bottom-up practice of deliberation might lessen the perceived isolation of managers charged with making tough decisions. As we saw, casuistry is a consensus-driven process of moral deliberation. Though it seems to be highly authoritarian, casuistry's moral authority ultimately rests (like the highly normative Ten Commandments) not in top-down edicts but in bottom-up consensual agreements.[49] Managers who use casuistic forms of deliberation, then, are likely to find support in others for their decisions. Although pluralism certainly introduces challenges to the exclusive use of one particular form of casuistry, Jonsen's and Toulmin's experiences with the National Commission for the Protection of Human Subjects, for example, attest to the fact that agreement can be achieved in pluralistic settings through the use of casuistry. It is this agreement that might well support managers in their decision making.

Third, the adoption of casuistic practices in case-based decision making might minimize the prevalence of stalemates borne of relativism. As we have seen, the case method originated at Harvard during the late nineteenth and early twentieth centuries. This was a period of great change in the U.S. Northeast. At that time and place, Protestant churches were exhausting themselves over disagreements concerning their identification with and adherence to creeds, religious-affiliated educational institutions were rapidly secularizing, and American Pragmatism was being formulated and promulgated throughout a tightly knit scholarly community. The business case method that emerged then and there reflects many of these and other social changes that were sweeping through American centers of learning.

Of all these social trends, Pragmatism's influence on the business case method cannot be overly stressed. Rooted in classical utilitarianism, Pragmatism embodies the can-do, matter-of-fact spirit of Americans unlike other philosophies. Pragmatism is especially noteworthy for its emphasis on action and its claim that truth is preeminently tested by the practical consequences of belief. While these are important qualities for philosophy, Pragmatism cannot be used alone to resolve all moral problems because it is sorely lacking in moral content. Chief among Pragmatism's deficiencies is its reliance on the practical as a test of truth that leads it to produce relativistic stalemates.

Casuistry, while severely limited in its own right, offers a content-rich way around relativistic impasses. Casuistry insists that decision makers consider things other than practicality and usefulness in deliberations. Its clear taxonomy helps users advance discussions toward more defensible conclusions. Its narratives (or truth-bearing cases) help facilitate a broader understanding of situations. For these and other reasons, casuistry complements or acts as an alternative to Pragmatism as a practical and case-based method for moral deliberation.

Fourth, the incorporation of certain casuistic practices in business case-based discussions might advance communication across academic disciplines. As we saw, casuistries are based on meaningful narratives (truth-bearing cases) reflective of collective notions of right and wrong. Casuistries emerge through the efforts of many, are reflective of particular cultures, and are not necessarily delimited by particular academic disciplines. When applied to business problems, casuistic inputs can be generated from a wide range of academic disciplines and can be sourced outside the realm of business. This enriches discussions immeasurably and more accurately reflects the overall values of society thereby strengthening the outcomes of decision making.

CONCLUSION

Although management's adoption of certain casuistic practices makes a certain amount of sense, implementation will not be achieved easily. If an effective taxonomy of cases for business is to emerge, we will have to come together to settle on the particular stories (cases) that hold meaning for us and we will have to agree on the cases that fit our criteria of paradigm. We will have to collectively review our prevalent maxims and analogies for accuracy and we will have to gather, code, and order our existing cache of cases for their more efficient and meaningful use.

While the proposed task is large, it is not insurmountable. With today's advanced technology, academic disciplines are easier to bridge, ethical and business language is more commonly held, and case databases are easier to use. As we have seen, our maxims have already crossed disciplines. We need only build upon what is already present in nascent form. The real challenge then, seems to be our willingness to engage this process and to marshal those among us who find casuistry to be a practically useful and meaningful tool for moral and managerial deliberation.

QUESTIONS FOR DISCUSSION

1. What is a paradigm case and how is it used in casuistry? From the cases you have studied in your class, do any stand out as possible paradigm case candidates?

2. Casuistry uses analogical reasoning processes to arrive at conclusions that are more or less probable, rather than logically certain ones like many other ethical methods. What are the advantages and disadvantages of this approach in comparison to others you have studied?

3. What is a maxim? Think of some of the cases you have studied. Are there maxims that can be derived from any of these cases? Have you studied any other ethical theory that utilizes maxims to help apply the theory?

4. Casuistry de-emphasizes the logical certainty of ethical conclusions and focuses more on the practical moral probability of taking certain options over others. How might this be an advantage, especially when analyzing cases that include particularly complex circumstances?

5. What does the author mean when he asserts that casuistry relies on cumulative arguments in order to persuade the listener of the correctness of a moral action? Choose a case you have studied in your class and attempt to argue cumulatively from a number of different and disparate sources. You can use ethical theories, practical reasoning, policy statements, legal precedent, probable outcome, and so on.

NOTES

1. Alasdair MacIntyre, *After Virtue: A Study in Moral Theory*, 2nd ed. (Notre Dame, IN: University of Notre Dame Press, 1984) and Albert R. Jonsen and Stephen Toulmin, *The Abuse of Casuistry: A History of Moral Reasoning* (Berkeley: University of California Press, 1988).

2. Jonsen and Toulmin, *Abuse of Casuistry*, 257.

3. For the Merck and Co. river blindness case, see "Miracle Worker," *Time* 130 (2 November 1987): 78; K. O. Hanson and S. Weiss, *Merck and Co., Inc.: Addressing Third-World Needs* (Cambridge, MA: Harvard Business School Publishing, 1991), 9-991-021 to 024; Thomas Donaldson and Patricia H. Werhane, *Ethical Issues in Business: A Philosophical Approach*, 6th ed. (Upper Saddle River, NJ: Prentice-Hall, 1999), 148–53; and Gerald F. Cavanagh, *American Business Values with International Perspectives*, 4th ed. (Upper Saddle River, NJ: Prentice-Hall, 1998), 235–36. For the Plasma International blood sales case, see T. W. Zinmerer and P. L. Preston, "Plasma International," in *Business and Society: Cases and Text*, ed. Robert D. Hay, Edmund R. Gray, and James E. Gates (Cincinnati: South-Western Publishing, 1976), reprinted with updated numbers in Donaldson and Werhane, *Ethical Issues in Business*, 119–20.

4. Albert R. Jonsen, "Casuistry: An Alternative or Complement to Principles?" *Kennedy Institute of Ethics Journal* 5, no. 3 (1995): 241.

5. Jonsen, "Casuistry: An Alternative or Complement," 241.

6. Jonsen and Toulmin, *Abuse of Casuistry*, 252.

7. Jonsen and Toulmin, *Abuse of Casuistry*, 86 and 252.

8. Donald S. Klinefelter, "How Is Applied Philosophy to Be Applied?" *Journal of Philosophy* 21 (1990): 19.

9. Jonsen and Toulmin, *Abuse of Casuistry*, 253.

10. Jonsen and Toulmin, *Abuse of Casuistry*, 253–54, and Jonsen, "Casuistry as Methodology in Clinical Ethics," *Theoretical Medicine* 12, no. 4 (1991): 298.

11. Jonsen, "Casuistry as Methodology in *Clinical Ethics*," 304.

12. Richard B. Miller suggests five ways that circumstances impinge upon moral reasoning in *Casuistry and Modern Ethics: A Poetics of Practical Reasoning* (Chicago: University of Chicago Press, 1996), 22–24.

13. Klinefelter, "How Is Applied Philosophy to Be Applied?" 20.

14. Jonsen and Toulmin, *Abuse of Casuistry*, 16–19.

15. Jonsen and Toulmin, *Abuse of Casuistry*, 255–56.

16. Jonsen and Toulmin, *Abuse of Casuistry*, 257.

17. Jonsen and Toulmin, *Abuse of Casuistry*, 256.

18. Jonsen, "Platonic Insults: Casuistical," *Common Knowledge* 2, no. 2 (Fall 1993): 52.

19. John D. Arras, "Getting Down to Cases: The Revival of Casuistry in Bioethics," *Journal of Medicine and Philosophy* 16 (1991): 48.

20. C. R. Christensen quoted in Craig C. Lundberg, "Case Method," in *Mastering Management Education: Innovations in Teaching Effectiveness*, ed. Charles M. Vance (Newbury Park, CA: Sage Publications, 1993), 45.

21. Although there seems to be agreement about the general characteristics of the business case, there is little consensus about the case's proximity to reality.

Lundberg, for one, distinguishes between "true" cases based on real experiences and "near cases" that are fictional accounts of particular situations. In the latter category, he includes sets of actual organizational data and instances derived from business articles, journals, and newspapers. In his view, research that "explore(s) or elucidate(s) some phenomenon of theoretic or pragmatic significance" of real situations may enhance classroom discussion, but such research cannot be considered to be on par with actual experience. Lundberg, "Case Method," 47.

William Rotch, for another, seems to care little for such distinctions. He asserts that business cases may be based on interviews or observation in the field, obtained from readily available published resources (newspapers, magazines, court records, government documents, and so forth), or derived from one's own experiences. Rotch, *Casewriting* (Charlottesville: University of Virginia Darden School Foundation, 1989, Rev. 1992), UVA-G-0364.

James W. Culliton adopts the middle position that "at times cases are written exclusively from published sources; but experience indicates that, by and large, they are not so satisfactory as cases secured in whole or in part from personal interviews." Culliton, "Writing Business Cases," in *The Case Method at the Harvard Business School: Papers by Present and Past Members of the Faculty and Staff,* ed. Malcolm P. McNair (New York: McGraw-Hill, 1954), 256.

22. The points in this table are sourced in the following: Point 2: P. Lawrence quoted in Vance, *Mastering Management Education,* 46. Point 3: Charles I. Gragg, "Because Wisdom Can't Be Told," in McNair, *Case Method at HBS* and quoted in Vance, *Mastering Management Education,* 46. Point 5: Rotch, unpublished casewriting workshop handout, 20 May 1996. Point 6: Robert F. Bruner and Katarina Paddack, "Case Writing Project Overview: The Transformation of Allied Signal," in Rotch, unpublished casewriting workshop handout. Point 7: J. A. Erskine, et al., quoted in Vance, *Mastering Management Education,* 47. Point 12: Derek Abell, "What Makes a Good Case?" *ECCHO* (Autumn/ Fall 1997): 4–7. Abell sites ten features of a good case. His recommendations follow:

1. Make sure it is a case and not just a story.
2. Make sure the case tackles a relevant, important issue.
3. Make sure the case provides a voyage of discovery—even some interesting surprises.
4. Make sure the case is controversial.
5. Make sure the case contains contrasts and comparisons.
6. Make sure the case provides currently useful generalizations.
7. Make sure the case has the data required to tackle the problem—not too many and not too few.
8. Make sure the case has a personal touch.
9. Make sure the case is well-structured and easy to read.
10. Make sure the case is short (no more than eight to ten pages).

23. As noted earlier, there is disagreement over whether true cases must be based solely on firsthand experience.

24. Michael Leenders and James Erskine suggest further that a good business case supports the adage, "if you can't say it in ten to fifteen pages, it's probably not worth saying." Michael R. Leenders and James A. Erskine, *Case Research: The Case Writing Process,* 2nd ed. (London, Ontario: Research and Publications Division, School of Business Administration, University of Western Ontario, 1978), 43. William Rotch backs up Leenders and Erskine in asserting that "many faculty believe seven pages of text is maximum." Rotch, casewriting workshop handout. The University of Virginia's Darden Case Production and Style Manual, moreover, recommends that case writers use appendixes rarely and that "bibliographies be added only if a case makes many

references to works of interest to a student." Mark Reisler, et al., "Darden Case Production and Style Manual," *in Academic Support Handbook 1994–1995* (Charlottesville, VA: Colgate Darden Graduate School of Business Administration, 1994), 24–25.

25. Leenders and Erskine observe that "the present committee at Harvard, which investigates the types and uses of case materials, is in general agreement not to include solutions." Leenders and Erskine, *Case Research*, 44.

26. To be published, case-based articles increasingly must not only persuade, they must also withstand the epistemic scrutiny proper to science. One academic business journal's article review sheet, for example, asks the reviewer whether or not the article in question manifests sound judgment based upon data and a measure of "scientific quality." While this requirement makes sense for scientific articles, it may not befit case-based articles. To the contrary, instead of strengthening case-based articles, this requirement may weaken these sorts of articles by relegating the cases therein to the status of examples. In emphasizing principles or points of argument in a manner befitting science, abstraction is emphasized and cases become mere illustrations of theories. This changes the case's function, demotes the case, and undermines the role of narrative in argumentation. In the end, the scientific requirement weakens an instrument that expresses human relationships that are not quantifiable but nevertheless fundamental to business.

27. Leenders and Erskine affirm this notion when they observe that "during the past ten years cases have been getting longer [and] [t]he content is becoming more complex and the descriptions more elaborate." Leenders and Erskine, *Case Research*, 45.

28. Gragg, "Because Wisdom Can't Be Told," 7. Note: originally published in 1940.

29. The first four points are from Lundberg, "Case Method," 49. The fifth to ninth points are from Rotch, casewriting workshop handout.

30. For excellent summaries of the early history of the business case method, see Tom L. Beauchamp, ed., *Case Studies in Business, Society, and Ethics*, 4th ed. (Upper Saddle River, NJ: Prentice-Hall, 1998); Melvin T. Copeland, "The Genesis of the Case Method in Business Instruction," in McNair, *Case Method at HBS*, 25–33; and Louis B. Barnes, C. Roland Christensen, and Abby J. Hansen, *Teaching and the Case Method: Texts, Cases, and Readings* (Boston, MA: Harvard Business School Press, 1994), 38–50.

31. Arthur Stone Dewing, "An Introduction to the Use of Cases," in McNair, *Case Method at HBS*, 4.

32. Rotch, casewriting workshop handout.

33. Points 1–4: Rotch, *Casewriting*, UVA-G-0364. Points 5–7: Rotch, casewriting workshop handout. Point 8: Casewriting and casewriting workshop handout. Point 9: Wallace B. Donham, "The Case Method in College Teaching of Social Science," in McNair, *Case Method at HBS*, 245.

34. Rotch, casewriting workshop handout.

35. Donham, "The Case Method in College Teaching of Social Science," 245.

36. Jonsen and Toulmin point out that "from the eleventh to the eighteenth century, the problem of usury exercised the finest theological and canonical minds." Jonsen and Toulmin, *Abuse of Casuistry*, 181.

During this time, the very definition of usury changed from the Middle Ages' "where more is asked than is given" to St. Alphonsus Ligouri's (1696–1787) "interest taken where there is no just title to profit." Toulmin, *Abuse of Casuistry*, 193.

37. James F. Keenan, S.J. and Thomas A. Shannon, "Introduction," in *The Context of Casuistry* (Washington, DC: Georgetown University Press, 1995), xvi.

38. Jonsen and Toulmin, *Abuse of Casuistry*, 257.

39. Jonsen and Toulmin, *Abuse of Casuistry*, 256.

40. Ralph Waldo Emerson, "We aim above the mark to hit the mark" and "What you do speaks so loudly that I cannot hear what you say"; Anonymous, "A person who aims at nothing is sure to hit it"; and Spencer Ante, "The road of good intentions is paved with Hell," all available at http://ww.quoteland.com.

41. Gina Shaw, "Quality Is Job One, Says Presidential Commission," *AAMC Reporter*, May 1998, available at http://aamc.org/newsroom/reporter/may98/quality.htm; Computerised Numerical Controls (India) Pvt. Ltd., "Quality Is Job #1," available at http://www.india-pulse.com/cnc/quality.html; and Propagandhi, Where Quality Is Job #1, Recess Records, 1994, available at http://www.fatwreck.com/pgh/wherequa.htm.

42. Here, "business ethics" includes social issues in management and business, government, and society.

43. For the Merck and Co. river blindness case, see Donaldson and Werhane, *Ethical Issues in Business*, 148–53, and Cavanagh, *American Business Values with International Perspectives*, 235–36.

For the Plasma International blood sales case, see Zimmerer and Preston, "Plasma International," reprinted with updated numbers in Donaldson and Werhane, *Ethical Issues in Business*, 119–20.

For the Burroughs Wellcome and AZT case, see W. Emmons and A. Nimgade, *Burroughs Wellcome and AZT* (Cambridge, MA: Harvard Business School Publishing, 1993), 9-792-004, 9-793-114, and 9-793-115; Jeanne M. Liedtka, *Burroughs Wellcome and the Pricing of AZT* (Charlottesville: University of Virginia Darden School Foundation, 1993), UVA-E-0081; and Beauchamp, *Case Studies in Business, Society, and Ethics*, 235–43.

For the Johnson and Johnson Tylenol case, see Richard T. DeGeorge, *Business Ethics*, 5th ed. (Upper Saddle River, NJ: Prentice-Hall, 1999), 3–5; Rogene A. Buchholz, *Fundamental Concepts and Problems in Business Ethics* (Englewood Cliffs, NJ: Prentice-Hall, 1989), 212–32; and Cavanagh, *American Business Values*, 237–38.

For the Ford Pinto case, see W. Michael Hoffman, "The Ford Pinto," in *Business Ethics: Readings and Cases in Corporate Morality*, 3rd ed., ed. Hoffman and Robert E. Frederick (New York: McGraw-Hill, 1995), 552–59; Manuel G. Velasquez, *Business Ethics: Concepts and Cases*, 4th ed. (Upper Saddle River, NJ: Prentice-Hall, 1998), 71–72, 73–74, 76, 81–82, 119; DeGeorge, *Business Ethics*, 40–241; "Ethical Responsibilities of Engineers in Large Organizations: The Pinto Case," in *Ethical Theory and Business*, 4th ed., ed. Tom L. Beauchamp and Norman E. Bowie (Upper Saddle River, NJ: Prentice-Hall, 1993), 130–37; and Buchholz, *Fundamental Concepts*, 167–69.

For a complete analysis of the various Ford Pinto cases, see Werhane, "The Rashomon Effect," in *Perspectives in Business Ethics*, ed. Laura Pincus and Edwin M. Hartman (Chicago: McGraw Hill, 1998), 189–97.

44. Jonsen and Toulmin, *Abuse of Casuistry*, 252.

45. The COLIS web search mechanism can be found at through the European Case Clearing House website at http://www.ecch.cranfield.ac.uk.

46. The COLIS electronic library contains abstracts of over fourteen thousand cases studies and supplementary materials from the world's major case producing centers. See "What We Do" at http://www.ecch.cranfield.ac.uk.

47. Jonsen and Toulmin, *Abuse of Casuistry*, 251.

48. An extremely violent Oscar-nominated film, *Se7en* (a.k.a. *Seven*, 1995) tells the story of two homicide detectives' hunt for a serial killer who justifies his crimes as absolution for the world's ignorance of the Seven Deadly Sins. Akin to the Sword of God, the serial killer chooses seven victims who represent egregious examples of each sin (gluttony, greed, sloth, envy, wrath, pride, and lust). "Seven deadly sins. Seven ways to die. Seven ways to kill"—so the movie's promotional material states. Quote and plot summaries from IMDb database at http://us.imdb.com.

From the villain's applied principles viewpoint, each killing is an illustration of a manifest breach of what is considered to be good and right. However, from the detectives' viewpoint, each murder is an exercise in casuistry. The detectives must first figure out the killer's modus operandi (MO). The seasoned and cultured detective eventually researches the Seven Deadly Sins in an effort to understand the killer's MO. Once the MO (the killer's taxonomy) is established, the detectives can begin to search for resemblances to past crimes for clues to where the killer will strike next.

While the story line of pattern killing and problem solving through the use of resemblances is typical of detective stories, *Se7en* is interesting because it relies on a distinctive taxonomy (the Seven Deadly Sins) and shows how casuistry works. Most important, the overall method used in *Se7en* illustrates the sort of inductive method that is not present in business ethics today.

49. The Ten Commandments (Exod. 20:1–21), the point-by-point set of rules given to Moses by God, are often thought to be the ultimate set of top-down prescriptive norms for Jews and Christians. In reality, however, they are summary statements. They are not so much God's terse first principles to people as they are God's concluding expressions of love and commitment by God for His chosen people (the Jews).

Why is this so? Consider the history leading up to the effective establishment of the Ten Commandments. The commandments were delivered to the Jews after a period of slavery and liberation from the Egyptian pharaoh. They were given to the Jews after a prolonged relationship with Yahweh. However, even though God issued them, the Jews did not accept them at first. Instead, the Jews apostatized (Exod. 32:1–6). Moses then broke the commandment-bearing tablets in anger (Exod. 32:15–35). Afterward, lacking God's protection and care, the Jews suffered. They lamented when they realized that Yahweh was no longer with them (Exod. 33:1–6). Eventually, they returned to Yahweh who reaffirmed His passionate commitment to them through the remaking of the Covenant (Exod. 34:1–35). Through this back-and-forth process on the part of the Jews, the Jews learned to cherish and accept God's steadfast love for them as expressed in the norms of the Decalogue (Exod. 35–end). In today's terminology, God's principles became actualized (and God's love was accepted) only after a period of experimentation on the part of the Jews, that is, after a bottom-up process of discovery had been completed. Bruce M. Metzger and Roland E. Murphy, *The New Oxford Annotated Bible* (New York: Oxford University Press, 1977).

Part II

RELIGIOUS APPROACHES TO ECONOMIC LIFE

• 8 •

The Brave New World of Business Ethics?

Laura L. Nash

From a Christian perspective, Laura L. Nash reflects on the evolving role of faith in a global marketplace that has been so fundamentally transformed by information technologies. Christianity, especially its Protestant variety, had a profound influence on the hearts and minds of those who were pioneers in the earliest capitalist enterprises. Professor Nash examines what resources Christians bring to the table in the context of today's enormous fast-paced and high-tech markets. She concludes by offering the reader four "avenues" to help business leaders view faith not as a source of ready-made answers to ethical conundrums, but as a process that should constantly and actively intrude on their consciousness.

Gabriel's horn signaling the millennium is no longer a single trumpet blast, but thousands of networked pundits worrying about business, society, and the deeper meaning of current changes in economic life. One of the most pressing of these soul searches concentrates on the state of business ethics. The businessperson who seeks to do right faces a brave new cyberworld where none of the familiar moral reinforcements are stable. So many products with no previous history, newly minted mergers of businesses with no common culture, and no fixed geographic locality to answer to as neighbor.

Columnist James Burke suggests in his bit of punditry for *Forbes ASAP* that there are only two things we can count on in the future: first, a "great convergence" of information technology generating massive fragmentation of knowledge that will lead to "an innovative surge unlike any that went before," and second, a society totally unprepared for the effects of these changes.

Nowhere can we expect more rapid change than at business institutions. How prepared are business leaders to respond from a sufficiently humane and enlightened standpoint? Will Christianity make a difference in their preparation and ethical expertise?

The future is already here: Supermarkets are taking up banking; corporate mailrooms are turning into retail outlets as employees order goods through their office computers; whole office complexes are being abandoned in favor of teleconferencing among the "road warriors"; computer-to-computer transactions are conducted entirely without benefit of human "interference"—until Mrs. McGillicuddy discovers herself the proud recipient of four thousand tons of soybeans on her doorstep due to an erroneous keystroke during her daily e-trades!

What do obligation and responsibility mean in a world where traditional moral touchstones are undone by business innovation? One thing is certain: The current moral infrastructure is not secure enough to support these changes. Property rights, interpersonal trust, regulatory oversight, institutional loyalty, and long-standing reputation are all under spontaneous reconstruction. What role will Christian faith—by definition based on timeless truths—play in this new world that seems to leapfrog over history with startling speed? The short answer: It depends.

As familiar ethical reinforcements crumble and well-intentioned ethics programs lag behind new business conditions, faith will arguably take a more central role as moral navigator to the concerned. Already there is growing interest in spirituality (including the ethical assumptions that go along with spiritual revival) as a resource to business rather than a sidebar. But the distinctive aspects of Christianity in its many forms will only influence business to the degree that the faith can be seen to engage the new questions of business and society in practical, diverse ways.

There is an ironic dimness to our information pool on religion and business, despite the obvious history of Protestant dominion over earlier economic eras. Long relegated to one's private thoughts or seen as standing over and against business, Christianity has only recently come out of the closet as a force to be taken seriously and deliberately inside the workplace. First came the conservative Christians seeking to resurrect the sacred canopy in the marketplace. Many are in smaller companies whose founder/CEO breached the secular beachhead through the power of personal ownership. Some have aggressively dedicated their businesses to Jesus as a public statement of conviction. They advertise this commitment openly in corporate communications and seek to construct a corporate culture that replicates the language of the Bible. Some represent terrible business practices, playing on people's religious faith to push poor products and questionable financial schemes.

Many, however, are excellent companies, like ServiceMaster or the R. W. Beckett Corporation. Holding diverse political views and dedicating their businesses to the glory of God, they seek to establish a place for explicitly Christian values within mainstream business without silencing other forms of religious or agnostic faith. As business globalizes, these tensions are intensifying. One can only applaud those leaders who are keenly sensitive to the religious diversity within their own companies, who wrestle with the twin desires of ensuring freedom of expression and making a clear statement about their own commitments.

These evangelicals are somewhat of a surprise to the larger business culture, which tends to associate marketplace references to Jesus with hucksterism. On the contrary, ServiceMaster has been in *Fortune*'s top-10 service companies for a number of years, occupying the top slot in 1999. R. W. Beckett's quality and reliability have been legendary, as has its progressive parental-leave policies. Others lead in community outreach. For example, Paul Kuck, head of Regal Marine, has been extremely active in Chuck Colson's Prison Fellowship program, which has increasingly concentrated on job-skill preparation (including educational and emotional skills) as part of its mission.

They are not alone. There are many concrete examples of evangelical CEOs bringing their faith into practice. The lesson is not that Christian belief leads to a uniform stand on employee policies or corporate citizenship. Rather, faith sustains a tension of values around competition and service that stands in alignment with creative, dignifying forces rather than destructive exploitation.

The second major wave of religious resuscitation in business today is comprised of the many people professing many forms of Christian faith who feel that their religion should be personally relevant to their own decisions, the relationships they form, and the institutional structures they promote through business activity. They do not want to wear religion on their sleeve, nor are they satisfied with a faith that only issues political or economic directives.

In this search for religious relevance and deeper spirituality, many businesspeople are going it alone, convinced their churches are irrationally hostile to business or ignorant of the roles and responsibilities that go with the territory. They point to preaching that contains impossibly utopian economic views, as well as discriminatory policies and financial irregularities within church administrations and in faith-based organizations—and conclude the church is unqualified to discuss best practices in the business community. Even when these business leaders are close to their pastors on a personal level, their conversations rarely penetrate the realms in which they, as businesspeople, daily operate.

When the church does address business through social action, its activities are typically focused on negative actions: boycotts and demands for withdrawal from business activity. What the businesspeople seek is a perspective that will help them create solutions. As one CEO commented, "I'd like to do things differently, but it is not an option for me to adopt a strategy that suspends all the rules of capitalism and depends on charity to create a financially viable business. Can't my church offer something to say that doesn't put me out of business?"

For contrast, the oft-scorned secular spirituality programs have captured the imagination and conscience of millions of businesspeople. These programs position spiritual and ethical conviction as an addition to business thinking, not a negation of it.

The great information convergence raises acute questions as to how Christians and other people of conscience will retain a robust moral perspective in the face of new dimensions of scale and fragmentation. The megamergers in telecommunications are only the beginning of a general reordering that has already thrown compensation systems, organizational loyalties, and even market pricing mechanisms completely out of whack. Managers, who must think globally in order to capitalize on innovative potential, risk losing their sensitivity to the human scale. If you imagine the view of Earth from a spaceship, the problem becomes vivid: no people in the picture. Ethics and faith demand recovery of one's connectedness to people, whether or not they have a market affiliation.

However, the number one concern from businesspeople on all parts of the Christian spectrum (and from many non-Christians) is not about a particular issue but about how to exercise moral authority as a business leader. What are the proper parameters to religious belief in deciding what's right for oneself and in representing what's right for the corporation as a whole?

Some try to prepare themselves through ethical discussions, which tend to concentrate on decision-point problems. "Golden parachute" retirement packages while 5 percent of the workforce is laid off? Locate plants overseas and employ the desperately poor or stay in Middletown, USA? Fast-track employees recruited as the best and the brightest, but seemingly without conscience? They are right to see these as Christian concerns. But how can these "concerns" be brought down to ground zero in the daily decisions and policies of a business manager?

After endless unresolved debates at seminars and retreats for businesspeople, the greatest contribution believers will make to the transformation of business ethics is not captured in a policy question. Rather, faith will make its greatest contribution as a process—an active, intrusive force in the businessperson's consciousness.

This process can be engaged in the business realm in many ways. Below are four "first-level" avenues that will provoke the dynamics of faith as a process. Deeper questions of relation to God are raised by these avenues, connected like the networks we anticipate in more secular settings.

1. Articulation

There is ample evidence that business leaders need to signal the basic values of their faith more clearly. How many times have you been surprised to hear a devout Christian business leader publicly explain the company's adherence to the Golden Rule exclusively in terms of its economic good sense? This is a poor leadership strategy for inspiring ethical behavior in the marketplace, which depends on deeper convictions that drive the process of following the Golden Rule. When leaders fail to acknowledge this process, they morally shortchange their own corporate culture.

I am reminded of a recent *New Yorker* cartoon in which a couple is viewing an ultramodern painting. The woman barks, "If you can't say anything, would you at least exude something?" The cartoon advice holds good for businesspeople. If you feel religion is better expressed in a secularized form in the workplace, could you at least exude the moral impulse? Clearly we need to work on acceptable strategies and language for capturing the process of faith amidst a diverse group of people.

2. Personalization

Christianity can be a deep source of personalizing the increasingly de-personalized face of business. The convictions that every person is sacred and that human relations define values carry an impetus to deliberately notice the human factor in decisions and act upon it.

3. Valuing Details

In a religiously anchored consciousness, details have special moral meaning. Often the macrorepresentation of a business fails to capture the spirit of a corporate culture, while a small detail—such as how people are greeted says volumes about the value placed on people. In the current glamorization of global viewpoints, details are particularly devalued. Lawsuits blow up when "the system" fails to notice discriminatory practices that start in little exchanges between employees. Reviving a sensitivity to detail is itself a potentially dignifying process and a service to others.

4. Life Creation

The central, hopeful message of Christianity is life found even in the face of death. When businesspeople see their decisions and responsibilities as a process of life creation, many of the most dead-end ethical debates experience a breakthrough. Problems of scarce resources are met by demanding innovation of oneself, rather than finessing a deal or a political win. A life-creation mindset not only disturbs the believer out of accepting (or exploiting) the status quo, it offers the possibility of joy in one's working life. It is the heart of another Christian value: stewardship.

By seeing faith as a process, the businessperson finds new resources for exerting moral leadership in the workplace. Even those who are reluctant to apply specific religious, political, or economic positions in a business setting can tap into the dynamics of faith and share the process with others. Faith cannot produce a seamless web between Christian values and the marketplace, but the process of faith can help strengthen the connections between Christian social ethics and business.

QUESTIONS FOR DISCUSSION

1. What do obligation and responsibility mean in a world where traditional moral touchstones are undone by business innovation?

2. What role will religious faith—by definition based on timeless truths—play in this new world that seems to leapfrog over history with startling speed?

3. What are the proper parameters to religious belief in deciding what's right for oneself and in representing what's right for the corporation as a whole?

4. Can religion offer advice to businesspeople that doesn't put them out of business? Can religion offer recommendations to businesspeople that are both true to spiritual ideals and which can be practically implemented?

5. How might business leaders go about articulating the religious motivations that inspire many of their decisions without alienating those around them?

6. Why is personalization important in a business setting?

7. What sorts of values can religious traditions bring into a business setting that are both inspiring and helpful for the basic goals of enterprise?

8. How can a business leader engage in a process of life creation? What sorts of actions and policies might this entail?

· 9 ·

Business Ethics after MacIntyre

Dennis McCann and M. L. Brownsberger

British philosopher Alasdair MacIntyre has wielded an enormous influence in the field of ethics during the past twenty-five years. Since the publication of his seminal work, *After Virtue*, many ethicists have found it necessary to take account of his critique of modern systems of morality. MacIntyre's approach is based upon an attempt to recover the idea of virtue as rooted in social practices, which are in turn associated with institutions and traditions. In this essay, Dennis McCann and M. L. Brownsberger attempt to take account of MacIntyre's critique in order to argue in favor of the idea that management is a morally significant social practice that is deserving of careful ethical scrutiny. Using the work of management guru Peter Drucker, they argue that management is indeed a social practice that may allow businesses to be understood as social institutions in which virtue may be cultivated and in which human moral excellence is to be sought and expected.

 $\mathcal{A}$ lasdair MacIntyre's *After Virtue* has proved to be quite effective in undermining the claims of those ahistorical forms of moral philosophy typically referred to as "the standard account of morality."[1] In challenging the authority of the standard account, MacIntyre thus has become the ally of religious ethicists who find their own concerns almost entirely neglected by contemporary moral philosophy. Indeed, MacIntyre's accomplishment is not simply critical; he has also outlined a constructive program for developing an ethic of virtue that is open to the moral wisdom of various religious traditions. Such a program, however, may be a costly one. For in exposing the pretended universality of standard moral philosophy, MacIntyre may have exaggerated the problems of moral discourse in a pluralistic society so grossly as to render the potential contributions of any religious tradition irrelevant except to parochial gatherings of the faithful. Our task, however, is not to assess the overall philosophical adequacy of MacIntyre's program. Most of the reservations that we would raise are already expressed and dealt with impressively in Jeffrey Stout's *Ethics after Babel*.[2] Rather than simply echo what Stout has already done, we propose to test the adequacy of MacIntyre's constructive program in an important area of "applied" moral philosophy, business ethics.

Business ethics is a crucial test of MacIntyre's program because, in our view, business ethics focuses on the practice of management. The alleged moral bankruptcy of bureaucratic management, however, serves as a central premise of MacIntyre's denunciation of modern liberalism. Along with the therapist, it functions as the dominant model of character to which, in MacIntyre's view, educated persons conform their public lives in a modern society. We assume that those sympathetic to the therapeutic model are capable of defending themselves; our concern, however, is with MacIntyre's substantive views of management. For, if he is right about the moral meaning of management, then any program in business ethics that regards the current system of business enterprise as a viable context in which to practice the subtleties of moral discernment must be regarded as itself morally bankrupt. This conclusion follows, even if the proposed program of business ethics accepts MacIntyre's critique of contemporary moral philosophy and therefore develops its insights on some other basis than the standard account of morality. In order to set aside this conclusion in favor of a more benign view of management, we must come to grips with MacIntyre's normative understanding of a "social practice." For if some organized activity cannot be regarded as a social practice, then the processes of character formation and tradition-oriented ethical reflection that he describes cannot be cultivated within it. Or, if such processes are organized within an activity that falls below the minimum moral requirements of a social practice, then their yield will not be virtuous but only a tawdry imitation of virtue. In what follows, we accept the burden of giving reasons why business management may plausibly be regarded, on MacIntyre's own terms, as a social practice.

Clarifying the moral status of management is a necessary condition for doing business ethics after MacIntyre, but it is not sufficient. MacIntyre's suspicions regarding business enterprise in general must also be confronted, for he projects a consistently negative attitude toward not just the institutions of specifically modern capitalism, but also toward any form of market-oriented economic activity. Here the source of the problem lies deeper than the residual influence of Marxism on MacIntyre's views of modern society. It involves an uncritical assimilation of Aristotle's own prejudices against commerce. MacIntyre's intensive reading of Aristotle in the early chapters of *Whose Justice? Which Rationality?* is especially revealing.[3] For MacIntyre appears to endorse

Aristotle's view that injustice is virtually synonymous with a life devoted to moneymaking. MacIntyre is not alone in accepting Aristotle's prejudice; nevertheless, if business ethics is to be developed on a neo-Aristotelian basis, both MacIntyre and Aristotle need to be corrected by a more discerning interpretation of both the limits and the possibilities of a just market system. We therefore will challenge Aristotle's view of *pleonexia* ("simple acquisitiveness," according to MacIntyre) and its relationship to the actual practices of business management.

In what follows, then, we will consider, first, whether, on MacIntyre's own terms, managing a business can be considered a social practice; second, we will review MacIntyre on Aristotle's account of moneymaking as a way of life, and will explain why it is an inadequate basis for rendering a moral judgment on the system of business institutions as a whole. Having cleared away these substantive obstacles to a neo-Aristotelian program in business ethics, we will, third, suggest the outlines of such a program by showing how our conversation with MacIntyre has helped clarify a "theocentric" approach to business. Finally, throughout this presentation we're assuming that MacIntyre's enduring contribution to religious ethics is most likely to develop neither at the individual nor at the societal level, but at the intermediate level at which institutions like churches and synagogues, colleges and universities, labor unions, the whole range of business enterprises, and other forms of voluntary association flourish. The sheer scale of such voluntary activity as well as the intricacies of the interrelationships among these forms of association, however, require precisely the system of liberal political institutions and the ideological support of a liberal social philosophy that MacIntyre is wont to despise.

BUSINESS AS A SOCIAL PRACTICE?

First, let us consider whether business management can be considered, on MacIntyre's terms, a social practice. In order to answer this question, we must attend to his definitions of a social practice. The term is introduced systematically in his chapter on "The Nature of the Virtues" in *After Virtue*:

> By a "practice" I am going to mean any coherent and complex form of socially established cooperative human activity through which goods internal to that form of activity are realized in the course of trying to achieve those standards of excellence which are appropriate to, and partially definitive of, that form of activity, with the result that human powers to achieve excellence, and human conceptions of the ends and goods involved are systematically extended.[4]

In order to count as a practice, the activity in question must be socially established and cooperative; it must be governed by standards of excellence that are constitutive, at least partially, of the activity itself; and it must yield "internal goods" by meeting these standards of excellence. The definition implies an indispensable connection between virtue and social practices: "A virtue is an acquired human quality the possession and exercise of which tends to enable us to achieve those goods which are internal to practices and the lack of which effectively prevents us from achieving any such goods."[5] Thus, virtues are cultivated in the context of social practices: They are the habits that help us achieve the internal goods that an authentic social practice ought to produce.

Clearly, MacIntyre's is a normative theory of social practices. Not all human activities will meet his stipulations, but for different reasons: "Planting turnips is not a practice; farming is." Presumably, the difference is that planting turnips or anything else is but an element in a practice, an activity whose purpose can only be understood by placing it in the context of an integrated whole, in this case, farming. So, some activities are ruled out as practices because they are parts, but not wholes. On the other hand, as MacIntyre insists, "practices are not to be confused with institutions":

> Chess, physics and medicine are practices; chess clubs, laboratories, universities and hospitals are institutions. Institutions are characteristically and necessarily concerned with what I have called external goods. They are involved in acquiring money and other material goods; they are structured in terms of power and status, and they distribute money, power and status as rewards. Nor could they do otherwise if they are to sustain not only themselves but also the practices of which they are the bearers. For no practices can survive for any length of time unsustained by institutions.[6]

Institutions differ from the practices which they sustain in two ways: (1) Institutions characteristically generate "external goods," while genuine social practices are focused on internal goods. (2) Though institutions therefore organize the resources necessary for social practices, social practices are also thereby rendered vulnerable to the "corrupting power of institutions."

Clearly, there is a lack of symmetry in the relationship between institutions and social practices, as there is between external and internal goods. The problem of corruption, in both cases, seems to run only one way. It is easy to see why this would be the case in MacIntyre's view, when we consider his examples of the two types of goods. Throughout the discussion in *After Virtue*, justice, courage, and truthfulness are listed as goods internal to social practices, while money, power, and status are external goods provided by institutions.[7] Though MacIntyre is quick to affirm the desirability of such external goods and readily concedes that successful performance in the various practices is often rewarded with them, he must insist at the same time that external goods are a threat to virtue:

> Yet notoriously the cultivation of truthfulness, justice and courage will often, the world being what it contingently is, bar us from being rich or famous or powerful. Thus although we may hope that we can not only achieve the standards of excellence and the internal goods of certain practices by possessing the virtues and become rich, famous and powerful, the virtues are always a potential stumbling block to this comfortable ambition. We should therefore expect that, if in a particular society the pursuit of external goods were to become dominant, the concept of the virtues might suffer attrition and then perhaps something near total collapse, although simulacra might abound.[8]

This last observation, of course, nicely summarizes MacIntyre's view of the moral consequences of liberal modernity. We will return to it later as one striking indication of just how deeply MacIntyre's reservations about bureaucratic management and business enterprise are rooted in his general theory of virtue.

Though he has all but identified moral virtue with social practices, MacIntyre considers the possibility that there may be some practices that simply are evil. He tends to dismiss this possibility, but his reflections demonstrate that, in his view, what secures the virtuousness of social practices is their fit within a larger account of the moral life as a whole. There must be some telos to human life, a vision anticipating the moral unity of life, given in the form of a narrative history that has meaning within a particular community's traditions; otherwise the various internal goods generated by the range of social practices will remain in disorder. Without a community's shared sense of telos, there will be no way of signifying "the overriding good" by which various internal goods may be ranked and evaluated. The most significant indication of this shared understanding of an overriding good is the existence of a virtue—MacIntyre calls it "integrity or constancy"—which "cannot be specified at all except with reference to the wholeness of human life."[9] Social practices thus can be relied upon to instruct us in virtue to the extent that they possess the integrity that stems from the community's recognition of the telos that gives meaning to the moral life as a whole.

If managing a business is to be evaluated discerningly in terms of MacIntyre's theory of social practices, we must press him for further clarification of his understanding of the relationship between social practices and institutions. On a first reading, MacIntyre seems to suggest not only that a business enterprise could never be anything but an institution producing and distributing external goods, but also that there is no virtue, but only the threat

of corruption, inherent in managing such institutions. By paying careful attention, however, to MacIntyre's remarks on the virtue of justice, we can detect
the outlines of a more nuanced perspective. Even in *After Virtue*, MacIntyre
recognizes both the moral necessity of institutions and their power of corruption. In explaining their necessity, however, he must evoke the characteristics
of a social practice: "the making and sustaining of forms of human community—and therefore of institution . . . stands in a peculiarly close relationship
to the exercise of the virtues."[10] Indeed, the proper ordering of institutions requires the exercise of the virtue of justice, conceived in an Aristotelian fashion:
"For the ability of a practice to retain its integrity will depend on the way in
which the virtues can be and are exercised in sustaining the institutional forms
which are the social bearers of the practice."[11] So it is that institutions in some
sense are capable of promoting virtue, though perhaps not as unequivocally as
social practices seem to be.

When we turn to MacIntyre's later work, *Whose Justice? Which Rationality?*, this account is modified only slightly. Though this book has a narrower
focus than *After Virtue*, it unfolds as a historical, rather than systematic argument. The notion of social practice is not developed any further, though
MacIntyre may have helped clarify its function in his remarks on a particular
culture's "structures of normality": "[B]y making it unnecessary for almost
everybody almost all the time to provide justifications for what they are doing
or are about to do, they relieve us of what would otherwise be an intolerable
burden."[12] Besides challenging us with standards of excellence, social practices
thus lead us to virtue by making the pursuit of the relevant internal good so
habitual that normally we don't have to think about it. Despite MacIntyre's silence about social practices, we must pause to consider the more recent book's
abandonment of *After Virtue*'s distinction between external and internal goods.
In its place, based on the Homeric discernment of two related dimensions of
arete, "to excel" and "to win," he distinguishes between "goods of excellence"
and "goods of effectiveness," which still bear the moral contrast asserted in the
previous pair.[13] The change in categories is not explained, but unless MacIntyre
was simply trying to be more faithful to Greek tradition, he may have recognized that the distinction between internal and external goods is too relative to
shifting contexts to carry the moral burden that he tried to assign to it.[14]

Similarly, the moral contrast between social practices and institutions,
based on this distinction, is no longer featured in *Whose Justice? Which Rationality?* Once again, in trying to interpret MacIntyre's silences, we must keep in
mind that the later work is less systematic than *After Virtue*. Nevertheless, the
later work gives evidence of a deeper, more penetrating reading of Aristotle,
in which the relationship between justice and politics is fully understood. As
MacIntyre observes:

The only form of community which could provide itself with such a standard would be one whose members structured their common life in terms of a form of activity whose specific goal was to integrate within itself, so far as possible, all those other forms of activity practiced by its members and so to create and sustain as its specific goal that form of life within which to the greatest possible degree the goods of each practice could be enjoyed as well as those goods which are the external rewards of excellence. The name given by Greeks to this form of activity was "politics," and the polis was the institution whose concern was, not with this or that particular good, but with human good as such, and not with desert or achievement in respect of particular practices, but with desert and achievement as such.[15]

Justice, in other words, is characteristic of institutions, rather than the social practices within them; for justice is the appropriate activity of political coordination by which particular goods are ordered to the community's vision of an overriding or common good.

We are now in a position to ask where managing a business fits within MacIntyre's normative theory of social practices. A business enterprise, like a chess club or a university, is clearly an institution. But is managing such an institution a social practice? Furthermore, could not management be conceived as exercising a function analogous in businesses to that represented, as in the previous paragraph, by politics? Though a full answer to these questions is not possible until we confront MacIntyre's attitude toward commerce generally, a preliminary answer can be had by comparing moral descriptions of contemporary business management with MacIntyre's notion of a social practice. Is the fit between the two sufficiently plausible to set aside MacIntyre's own description of management? We think that it is.

THE PRACTICE OF MANAGEMENT

What, then, is business management? In order to explore this question, we find it useful to consider Peter Drucker's classic normative statement, *The Practice of Management*, which will give us reasons for accepting management as a social practice.[16] Drucker's approach is systematic, and Aristotelian in form, if not in substantive judgment. He defines management broadly as "the dynamic, life-giving element in every business,"[17] as the "specfically economic organ of an industrial society," whose functions are: (1) economic performance: "managing a business," (2) the transformation of human and material resources: "managing managers," and (3) organization of productive activities: "managing workers and work."[18] Each of these three functions structures a major area of Drucker's statement as a whole.

The first function, economic performance, recognizes the specific difference between a business enterprise and other institutions serving society. Given the fundamental and pervasive fact of scarcity, business enterprises are specifically designed to organize as efficiently as possible the human and material resources required for the production and distribution of economic goods.[19] The purpose of a business, however, is "to create a customer";[20] it is not to make a profit, though profit clearly is "the test of [the] validity" of this institution's activities.[21] Drucker's way of defining economic performance as transactions creating a relationship between market institutions and their customers is important for what it implies regarding the limits of business ethics. First of all, it suggests that the moral meaning of business management is contingent upon society's general attitude toward the marketplace: The purpose of a business is unintelligible apart from the market system that defines the scope of its activities. Second, by understanding this purpose relationally, that is, as an activity constitutive of customers and suppliers, it opens up the possibility that managing such an activity could be regarded as a social practice, on the one hand, if the telos of society, the common good, is furthered through such activity, and, on the other hand, if the practice of management can succeed in this purpose only by achieving the internal good appropriate to it. Third, by recognizing the profit motive not as the purpose of a business but as the test by which economic performance is measured, it implies that, at least in Drucker's view, the external good is subordinate to the internal good, as it would have to be, were managing a business to count as a social practice.

When we turn to Drucker's other two functions of business, this pattern of teleological definition is confirmed; furthermore, his specific observations on "managing managers" and "managing workers and work" suggests not only that business management could be a social practice but that it must be such, if managers are to succeed even in meeting their employers' economic goals. It is clear that Drucker's approach to human resources is anything but manipulative, in MacIntyre's sense of managerial "effectiveness." Drucker regards every employee as potentially a manager, and he hopes to achieve a state of industrial organization in which "self-control" or self-management is the normal condition. Such a scheme requires "responsible workers" whose potential contributions can be actualized if their supervisors learn to motivate them through "careful placement, high standards of performance, providing the worker with the information needed to control himself [sic], and with opportunities for participation that will give him [sic] a managerial vision."[22] Here the policies that Drucker advocates seem to presuppose that there is an institutionally significant distinction between effectiveness based on manipulation and that based on informed consent. Though he is careful to point out the limits to worker participation in managerial decision-making processes, he insists that the only way to increase the productivity of human resources over the long term is to manage them for mutual accountability.[23]

Finally, there is Drucker's insistence upon the indispensable link between managerial success and personal integrity:

> One can learn certain skills in managing people, for instance, the skill to lead a conference or to conduct an interview. One can set down practices that are conducive to development—in the structure of the relationship between manager and subordinate, in a promotion system, in the rewards and incentives of an organization. But when all is said and done, developing men [*sic*] still requires a basic quality in the manager which cannot be created by supplying skills or by emphasizing the importance of the task. It requires integrity of character. . . .
>
> It may be argued that every occupation—the doctor, the lawyer, the grocer—requires integrity. But there is a difference. The manager lives with the people he [*sic*] manages, he decides what their work is to be, he directs it, he trains them for it, he appraises it and, often, he decides their future. The relationship between a merchant and a customer, professional man and client requires honorable dealings. Being a manager, though, is more like being a parent, or a teacher. And in these relationships honorable dealings are not enough; personal integrity is of the essence.[24]

Such integrity, however, is not the result of taking courses in business ethics. Drucker argues that here is "one qualification that the manager cannot acquire but must bring with him [*sic*]." Rather than counting against our view that managing a business is a social practice, we understand Drucker to be saying that the telos that ought to govern the activities of managers lies beyond the scope of management itself. At the same time, however, Drucker insists that ultimately the task of management is educative: "The one contribution he [*sic*] is uniquely expected to make is to give others vision and ability to perform. It is vision and moral responsibility that, in the last analysis, define the manager."[25]

This brief outline of Drucker's interpretation of the practice of management fails to do it justice, for it is in the details of the analysis that his vision of the moral meaning of management becomes plausible, descriptively as well as normatively. Nevertheless, what little we have presented of his thought should be a sufficient basis from which to infer Drucker's response to our question: Is management a social practice, in MacIntyre's sense of the term? "How could it not be a social practice?" might be Drucker's reply. Analytically, we might press him to specify the internal good that is achieved by the practice of management. His answer, we infer, would be "service," understood as a form of empowerment. Nevertheless, Drucker's view of the manager's internal responsibilities suggests a view of service that is not completely symmetrical with the one operative in the business's external relationship of service to its customers.

In their internal operations, managers serve their fellow employees by helping them to become participants in a cooperative endeavor whose scope would have remained beyond the capacities of any of them, considered as individuals. Clearly, Drucker's assumptions regarding this type of managerial empowerment involve normative beliefs about human nature and the common good not significantly different from those that inform MacIntyre's neo-Aristotelian perspective. They also, not surprisingly, seem to have anticipated, in substance, if not in terminology, the perspective on human work currently advocated by Catholic social teaching.[26] Where Drucker parts company with MacIntyre and, to some extent, Catholic social teaching, is in his understanding of the form of empowerment operative in the ultimate purpose of business enterprise, namely, creating a customer. For his questions—"What is our business?" and "Who is the customer?"—are answered by appealing to consumer sovereignty rather than an overriding notion of the common good. Both questions determine the specific meaning of the service a business provides by asking what the customer actually values and whether the business is capable of fulfilling those expectations profitably, rather than by reflecting on what is intrinsically good either for the customer or for society as a whole.[27] Managers serve customers, in short, by empowering them to decide for themselves what the meaning of the good life may be, subject to the constraints imposed by law and the limits of their financial resources. Such a view of consumer sovereignty is hardly indefensible, but it does rest upon arguments of the philosophically liberal type, concerning a just market system, that MacIntyre disparages. As a result, any strict analogy between management and Aristotelian politics breaks down at this point. Nevertheless, despite the lack of symmetry in Drucker's understanding of the meaning of service, we believe that it does represent a genuine internal good, whose moral characteristics entitle us to qualify managing a business as a social practice.

VICE AND VIRTUE IN THE PRACTICE OF BUSINESS

Let us turn briefly to the larger question, as it is unfolded in MacIntyre's endorsement of Aristotle's critique of moneymaking laid out primarily in Book I of *The Politics*. It is not our view that MacIntyre has misunderstood Aristotle. Aristotle, indeed, does regard trade or moneymaking to be unnatural and therefore immoral. But we also think that MacIntyre's appeal to Aristotle on economic questions is seriously undercut to the extent that he fails to consider the way in which slavery figures in Aristotle's alternative to commerce, as part of the "natural" pattern of acquiring goods. Obviously, two wrongs don't make a right; and perhaps our alternatives are broader than either modern managerial capitalism or the slavery regarded as indispensable to the prosperous Greek *oikos*. Our focus here, however, is limited to MacIntyre's interpretation of the place of moneymaking in the good life. Does Aristotle's view of *pleonexia* ("simple acquisitiveness") adequately describe the basic motive for going into business, with the result that managing a business, no matter how enlightened the management, inevitably must fail to meet the moral standards implicit in MacIntyre's notion of a social practice? We think not; and here are our reasons why.

First of all, we have no quarrel with MacIntyre's conclusion that simple acquisitiveness, that is, "acting so as to have more as such," when pursued to the exclusion of all the other purposes that together constitute the good life, is a vice, and inevitably an offense against justice.[28] The question, for us at least, is whether such acquisitiveness can be identified with the structural imperative of successful economic performance that is, as Drucker insists, the essence of a business enterprise. Can simple acquisitiveness account for the situation that MacIntyre apparently regards as typical of business management, that is, the structural pathology in which a desire for external goods (or the "goods of effectiveness") completely overshadows a person or a group's presumably natural affinity for internal goods (or the "goods of excellence")? We are skeptical about both the explanation and just how typical this pathology is among business managers.

Secondly, if MacIntyre is right about *pleonexia*, then Drucker is necessarily wrong about the limited role of "profit" in explaining the purpose of a business. We think that Drucker is right, though some economists, such as Milton Friedman, who fancy themselves the defenders of "free enterprise," seem to defend the notion that the only sufficient motive for business activity is "profit-maximization."[29] To the extent that these views are coherent, they seem to point to the fact that within the discipline of neoclassical economics there are no theoretical limits to the pursuit of higher profits. But, as Drucker insists, certain practical constraints are operative, to the extent that the firm wishes to remain in business.[30] For "profit-maximization," when pushed to the limit, would entail a complete sell-off of business assets without which the firm can hardly remain in business. The next balance sheet might look impressive; but it would also be the last one the firm will ever issue. Drucker's nuanced view of the role of profit relative to the purposes of a business enterprise, therefore, cannot be dismissed as an idealist's special pleading. If management is to fulfill those purposes, its practices cannot be motivated by *pleonexia*.

Thus, if profit is merely the standard by which an enterprise's success in meeting its objectives is measured, then not only is the so-called profit motive only marginally relevant for explaining managerial behavior, but it can hardly be identified with MacIntyre's simple acquisitiveness. Nevertheless, we believe, thirdly, that the appearance of a connection between the two is so impressive that we must explain the simulacrum of vice, if you will, inherent in common perceptions of profit. We believe that, though this explanation does point to a serious systemic challenge to our view of business management as a social practice, it also completely disqualifies Aristotle's interpretation of commerce as a basis for understanding the moral meaning of managing a business.

In order to advance this argument, let us ask ourselves what is the actual context in which profit functions as a measure of successful business performance. This measurement is unlike the rating systems used to measure the performance of athletic teams, such as the coaches' poll for the fictive "National Championship" in collegiate football. Though a school's ranking in such ratings may have a significant impact on its ability to attract a range of external goods, including unrestricted endowment funds, the standard of measurement itself is not calibrated in such goods. The profits reported in a business's quarterly report, however, are stated as quantities of real money, which are disbursed to those investors who have title to them through some sort of shareholding. Among its customary moral obligations, management has a fiduciary responsibility to these shareholders, the ultimate owners of the enterprise, to maximize the return on their investment, consistent with the overall objectives of the business. The simulacrum of simple acquisitiveness is explained, we believe, by the fact that there is, in the nature of the case, no fixed standard of profitability. Managers are confronted, instead, with the volatility of our increasingly competitive capital markets, dominated by institutional investors whose own fiduciary responsibilities apparently commit them to short-term strategies for managing investments that are in competition with one another. As a result, business managers can never rest content with the secure knowledge that, with regard to their own firm's profitability, enough is enough. The dynamics of the capital markets in which businesses compete for investors may change virtually overnight, and a rate of return that was sufficient to attract investors in one set of circumstances may no longer be competitive.[31] What may appear to the outside observer as either greed or, in MacIntyre's terms, "acting so as to have more as such," seems just as plausibly explained by the understandable anxiety that managers must experience in trying to chart reasonable goals for the firm while coping with the basic instabilities of the capital markets.

We are not asserting, therefore, that business managers are entirely innocent of simple acquisitiveness. An insightful characterization of the moral situation should be more realistic than that. It would affirm, along with Reinhold Niebuhr, that just as sin, generally, is an inevitable but hardly necessary outcome of the basic anxiety provoked by our experience of finitude and freedom,[32] so something like the vice of *pleonexia* may well result from a manager's protracted struggle to still the anxiety produced by the uncertainties of securing a business's finances. We insist, however, that such irresponsible behavior is not a necessary consequence of managing a business's finances; it is just that in the ordinary course of business here is where *pleonexia* is most likely to take root.

If this analysis of the so-called profit motive is on target then, as we've indicated, the challenge that it represents for the practice of management is a systemic one. Drucker, you will recall, wisely counsels managers to seek a balance among the various objectives of a business, including its performance for shareholders; and this balance, he repeatedly insists, finally rests upon the moral and intellectual integrity of management. He also notes that integrity can neither be taught to managers nor produced by them; inasmuch as they must bring it with them to business, it remains beyond a business's capacity to control.

Our analysis suggests that the likelihood of achieving this balance may depend upon still another factor not entirely within management's control, namely, the firm's vulnerability to the vicissitudes of the capital markets. To the extent that the volatility of these markets directly contributes to a demoralizing instability in business management, their current mode of operations is a systemic obstacle to actualizing Drucker's vision of management as a social practice. A significant part of the challenge represented by managing a business today involves overcoming this obstacle. Nor are plausible approaches to this challenge lacking, even though the operations of the capital markets are beyond the capacities of any single business or group of businesses to control. Among the strategies seeking to enhance the stability of management are taking a company private by buying back its outstanding stock and/or initiating employee stock ownership plans in which the firm increasingly is owned by those who work for it.[33] Since such strategies can only succeed in particular cases, a truly systemic overhaul of the regulatory framework in which our capital markets operate may be required for the common good.

ARISTOTELIAN CONCEPTIONS OF COMMERCE

Whatever the precise solution to the problem of enhancing the stability of business management, our analysis clearly indicates the irrelevance of Aristotle's view of commerce, at least in its classical form. However comforting it may have been to MacIntyre, Aristotle's declaration that moneymaking is to be despised as an "unnatural" way to obtain wealth is simply innocent of any true understanding of business economics. The interest paid to lenders, contrary to Aristotle, should be regarded as a "user fee" for capital. The accumulation of savings is socially necessary, for without it there can be no investment, and without investment over the long run the level of business activity is likely to

stagnate and society's living standards fall. To receive a return on one's investment is to be compensated for the opportunities foreclosed by trusting one's
savings to this enterprise rather than to another. There is nothing inherently
unnatural about profiting from the productivity of money, unless all the strategies designed to produce an increase of goods or economic growth are also
suspect morally. Aristotle forgets that money saved and invested is still just as
much a means of exchange as money spent on some good to be used or con-
sumed immediately.

We could extend our critique of Aristotle into the area of comparative
economic systems and ask ourselves which basic strategy of allocation best
serves the common good; but the debate about the relative merits of capitalism versus socialism for all practical purposes was brought to an end by the
processes of economic and social change unleashed in Eastern Europe by
Mikhail Gorbachev. Abraham Lincoln may have played a similar role in concluding the debate over capitalism versus slavery over a century ago. At any
rate, by ignoring what history and experience have to tell us about the actual
performance characteristics of various economic systems, MacIntyre tends to
moralize Aristotle's argument, with the result that our righteous desire to avoid
the vice of *pleonexia* becomes an excuse for not investigating very carefully the
moral meaning of the social practices upon which the welfare of the community inevitably depends. Neither Aristotle nor MacIntyre, to conclude, give us
sufficient reason for thinking that commerce is any less moral than any of the
other organized activities that constitute our public world. The playing field,
upon which the perennial struggle between vice and virtue unfolds, is just as
level in business management as it is in religion, education, politics, medicine,
or any other social practice we care to imagine.

If those formal characteristics of an ethic of managerial responsibility are
best understood by examining the origins of the concept of public responsibility in *The Federalist Papers*, and the seven institutional conditions for responsibility we extrapolated from Herbert Spiro's *Responsibility in Government: Theory
and Practice* which, in our view, are applicable to all forms of bureaucratically
organized activity. Furthermore, we still find it useful, on a formal level, to note
three general areas of responsibility, those related to one's role or professional
identity (role responsibility), to one's loyalty to the institution with which one
is associated (institutional responsibility), and to those civic obligations implied
in one's membership in the political community (social responsibility), in order
to seek an appropriate balance among them in situations where they conflict
as well as overlap one another. Nevertheless, precisely because these dimensions of the ethic of responsibility remain abstractly general, we also insisted
on construing business dealings specifically, in order to confirm whether our
notion of responsibility is relevant to business ethics.

This current reading of MacIntyre and Drucker, we believe, contributes most effectively to the effort to construe business dealings. Business is a form of voluntary association, which like all voluntary associations is differentiated according to its "medium of exchange." Although all forms of voluntary association necessarily have an economic dimension insofar as all are held to the constraints of a budget, businesses are distinctive in that their purpose is economic as such. The motive for doing business is to make money, and all the other good things achieved by a business are consequences of making money. Indeed, a detailed reading of our previous paper[34] might suggest that, in order to assert that business is a social practice, we have been forced to abandon the construal of business that we held earlier. Again, we think the truth lies in a different direction.

The neo-Aristotelian theory of social practices makes it possible to concretize the ethic of responsibility in business, but only on the condition that what MacIntyre calls the internal good, which is always substantive, can plausibly be identified. Furthermore, for this view of business to be regarded as likely, the internal good identified must represent a genuine constituent of the common good and not simply a simulacrum of it. When asked to state what the purpose of a business is, however, most people may say, offhandedly, that it is "to make money" rather than "to create a customer," or that the latter is merely a means to the former. Drucker's insistence on precisely the opposite conclusion is not a convenient exercise in verbal gymnastics, but a true ordering of the actual causes of business activities. In order to reconcile our own previous speculation on this matter with the position outlined here, as well as to answer the common opinion, we now find it necessary to construe business in terms of the neo-Aristotelian understanding of causality. This move, we believe, is inherent in the task of understanding business management as a social practice.

Traditionally, Aristotle is understood to have asserted four dimensions to causality: the material and formal causes of an object or act, its efficient cause, and its final cause. Students of theology may recall the most familiar examples of this analysis. In the sacrament of baptism, for example, the pouring of water or the initiate's immersion in it would be the material cause; the actual words of baptism, the formal cause; the initiate's desire to become a member of the Christian community, the efficient cause; and the unfolding of the divine life of grace, the final cause. The final cause, of course, signifies the ultimate telos of the act, which is constitutive of the other three causal dimensions and without which they are unintelligible. Were we to extend this pattern of analysis to business activity in general, the material cause might be the products marketed by the firm; the formal cause, the actual exchange of goods or services for money, as signfied in a bill of sale, or promissory note, with all the institutional mechanisms in place that facilitate the actual exchange; the efficient cause, for both parties to the exchange, would be the desire to be better off—for business, specifically, the profit motive; and the final cause, for the business at least, would be to actualize that kind of market relationship or association that Drucker refers to as creating a customer. Here, too, without the final cause, creating a customer, business activity is unintelligible, and if it remains unintelligible to those managing the business, it is likely to be mismanaged.

MANAGEMENT AND STEWARDSHIP

Were we to demonstrate in detail a religious orientation to business ethics, consistent with the neo-Aristotelian point of departure we've outlined in this chapter, we would organize our remarks around the theme of stewardship as a fitting response to the manager's vocation. Along with Gustafson and his conversation partner from the business world, Elmer Johnson, we would interpret stewardship in a theocentric perspective which confesses that business organizations themselves, in principle, like all human institutions, are aspects of "divine governance" in the world.[35] Such an "in principle" affirmation needs to be specified concretely in terms of an appropriately religious construal of the economic purpose of business organizations, which may require developing the kind of theological interpretation of economic scarcity as inherent in God's activity of creation, such as McCann has suggested elsewhere.[36] Were this proposal to be accepted, the way would be open toward understanding business management as stewardship in dynamic and transformative terms that are closer to Max Stackhouse's recent work than to Gustafson and Johnson.[37] By thus answering the question of what God is doing in business, Drucker's analysis of the practice of management can be appropriated to spell out the orientations entailed by the business manager's vocation of stewardship.

A fresh perspective on stewardship and vocation hardly exhausts a religious approach to business ethics, but it does provide an adequate theological orientation to management conceived as a social practice. Consistent with MacIntyre's proposals, such an approach would develop business ethics with less emphasis on courses that fit into the curricula of college and university programs, and more on facilitating mentoring relationships and a sense of communal tradition within business organizations themselves. Senior managers who understood their stewardship responsibilities, we believe, would welcome the opportunity to assist in the professional development of their younger colleagues by helping to envision properly the social practice of management. The communal moral traditions that distinguish one business organization from another would become a matter of common concern, encouraged through processes of open reflection and critical conversation structured into the ordinary course of business activity.[38]

The common understanding of the specific purposes of the business might find formal articulation in a corporate "credo," whose seriousness is demonstrated by its role in ordering the criteria by which individual and group performance are evaluated and rewarded within the firm. These strategies for doing business ethics within the firm have already been tested here and there in various businesses. Our proposal for understanding management as a social practice merely offers a framework for ordering them more coherently.

CONCLUSION

Let us conclude this essay by returning to the problem of pluralism inherent in advocating a religious approach to business ethics. As we mentioned in our introduction, both to this chapter and its predecessor, the major advantage claimed for doing business ethics on the basis of the standard account of morality is that it avoids the problem of pluralism allegedly created by appeal to religious warrants in moral argument. Part of MacIntyre's appeal is that he demolishes the claim of modern moral philosophy to deliver an approach to morality upon which all rational agents can agree. In order to advance the discussion of business ethics after MacIntyre, we are forced, as our remarks clearly demonstrate, to make substantive claims embedded in social practices and communal traditions about which moral disagreement may be interminable. Such an approach might yield a critical conversation with Drucker's perspective on management, but isn't the problem exacerbated by incorporating that perspective into an explicitly theocentric construal of reality? We don't think so; but in order to demonstrate why it isn't so, we would have to exhibit a fully developed theological model of business ethics and show how it would tend to enhance the internal conversation in business organizations rather than further inhibit it. Such a project is well beyond the scope of this chapter, but were it to be carried out, we do anticipate that the relevant model would be that of a public theology and, MacIntyre to the contrary notwithstanding, the public institutional framework would be conceived as liberal. Business ethics after MacIntyre is possible if, and only if, MacIntyre's neo-Aristotelian theory of virtue cultivated within social practices can be detached from his idealizing nostalgia for the Greek polis and grafted onto an unjaundiced view of the opportunities for communal existence opened up by characteristically modern forms of voluntary association. Business organizations are but one of those forms of association.

QUESTIONS FOR DISCUSSION

1. What is a social practice according to MacIntyre? How are social practices related to institutions? What kinds of things do and do not qualify as social practices? Why must social practices be oriented to "intrinsic," but not "extrinsic" goods? What difficulties does this create for business ethics, according to MacIntyre and Brownstein?

2. How is the conception of justice related to social practices? How is this related to questions of the common good?

3. What, according to Peter Drucker, is the purpose of a business? How is this purpose related to the profit motive?

4. Is management a social practice? How does a manager's relationship to his employees reflect elements of MacIntyre's conception of a social practice, according to McCann and Brownberger? Must management be manipulative in order to be effective? Why or why not?

5. What is the connection between management and personal integrity according to Drucker? How does this contrast with MacIntyre's conception of management in modern society? Is it possible to be a "virtuous" manager?

6. What difficulties are there in an Aristotelian conception of business enterprise, according to McCann and Brownberger? Should business be regarded as "simple acquisitiveness"? Why or why not? What difficulties are there in an economic theory rooted in "profit maximization," according to McCann and Brownberger?

7. What are the three areas of managerial responsibility identified by McCann and Brownberger? Do you agree that these are genuine responsibilities? Why or why not?

NOTES

1. Alasdair MacIntyre, *After Virtue* (Notre Dame, IN: Notre Dame University Press, 1981).

2. Jeffrey Stout, *Ethics after Babel* (Boston: Beacon Press, 1988).

3. Alasdair MacIntyre, *Whose Justice? Which Rationality?* (Notre Dame, IN: Notre Dame University Press, 1988).

4. MacIntyre, *After Virtue*, 175.

5. MacIntyre, *After Virtue*, 178.

6. MacIntyre, *After Virtue*, 181.

7. MacIntyre, *After Virtue*, 181.

8. MacIntyre, *After Virtue*, 183.

9. MacIntyre, *After Virtue*, 189.

10. MacIntyre, *After Virtue*, 181.

11. MacIntyre, *After Virtue*, 182.

12. MacIntyre, *Whose Justice? Which Rationality?*, 25.

13. MacIntyre, *Whose Justice? Which Rationality?*, 32.

14. MacIntyre's shift to a distinction between "goods of excellence" and "goods of effectiveness" may also be a reflection of his inability to specify the type of good achieved by the management of institutions. M. L. Brownsberger has taken up this point in MacIntyre's theory and proposed a third category, namely, "opportunity goods," in order to describe the characteristic achievement of institutions relative to social practices. His proposal is sketched in an unpublished paper, "Ethos, Incarnation, and Responsibility: A Field Encompassing Model for Clergy Ethics," done for the Clergy Ethics Study Group, sponsored by the Park Ridge Center, March 5, 1989.

15. MacIntyre, *Whose Justice? Which Rationality?*, 33–34.

16. Peter Drucker, *The Practice of Management* (New York: Harper & Row, 1954).

17. Drucker, *Practice of Management*, 3.

18. Drucker, *Practice of Management*, 6–17.

19. The question of economic scarcity deserves fresh theological examination. Dennis P. McCann has tried to understand scarcity as part of Creation, rather than the Fall, in an unpublished paper, "The Unconstrained Vision of Pope John Paul II," done for a conference on Catholic social teaching, sponsored by the Center for Ethics and Religious Values in Business, University of Notre Dame, April 24–26, 1989.

20. Drucker, *Practice of Management*, 37.

21. Drucker, *Practice of Management*, 35.

22. Drucker, *Practice of Management*, 304.

23. Drucker, *Practice of Management*, 365.

24. Drucker, *Practice of Management*, 348–49.

25. Drucker, *Practice of Management*, 350.

26. Drucker's concept of management as an organ of the business enterprise as a whole entails regarding all persons working for the business as, in principle, managers, insofar as all of them must be responsible, however minimally, for their own actions. The effect of this view is to collapse the distinction between management and labor, as Drucker himself seems prepared to admit, when envisioning a situation in which all a firm's employees will be managers. The same tendency is evident in his definition of management as a form of self-control. For similar tendencies in Catholic social teaching, see Pope John Paul II's encyclical, *Laborem Exercens*, which, in arguing for the priority of labor over capital, regards all employees, including managers, as labor (par. 12). The American Catholic bishops' pastoral letter, *Economic Justice for All: Catholic Social Teaching and the U.S. Economy*, seems to advocate a similarly collaborative and inclusive view of work, especially in its chapter on "A New American Experiment: Partnership for the Public Good" (pars. 298–306).

27. Drucker, *Practice of Management*, 54–61.

28. MacIntyre, *Whose Justice? Which Rationality?* 111.

29. Cf. Milton Friedman, "The Social Responsibility of Business Is to Increase Its Profits," *New York Times Magazine*, September 13, 1970. Note that even Friedman's

position recognizes the practical constraint on profit maximization represented by civil and criminal law.

30. Drucker, *Practice of Management*, 35–36.

31. The relatively high rates of real interest throughout the 1980s helped to exacerbate the anxiety level for most business managers. With the cost of capital remaining relatively high, managers are forced to promise higher rates of return. Such promises add to the pressures toward a "bottom-line" orientation that distorts the balance of business objectives that Drucker advocates. The current struggles between institutional investors and management teams for control of various publicly held corporations is another symptom of the instability that will tend to demoralize management. Similar results are apparent from the unusual levels of leveraged buyout activity that only recently seem to have peaked. For an informed discussion of the relationship between financial markets and other businesses, as well as various attempts to assess the morality of financial markets, see the symposium edited by Oliver Williams, Frank Reilly, and John Houck, *Ethics and the Investment Industry* (Savage, MD: Rowman and Littlefield, 1989). Among other things, this volume contains Dennis McCann's essay, "The 'Accursed Internationalism' of Finance: Coping with the Resources of Catholic Social Teaching" (127–47).

32. Cf. Dennis McCann, *Christian Realism and Liberation Theology* (Maryknoll, NY: Orbis Books, 1981), 55–62.

33. For an explanation of employee stock ownership plans (ESOPs) and other strategies designed to expand the ownership of American business, see Stuart M. Speiser's *Ethical Economics and the Faith Community* (Bloomington, IN: Meyer and Stone, 1989).

34. Dennis McCann and M. L. Brownsberger, "Management as a Social Practice: Rethinking Business Ethics after MacIntyre," *Annual of the Society of Christian Ethics* (Collegeville, MN: Society of Christian Ethics, 1990): 223–45.

35. We have come to recognize that the view of business ethics in a theocentric perspective that we are advocating is substantially similar to that outlined by James M. Gustafson and Elmer W. Johnson, "The Corporate Leader and the Ethical Resources of Religion: A Dialogue," which appeared in the symposium edited by Oliver Williams and John Houck, *The Judeo-Christian Vision and the Modern Corporation* (Notre Dame, IN: University of Notre Dame Press, 1982). The differences between them are a matter of emphasis: ours is upon the structural dynamics of business organizations; theirs, upon the personal characteristics of those who manage such organizations.

36. See note 19.

37. Max Stackhouse's approach to business ethics can be inferred from his essay, *Public Theology and Political Economy: Christian Stewardship in Modern Society* (Grand Rapids, MI: Wm. B. Eerdmans, 1987).

38. Such processes of critical conversation have already been implemented in some not-for-profit corporations, including DePaul University's Center for the Study of Values, for which Dennis McCann serves as codirector. Among the center's projects are various in-house retreats and "town meetings" designed to recover the community's lived sense of its own mission as an "urban, Catholic, Vincentian" institution. Similar experiments have occurred in various businesses, some of which are documented in the Business Roundtable Report of 1988, "Corporate Ethics: A Prime Business Asset."

Six Economic Myths Heard from the Pulpit

Robin Klay and Christopher Gryzen

It is not uncommon for religious leaders to speak to issues of economic concern. Given the human impact of economic policy, many clergy feel compelled by their faith to critique those economic strategies that seem likely to cause harm. In this article, Robin Klay and Christopher Gryzen attempt to debunk several of the most commonly heard economic misunderstandings that arise in the preaching of socially concerned religious leaders. These myths, they argue, often arise from an improper analysis either of the economic realities to which religion should respond or of the religious requirements to which believers are obligated to adhere. They do not argue that religious leaders should refrain from making economic arguments, but they assert that such arguments should be understood in the context of a properly conceived understanding of both the economy and religion.

*E*conomists and clergy have often been at loggerheads. In the early nineteenth century, economists were accused of practicing the "dismal science," a reputation that flowed from Thomas Malthus's deeply pessimistic predictions. He warned that world population pressures would inevitably perpetuate grinding poverty. Today, in contrast, morally sensitive people accuse economists of being too optimistic about economic growth and the benefits of technology. To outsiders, they seem to be technicians coldly manipulating models.

But despite their limited perspective, economists have useful insights about practical matters. They evaluate such things as what kind of tax will do the least harm, or what environmental-protection measures will least impede economic growth. They consider what approaches to welfare best preserve incentives to work and save, or what type of banking system does the best job of getting money from the people who save to those who can put it to productive use. They concern themselves with how policy design and implementation in all these matters affect income and opportunity gaps between the haves and have-nots. Clearly, these are all social issues with important moral implications. As a result, those who address our moral obligations and spiritual destiny need to understand economics.

The oldest dispute between clergy and economists regards the ethics of charging interest. The early Christian church believed that the scriptures clearly forbid interest; it cited the Old Testament law stating that Israelites must not charge interest on loans to each other. The church decided that Jesus' teaching about loving our enemies superseded even the Old Testament provision allowing Israelites to charge interest on loans to foreigners. Over the centuries, theologians such as Thomas Aquinas reaffirmed this stricture against interest—or usury, as it was called.

Only toward the end of the Middle Ages and in the early years of the Reformation did Catholics and Protestants relax this standard. Calvin, looking at the context of the Old Testament law, decided that the point of the ban on usury was that we should treat poor people with generosity. The needs of the poor were not to be occasions for profit making. He observed that the scriptures actually said nothing about business loans. Further reflection on the fruitfulness of money as business capital convinced most Christians to accept interest. Since business loans make increased profits possible for borrowers, it is only fair that lenders share in the profits. Furthermore, lenders deserve to be compensated for foregoing the use of the funds in their own businesses or for their own purchases.

Even so, there are still organizations today, like Habitat for Humanity, that refuse to charge interest on loans to poor families. Habitat families invest their "sweat equity," working alongside volunteers in constructing their own homes. Habitat takes the scriptural teaching against interest seriously, but not because its leaders are economically illiterate. They understand that the Old Testament teaching on this subject was meant to ensure that God's people, recalling their own deliverance from bondage, looked after the needs of poor families.

Economists began to carve out their own intellectual domain only in the late 1700s, separating their discipline from that of moral philosophy. The founder, Adam Smith, had a rather cheerful view of human economic activity, especially in societies in which strong moral foundations guide public behavior and free, competitive markets reward with better profits and higher wages those producers and workers who make good decisions. In *The Wealth of Nations*, Smith wrote:

> Every individual is continually exerting himself to find out the most advantageous employment for whatever capital he can command. It is his own advantage, indeed, and not that of the society which he has in view. But the study of his own advantage naturally, or rather necessarily leads him to

prefer that employment which is most advantageous to the society. . . . He generally, indeed, neither intends to promote the public interest, nor knows how much he is promoting it. . . . He intends only his own gain, and he is in this, as in many other cases, led by an invisible hand to promote an end which was not part of his intention.

Many pastors from Smith's day down to our own time have questioned this conviction that the powerful incentive of self-interest is a servant of the public good. Yet most economists, as well as many people living in countries newly committed to economic reform, overwhelmingly affirm Smith's views on the importance of free markets. They are unparalleled in their power to unleash the creative energies that can raise living standards above subsistence.

A large part of the misunderstanding between clergy and theologians on the one hand and economists on the other is simply the result of their different focus on human choice. Christian thinkers concern themselves with the motives underlying individual choices about working, buying, producing, and sharing the economic pie. We are called to do all these things as unto God, in grateful stewardship of God's gifts and for God's purposes. Economists, on the other hand, take human motives—both high and low—for granted. They then analyze the effect of such things as changes in prices, wages, interest rates, time scarcity, and taxes on the choices we make, the incomes we earn, and our present and future living standards.

Some common misunderstandings about economics interfere with Christians' ability effectively to express their moral concerns and calling in their private economic choices and in influencing public policy. One need not fear that dispelling certain myths will rob pulpits of their power to teach and challenge. No economic system, however well articulated, mimics the kingdom of God. Nonetheless, a better understanding of both the salutary and corrosive impacts of economic forces should prepare pastors and lay Christians to discern where the real moral issues and grace-full opportunities lie.

HUMANS COMPETE OVER A FIXED PIE

Should those who care about the welfare of the poor adopt simple lifestyles because by so doing they make available more food, energy, and other resources to less-developed countries? Those who answer yes usually present the following scenario: We Americans use X percent of the world's resources. If we would constrain our demands, more could be used by poor people. This view of the world assumes that only a limited amount of energy is available; consequently, if one country's citizens use more, the people of other countries will have less. But this is not true. There is *not* a fixed pot of energy. Rather, there are known supplies of oil, coal, and other natural resources whose quantities tend to expand as their prices rise, making it more profitable to explore for new deposits. These price increases also encourage the development of substitutes. For example, petroleum-based kerosene replaced whale oil for lighting in the nineteenth century, and then electricity took its place in the twentieth century. That prices of non-oil commodities are today 30 percent below their 1980 level suggests that our ability to use technology to reduce our dependence on raw materials is far greater than the "no growth" pessimists of the late 1970s thought.

Even less is it true that when, for example, U.S. livestock producers buy more soybeans from Brazil, the result is less food for Brazilians. When the international market pays a good price for bean exports, then land, labor, and other resources are drawn into production. The land may previously have been uncultivated or used for some other crop, perhaps food. Not only does the land now earn more, but labor devoted to bean production and processing is also better rewarded. The higher wages, profits, and rents earned in soybeans allow the workers, farmers, and input suppliers to buy more food and other necessities—either domestically produced or imported.

Where this does not happen, it's usually because of poor government policy and counterproductive regulation, not immoral market motives and behavior. For example, in many third-world countries women raise most of the food crops but are not allowed to own property in their own names. Without title to their land, enterprising farmers don't have the collateral to apply for loans for fertilizer, irrigation wells, and other equipment that can increase their output. Furthermore, in many developing countries price regulation in favor of providing cheap food for urban residents has been a devastating disincentive for food producers to increase their production. But when few regulatory and legal barriers to production exist, both buyers and producer/sellers benefit from trade. It is not a win-lose situation.

Simple living has much to recommend it on spiritual grounds, since it may liberate us to focus on God's nonmaterial riches and priorities. There is even some truth in the contention that our adopting a simple lifestyle can help the poor here and abroad. However, that benefit can come only if we use the savings in our living costs to assist poor people in acquiring the resources and skills needed to support themselves. When our mothers said, "Clean your plate, because children are starving in China," they meant to teach us something about manners and gratitude. They did not expect that cleaning our plates would solve world hunger. Similarly, the best economic rationale for simple living is not that it leaves more natural resources on the plate for others, but that it increases our capacity to give. This motive, firmly rooted in biblical teaching, is the issue to which we now turn.

PROPERTY RIGHTS ARE ABSOLUTE

Some Christians claim that the Bible says little about economics and that it uniformly endorses private property rights. Indeed, they argue, God so much affirms the institution of private property that one of the Ten Commandments denounces stealing as a major sin. Furthermore, some claim that when the Bible urges us to help poor people it refers only to voluntary charity, not to government-mandated (coerced) aid.

Though the Bible does indeed look dimly on stealing, it also qualifies the use of property in ways that do not fit well with a completely hands-off view of government. This is especially true of the Old Testament law, which required the people of God to pay tithes to support temple worship and to help the poor. It instructed farmers to leave a corner of their fields unharvested for the poor to glean. This was more than voluntary charity. It was a sort of communal tax, designed to provide for those unable to feed themselves. It's the Bible's version of a "safety net."

Some Christians argue that these Old Testament laws do not apply to a secular society like ours. However, the spirit of the scripture requires every decent society to institute mechanisms to protect the poor, who "will never cease out of the land" under any economic system. Societies that neglect to do this will, the scripture says, answer to God for their hardheartedness. Of course, the Bible sets an even higher standard for those who follow God. Over and over again, the people of God are reminded that they must express their gratitude for having been rescued from slavery and sin by being openhanded toward those in need.

There is room for debate about how comprehensive the safety net should be and whether it is best funded and managed by local or national governments or by private voluntary agencies. Conservatives rightly emphasize that generous welfare payments may have the serious moral and economic consequences of making people dependent or disinclined to work. They know that a "war on poverty" cannot be won through the technical prowess that put "a man on the moon." Human freedom, motivation, and social relationships make poverty extremely complex. Liberals, on the other hand, remind us of the biblical caution that people do not always deserve either their wealth or their poverty, and that pulling oneself up by one's bootstraps is often impossible without help. Communities are strongest when a portion of the gap in resources available to rich and poor is bridged, and when each generation is presented with the opportunity to "make good."

THE RICH ARE RICH BECAUSE THE POOR ARE POOR

Is capitalism the exploitation of the "have-nots" by the "haves," as some critics claim? This, of course, is the classic Marxist position. However, both Catholic and Protestant liberals have flirted with similar interpretations. Their concern is appropriate since the single most prominent economic theme in the Bible is God's desire that the critical needs of the poor be met through both systematic and voluntary remedies. Even so, there are some built-in errors in the liberal position.

Studies do not confirm the assumption that over time capitalism widens the gap between the rich and poor. Economic growth under capitalism can either widen or narrow income gaps. Whether it does one or the other depends largely on how widespread is the access to such valuable assets as land, education, credit, and basic health care. With primarily market-driven economies, South Korea and Taiwan have exhibited both rapid economic growth and a narrowing of income gaps between rich and poor. Their progress points to the virtue of a "trickle-up" approach to development, one that unleashes the productive powers of the poor through land redistribution, education, and regulatory reform.

By contrast, Mexico, Brazil, and most other Latin American economies (which have only recently begun to break out of a sort of bastardized, patrimonial capitalism) exhibit greater degrees of income inequality. Fifty-one percent of Brazilian and 40 percent of Mexican incomes go to the richest 10 percent of the population, in contrast to only 28 percent of South Korean incomes. These results illustrate the inadequacy of a purely "trickle-down" approach to economic development that fails to remedy the problems of wealthy families' favored access to public services and markets.

It is also inaccurate to think of market exchange as a case of one party (such as an employer or seller) ripping off another (a worker or consumer). People take certain jobs and not others or buy from one source instead of another in order to maximize their own gain from these exchanges. The employer's choice of a worker and the seller's choice of a customer are governed by similar intentions. Both parties gain. Furthermore, the enlargement of markets, which occurs when either transportation costs fall or artificial barriers to international trade are lowered by mutual agreement, tend to increase the net gains of all parties. Why? Because competition opens up new options to buyers of goods and sellers of labor. It also makes possible growth in the economic pie, as people and resources move toward activities in which they are more productive.

The best news is that the economic development that can quickly raise Third-world standards of living far beyond subsistence are already happening.

In the eighteenth and nineteenth centuries, average incomes in the United States and the United Kingdom doubled every fifty to sixty years. Today the doubling rate for income in South Korea and China has fallen to ten to eleven years. Asia's recent economic growth makes plausible the *Economist*'s projection that "within a generation, perhaps half of today's poor nations could be rich by current standards." Not surprisingly, this outcome for third-world people will also entail better markets for rich countries like our own. Economics is about win-win growth, not about winners and losers; across the world, the gaps between rich and poor nations are closing.

COOPERATION IS GOOD, COMPETITION IS BAD

Is cooperation more Christian than competition? Some people believe that competition in business (unlike sports) is unhealthy and often immoral—an effort to "do in" other producers in the same market. Competition is often criticized even if the means employed are legal and ethical, such as offering lower prices or better quality.

What is the basis for these moral qualms about business competition? Perhaps it's a presumption of unworthy motives, such as the desire to win at someone else's expense. Yet this need not be either the motive or the result of competitive behavior. Using their special knowledge of markets, many responsible entrepreneurs aim to provide useful, high-quality products and services to consumers. In coordinating human and material resources and technology, they respect the integrity and creativity of their workers, as well as the health and character of the communities in which they operate. Furthermore, competition may actually enlarge the market for a product so that many producers gain, as has been the case with audio and video recording.

Competition does result in the failure of firms unable simultaneously to serve customers well and earn competitive incomes for their workers and stockholders. Is this bad or avoidable? Surely business failures mean real costs to workers who lose their jobs, to materials suppliers who lose sales, and to stockholders who lose on their investments. On the other hand, attempts to stifle competition ostensibly to "save jobs"—as with trade restrictions, government bailouts, or regulations to make shutting down very difficult—ultimately weaken incentives for producers to energetically serve consumers' interests. Thus, during OPEC's big oil price hikes, Detroit producers, protected by quotas on Japanese imports, were sluggish and unimaginative in meeting consumer demand for fuel-efficient cars. Furthermore, European regulations that make going out of business difficult and costly contribute to the slower growth of new business and the higher rates of long-term unemployment there. By increasing the size of potential investor losses if the business is not successful, these regulations reduce the number of new business ventures and job growth.

Rather than stifle competition for the sake of existing industries, governments do better to stand out of the way so that people and money released from failed businesses can flow into more productive, expanding sectors. Of course, the widespread social benefits of vigorous competition make it appropriate for a society to use public- and private-sector initiatives to cushion the most vulnerable people from the worst effects of job loss. Such is the intent, for instance, of laws that yoke the lowering of trade barriers with programs to retrain and relocate workers.

But though competition is socially useful and may be entered into with the highest of motives, isn't cooperation more Christian? Well, markets do involve lots of healthy cooperation within firms and between firms and their suppliers. It's what we commonly refer to as "teamwork" in business. In many ways, the spirit of common purpose and sharing that makes some of us nostalgic for the past is present within the best modern firms. In other firms the competitive environment has been used as an excuse to weaken the bonds of community among fellow workers. Such firms can gain a great deal by developing a spirit of mutual cooperation rather than ruthless, personal competition.

Still, we might wonder whether cooperation among car manufacturers or steel firms or furniture makers or computer chip producers wouldn't be a moral advance over competition. Research in economics and industrial organization suggests otherwise. Adam Smith observed that producers often conspire to take advantage of consumers. Building on his insight, modern economists can demonstrate how great is the temptation (and financial reward) for producers whose control of a market allows them to restrict production and overcharge consumers. Not all collaboration by firms in the same industry is at the expense of consumers, but this is always a danger. It is widely recognized and dealt with in antitrust law and in the deregulation that has introduced competition into the telecommunication, transportation, and banking industries.

PROFITS ARE A FORM OF EXPLOITATION

Are profits "unearned income," extracted through some form of exploitation of the poor? Many who criticize capitalists assume that they simply put their money into operations to which others contribute their labor. Capitalists are said to take unfair advantage of their special knowledge about markets in order to make profits at someone else's expense. But the essence of capitalism is the use of the head (*caput*) to put practical knowledge to work. In any economy, a crucial resource is knowledge—practical knowledge of untapped talents, un-exploited resources, and unmet consumer wants and needs.

No economic system can harness this knowledge for the social good without providing incentives to those who possess it. Profits reward efforts to acquire and employ knowledge. They can be excessive when they result from unfair leverage over workers, suppliers, or consumers. They may even be artificially inflated by government restrictions on competition or guarantees against losses. But in a reasonably competitive economy, profits are essential rewards attracting producers into needed industries. In this sense, Adam Smith's "invisible hand" does work to promote the general good, though it is not in itself sufficient.

INDIVIDUAL FREEDOM IS THE HIGHEST GOOD

Is total freedom for the individual pursuit of self-interest in the marketplace the best guarantee of morality and progress? Though this idea may not be preached from many Christian pulpits, it is espoused by some Christian (as well as lib-ertarian) economists. At the same time, a striking argument to the contrary is being made by other conservative voices, like that of Michael Novak. In *The Catholic Ethic and the Spirit of Capitalism* Novak argues that neither democratic institutions nor markets can by themselves make human beings flourish. They must be balanced by strong moral and cultural institutions, such as families, schools, churches, and other voluntary associations that serve the common good. These institutions habituate us to the practice of essential private and social virtues, like honesty, self-control, and kindness, without which neither markets nor democratic governments can function well.

Novak argues that Jewish and Christian scriptures and teachings provide the firmest grounds for the American belief in fundamental human rights and for the free exercise of human creativity encouraged by the system of market rewards. These religious traditions also teach us that human beings seek both self-interest and the common good. We each possess unique talents, knowledge, calling, and destiny, yet we are also social creatures with a common Creator and a common destiny. We are subject to the shared liabilities of finitude and sin. Much more than any unitary socialist system, the threefold system of democratic capitalism—which honors political, economic, and moral-cultural freedoms—tends to call forth individual and collective efforts that contribute to the common good.

Citing Pope John Paul II, Novak says that humans are made not for the freedom of the libertine but for the ordered liberty that respects human nature and vocation. He opposes "primitive capitalism," characterized by ruthlessness.

Total reliance on markets is not morally adequate, since some human needs go unmet by markets, some things should not be bought and sold, and some groups lack the resources necessary to participate in markets. Markets must, therefore, be tamed, guided, and supplemented by democratic and moral-cultural institutions.

In an economy that deemed individual freedom of choice the highest value, markets in sex, divorce, and babies for adoption would be directed purely by the forces of supply and demand. However, a society that honors human nature accepts some trade-offs between individual freedom and social well-being by, for instance, outlawing or heavily regulating such markets. Thus, babies available for adoption do not go to the highest bidder; prostitution is banned or regulated; and neither divorce nor abortion is available on demand.

Furthermore, humane societies do not leave socially, psychologically, and physically handicapped people at the mercy of the brute forces of Darwinian competition. Through some combination of public and voluntary efforts, these people are given subsidized jobs or are otherwise provided with the physical and social necessities of life. Children whose families are unable to give them the education necessary for productive lives are helped with scholarships, loans, and direct provision of education by governments or churches and other voluntary organizations.

In addition, humane societies seek to cushion workers who lose their jobs due to recessions, foreign competition, and technological change by offering them short-term unemployment benefits and financial assistance for retraining and relocating. Finally, through private and public insurance, as well as by direct provision of services, those whose health, old age, or youth prevent them from fully supporting themselves receive the help they need to live in dignity. In all these ways, moral and democratic forces work to balance and tame markets for the sake of social justice and well-being.

Readers may have noticed that we have not balanced myths "on the left" with an equal number of myths "on the right." This is not meant to suggest that the errors of liberals are more dangerous than the errors of conservatives. They do, however, tend to enjoy greater currency among intellectuals generally and Christian leaders in particular, and thus need to be discussed in greater detail.

Even so, it would be foolish to abandon the errors on the left only to fall prey to those on the right. Moral leaders must continually teach that individuals have responsibilities to each other in a humane society. Narrow self-interest, though a powerful incentive for the production of material wealth, does not cement communities. We all need encouragement to exercise a new vision of the public good and to join with others in sacrificial efforts to achieve that good in concrete ways, ranging from providing housing for the homeless to parks for everyone and enriched educational environments for disadvantaged children. Learning to understand economics can assure Christians that working together and individually they can make a difference—one which does not depend for its outcome on some far-off systemic revolution.

QUESTIONS FOR DISCUSSION

1. Where does the conflict between economists and clergy come from? Have clergy been justified in their suspicions of economics as a discipline? According to Klay and Gryzen, what benefits do economists offer to society?

2. What are the ethical problems involved in the charging of interest? Why has the Christian church historically been opposed to the charging of interest? Should prohibitions on the charging of interest be reestablished in society? Why or why not?

3. Why do the authors argue that property rights are not absolute? What are the grounds for this argument? Are these grounds persuasive? Why or why not?

4. What critique do the authors make of the idea that the rich are rich because the poor are poor? Why do they not find this idea persuasive? Do you agree or disagree? Why or why not?

5. Why might cooperation among producers be worse than competition? What effect might such cooperation have on consumers? What kind of understanding of humanity is reflected in the belief that cooperation is morally superior to competition?

6. What value should be placed on individual freedom in society? Should this idea be the basis for how we organize our economic system? If not, what other principles should be considered in creating a just economy?

• 11 •

Zen in the Workplace:
Approaches to Mindful Management

Gerry Shishin Wick Sensei

In this chapter, Gary Shishin Wick Sensei takes a look at management attitudes and practices through the lens of Zen Buddhism. He identifies four ways that good managers act to benefit themselves, others, the organization, and the entire world. He claims that good managers will model themselves after the bodhisattva—the one who uniquely embodies the virtues of the Buddha in this plane of existence. The manager who is like the bodhisattva will engage in acts of *giving*, will use *loving words*, will take *beneficial actions*, and will *identify with others*—recognizing that we are not many, but really all one. By applying these simple practices to everyday issues in the corporate context, employees, managers, and executives can create a peaceful and balanced enterprise that serves the needs of all.

When the country prospers, the king's name is unknown. It is only when there are problems that everyone knows who is to blame. It is the person in charge, the ruler: the king, the president, or the manager. When the king is more important than the country; the country will not prosper. When the manager is more important than his or her employees, then the company will fail. If a manager is doing his or her job properly, then the company should run smoothly. The manager will become like a forgotten person, which is what a manager should strive for. Too many managers believe that they must have all of the answers and control every situation.

Zen Master Jizo said that not knowing meant to be open to all eventualities, to not prejudge a person or situation. If your mind is full of preconceived notions, there is no room for an unbiased view. It is like when your hands are full of objects—you cannot pick up anything new. A closed mind causes separation and suspicion. Like an umbrella, a mind is only useful when it is open.

211

The first step toward maintaining an open mind is to understand the nature of mind or self.

In his *Genjo Koan* Master Dogen wrote, "To study the Buddha Way is to study the self. To study the self is to forget the self." To forget the self means to let go of our schemes either to aggrandize or to pity ourselves. These schemes are so pervasive and subtle that they require careful examination. One needs to see the nature of these schemes. By studying the self one sees that all schemes are hollow fabrications that arise and disappear with each thought. The thoughts themselves are mere phantoms with no substance. The same is true with feelings, sensations, perceptions, and conceptions.

Recently, I met a seasoned high-level manager. He has run departments of many hundreds of people for multimillion-dollar corporations. During the course of our interaction, he expressed an interest in Zen and Zen practice. After he was practicing *zazen* for a while, I asked him the famous koan of the sixth patriarch, "Thinking neither good nor evil, what is your true self?" He has been reflecting on this for a year and during that time his interactions with both his superiors and his employees have dramatically changed. Rather than coming to a meeting with preconceptions, he can clear his mind and just be present and participate. He is not so carefully guarded and protective. His interactions flow more easily and as a result he is able to get his points across with less resistance.

If you "think neither good nor evil," you can just be present and reveal your innate wisdom. If you are constantly thinking about how your colleagues or bosses are evaluating you, you are putting a filter between you and yourself, and between you and others. You will be in touch with neither yourself nor your situation. Thinking neither good nor evil is the same as forgetting the self. "To forget the self is to be enlightened by the ten thousand things." When we can truly let go of our attachments to the self, every activity in the ten directions is the enlightened action and every place is *nirvana*, including the boardroom or the laundry room. Every good manager is a bodhisattva. I did not comprehend the immensity and seriousness of being a bodhisattva until I heard Trungpa Rinpouche say that a bodhisattva does not reserve any time for himself or herself. A bodhisattva cannot even allow himself the luxury of reading *Time* magazine while sitting on the commode. Sometimes it takes good examples to drive the point home. Dogen Zenji wrote that there are four ways a bodhisattva acts to benefit human beings. They are giving (*fuse*), loving words (*aigo*), bene-ficial actions (*rigyo*), and identifications with others (*doji*). A bohisattva serves others. And part of that serving is giving. There are many different kinds of things that can be given. A manager is capable of giving all of them. The first thing to give is material things and comfort. The salary that an employee earns provides the necessary material things required for survival and comfort. A good manager will also make sure that his employees have the necessary state-of-the-art equipment and a suitable space in order to fulfill their job. That's one aspect of giving. Another type of giving is to give to the *dharma*. The *dharma* is the teachings of the Buddha. It can take many forms. Giving employees the training they need in order to be successful is giving the *dharma*. Empowering employees to make their own decisions is giving the *dharma*. Allowing employees to learn by making mistakes is giving the *dharma*. Employees who are given opportunities become more capable. Conscientious employees always rise to the occasion when they feel that they have the encouragement and support of their boss.

The last and most important thing that a bohisattva can give is "no fear." A manager cannot give "no fear" unless he or she has "no fear" to give. "No fear" is the same as "forgetting the self." If there is no self to protect or aggrandize, what is there to fear?

The second way a bodhisattva acts to benefit human beings is called "loving words." When a bodhisattva sees another person, compassion is naturally aroused and he or she uses loving words. Compassion is the natural functioning of wisdom. The clearer one sees, the more readily one uses loving words. Loving words can take all kinds of forms. "Loving words" doesn't always mean being sweet and solicitous. Sometimes a loving word can be a very harsh word, but it is always according to the situation.

The third bodhisattva way is "beneficial action." Beneficial action means to take care of every person whether of high or low position. Some people are good at managing their managers and other people are good at managing their subordinates. But you have to manage in both directions. One of the reasons there is so much dissension in companies is that people think that if somebody else gains or moves forward it's at their loss. Beneficial action is a win–win scenario. If you support the people who work for you, they will push you up. If you support your superiors, they will pull you up.

The fourth way is "identification with others." Whenever I felt alienated from a situation and the people at work, I would chant "not two." Heaven, Earth, and I have the same root: Self and others are not two. That is one of the revelations of the Buddha: that there is no separation between oneself and others. There is no formula to being a good manager. The Buddha called this lack of formula *upaya*, or skillful means. Each situation is different and each person is different. *Upaya* is employed by a bodhisattva to awaken others. A manager uses *upaya* to bring the best from his or her employees.

Years ago an old teacher gave me three pieces of advice about how to bring practice into one's life. The first thing he said was to see everybody as the Buddha. It doesn't have to be Buddha; it can be anybody for whom you have an image of respect and appreciation. The second thing he said was to hear everything as the *dharma*. The *dharma* in this sense means the teachings of the Buddha. The third thing he said was to reveal every place as *nirvana*. *Nirvana* means the enlightened place—the place of clarity, peace, and comfort. How would we function if we held those principles all the time?

See everybody as the Buddha. When you are stuck in a traffic jam on the Los Angeles freeway, can you look at all the other drivers, particularly the ones who are weaving in and out of lanes, and see them as the Buddha? In a work situation, if you have a particularly cantankerous boss who you think is a complete idiot, can you look at the person for whom you are working as the Buddha?

I don't mean that we should react to everybody in the same way, because we have to react according to our wisdom. Our wisdom evolves over time and has to be in accord with our activity or our action. There is an expression in Zen that wisdom and compassion need to be well balanced. Compassion doesn't always mean being nice to people. Sometimes the best thing you can do in a situation is to be rough with someone. We have to be balanced in accord with each situation.

A manager needs to see each situation clearly and act accordingly. A decision may be correct today and incorrect tomorrow. A decision may be correct with one person and incorrect with another. Each decision depends upon conditions, the time, the place, the people involved, and the intensity of the situation.

The second guiding code of conduct is to hear every sound as the *dharma*. There was a famous Chinese Zen master named Joshu. At the age of sixty he was extremely well accomplished as a Zen master, but he felt he needed more seasoning. So he told himself that he was going to go on a pilgrimage and if he met a man of eighty whom he could teach, he would share with him; if he met a child of eight whom he could learn from, he would learn from that child. By being that open, he further seasoned himself for twenty years until he was eighty years old, and then he decided that he was ready to teach others. And he taught for another twenty years.

To hear every sound as the *dharma* means just to pay attention. Listen to what people are saying when they are talking to you. We are usually so busy trying to say something that will impress them that we don't really listen to what they are saying. It is easy to give an appropriate response if we are really listening.

When you meditate you can see how difficult it is just to pay attention. Just to pay attention to breathing is not easy. Until you can quiet your mind it's almost impossible to really listen to what other people are saying.

People like to get away from the city and enter the mountain for *zazen* because they think it's quiet. Actually, when the squirrels and the blue jays get going, it is quite a racket. What's the difference? We think that some sounds are pleasant sounds and other sounds are not pleasant sounds. It is true that there is something attractive about the trees and the lack of congestion. Why is that? Is it something that's basically biological or is it something in our own minds? Listening to the flowing water is very soothing. If you think that passing cars are smelly, noisy traffic, then it's going to be unpleasant. The point is that we interject so many filters. If we can just let those go and be present, then every sound is the sound that can enlighten us.

The third principle is to reveal every place as *nirvana*. Where you sit right now, that place is *nirvana*. One Zen ancestor said, "Neither try to eliminate delusion nor search for what is real. This is because ignorance, just as it is, is the Buddha nature. This worldly body itself, which appears and disappears like the phantom in this world, is nothing other than the reality of life, there is not any particular thing that you can point to and say, 'This is it!'"

A couple of points here are worth absorbing. One is that people try to change themselves. "If I could only change, if I could be a different person, then everything would be okay." What's the difference between that and thinking that if you had a new stereo, you would be okay? Or if you had the right automobile of the right color and the right make and model? Our practice is to appreciate who we are, rather than to become somebody who we are not.

The ignorant, deluded self, just as it is, is no other than the enlightened self. If you can appreciate that, then this practice is a simple matter. If we deny ourselves, right there we are denying the very vehicle that reveals to us our innate true self. It is no other than our body and mind. This very body and mind in this very place is the enlightened one. If you reject in any way, you are rejecting that enlightened self. So rather than trying to eliminate delusion, just be attentive to each moment.

QUESTIONS FOR DISCUSSION

1. How does the virtue of *giving* lead to good management practices? What examples of *giving* does our author use? Discuss other concrete practices that reflect the virtues of *giving*.

2. How does a good manager employ *loving words* in the workplace? Does it always entail saying nice things? Think of some instances where one might need to use harsh words.

3. How do *beneficial actions* enhance the workplace? What kinds of *beneficial actions* have you encountered in a business setting?

4. What does our author mean by the virtue of *identification with others*?

How might a deeper sense of oneness with each other and with the entire universe change business practices?

5. If we approached our work with the expectation that every sound we heard was *dharma*, how would this change our perception of ourselves and those with whom we work?

6. How can the modern workplace be *nirvana*?

Confucian Trustworthiness and the Practice of Business in China

Daryl Koehn

It is no secret that China represents the largest single emerging market in the global capitalist economy today. From the perspective of business ethics, this emerging economic powerhouse will not only have a profound effect on the commercial dimensions of the economy, but more importantly for our purposes, it could conceivably impact the philosophical underpinnings of corporate capitalism. In this chapter, Daryl Koehn examines the philosophical differences between a Western capitalist understanding of contractual trustworthiness and a Confucian perspective on trustworthiness. This fascinating exercise in comparative ethics opens the door to a different way of understanding contractual relationships, possibly enriching our more narrow notions of procedural trust with the ethic of mindfulness and being trustworthy.

Confucius's teachings fall under four headings: "culture, moral conduct, doing one's best, and being trustworthy in what one says." Trust, or, more precisely, being trustworthy, plays a central role in the Confucian ethic. This chapter begins by examining the Confucian concept of trustworthiness. The second part of the chapter discusses how the ideal of trustworthiness makes itself felt in business practices within China. The chapter concludes by raising and addressing several objections to the Confucian emphasis on trustworthiness.

It is not the failure of others to appreciate your abilities that should trouble you, but rather your own lack of them.

—Confucius

PART ONE: THE CONCEPT OF TRUSTWORTHINESS IN
THE CONFUCIAN ETHIC

*C*onfucius contends that individuals are ethically obligated to refine themselves and to become exemplary human beings. Such refinement (*jen*) requires education. Becoming an educated and influential individual depends, in turn, upon establishing trust: "Only after he has gained the trust of the common people does the gentleman work them hard, for otherwise they would feel themselves ill-used. Only after he has gained the trust of the lord does the gentleman advise him against unwise action, for otherwise the lord would feel himself slandered" (19/9).[1]

At first glance, Confucius appears to think of trust in a manner not all that different from Western theorists. Trust is the trustor's expectation of good will on the part of the trustee. Trust is something we can bestow on or refuse to other people. Trust must be gained and, if we are not careful when reposing trust, we will feel ourselves betrayed. On closer examination, though, we find that Confucius diverges from many Western theorists because he regards the virtue of trustworthiness as more important than trust per se.

To be worthy of our trust a person does not have to cater to our needs. While a good leader will try to ensure that those ruled have enough to eat and drink, people will still honor a leader in hard times: "Death has always been with us since the beginning of time, but when there is no trust, the common people will have nothing to stand on" (12/7). This saying suggests that we should trust as long as the goodwill of the trustee is evident, regardless of whether the trustee promotes our material well-being or conforms to our expectations. Virtuous persons, who look beyond their own narrow self-interest and who seek the spiritual as well as merely material welfare of all of their fellow citizens, merit our trust. Cultivated individuals display goodwill by never treating the multitude with contempt. Instead, such persons always praise the good while taking pity on the backward (19/3). To excessively hate those who are not refined only provokes them to unruly behavior (8/10), and the trustworthy person seeks to avoid war and conflict (7/13).

Those who are devoted to the way of virtue take instruction from anyone who speaks well. Anyone who truly is trying to be virtuous is eager to learn, and she never dismisses what is said on account of who is speaking (15/23). The person of *jen* will even speak with a madman (18/5). In general, the person of *jen* is intent upon helping others realize what is good in them (12/16). He neither looks for the evil nor denounces others as evil (17/24). He hates evil, not evil people: "To attack evil as evil and not as evil of a particular man, is that not the way to reform the depraved?" (12/21). If we focus upon evil persons, we will not discern opportunities for realizing the good in others. We will not merit the trust of others because we will not be acting so as to refine people. Instead, our judgments will foster hatred and discord.

Many Western ethics of trust contend that we are justified in accusing of betrayal those who fall short of our expectations.[2] Confucius asks us to consider instead whether we have demanded more of those we have trusted than we should have. We ought to err on the side of making allowances for people (15/15), remembering that individuals have different strengths. Virtue exists as a continuum. The person of *jen* has good relations with others precisely because she does not expect complete virtue from everyone:

> A man good enough as a partner in one's studies need not be good enough as a partner in the pursuit of the way; a man good enough as a partner in the pursuit of the way need not be good enough as a partner in a common stand; a man good enough as a partner in a common stand need not be good enough as a partner in the exercise of moral discretion (9/30).

It is up to us to choose our partners and friends carefully. In some cases, our business associates, friends, and family members may fail to keep their promises to us or may not show us due respect. However, we should not waste our energy accusing them of being untrustworthy. It is not the failure of others to appreciate our abilities that should trouble us, but rather our own lack of abilities (14/29). The Confucian ethic sees the value of trust but always directs our attention back to our own performance and attitudes. When there is trouble, we should look inward (4/17) and bring charges against ourselves, instead of blaming or scapegoating others (5/26).

The Confucian ethic takes the energy out of our anger at others for slighting us and redirects that energy back into self-examination. This redirection is appropriate for several reasons. First, there is little point in getting angry with others. If they have harmed us out of ignorance, then the correct response is to try to educate them, not to harm them in return. If they intend us harm, we should still try to dissuade them, rather than retaliate in kind. Second, even if others persist in trying to wrong us, we should not let their actions distract us from the arduous work of becoming an authoritative person. Since refinement or *jen* is within our control, we always should look to our own behavior and not worry overly much about what others are or are not doing to us. Warned that Huan T'ui would try to assassinate him, Confucius retorted: "Heaven is the author of the virtue that is in me. What can Huan T'ui do to me?" (7/23). The person of *jen* is free from anxieties (7/37) because he keeps his eye on what is most important: "If, on examining himself, a man finds nothing to reproach himself for, what worries and fears can he have?" (12/4). Confucius was famous for maintaining his composure in the face of insults: "To be transgressed against yet not to mind. It was towards this end that my friend [Confucius] used to direct his efforts" (8/5). It is our trustworthiness, not others' machinations or venom, that should be our primary concern.

Third, it is easy to misjudge another. We may think, for example, that someone is not a good leader because the community or corporation he leads is in disarray. Yet "even with a true king, it is bound to take a generation for benevolence to become a reality" (13/12). Or we may conclude we have been betrayed when a trusted party deviates from a stated plan of action. Sometimes, though, to change one's mind is the right course. A "man who insists on keeping his word and seeing his actions through to the end . . . shows a stubborn petty-mindedness" (13/20). We cannot hope to assess accurately the "betrayals" of other people if we are not striving simultaneously to be as mindful as possible (15/8). Followers have a responsibility, therefore, to be as thoughtful as their leaders. If those who are led are not mindful, they will not be able to grasp the wisdom in what the leader is saying and simply may dismiss her out of hand.

Finally, we humans are only too prone to self-deceit. Scrupulous self-examination is necessary if we are not to err. For example, we may be inclined to dismiss younger workers as undisciplined and undeserving of our trust and regard. Yet, we are far from infallible. How "do we know that the generations to come will not be equal of the present?" (9/23). In other cases, our judgment may be motivated by bad faith. One should never oppose a lord or ruler without first making certain of one's own honesty (14/22). If all of us would engage in routine self-scrutiny, we would be more worthy of trust. We then would trust one another more fully. With more trust, we would be able to educate each other even better, thereby increasing the level of trustworthiness and engendering still more trust. If people are failing to live up to their potential and living in discord, then perhaps it is because we are failing to lead by example (13/4). When Confucius wanted to settle in the midst of the "barbarians," one of his disciples asked, "But could you put up with their uncouth ways?" Confucius bitingly retorted, "Once a gentleman settles amongst them, what uncouthness will there be?" (9/14).

For all of these reasons, Confucius warns that to love trust without loving learning can lead an individual to do harm (17/8). Judging other people's goodwill without simultaneously turning a critical eye on our own standard and trustworthiness is a recipe for disaster. It does not follow that we should tolerate any and all abuse. The person of *jen* is not angered by abuse, but neither does she stick around to be mistreated. She tries to choose her friends carefully, refusing to accept anyone as a friend who is not as good as herself (9/25; see also 16/4). That does not mean she chooses only completely virtuous individuals as her friends. It does mean she looks for others who are as critically mindful as she is. Her friends should be eager to learn. She advises them as best she can but stops if her advice is not being heeded. She does not ask to be snubbed (12/23) and does not waste her words on those who are incapable of improving themselves (15/8). The superior person does not look for evil but she quickly discerns it because she is thoughtful. So, "without anticipating attempts at deception or presuming acts of bad faith, [she] is, nevertheless, the first to be aware of such behavior" (14/31). Her responses to others' acts are similarly nuanced. An injury should not be taken personally but neither should it be rewarded. Confucius rejects a student's suggestion that one should repay an injury with a good turn. For if you did so, then "what do you repay a good turn with? You repay an injury with straightness, but you repay a good turn with a good turn" (14/34).

By judging and responding with a high degree of discretion, we show ourselves to be worthy of trust. In turn, we should trust those who are consistently thoughtful. There probably is no such thing as a perfect friend or colleague. However, if we use good judgment and do not expect too much of our colleagues and associates, and if our friends use good judgment as well and do not take on too much responsibility, then we can have strong, secure, and trusting relations with our fellow employees and friends.

Notice that for Confucius trust cannot be based on conformity to rules such as "Always keep promises," "Avoid conflicts of interest," and the like. A friend might become even more trustworthy in our eyes if she were to break a promise. Suppose she had promised to help her best friend paint his house. On the way over, she comes across a child badly hurt in a bicycle accident. She takes the child to the hospital and as a result never gets over to his house. Although she did not keep her word, her friend might conclude she is even more deserving of his trust because she used good judgment. To take an example from business: Oskar Schindler lied about the health and productivity of the Jews he employed in order to save them. This willingness to lie to the Nazis was exactly what endeared him to his employees.

From the Confucian perspective, there can be no algorithm for assessing other people's trustworthiness. We must always judge the particular action, looking at the context in which the actor operated and at the relevant factors. There are some general guidelines for assessing the agent's judgment: Is the person thoughtful? Does he rush to judgment or does he stop to examine his own motives and assumptions? But these guidelines are not exhaustive and never will be so because the person of *jen* will often act in such a way as to make us completely rethink our presuppositions. Although the ethical order has certain changeless injunctions—for instance, "Do not let your word outstrip your deed" (14/27) or "Be resolute" (13/27)—it is always up to the individual to decide what these injunctions actually mean in a particular context. As Aristotle would put it, the decision lies with perception or *aisthesis*. The person of *jen* acquires authority because she is able by her actions and speech to disclose new, relevant possibilities to her peers. Confucius's own discourse, for example, makes us consider what it means for our deeds to conform to our words. He berates those who keep to their word in a literal way as petty and stubborn-minded. So he clearly does not favor honoring any and all of one's past promises or claims. What does he mean then when he urges us not to let our words outstrip our deeds?

The example given above is helpful: Although the woman failed to keep her promise to help her friend paint his house, her words did not outstrip her deeds. In volunteering to assist her friend, she spoke as a true friend would because friends seek to benefit each other. In helping the child, she acted as a humane person would. In both cases, her words and deeds reflect her commitment to *jen*. Only a small person would accuse her of betraying her friend. Those who are critically mindful would see her behavior as exemplary (*jen*) because her choices and actions serve to disclose what it means for words and deeds to be congruent.

PART TWO: EXAMPLES OF THE CONFUCIAN ETHIC AT WORK IN BUSINESS SUSPICION OF CONTRACTS

Like the Japanese, the Chinese historically have been loath to rely upon contracts. They often will not even read long contracts and may insist the document be shortened. A contract is merely a commercial agreement not to be taken as the gospel: "You might say they [the Chinese] sign long complicated contracts only as a formal confirmation that they intend to do business with you, not how they are going to conduct the business."[3] The Confucian emphasis on trustworthiness makes reliance on contracts less attractive for several reasons. First, use of detailed contracts encourages parties to think of the contract as the basis for trust. The parties then feel entitled to accuse each other of betrayal whenever one appears to the other to have deviated from the terms of the contract. The contract thus contributes to an atmosphere of distrust. By contrast, if people enter into relationships and transactions with the understanding that they will need to work hard to accommodate their partner's interests and to keep their own biases and self-righteousness in check, then they will have put their relationship on a sounder footing. They may still decide to use some simple written document to lay out key terms or to serve as a talking document, but they will not make adherence to a contract the entire basis of the relation.

Second, reliance on contracts can prevent people from focusing on the larger picture and from being as mindful as they should be. A number of disputes between the Chinese and their joint-venture partners have involved transfer of technology issues. The foreign partner typically accuses the Chinese side of failing to meet contractual requirements to supply land or capital, while the Chinese claim that the foreign partner has not provided the technical training the two had agreed upon. The foreign partner has generally viewed this counterclaim as a fabrication. It did provide training and the Chinese are simply trying to justify their own breach of contract. While that might be true in some cases, the person of *jen* would look beyond the contractual dispute to the larger cultural and economic issues.[4]

The Chinese have good reason to be sensitive about technical training. The government has made a conscious decision to modernize the country by importing technology and then adapting it to suit their needs and their level of development. Mao Tse Tung imported "turnkey" facilities—that is, entire factories. The current policy is to build their own facilities using imported technology. In an effort to acquire technology as cheaply as possible, the Chinese have been willing to acquire slightly older hardware and software in the secondhand market. This modernization strategy obviously will not succeed if they do not also learn to use the technology. Therefore, the Chinese place great emphasis on *jishu jiaoliu,* or technical presentations conveying technical information. They will bring in successive groups. Each group asks most of the same questions their predecessors posed. The Chinese use these sessions not only to brief all members of their team on the status of the project but also to train their people in the technology.[5] They do not see themselves as "using" these presenters for their own purposes. They simply see themselves as obtaining an education that any person of genuine goodwill would wish to help them obtain.

Given their history of being colonized, the Chinese are understandably afraid of being exploited. Many have noted that, as late as the beginning of World War II, Shanghai's British quarters still had signs proclaiming, "China-men and dogs are not permitted to enter."[6] They do not want to give up hard currency and to provide land and other resources to their former masters in exchange for technology they are unable to use. Nor do they want to become a dumping ground for obsolete or nonfunctioning software. If they cannot get the software to run, they naturally suspect that they have been duped. What Westerners view as a rather cut-and-dried contractual dispute—did the Chinese live up to their end of the bargain or not?—is a major cultural issue for the Chinese. The future of China and Chinese pride and self-respect is at stake in each of these deals. Contracting to do business with the Chinese will never build trust unless each side consistently looks beyond the contract to discern the economic, psychological, and cultural factors at work.[7] Parties will be more inclined to take this broad and more generous point of view if they remind themselves that they may not know as much about the situation as they think they do. Contractual disputes will prove more resolvable if each side shifts its attention away from the other's alleged betrayal and to the question of whether it has been behaving trustworthily.

The Prominence of Guanxi

The Chinese reliance on connections or *guanxi* is another important feature of the Chinese business scene. Does the Confucian ethic endorse such a reliance? *Guanxi* is typically seen as an outgrowth of the Confucian emphasis on personal relations. And it is true that, for Confucius, good order requires that each person fulfill his particular role-based duties. Children should be filial. The ruler should be a ruler and a father should be a father (12/11). Persons should acknowledge their role in the hierarchy. Historically these roles were relatively fixed by custom. There was little public law to which people could appeal if the authorities abused their power. In such a system, it became vitally important to cultivate relations with powerful people in the event one needed some sort of help from an authority. Family and local ties were especially important. To this day Chinese businesspeople will often treat classmates, friends, and family members preferentially when making hiring or other business decisions.[8]

Public authorities, especially local authorities, continue to exercise a phenomenal degree of power in China. Kristoff and Wudunn argue that China still has an imperial system. The party leader is the new emperor, but local chieftains share in this absolute power:

> Each lower official acts like a prince on his own turf, from the ministry to the department to the section to the team, from the factory manager to the production manager to the workshop director. The petty autocrats are often the worst, as well as the most difficult to escape. In many villages, the local chief rules even more absolutely than [the national leader], for he decides who can marry, who can get good land, who can get water for irrigation, who can be buried where. He is almost as powerful as God, but not so remote.[9]

Businesspeople, therefore, are well advised to cultivate *guanxi*. However, it would be a mistake to conclude, as Francis Fukuyama does, that China is a low-trust, family-oriented society whose members have little practice or interest in interacting with outsiders or in dealing with others on an equal basis.[10] If this were true, the Chinese would never have been able to achieve their economic miracle: China now ranks first in the world in the production of coal, cement, grain, fish, meant, and cotton; third in steel production; and fifth in crude oil output; its annual growth rate has averaged more than 9 percent since 1978.[11]

The Chinese would never have succeeded if they had not imported their technology and had not formed numerous joint ventures with foreign companies. Nearly 10 percent of China's industrial output comes from foreign-owned and private businesses.[12]

It should also be noted that the fastest-growing countries during the last decade—China, Japan, Hong Kong, Singapore, Taiwan, and South Korea—either have a large Chinese population or have been heavily influenced by Chinese culture. The ethnic Chinese may be the most economically successful ethnic group in the world. Although they constitute only 1.5 percent of the Philippine population, they are responsible for 35 percent of the sales of locally owned firms. In Indonesia, they are 2 percent of the population, but may own as much as 70 percent of private domestic capital.[13] Again, these minority Chinese populations would never have done as well as they did if they had refused to deal with nonfamily members.

While Confucianism certainly stresses the need for respect for family, Confucius never says, "Trust only your intimates." On the contrary, a trustworthy person willingly associates with anyone else who is eager to learn. Confucius chides his students who presume to condemn a fellow student with an undesirable background (7/29). Moreover, filial piety is not desirable if it functions in an exclusive manner. Filial piety should lead to respect for others and for true rulers and to a general climate of trust and good will. A Confucian ethic encourages open rather than exclusive relations rooted in suspicion of other people. It supports *guanxi* with everyone.

The Chinese openness to new relations, their reliance on *guanxi*, and their emphasis on being trustworthy are evident in their response to Western marketing. On the one hand, the Chinese are certainly willing to buy goods from foreigners. There is not any xenophobia when it comes to purchasing from strangers. On the other hand, the most effective Western marketing focuses more on the company and its character and less on the product.[14] The consumers want to know with whom they are dealing. This desire is a natural outgrowth of a Confucian ethic emphasizing relations of mutual development and refinement instead of desire satisfaction. Any company can sell a product, so pushing the product does not make the company trustworthy. Advertising of the company's character, by contrast, may foster trustworthiness. The consumer sees that the company is self-conscious and aware of the effect its behavior has on consumers and other stakeholders. Since the advertising may turn out to be deceitful, we cannot say that all such advertising is intrinsically ethical. Nevertheless, from the perspective of the Confucian ethic, corporate image advertising would be more ethical than mere promotion of products because ultimately the consumer and other stakeholders are in relation with the company, not its output.

An Emphasis on Trustworthy Leaders in Politics and in Business

The Confucian value of trustworthiness both illuminates certain Chinese business practices and enables us to critique them. Consider the question of who is a good business leader. In one respect, Confucian leadership resembles so-called servant leadership. There are no leaders when there are no followers. One leads best when one rules in the interest of the ruled. A ruler will be able to accurately perceive the interests of the ruled only if he is able to live in such a way as to remain sympathetic to other people's concerns and problems. Since so many people have been poor throughout China's history, the Confucian ethic would recommend that a business leader live frugally and unostentatiously. The ethic does not necessarily favor absolute egalitarianism. Neither does it promote asceticism. As the standard of living of those one is ruling or managing improves, a leader can opt to live more comfortably, although virtue rather than material comfort should always be her primary concern.

The Chinese students protesting government corruption at Tiananmen Square were on sound Confucian ground. After Deng Xiaoping made his famous 1992 trip to the south and urged people to embrace capitalism even more quickly, the whole country seemed to be gripped with *baijinzhuyi*, or money worship.[15] Minister-level officials plus many of the leader's children went into business for themselves. The army ran factories making clocks and refrigerators, and the Army General Staff Department became the part-owner of a luxury Chinese hotel. Government officials were sometimes able to enrich themselves because they could take advantage of their contacts and their control over land to secure contracts or to gain a share in joint ventures. Relatives of senior Communist officials have become some of the richest people in China. The Confucian ethic would condemn those who have sold state assets to enrich themselves and would question whether such ruler-managers are true or legitimate rulers.

In addition, the Confucian ethic of trustworthiness would have us look beyond the material successes of leadership. Modern Chinese leaders are sometimes praised for destroying the feudal system, reducing infant mortality, and extending adult life span. If Hitler was right and if "success is the sole earthly judge of right and wrong," then Mao, Zhou Enlai, and Deng Xiaoping would deserve praise for their achievements. Confucius does not dismiss success, but he would have us ask: Success at what? A leader should excel at leading human beings. Guaranteeing people an "iron wage" and an "iron rice bowl" is no proof of outstanding leadership. It is true that starving people have a hard time caring about virtue. But feeding them does not by itself help them to realize their human excellence. Even animals feed their young, so there is nothing especially humanizing about providing material subsistence (2/7). As I noted earlier, Confucius insists a true ruler can ask people to forego food without forfeiting their trust as long as the ruler's goodwill is evident. A trustworthy ruler never loses sight of the distinctively human capacity to choose. People will endure all kinds of hardships as long as they are not oppressed.

A famous Confucian anecdote nicely illustrates this point. According to the *Li Ji*, a Confucian classic, Confucius and his students were walking through the forest and came across a woman sitting next to an open grave. She was weeping profusely. When one of the students asked her why she was crying, she replied, "First, my father-in-law was killed by a tiger. Later the tigers ate my husband. Now they have eaten my son as well." Confucius asked her why she didn't leave the forest. The woman replied, "At least there is no oppressive government here." Confucius turned to his students and said, "Remember this: Oppressive government is more terrible than tigers."

This story bears close analysis. The woman was dependent upon these menfolk to provide her with a livelihood. The tigers had beggared her and were a threat to her very life. Yet she would rather face material devastation than lose her freedom. If a true ruler serves the interests of the human beings he rules, and if, as this story suggests, freedom is the primary interest of human beings, then the only trustworthy ruler is the one who always takes care to respect and promote freedom. Freedom generally "trumps" economic well-being in the Confucian scheme of values. The ethic might sanction a forced redistribution of land, but it would never approve of the murder of the citizenry. Freedom has value because it enables us to make the thoughtful choices through which we realize *jen*. Given that the dead have no freedom and no opportunity to excel at deliberation, a policy of killing some people in order to improve the people's standard of living is never justified in this ethic.

Confucius, therefore, would not judge anyone a great leader just because he or she improved people's standard of living. Nor would he be especially enamored with some who are being touted as exemplary business leaders in China today. Take the case of Zhang Guoxi ("Boss Zhang"). "Boss Zhang," possibly the richest man in China, is so esteemed that an asteroid discovered at the Jiangxi observatory was named after him. Why is he greatly admired? During the Cultural Revolution, he sold the family home and used the capital to start a business carving wooden chests. These chests found a market in Japan, and Boss Zhang expanded his product line to include gilded Buddhist altars. The Guoxi Group grew to include trading operations in Japan, Germany, and Hong Kong. Confucius would acknowledge Boss Zhang's initiative, his ability to seize opportunities, and his flexibility and adaptability. But he would not judge Zhang a great business leader. Zhang appears to care little for politics. As long as the government leaves him alone so he can pursue his vision of business grandeur, Zhang is content. He does not bother to consider whether the government is the right sort to help as many people as possible realize their humanity. Nor is he in the least bit interested in any form of public service. As a result, he fails to realize himself as a full human being worthy of the trust of his peers.

The point is not that every leader must be ethically pure. When one of Confucius's students criticizes a minister who transferred his allegiance from his murdered lord to the new ruler responsible for the murder, Confucius rebuts the criticism. The advice this same minister gave to the new lord saved the kingdom. If it were not for that minister, Confucius and his students would all be living and dressing like barbarians (14/17). The minister deserves praise not because he was effective but because he kept his eye on what was important—the freedom of his people. The old lord was dead. The enemy was threatening. So the minister made what he could of the situation at hand, giving good advice to the new lord.

The Confucian ethic favors ethical leadership (7/16; 8/13), but "ethical" is not equivalent to "rigidly principled." In his own way, Confucius is every bit as worldly as Boss Zhang. He knows we often must act under less than optimal circumstances. We do not get to choose our venue. Refusing to act because one wants to keep one's character unsullied does little to improve a bad situation. It may even make the situation worse than it would have been if we had acted. The businessman Oskar Schindler was not a paragon of virtue. Yet, by negotiating with and deceiving the Nazis, this hard-drinking womanizer managed to save the lives of hundreds of Jews. Schindler's actions embodied the Confucian ethic. Schindler did not worry about his character or reputation. He did concern himself with what he could and should do to alleviate the suffering of those less fortunate than himself. He was entrepreneurial like Boss Zhang but, unlike Zhang, he put his talents in the service of the larger cause of securing people's dignity and freedom. Schindler implicitly understood that the common people are the touchstone by which leaders are kept to the straight path (15/25).

PART THREE: OBJECTIONS TO THE CONFUCIAN IDEA OF TRUSTWORTHINESS

Is the Confucian idea of trustworthiness defensible? In order to answer that question, we need to consider several possible objections.

Objection 1: Confucian Filial Piety Encourages Distrust and Impedes Economic Development

Some critics have suggested that Confucianism has functioned as a drag on the economic development of China. The ethic's emphasis on filial piety and on nurturing specific relationships supposedly leads citizens to defer to authority and prevents them from developing a more universal ethic capable of nurturing and sustaining trusting relations with strangers. Those making this objection clearly have not read Confucius. His ethic favors filial piety precisely because and to the extent that it instills habits of respect and care capable of being transferred to people outside of the immediate family. Moreover, Confucius certainly did not approve of either patriarchal tyranny or abject submission to the will of authority figures. One should never do unto others what one would not have them do to oneself (15/24). While China has unquestionably known many centuries of tyrannical rule, such authoritarianism is not Confucian and certainly is not limited to China.

In some respects, Confucian values have helped to make possible the recent "economic miracle" in Southeast Asia. Given that these values existed prior to the twentieth century, and given that there are many sources of values within the huge region of Asia, it would be simple-minded to cite Confucian values as the sole or perhaps even major cause of the rapid industrialization of China, South Korea, Indonesia, and so on. Specific historical events have been crucial factors in development. For example, it was only after Maoism destroyed the feudal infrastructure in China that the country was able to modernize. Nevertheless, the Confucian emphasis on health and education—an emphasis resurrected by Mao—has produced a relatively healthy and well-educated work force. People are able to work hard and have many of the literacy skills necessary to succeed in an increasingly complex economy. The assertion, then, that Confucian values are intrinsically hostile to modern capitalism is absurd.

Objection 2: Confucian Ethic Ignores the Role of Competency and Shared Values in Trust

Modern leadership studies suggest a more interesting and compelling objection to the Confucian ethic. This ethic centers on trustworthiness, more than on trust, and emphasizes self-scrutiny as a method for making oneself worthy of other people's trust. But can we avoid considering others' character traits and their substantive commitments? Shouldn't our rulers have to demonstrate competence and a commitment to values we, their followers, hold? No one would trust a doctor who did not know how to diagnose and heal illness. By analogy, stakeholders surely should not trust business leaders who are unable to inspire and empower workers and to articulate a vision capable of molding the company into a prosperous and profitable organization. Furthermore, a business leader will not be successful unless she is able to speak to the deeply held values of those she must motivate. If she is not able to convince her colleagues that she shares those values, she likely will find it hard to work with them, much less inspire and coordinate their activities. We might contend, therefore, that the Confucian ethic badly errs in overlooking the important role competency and shared values play in bolstering the authority of a leader and making her appear credible and trustworthy.

While it is true that Confucius says little about shared values, his account of trustworthiness is far from worthless. The Confucian ethic anticipates new developments in leadership theory. Some scholars have begun to challenge the standard management assumption that leadership is a matter of mastering certain teachable core competencies. For example, Peter Vaill contends that "managerial leadership is not learned; it is learning."[16] Today's leaders must deal with a huge array of stakeholders. The various groups have heterogeneous missions, interests, and organizational structures. These features of the stakeholders' groups are in continual flux as the economy and society evolve in surprising ways. The most "competent" leader may not be the party with the most number of techniques but the person who is most able to challenge commonplace assumptions and to see things in a fresh manner.

Confucius would agree entirely. His ethic of mindfulness aims at instilling habits of thoughtfulness. The truest ruler is the one who knows one thing: "[I]t is difficult to be a ruler, and it is not easy to be a subject either" (13/15). There is no technique for guaranteeing prosperity, but those who keep this saying before them have the best chance of success. One who meditates on these difficulties will listen to others because he will be open to insight, whatever its source. Such a leader can perceive the old in a new light and is thus well equipped to at least discern change. Those who can see the past anew will not be inclined to assume the future will merely repeat the past.

By basing trustworthiness on a willingness to learn and to be self-critical, Confucius lays the groundwork for a very different but perhaps quite profound understanding of human relations. During the past decade, management gurus have argued for empowerment of the workforce. Empowerment is understood roughly as granting responsibility for decisions to subordinates and then allowing the subordinates to make and to learn from their mistakes. This description of empowerment makes it seem as though it were a one-time act. The executive grants authority and responsibility to subordinates and then steps back to wait for the benefits. But of course matters are never so simple. Leaders and followers alike have had to learn what empowerment does and does not mean. It does not mean giving employees carte blanche to make any and all decisions. Bank tellers should not be granting loans; phone marketers should not be diagnosing problems with a customer's phone line. Employees should not make promises they are unable to keep or presume to possess knowledge and expertise they lack. Leaders have had to learn some hard lessons as well. They cannot tell subordinates they are empowered to design and produce a product and then refuse to give them a budget for production. Empowerment is a sham unless employees are given genuine discretion to do what needs to be done for a project to be successfully completed. In short, empowerment is not a technique. It is an ongoing process of learning by leaders and followers about power, appropriate limits, and discretion. It is indeed hard to be a ruler and it is hard to be a subject.

Objection 3: Self-Scrutiny Too Easily Becomes Dangerous Self-Criticism

A third concern has gone largely unremarked by expositors and critics of a Confucian ethic. The ethic demands that agents be both highly self-conscious and self-critical. While this requirement can lead to greater thoughtfulness, it also can make reform difficult. Instead of finding fault with other people or with institutions, the agent is to look inward and seek to improve herself. This duty of self-criticism can be used by unscrupulous authorities to derail any attempts to criticize or reform existing power structures. The Chinese Communists under Mao would remind the middle and upper classes of the many privileges they had enjoyed. Having cunningly played on people's feelings of guilt, the Communists would then demand that these "guilty" parties write self-accusations describing their faulty actions and thoughts. People were not allowed to criticize the authorities. They were supposed to monitor and rectify their own thinking instead. To this day employees in Chinese firms still are routinely required to produce self-criticisms when they conflict with fellow employees or managers, even if the court or arbitration board has found the other party to be at fault.

To be fair, Confucius himself never requires people to accuse themselves. Neither does he forbid criticism of others. Criticism is permitted, provided the mode of criticism is correct. We should offer constructive criticism and should always attack evil, rather than persons. However, in some cases, a corrupt system may be more to blame than those who are captives of this system. The Confucian ethic fails to recognize the ways in which the practice of self-criticism may be manipulated and abused. People need to be able to confront and challenge authorities without having to fear that they suddenly will become the accused. Here we have a case where Confucian ethics can be usefully supplemented by Western rights theory. People have a duty to critically examine their actions and motivations and to be judicious when criticizing other people's behavior. However, they also have a right not to be forced to incriminate themselves.

Can the Confucian ethic accommodate this insight? Although the language of rights is foreign to Confucianism, the impulse underlying a right to avoid self-incrimination is not. A right not to incriminate oneself is yet another expression of the thoroughly Confucian belief that the individual ultimately transcends societal categories. The categories can never determine who a person is because these categories change in response to an individual's actions and thoughts. Today's counterrevolutionary is tomorrow's hero. To require people to incriminate themselves is to demand that they reduce themselves to categories they transcend. No thoughtful person would choose to engage in such a charade. The duty to be self-critical can coexist with the duty to be thoughtful only when individuals are not forced to incriminate themselves—that is, only if they have a right against self-incrimination. In addition, people will trust each other's words more if they have good reason to think the speech has not been uttered under duress. In this respect, the conditions for being worthy of trust are identical with those for reposing trust.

CONCLUSION

Although recent Western discussions of trust have tended to focus on conditions for reposing trust, Confucius asks us to see trustworthiness as the more important phenomenon: How should we behave if we are to make ourselves into beings truly worthy of trust? What responsibility do we have for ensuring that our judgment of someone's trustworthiness is sound? The Confucian ethic calls into question whether a business leader can earn the trust of her followers simply by adhering to select rules (e.g., "avoid conflicts of interest") or by adopting certain techniques. Being thoughtful is ultimately the only way to earn and merit the trust of one's fellow citizens.

QUESTIONS FOR DISCUSSION

1. What are some elements of Confucian trustworthiness that distinguish this ethical virtue from the notion of trust found in the West?

2. In some Western traditions, ethics is reduced to adhering to a behavioral algorithm or following rules that are true in all circumstances—like Kant's Categorical Imperative. How would a Confucian ethicist respond to someone who was convinced that trustworthiness was simply a matter of following rules?

3. The author claims that the Chinese have been suspicious of contracts that spell out in great detail the rights and responsibilities of each party. What are the Confucian values that are jeopardized by this model of contractual arrangement? What type of contract would be preferable from the perspective of a Confucian ethicist?

4. How might the Confucian reliance on *guanxi*—close personal relationships—affect the ways some Chinese approach corporate relations? How does one cultivate *guanxi* in a business setting?

5. What are the arguments used by those who believe Confucianism has functioned as a drag on Chinese economic development? How does the author counter these naysayers?

6. Does Confucianism ignore the role of competency and shared values of trust? If so, in what ways? Does Confucianism have an answer to this apparent shortcoming?

7. Can self-scrutiny in Confucianism too easily lead to ethical passivity in the face of incompetent or immoral leadership? Can self-criticism be manipulated or abused by authority to ensure obedience and derail reform? How might this happen?

NOTES

1. All references to Confucian sayings are to the chapter and paragraph listing in *Confucius, The Analects*, trans. D. C. Lau (London: Penguin Books, 1979).

2. See, e.g., Annette Baier, "Trust," in *Tanner Lectures on Human Value*, ed. Grethe B. Peterson, vol. 13 (Salt Lake City: University of Utah Press, 1992), 107–36; Trudy Govier, "An Epistemology of Trust," *International Journal of Morality and Social Studies* 8 (Spring 1993): 155–74.

3. Boye Lafayette De Mente, *Chinese Etiquette and Ethics in Business* (New York: NTC Publishing Group, 1994), 121.

4. Of course that is not to deny that some unscrupulous persons may abuse one's trust. Mente contends: "The Chinese continuously emphasize that all agreements should be based on friendship and goodwill, making finely detailed contracts unnecessary. However, in any disagreement, they take a legalistic view of contracts and do not feel bound by anything that is not explicitly stated in a contract." Mente goes on to complain that the Chinese will always try to make business relationships conform to the laws of their own country. Mente, *Chinese Etiquette*, 121. However, given that Americans, English, and Germans also prefer to do business in accordance with the laws of their respective countries, this last point hardly counts as evidence that the Chinese are more grasping or unjust than other peoples.

5. Mente, *Chinese Etiquette*, 119.

6. Chin-Ning Chu, *The Asian Mind Game* (New York: Rawson Associates, 1991), 171.

7. Asians consistently complain about Americans' impatience and their preference for studying trade statistics and neglecting cultural and historical studies. Some Chinese describe Americans as *tean-zu*, a term meaning "childlike." Americans have been blessed with growth and peace and have not known the level of suffering the Chinese endured for centuries. Their optimism can lead them to a superficial understanding of other

people's positions. Chu, *Asian Mind Game*, 172.

8. Mente, *Chinese Etiquette*, 90.

9. Nicholas D. Kristoff and Sheryl Wudunn, *China Wakes* (New York: Vintage Books, 1995), 96.

10. Francis Fukuyama argues the Chinese are a low-trust society in *Trust* (New York: Free Press, 1996), *passim*. The same point has been made by Mente, *Chinese Etiquette*, 90.

11. Kristoff and Wudunn, *China Wakes*, 316.

12. Kristoff and Wudunn, *China Wakes*, 344.

13. Kristoff and Wudunn, *China Wakes*, 317.

14. "P&G Wants to Be on Tip of Tongues in, Let's Say, Tianjin," *Wall Street Journal*, August 24, 1998, B8.

15. Kristoff and Wudunn, *China Wakes*, 141; Lu Xiaohe, "On Ethical and Economic Value" at http://www.stthom.edu/cbes.

16. Peter B. Vaill, "The Learning Challenges of Leadership," in *The Balance of Leadership and Followership*, Kellogg Leadership Studies Project, July 1997, 71–83.

Part III

RELIGION AND QUESTIONS OF CONTEMPORARY BUSINESS

• 13 •

The Potential for Building Covenants in Business Corporations

Stewart W. Herman

Covenants have a long and deep history within a number of the world's major religious traditions. Like a contract, a covenant is an agreement between two parties. However, a covenant tends to be more descriptive of the quality of the relationship in question and the norms that ought to govern it. By contrast, a contract tends to concentrate on the narrow legal prescriptions that restrict the behavior of parties to a business relationship. Therefore, covenants, by their very nature, tend to give more details and better direction in regard to the moral character of a relationship and the interpersonal dimensions of an agreement. It follows then that covenants represent a largely untapped ethical resource when businesses enter into agreements with one another, with employees, with consumers, and with investors. In this article, Stewart Herman will explore some of the possibilities for using covenants to help us insert richer moral elements into business agreements.

COVENANTS AND CORPORATIONS

*W*hat exactly is the potential for covenantal relations in modern business corporations? The question arises because during the last several years, at least five theologically minded business ethicists have proposed the idea of covenant as a normative model for explaining how large bureaucratic corporations ought to function.[1] These prescriptions are challenging because covenantal norms hold business practitioners to a morally higher standard than the quid pro quo of contractual obligations. Douglas Sturm holds corporations to the norms of peace, justice, and steadfastness, while Charles McCoy and William May challenge executives to exercise moral leadership.

I am inclined to agree with these ethicists that a covenantal potential exists in corporations. Yet this potential is not obvious, for it is generally eclipsed by contract as the central term that explains how corporations operate. The contractual bond is the primary source of legal and moral leverage against malfeasance in corporations, because it is the primary description of the relationship between management and employees. Covenant-minded business ethicists therefore face the difficult task of making a covenantal basis to corporations appear as real and as firm as this contractual basis. I suspect the contractual description is too firmly established to be displaced, but it could be supplemented and modified by a covenantal description. What is needed then is to demonstrate how the idea of covenant captures a descriptive dimension of corporations that the idea of contract misses. If Clifford Geertz is right that religious moral visions become compelling insofar as they appear "really real," the covenantal norms asserted by Sturm and others will become more persuasive as they are grounded in a description of the corporation that renders those norms obvious and compelling.

Here, I will focus on the relationship between managements and employees rather than, as is often done, the relation between corporations and society. My principal claims are that corporate settings involve managements and employees in relations that are more than contractual and that this "more than" opens the door to develop a plausible and powerful covenantal ethic for management–employee relations. This redescription and appraisal of the corporation in covenantal terms proceeds in three steps. First, I will argue that the cement that holds corporations together is not simply contracts, but a broad array of "influence strategies," which managements and employees apply to shape each other's thinking and acting. For an account of these strategies, I draw upon organization theory and organizational behavior, two closely related social-scientific fields which attempt to explain how large organizations function.[2] This redescription renders the logic of covenanting directly relevant to explaining how corporations function, because one signal feature of covenants—in contrast to contracts—is that they are vehicles through which parties aim at forming, even transforming, the character and actions of each other. Second, I will interpret the biblical history of divine covenant-building from an organizational perspective in order to generate a normative model for covenant-building in corporations. Managements and employees are driven to influence each other by a logic of interdependence compounded of vulnerability and contingency. This dynamic correlates with the logic of divine covenant-building attested to in the canonical record of God's history with God's people. The important fact for organizational struggles is that the influence strategies used by God affirm the moral agency and freedom of God's people by not attempting to vanquish or manipulate the contingency that these stubborn covenant partners pose to

God. Third, I abstract from this normative model two general guidelines: that authentic covenant-building requires that managements and employees acknowledge their vulnerability to each other, and that they be generous in their application of influence strategies to each other.

In theological ethics the social origin and character of selfhood is commonly affirmed. Yet rarely do we pursue the full implications of this insight: that the dynamic, interactive aspects of human action indeed be the focus of our analyses. This insight is beginning to emerge in discussions contrasting the covenantal and social-contract bases of our social polity.[3] It appears late, if undeveloped, whenever ethicists turn to the question of how character and virtues are shaped. Still missing, however, is a systematic discussion of what here will be termed "influence strategies": intentional devices parties use to shape the thinking and acting of each other. We are subject to such efforts all the time, whether by consent or not. Intentional influences, ranging from the impersonal marketing strategies of Madison Avenue, to the communal efforts of sectarian religious academies, to the interpersonal tactics reported by social psychologist Erving Goffman, are ubiquitous, but they are rarely raised for discussion in theological ethics.

Corporations as Constructed of Influence Strategies

The modern corporation, perhaps more than any other form of association, exemplifies the dense interplay of intentional efforts to shape human action and character—and efforts to resist such shaping. A corporation comes into being when two or more people seek to coordinate their behavior toward particular productive or economic ends. The basic units in this form of association are human action of two sorts: particular productive tasks, such as operating a drill press or processing insurance claims at a video display terminal, and the actions that direct, coordinate, and motivate individuals to perform such tasks. If productive tasks are the bricks, and are performed by employees, the coordinating actions constitute the mortar of a business enterprise, and are performed by management. (The distinction is relative in that most individuals in corporations are both employees and part of management, depending on whether they look up or down the corporate hierarchy.)

In explaining how large organizations function, most organization theorists have been preoccupied with the mortar. They have asked, how does the needed coordination of human action come about? What orients and integrates human action around particular purposes? What motivates employees to perform work designed by managements? And how do employees affect managerial expectations about the content of work and other terms of the relationship? Organization theorists realized early that if the coordination and performance of productive tasks required no more than strictly mechanical behavior, corporations would need to be held together by no stronger glue than contracts.

Contracting partners take the character of each other as given and seek only particular performances from each other, as Joseph Allen has noted.[4] But the organization theorists have been no more satisfied than theological ethicists with the conventional idea that contracts suffice to explain human action in corporations. For reasons spelled out in the next section, neither managements nor employees can confine themselves to explicitly defined contractual relations. They seek to shape the manner in which they are valued by each other in order to further their respective chosen ends. In so doing, they engage in forming and even transforming each other—and themselves.

The Influence Strategies Used in Corporate Settings

A brief catalogue will serve to illustrate the dense interweaving of influence strategies in organizational settings. A series of psychologists (beginning in the 1920s, social psychologists in the 1930s), sociologists (1940s), political scientists (1950s and 1960s), and economists (1970s) have brought the tools of their disciplines to bear upon organizations. They have discovered at least eight of these strategies. The concept of an influence strategy has not yet emerged as a comprehensive organizing principle in the fields of organization theory or organizational behavior, but it does appear to be a useful rubric for sorting through the profuse accumulation of concepts and theories in these fields. While the first two (exchange and bureaucracy) reflect a contractual understanding of the relationship, the remaining six (leadership, therapy, delegation, socialization, bargaining, and resistance) cannot be shoehorned into exacting stipulation-centered thinking.

The first influence strategy identified by theorists is that of "exchange," through which managements seek to shape employee thinking about the value of their labor. As early as 1903, Frederick Taylor, an engineer, was arguing that sufficient pay would render employees willing to accept a second form of influence: "bureaucracy."[5]

Here, "bureaucracy" refers to the procedures, rules, and commands through which managements seek to channel the actions of employees. These first two strategies lend themselves to contractual specification and provide the basic cement, as well as the basic explanatory paradigm, of corporations. But they provided only the point of departure for those early theorists who began to appreciate that contractual descriptions hardly sufficed to explain how large organizations survived and flourished.

The early theorists aimed to improve organizational practice rather than provide value-neutral descriptions. They recommended, rather than simply reported, the use of influence strategies. Executives such as Henri Fayol, James Money, and Chester I. Barnard urged managers to exercise bold and visionary "leadership" in order to unite the energies of employees in pursuit of a coherent vision of organizational purpose.[6] In a different vein, social scientists began half a century ago to prescribe a "therapeutic" strategy, in two versions. Social psychologists identified with Harvard University during the 1930s and 1940s suggested that management could render workers more productive by making them happy by immersing them in small workgroups which would serve to dispel the neuroses of isolated individualism.[7] During the 1950s and 1960s, humanist psychologists counseled managers to assist employees to "realize" their innate potentials in order to liberate their energies in the direction of achieving managerial goals.[8] Somewhat similarly, business consultants such as Peter Drucker began to urge managements to "delegate" managerial work to employees as a means of fostering managerial commitment and drive in them.[9]

So far, these strategies represent the recommendations of theorists bent upon improving managerial practice by prescribing how human action should be shaped. During the 1950s, organization theory turned from prescription to description, with the result that more influence strategies were discovered. Theorists, beginning with Herbert A. Simon at Carnegie Mellon University, drew upon cognitive psychology to suggest that managements "inculcate" employees by establishing an environment of perception and purpose that shapes their thinking and acting.[10] More recently, organization theorists influenced by cultural anthropology have observed a more comprehensive "socialization" strategy, where managements integrate employees into cohesive "corporate cultures."[11] But in organization theory, perhaps the most prominent model of strategic influence today is "bargaining." This strategy emerged first in the 1960s, when theorists realized that influence does not work simply from top down, but in both directions.[12] These theorists turned to interest-group theory to argue that managements and employees cultivate discrete bases of power and attempt to shape each other's expectations in order to secure their own interests.

Of course, any of the seven influence strategies described so far could be used to manipulate or coerce compliance rather than induce cooperation. Radical organization theorists, always suspicious of managerial strategies, have contributed an eighth strategy: "resistance," or the multitude of ways in which employees strive to reduce managerial control and change managerial thinking. Resistance strategies range from mild measures to safeguard employee autonomy, such as stockpiling parts on an assembly line; through the use of work rules, planned absenteeism, and covert showdowns to frustrate management control; to more extreme measures such as needless waste or sabotage.[13]

This catalogue of influence strategies suggests that descriptions of how corporations function are impoverished to the extent that they are reductively contractual. Contrary to the principal assumption of the contractual paradigm, contracts are not likely to induce either managements or employees to abandon their attempts to control or influence each other. The contractual paradigm ignores the question of what extracontractual influence strategies are used coercively in a manner to which contract law is blind. If academic and other observers are to be believed, the coercive impact of these strategies can be powerful. Some strategies—particularly bureaucracy and socialization—have been pilloried precisely for their capacity to oppress or warp the moral character of managements and employees.[14]

Of course, it would be foolish to assume that managements and employees are always fiendishly clever and successful in cultivating and eliciting particular tendencies for thinking and acting. But neither should the intended outcomes of willed strategies be the only focus of concern. An important subtheme in the organizational literature is that influence strategies shape those who apply them as much as those who are targeted. Robert Merton in his classic 1940 essay explained how individuals imprint themselves with a "bureaucratic personality" by exercising bureaucratic influence. William H. Whyte Jr. outlined how a typical 1950s manager became an "organization man" by participating in, rather than resisting or exploiting, the human-relations conformity pressed upon him. More recently, Michael Maccoby has explained how managers enact four types of personality they bring to corporate settings. Recent best-selling success manuals advise ambitious individuals to shape their own characters in the direction of becoming expert bargainers.[15]

It is this connection between corporate settings and character that makes for relationship between managements and employees. The signal difference between contract and covenant as associational terms is that contracts aim no higher than to secure stipulated behaviors from each contracting party, while covenanting partners seek to form, even transform, each other in the direction of a more adequate relationship. The two terms are not entirely disjunctive. Like a contract, a covenant has a prehistory of negotiation, where one or both parties seek to institute the relationship in formal terms. But this dynamic quality is reduced or eliminated in a contractual relationship once the terms of performance have been spelled out. A covenant, in contrast, remains a dynamic, interactive relationship. The consent of both parties simply formalizes and ratifies the continuing history of the efforts by both parties to render each other more adequate covenant partners. The relationship between managements and employees trespasses from contractual onto covenantal terrain when neither party is satisfied with hands-off contractual relations, and therefore seeks to shape the manner in which each values the other. In so doing, they engage in forming and even transforming the character of themselves and each other.

DIVINE COVENANT-BUILDING FROM
AN ORGANIZATIONAL PERSPECTIVE

So far I have used "covenant" as a descriptive, operational, and not necessarily theological term. Once provided with this term for describing how character is shaped in corporate settings, covenantal theorists can proceed to ask when such influences work in the direction of fostering a theologically genuine covenantal relationship ("Covenant") between managements and employees. To render the divine Covenant a compelling prescription, some strong correlation must be found between the logic behind the intentional strategies of influence that managements and employees apply to each other and the process by which God and God's people influence each other in the direction of covenantal mutuality.

Theologians have proposed a variety of ways to conceptualize, in terms analogous to human intentionality, how God seeks to shape the character of God's covenant patterns. Augustine and Aquinas outline a persuasion aimed at reason and beyond reason; Luther envisions a dialectic of love and wrath; Calvin, a tutelage in unchanging divine precepts; Barth, a divine command which paradoxically functions also as permission. No doubt a theologically informed Covenant between managements and employees might be conceptualized on the basis of any of these divine influence strategies, as when the National Conference of Catholic Bishops applied the Thomistic model of persuasion to unite managements and employees around the value of human dignity, justice, and the common good.[16]

Here I will review the influence strategies God applies to God's people in the biblical narrative accounts of divine covenant-building. But in order to draw the correlation between the biblical material and management–employee relations most closely, I will redescribe the covenantal history through what might be termed an organizational perspective. First I will outline the logic that impels managements and employees to influence the action and character of each other; then I will use that logic as a lens through which to interpret the covenant-building strategies of God.

The Logic of Vulnerability and Contingency in Corporations

Why are managements and employees engaged in applying influence strategies to each other? The answer lies in what often blandly is termed their "interdependence." Emile Durkheim celebrated the division of labor as a means to render individuals more altruistic by making them more dependent upon each other.[17] Subsequent theorists have found such interdependence to be more ambiguous. From the perspective of organization theory, "interdependence" refers less to a constructive relation of mutual complementarity than to the often distasteful state of having one's autonomy of action circumscribed by functional dependence upon another actor. Markets, technologies, and the division of labor they spawn force managements and employees to interlink their action in a way that renders them closely reliant upon each other. As a result, large organizations such as corporations are often fragile coalitions of participants who individually and in groups are pulling in different directions in pursuit of dissimilar projects and interests.[18] Carefully cultivated corporate facades of unity, stability, and permanence only obscure the reality of the perpetual struggle of individuals and groups, in a context of tightly linked functional interdependence, to guard and enhance their zones of autonomous action.[19]

The market-driven need of management for employees and of employees for management enmeshes all parties in intricate webs of what here will be termed "vulnerability" and "contingency." The term "vulnerability" here is used not in personal terms, to indicate susceptibility to emotional hurt, but in impersonal terms, to point to the gap between expectations and fulfillment that opens up whenever a party has an interest or takes on a project. For example, a management committed to produce machine tools but unable to secure all the skilled workers it needs is vulnerable, in an impersonal sense, to the demands of those workers it already has. Where such dependence is great, it confers power upon one party to dominate and exploit the other. If managements and employees had no projects or interests to pursue, and therefore no functional need for one another, they would have no vulnerability to each other. Vulnerabilities of this impersonal sort open up not only because managements and employees are functionally interdependent, but also because they are beings endowed with will. Because both possess the capacity to exercise some degree of choice, managements and employees present themselves to each other as unpredictable, and to that extent uncontrollable.

It is, therefore, not surprising that bureaucratic managements have been engaged in a century-long quest—assisted by organization theorists—to iron every last bit of contingency out of the behavior of employees.[20] Managers rarely take employees as they are and simply specify tasks and roles. They seek to motivate employees, whether through exchange, therapy, or other strategies that provide rewards unrelated to the content of work or managerial purpose. Or they seek to energize their wills by inspiring employees with managerial aims, as in the leadership, delegation, or socialization strategies. Employees, for their part, do not simply accept directions and orders, but seek to shape the expectations managers hold regarding the quantity and quality of work to be done, or the manner in which they as employees are to be treated. They consent to the motivational strategies, or develop strategies of resistance in order to co-opt or thwart them.

The Logic of Vulnerability, Contingency, and Influence Strategies in Divine Covenanting

It is risky if not foolhardy to abstract comprehensive themes from the whole biblical canon, particularly from the millennium-long series of texts that narrate the history of God's people. An organizational perspective elicits one generalization that appears defensible, however. The "historical" texts that narrate the history of Israel and of the church assume the relationship between God and God's people evolves amid conditions of vulnerability and contingency on both sides.

The people are subject to a host of vicissitudes, collective and personal. In rough order of appearance, these include slavery, hunger and thirst, tribal warfare, economic exploitation, personal enmities, invasions, deportations, diseases, and "evil spirits." Since God, in God's sovereign freedom, intervenes at particular times and in particular ways to rescue the people from their vulnerability, God presents the people with a contingency that exceeds their control. At the same time, God is vulnerable because the people present God with contingency. They are promiscuous in their search for powerful divine aid to cope with their vulnerabilities.[21] Their memories are short, their fears great, and their hearts often rebellious. Their pride and weaknesses lead them into harming themselves and others, sometimes in the same unspeakably cruel ways by which their enemies harm them.[22] At the same time, the people are resilient and capable of change, even fundamental change. Sometimes they thirst for God, and their hearts can be converted to covenantal trust and loyalty. From within their midst God lifts up heroes of exemplary righteousness.[23]

An organizational perspective on the biblical narratives emphasizes the vulnerability of God to the contingencies presented by the people. The vulnerability of God can be acknowledged in two senses. First, God suffers, on the analogy of human pathos, when the people suffer, and particularly when their apostasy inflicts pain upon God.[24] This insight, long obscured by theological claims of divine impassibility, recently has been argued powerfully by Abraham Meschel and Jürgen Moltmann, among others. Second, and more important for covenantal business ethics, God is rendered vulnerable in an impersonal, teleological sense by the gap between the divine intention to Covenant and the fulfillment of that intention. Whether the fulfillment is seen as historical or eschatological, its not-yet character provides the people ample scope in history to fall short of the fidelity and righteousness God expects from them, and so to frustrate and delay God's intention to shape God's people into faithful Covenant partners. This dynamic has been obscured in the theological tradition by claims of divine omnipotence, but appears defensible to the extent that God's people enjoy moral freedom, and therefore present

God with contingency.

God copes with the contingent behavior of the people by applying strategies intended to elicit their faith as trust and loyalty. More than one strategy is needed because the changing situations of their lives preclude the evolution of one universal mode of influence. Following mainstream literary scholarship, four relatively distinct periods of covenant-building can be distinguished, corresponding to the works of the Jahwist (J) and the Elohist (E), the Deuteronomist (D), the Priestly writer (P), and the four evangelists. Each expresses a distinctive emphasis in divine strategy.[25]

> 1. From the time of the patriarchs throughout the Exodus and wandering (the Jahwist and Elohist texts), the people of God are nomads or slaves—exceedingly vulnerable to their neighbors or masters and largely unfamiliar with God.[26] God applies a dialectic of "promising" and "testing" to establish and sustain the Abrahamic and Mosaic covenants. Abraham, Moses, and the people respond in kind by questioning, bargaining with, and testing God to determine the degree of God's commitment and power.[27] The point of these strategies is for both parties to determine the character and reliability of each other.
>
> 2. Between the Conquest and the end of the Monarchy (the Deuteronomic texts), Israel becomes an increasingly stubborn and rebellious nation.[28] To cope with this increased contingency and bring Israel back to covenantal fidelity, God seeks to "deter" abuses of kingly and priestly power. These deterrent strategies include the Ancient Near East formula of curses and blessings, an emphasis not evident in the earlier J and E covenantal texts; the "covenantal lawsuit" or indictments announced by the pre-exilic prophets; and threats of future punishment.[29]
>
> 3. The Exile (Priestly texts) costs the people not only their political sovereignty, but more important, their confidence that God would never abandon the Covenant.[30] A radical redirection of divine strategy is called for. God applies various strategies of "affirmation." Prior covenants with Noah and Abraham are revised into radical promises binding God to Israel in perpetuity.[31] The exilic prophets use terms of intimate sympathy to comfort the people in their extreme vulnerability. However, once the people are restored to Jerusalem, the post-exilic prophets and Nehemiah return to a dialectic of deterrence (indictments of sin) and promises (hope).[32]
>
> 4. During the Roman occupation (Gospels), the self-righteousness and exploitation by religious elites invite prophetic denunciation by Jesus and renew God's enigmatic strategy of "hardening."[33] But the principal divine influence strategies appear to be more affirmative, in that they assume

a readiness of at least the disciples to renew the Covenant. Jesus applies "teaching" to elevate and refine their understanding of covenantal law (Matthew) and God's partiality to the vulnerable (Luke). And Jesus uses "recruitment" to transform the disciples into willing instruments of the kingdom, preparing them for the "delegation" needed to sustain the fellowship (John) or carry God's covenant-building mission to the ends of the world (Luke-Acts).[34]

The moral significance of these situationally tailored strategies lies in the remarkable fact that they do not extinguish, nor even reduce, God's vulnerability to the contingency posed by the people. None of the strategies serves to crush or undermine the moral freedom of the people. To be sure, coercion is present. The people are not free to immunize themselves against divine strategies, nor are they free to exit the relationship, nor, for that matter, are they free simply to surrender or abdicate their wills to direct divine control. Rather, the strategies indicate a broad channel along which human agency is moved toward a right covenantal relationship with God. This channel is bounded on the one side by efforts of God to nourish and encourage the human to restrain that same will when it overasserts itself. This overall strategy reflects the commitment of God to accept, rather than suppress, the contingency posed by wayward and unreliable Covenant partners.

Indeed, the logic of covenanting generates a profound irony. Covenant, as the very instrument God employs to render the people trustworthy, renders God vulnerable to their oft-repeated failure to be trustworthy Covenant partners. The long canonical history of broken Covenants and revised influence strategies suggests that nothing short of the unreserved vulnerability of God to human contingency will serve to elicit the fundamental trust and loyalty appropriate to Covenant partners. Hence, the incarnation, and of course, the cross. Of course, this logic of vulnerability and contingency in covenanting is not universal in the canonical text; it is more evident in the Prophets than the wisdom literature, more evident in Hosea than Amos, more the synoptic Gospels than in John. Moreover, a supercessionist argument is not being made here. From Abraham to the Resurrection there is no essential change in God's strategy to create Covenant partners from the widening circle of God's people. The vulnerability of God to the covenantal infidelities of God's people is evident from Sinai on. There is no essential difference between the refusal of God to abandon or destroy God's unworthy people in the Pentateuch and the unqualified vulnerability of Jesus Christ in the New Testament. The long historical arc is relevant principally because it is the lengthening continuity of such vulnerability that establishes covenantal fidelity.

NORMATIVE GUIDELINES

The major aim of a covenant-building ethic within a corporation will be to foster the growth of a genuine, inclusive mutuality and trust between employees and managements in a manner consistent with loyalty to God's Covenant. The heuristic value of such an ethic will reside in its capacity to make two kinds of discriminations. The first is the relatively obvious distinction between covenantal and overtly anticovenantal relations, as when managements openly exploit employees or employees categorically refuse to extend any trust toward well-meaning and honorable managements. The second is the less obvious distinction between inauthentic and authentic covenantal relations, as when some participants in a corporation bind themselves in a mutuality that excludes or devalues other parties inside or outside the corporation.

Constructing such an ethic involves more than articulating norms, which are static. In keeping with its focus upon interactive behaviors, it needs to be asked: When do the influence strategies management and employees apply to each other serve to generate an authentic covenantal quality of trust and trustworthiness? In formal outline, the answer appears simple: when the influence strategies they use reflect the influence strategies God applies. The biblical model suggests that such an ethic will need to make reference to both deterrent and affirmative strategies, as situationally appropriate. On the one hand, anticovenantal or inauthentic covenantal relations often call for the deterrent strategies of prophetic indictment and threat. These strategies, which clearly are part of the covenant-building process, long have been used by critics of business. Recent examples include the work of Karen Bloomquist and Prentiss Pemberton and Daniel Finn, who endorse strategies of nonviolent "resistance" in order to build a covenantal community inside or outside the corporation.[35]

On the other hand, the sincere covenant-building efforts of managements and employees call for affirmative strategies as well. Perhaps the dominant trend in recent theologically minded business ethics had been to foster such efforts. William F. May, Charles S. Conroy, and Oliver S. Williams recommend that executives develop leadership and socialization strategies in order to shape the organizational character of managers and employees. Elsewhere I have suggested that these efforts are too ambitious, in that they call employees to broad loyalties without explaining the conditions that might warrant the mutual trust necessary to support such loyalties.[36] But these ethicists remind us that there are managements and employees who are genuinely interested in cooperating rather than exploiting each other's vulnerabilities. For the balance of this chapter, I will propose and explore two general normative guidelines appropriate to such good-faith efforts.

Mutual Vulnerability

First, the most genuine Covenants are built as the influence strategies managements and employees apply to each other acknowledge and reflect mutual vulnerability as well as power. This guideline may appear otherworldly, because no fact is more evident to managements and especially to employees than their manifold vulnerability to the contingencies posed by each other in a market environment. Hundreds of thousands of managers and employees have lost their jobs, and shrewd strategies appear needed by individuals in thousands of other threatened positions. No norm could appear more unrealistic than one that exposes managers or employees to more risk than is avoidable. In the hard-headed business world, prudence dictates that managements and employees always be on guard against the exploitative tendencies of the other. The prudential imperative of self-preservation exerts a powerful, even moral, pull in business corporations.

Many managements now encourage employees to think of themselves as rugged entrepreneurs or consultants, with only temporary attachment to their companies. The more compassionate managements in this recessionary era are tempted to build paternalistic covenants, which they claim will take care of their employees. While such covenants certainly improve upon compacts of convenience, they pose a particular insidious danger. Paternalistic covenants come about when economic conditions endow managements with enough power to veil, offset, and deny their dependence upon employees. While such managements commendably may commit themselves to the benign and considerate use of their power, such unilateral covenanting encourages self-deception and the abuse of power. Paternalistic covenant-making serves to obscure or mask the true balance of vulnerability between management and employees, tempting managements to apply leadership or socialization strategies in a mendacious fashion. A recent Oscar-winning documentary on General Electric's nuclear operations juxtaposes management's apparently callous disregard for the health of workers with CEO Jack Welch's enthusiastic public assertions that GE workers are treated as valuable team players.[37]

Covenant-making becomes especially vibrant to the extent that the relations between managements and employees are more symmetrical—where both sides recognize, or are forced to recognize, that they possess vulnerability and power in some degree. The fascinating, and for a covenantal ethic encouraging, feature of business corporations is that all sides usually are vulnerable in some degree to contingencies posed by the other. While employees are vulnerable to management for wages, safe working conditions, and some degree of meaning in their work, managements are vulnerable to employees for some degree of efficiency, honesty, and reliability. The mutuality of these vulnerabilities provides the occasion for authentic covenantal trust-building measures. For example, a significant potential for building covenants resides precisely where management employees are locked in a stalemate. Consider the following 1987 letter by an hourly employee of General Motors to a high-school classmate who had become a member of management.

> Knowing that I never had a chance to do anything within the company. . . . I don't trust management and I don't feel that they have ever trusted me. . . . So when I hear these signals and am asked to get involved, I am torn between a spirit of cooperation and a spirit of rebellion against a company that has caused my guts to burn and my hair to thin and turn gray through years of mistrustful dealings.
>
> I now became the Champion of the Faith and the Defender of the Truth as I inflicted pain and doled out agony to management people that chose not to agree with me. I picked on bad management and good management people. It made no difference. I learned to justify my hatred every step of the way and through a seventeen-year process became a very bitter, bitter person.
>
> The one morning, shortly after my last election, I woke up with a different attitude. . . I was tired. I thought there must be a better way. —I'm ready for a change.
>
> There is a whole lot wrong with both sides. We have to truly change if we are to survive. We have to care about the consumer. We have to care about the stockholders. We have to care about the people we represent. But the most important, management people and the workers have to care about each other. . . . The leadership, both management and union, had better show the world that the employees are their most important asset.[38]

The route to covenanting lies through the realization that neither management nor employees can fully control the other, even if the power to ruin the other's projects or interests always remain available. The parties then may find themselves in a position where they must entrust themselves to each other in some degree, and a new history of trust-building gestures may begin. Mutual vulnerabilities can serve to present covenantal self-entrustment as a reasonable alternative to the kind of rigid defenses that work against the interest of all parties.

Generous Use of Influence Strategies

A second, much different recommendation is suggested by the biblical logic of covenant-building. Corporations will be more covenantal to the extent that managements and employees are generous and comprehensive in their application of influence strategies to each other. The generosity and comprehensiveness is mandated by the plentitude of God, who applies a full range of influence strategies, as situationally appropriate, to share with the people of God.

The strategies abstracted from the biblical narratives are not to be lifted directly into corporate contexts, of course. Rather, the ideas of promising, testing, warning, teaching, and so forth ought to be considered themes that might find expression in strategies more appropriate to the task-driven, densely interactive nature of corporations. The eight strategies described earlier have evolved specifically in organizational contexts. Each is an appropriate vehicle of influence because each pertains to a particular slice of human motivation elicited by participation in organizations. Exchange appeals to material desires and wants; bureaucracy to a penchant for obedience; leadership to expansive vision; delegation to the drive for mastery; therapy to the urge for psychological security and self-realization; inculcation to habitualness; socialization to the desire for moral order and meaning; bargaining to the desire for autonomy; and resistance to an egalitarian impulse.

Nevertheless, any one of these strategies applied in abstraction from consideration of the others implies a devaluation of its target. For example, the fault with bureaucratic management is less the apparatus of rules and procedures itself than the arrogant managerial assumption that rules and procedures constitute the only appropriate means of shaping the behavior of employees. Alternatively, the fault with resistance is less the opposition offered to management, which often is warranted, than the rigid underlying assumption that managements want nothing more than to exploit employees. A covenantal ethic seeks to transform suspicious, antagonistic relationships by broadening the basis upon which managements and employees value each other.

Charles McCoy, William F. May, and Oliver F. Williams move the covenantal project along by searching for ways managements and employees might value each other by a more commodious use of the influence strategies of leadership and socialization. However, these modes of influence should be emphasized only in proportion to their realistic capacity to affect organizational practice, a potential that I suspect is rather small. A larger potential resides within the basic strategies—exchange, bureaucracy, bargaining, and resistance. These strategies ought to be scrutinized for latent covenant-building elements within them.

One illustration will have to suffice. On the surface, bureaucracy appears a strategy that is exceedingly resistant to Covenantal use. This powerful anticovenantal potential cannot be extirpated from bureaucratic influence strategies, for it is rooted in impersonality, distance, and segmentation, to which bureaucracy also can inculcate universalistic, fair-minded habits of normative thinking. Objective structures of rules and policies can serve as tools and resources for individuals to demonstrate their trustworthiness by protecting others from arbitrary treatment. For example, sociologist Vicki Smith recently described how branch managers used the bureaucratic apparatus of a large California bank, at some risk themselves, to protect employees from attempts by senior management to engage in wholesale, unwarranted layoffs. These branch managers co-opted the device of training seminars to build solidarity among themselves and made constructive use of the difficult objectives imposed by senior management to organize and motivate employees for greater achievement, and in general used what margin of discretion the bureaucratic apparatus permitted in order to deflect the harsh policies of senior management.[39]

Applications to Business Ethics and Beyond

The relevance of the idea of Covenant to business ethics derives from a correlation between the logic of contingency, vulnerability, and influence strategies evident in the biblical history of covenant-building and a similar logic in management–employee relationships. In effect, Covenants of one sort or another are being made and broken daily in corporations, as managements and employees seek to shape each other's actions and expectations; like God and God's people, managements and employees are vulnerable to the contingencies they pose to each other. This vulnerability encourages them to influence, if not seek to control, the thinking and the acting of each other. They are strongly tempted not to let their relationship be confined to the strict quid pro quo of contracts. The long canonical history of covenant-making suggests that the only viable way for managements and employees to cope with the often irascible, prickly, and stubborn contingency of human nature is to apply a dialectic of deterrent and affirmative influence strategies that protect, rather than undercut, the moral freedom of Covenant partners.

Such protection appears to be a specification of the covenantal norm of "participation" prescribed by Robin Lovin, and of the covenantal love dissected by Joseph Allen, and of the covenantal norms of righteousness and justice prescribed by Douglas Sturm.[40] This chapter generates no new knowledge regarding the specific content of covenantal norms. But it outlines a means of "operationalizing" the idea of Covenant so that managements and employees might have some idea how Covenants actually are built—or vitiated—in corporate settings. In so doing, it suggests a new direction for approaching the question of character so central to discussions in Christian ethics today. Just as the characters of God and God's people emerge from a long history of efforts to shape each other, the characters of managements and employees emerge from the influence strategies they apply to each other. One task of ethics, then, is to borrow from organization theory and other social-scientific sources descriptions of what influence strategies operate in different forms of human association. Such data will enable ethicists to construct compelling accounts of how relationships in a variety of social contexts might become covenantal.

This conversation between organization theory and covenantal ethics has been less than fully interdisciplinary in that normative theological claims have been privileged—not subjected to criticism by organization theory. Organization theorists might object, for example, that another normative standard besides covenantal mutuality is more appropriate to their subject matter. That may be; at least one organization theorist argues that individual libertarian freedom is the norm most appropriate to organizations.[41] Economics as a normative discipline may hold corporations to the standard of economic efficiency; political science may hold them to the standard of distributive justice. A covenantal ethic rejoins, from a theological perspective, that whatever else corporations are, they are constructions for fostering genuine trust and trustworthiness among their participation. The point here is not to make exclusive normative claims. Other normative models are welcome to the conversation. The limited task in this chapter is to apply a norm most appropriate from a theological point of view.

Corporations may be the most obvious but are not the only forms of association in which participants are engaged in shaping the action and character of each other. Ethicists interested in the cultivation of character and virtue have attended to the family, church, and the broader political community as the principal institutional loci in which the opportunity to form moral persons is taken up or neglected. These explorations are usually undertaken at the expense of attention to the business corporations in which millions of people send the largest portion of their waking hours. The interactive model of covenant-building proposed here could serve to push such analyses forward and perhaps to nuance moral appraisals of instrumental associations such as corporations. For example, it might be discovered that the influence strategies appropriate to one kind of institution are inappropriate and even pernicious when used within another. Rather than judging some institutions inferior to others, it then would be more appropriate to argue, as Michael Walzer has done regarding the enormous power of money, that influence strategies be restricted to use within their proper spheres.[42]

This project of developing an interactive model of covenant-building also has relevance to the question of how religious convictions can find expression in the secularized, empty public square of a social-contract society. As Robin Lovin notes, a covenant society, such as that of the Puritans, authorizes its members to "encourage, exhort and perhaps even coerce" citizens to understand and adhere to a substantive vision of the good.[43] Ironically enough, the social contract liberates individuals from the state-sanctioned monopoly on such persuasion only to dump them into a vast cacophonous marketplace of efforts to shape behavior and character in a bewildering variety of directions. This array of influence strategies remains terra incognita. A theory of religion in public life might analyze the civil discourse of persuasion recommended by

Lovin[44] in the context of other influence strategies now at work in order to assess which other strategies might also be appropriate devices for introducing religious discourse into public life.

We are surrounded by intentional efforts, whether interpersonal or impersonal, to shape our beliefs, actions, and characters. Corporate settings present an intense, often suffocating, environment for such shaping. Nevertheless, this interactive state of affairs is not to be deplored, at least in principle. To evacuate attempts at influence in social relationships would be to assume that each individual already possesses the knowledge, wisdom, skills, and motivation to negotiate every challenge in life. The alternative to a social life rich in attempts by individuals to shape the action and characters of each other is the Hobbesian vision of atomistic monads randomly bumping into each other. The question, as usual, is how to discriminate between good, too much of a good, and the perverse and inhuman.[45]

QUESTIONS FOR DISCUSSION

1. What role should character and virtue play in defining our relationships to one another in a business setting? Should these be part and parcel of the agreements we sign as investors, employees, managers, and partners?

2. How can covenants help incorporate important influence strategies used by both management and employees that are not currently covered in traditional contracts?

3. How does covenant function in biblical relationships to address issues of vulnerability and contingency in the various influence strategies chosen by God and the people of Israel? In what ways can we say both God and the people are "vulnerable" and present each other with "contingencies" that address these vulnerabilities?

4. What kinds of coping strategies does God apply in order to address the contingent behavior of the people and elicit faith?

5. Why is the acknowledgment of mutual vulnerability so important to establishing healthy covenants between management and employees?

6. Our author claims that good covenant relations between management and employees demand they be both "generous" and "comprehensive" in their application of influence strategies on one another. What does this mean and how can this be accomplished?

7. Imagine a kind of influence strategy that you have experienced at some time in your life. How might an extracontractual covenantal agreement be struck that might help address the way this influence strategy affects both management and employees?

NOTES

1. William F. May, "Moral Leadership in the Corporate Setting," in *Profits and Professions: Essays in Business and Professional Ethics*, ed. Wade L. Robison et al. (Clifton, NJ: Humane Press, 1983); Charles S. McCoy, *Management of Values: The Ethical Difference in Corporate Policy and Performance* (Boston: Pittman, 1985), 223–24; Max L. Stackhouse and Dennis P. McCann, "A Post-Communist Manifesto," *Christian Century* 108 (January 15, 1991): 44–47; Douglas Sturm, "Corporation, Constitutions and Covenants: On Forms of Human Relation and the Problem of Legitimacy," *Journal of the American Academy of Religion* 41 (1973): 331–54.

2. Since organizational behavior is the more recent of these fields, I will use only the term "organization theory," for the sake of simplicity.

3. Robin W. Lovin, "Social Contract or a Public Covenant?" in *Religion and American Public Life: Interpretations and Explorations*, ed. Robin Lovin (Mahwah, NJ: Paulist, 1986).

4. Joseph L. Allen, *Love and Conflict: A Covenantal Model of Christian Ethics* (Nashville, TN: Abingdon Press, 1984), 292.

5. Frederick W. Taylor, *Scientific Management* (New York: Harper, 1947 [1903, 1911, 1912–1913]). This volume collates three earlier texts with their separate pagination retained. (The dates in brackets indicate original publication dates.) The reference here is to "Shop Management" (1903), 45–46, and "Principles of Scientific Management" (1911), 121.

6. Henri Fayol, *General and Industrial Management*, trans. Constance Storrs (London: Sir Isaac Pitman, 1949 [1919]), 73, 76, 97–98; James D. Mooney, *The Principles of Organization*, rev. ed. (New York: Harper & Bros., 1949 [1931]), 8–13, 30–31; and Chester I. Barnard, *The Functions of the Executive* (Cambridge, MA: Harvard University Press, 1939), chap. 17, especially 279–84.

7. Elton Mayo, *The Human Problems of an Industrial Civilization* (Boston: Harvard University Press, 1933), chaps. 7–8; and F. J. Roethlisberger and William J. Dickson, *Management and the Worker: An Account of a Research Program Conducted by the Western Electric Company, Hawthorne Works, Chicago* (Cambridge, MA: Harvard University Press, 1939), chaps. 22–25.

8. Daniel Katz and Robert L. Kahn, *The Social Psychology of Organizations* (New York: Wiley, 1966), chap. 12; and Douglas McGregor, *The Human Side of Enterprise* (New York: McGraw-Hill, 1960), chap. 4.

9. Richard Edwards helpfully subdivides the strategy here termed "bureaucracy" into its three components: "direction," "evaluation," and "discipline," in *Contested Terrain: The Transformation of the Workplace in the Twentieth Century* (New York: Basic Books, 1979), 18.

10. Herbert A. Simon, *Administrative Behavior: A Study of Decision-Making Processes in Administrative Organization*, 3rd ed., enl. (Glencoe, IL: Free Press, 1976 [1945]), chap. 10, especially 103; and James G. March and Herbert A. Simon, *Organizations* (New York: Wiley, 1958), chaps. 5–6.

11. William G. Ouchi, "Markets, Bureaucracies and Clans," *Administrative Science Quarterly* 25 (1980): 129–41; Terrence E. Deal and Allan A. Kennedy, *Corporate Cultures: The Rites and Rituals of Corporate Life* (Reading, MA: Addison-Wesley, 1982).

12. March and Simon, *Organizations*, 129–31; Michael Crozier, *The Bureaucratic Phenomenon* (Chicago: University of Chicago, 1964), chap. 5; and James Thompson, *Organizations in Action* (New York: McGraw-Hill, 1967), chap. 8.

13. Edwards, *Contested Terrain*, 154–55. For a detailed account of the intricacies of struggle on the shop floor, see Michael Burrawoy, *Manufacturing Consent: Changes in the Labor Process under Monopoly Capitalism* (Chicago: University of Chicago Press, 1979), esp. chaps. 4 and 10.

14. Regarding bureaucracy, see Barbara Garson, *All the Livelong Day* (New York: Doubleday, 1975); or a theoretical treatment by Kathy E. Ferguson, *The Feminist Case against Bureaucracy* (Philadelphia: Temple University, 1984). Regarding socialization, see Diane Margolis, *The Managers: Corporate Life in America* (New York: William Morrow, 1979), esp. "Earl Shorris: Scenes from Corporate Life: The Policies of Middle Management."

15. Robert Merton, "Bureaucratic Structure and Personality," *Social Forces* 18 (1940): 560–68; William H. Whyte Jr., *The Organizational Man* (Garden City, NY: Doubleday, 1956), parts 1–3; Michael Macoby, *The Gamesman: The New Corporate Leaders* (New York: Simon & Schuster, 1976); and Michael Korda, *Power! How to Get It; How to Use It* (New York: Random House, 1975).

16. National Conference of Catholic Bishops, *Economic Justice for All: Pastoral Letter on Catholic Social Teaching and the U.S. Economy* (Washington, DC: United States Catholic Conference), 52–59.

17. Emile Durkheim, *The Division of Labor in Society*, trans. George Simpson (New York: Free Press, 1933 [1893]), 226–29.

18. Michael Keeley, *A Social Contract Theory of Organizations* (Notre Dame, IN: University of Notre Dame Press, 1988), 12, 46–50.

19. Crozier, *Bureaucratic Phenomenon*, chap. 5; and Thompson, *Organizations in Action*, chap. 9.

20. For the classic account of how Frederick Taylor's "scientific management" initiated the "de-skilling" of U.S. workers, see Harry Braverman, *Labor and Monopoly Capital: The Degrading of Work in the Twentieth Century* (New York: Monthly Review Press, 1974), chaps. 1–6.

21. For example, see Exod. 32, Num. 11–21, and, Deut. 9 regarding the years of wandering, and Judges and 1 and 2 Kings for periods of apostasy after the Conquest and during the Monarchy.

22. See, for example, how Jeremiah indicts the people of Jerusalem for child sacrifice (Jer. 7:30–34, 32:35); child sacrifice was also performed by King Ahaz (2 Kings 16:3) and Manasseh (2 Kings 21:6).

23. Exemplary cases of *metanoia* include the repentance and reform of Josiah (2 Kings 22) and the conversion of Paul (Acts 9). See Ezek. 18 for a striking endorsement of individual reformation.

24. For example, Hos. 11:8–9 or Isa. 43:1–7.

25. The biblical narratives, particularly in the Old Testament, carry forward two kinds of Covenants: covenants which obligate God and covenants which obligate God's people. See George Mendenhall, "Covenant" in *Interpreter's Dictionary of the Bible* (New York: Abingdon Press, 1962), vol. 1, 714–23, especially 717–18. The covenants which obligate God include the early Noachic (Gen. 8:21–22), the early Abrahamic

(Gen. 15:1–5), and from the Priestly writer, the later Noachic (Gen. 9:8–17), the later Abrahamic (Gen. 15:1–5), and the Davidic (2 Sam. 7:8–16). The covenants that obligate God's people include the Mosaic (Exod. 20:1–24:8), renewed by Moses on the plain of Moab prior to the Conquest (Deut. 5–30), by Joshua at Shechem (Josh. 24:1–28), by King Josiah in Jerusalem (2 Kings 23), and by Nehemiah in the rebuilt Jerusalem (Neh. 9:38–10:31). One implication of this dual line of covenant-building is that the lack of an exactly specified linkage between the two sets of obligations serves to resist a contractual interpretation of the relationship.

26. The Jahwist and Elohist texts include much of Genesis, except for the portions attributed to the Priestly writer (see note 30 below), and much of Exod. 1–24 and Num. 11–14.

27. In the Jahwist and Elohist strands, God tests Abraham after the covenant is concluded by requiring the sacrifice of his son Isaac (Gen. 22); Abraham, for his part, tests God with questions (Gen. 15:2–3, 8) and with bargaining over the fate of Sodom (Gen. 18:16–33). Moses tests God with more pointed queries (Exod. 3:13–4:20). God tests the Hebrew slaves liberated from Egypt with deprivation in the desert, while they respond with murmurings (e.g., Num. 11:1), necessitating Moses' bargaining with God to stave off their destruction (e.g., Num. 14:11–19, 16:20–22).

28. The Deuteronomist materials, often attributed to the late Monarchical period (the reign of Josiah), include the books of Deuteronomy, Joshua, Judges, and the "historical" books from 1 Samuel through 2 Kings—that is, from the Conquest through the end of the Monarchy. Included here also are the pre-exilic prophets, principally, Hosea, Amos, first Isaiah (1–40) and portions of Jeremiah and Ezekiel.

29. For examples of curses, see Deut. 28:15–68 and Josh. 23:12–16; for examples of the "covenantal lawsuit," see Mic. 6:2 or Isa. 3:13–15; for an example of threats, see Isa. 5 and much of Jeremiah.

30. The Priestly materials and editing, often attributed to the period of the Exile, include a considerable portion of the book of Genesis (1:1–2:4a, 5, 6:9–22, 9:1–17, 10, 17, 36, 46:6–27), Exod. 25 through Num. 10, the book of Leviticus, and other materials not relevant to this analysis.

31. Regarding the Noachic covenant, compare Gen. 8:21–22 (Jahwist) with Gen. 9:12–17 (Priestly); regarding the Abrahamic covenant, compare Gen. 15:1–5 (Jahwist) with Gen. 17: 1–27 (Priestly).

32. In Third (post-exilic) Isaiah, compare chapters 59 and 63. See also Neh. 9 for a post-exilic renewal of the indictment language.

33. For the language of hardening, see John 12:36b–41. For examples of prophetic indictments related to the Abrahamic covenant, see Matt. 3:7–10; 8:11–12; John 8:31–59, as this covenant is revised polemically by John the Baptist and Jesus. For examples of warnings related to the Mosaic covenant, see Luke 16:19–30 (voiced, interestingly enough, by Abraham) and Matt. 5:17–20.

34. "Delegation" occurs both in the middle of Matthew and Luke, when Jesus commissions the disciples to preach and heal (Matt. 10:5–23; Luke 9:1–6) and in the greater commission bestowed just prior to or subsequent to the Crucifixion and Resurrection (John 13:31–17:26, see especially 15:15; Matt. 28:16–20). For Luke, this commissioning occurs at the Pentecost (Acts 2).

35. Karen L. Bloomquist, *The Dream Betrayed: Religious Challenge of the Working Class* (Minneapolis, MN: Augsburg Fortress Press, 1990), chap. 6; and Prentiss L. Pemberton and Daniel Rush Finn, *Toward a Christian Economic Ethic: Stewardship and Social Power* (Minneapolis, MN: Winston Press, 19985), chap. 9.

36. May, "Moral Leadership," 204–11; McCoy, *Management of Values*, chap. 8; Oliver F. Williams and Patrick E. Murphy, "The Ethics of Virtue: A Moral Theory for Marketing," *Journal of Macromarketing* 10, no. 1 (Spring 1990): 19–29. Stewart W. Herman, "The Modern Corporation and an Ethics of Trust," *Journal of Religious Ethics* 20, no. 1 (Spring 1992): 111–48.

37. "Deadly Deception" (Boston: Infact Productions), 1991.

38. As quoted in James M. Gustafson and Elmer W. Johnson, "Efficiency, Morality and Managerial Effectiveness," in *The U.S. Business Corporation: An Institution in Transition*, ed. John R. Meyer and James M. Gustafson (Cambridge, MA: Ballinger, 1988), 199–200.

39. Vicki Smith, *Managing in the Corporate Interest: Control and Resistance in an American Bank* (Berkley: University of California Press, 1990), chap. 4.

40. Robin W. Lovin, "Covenantal Relationships and Political Legitimacy," *Journal of Religion* 60 (January 1980): 1–16. According to Lovin, the covenant paradigm emphasizes "participation," which entails that all parties recognize each other as "independent and equal centers of recognition" (12). For Sturm, corporations "must incorporate the procedures of constitutionalism to secure the participation of all populations affected by its operation" (Sturm, "Corporations, Constitutions and Covenants," 352). For Allen, covenant love includes: "always to see self and others as essentially belonging together in community . . . to affirm the worth of each covenant member . . . to include every category of person in the covenant community . . . to seek to meet the needs, both ultimate and proximate, of each person . . . to be faithful in our commitments to others . . . [and] to seek reconciliation wherever alienation exists" (Allen, *Love and Conflict*, 77–81).

41. Keeley, *A Social Contract Theory*, 216–25; see also 32, 52–53, 180, 203–5.

42. Michael Walzer, "In Defense of Equality," *Dissent* 20 (Fall 1973): 399–408.

43. Lovin, "Covenantal Relationships," 137.

44. Lovin, "Covenantal Relationships," 141–44.

45. I am grateful to Joseph Allen, Harlan Beckley, Dennis McCann, Douglas Ottati, anonymous reviews and lively discussants from the SCE, the members of the Concordia Religion Department, and especially to Paul Camenisch for their critical comments on earlier drafts.

· 14 ·

How Green Is Judaism?
Exploring Jewish Environmental Ethics

David Vogel

David Vogel draws on ancient and medieval Jewish texts to explore the role of the physical environment in Jewish thought. It situates Jewish teachings in the context of the debate between anthropocentrism (the belief that the natural world is valuable insofar as it is beneficial to human flourishing) and ecocentrism (the belief that the natural world has intrinsic value independent of the benefit it might have for humans). The chapter also discusses the Jewish view of nature and reviews various interpretations of an important biblical precept of environmental ethics. It argues that while Jewish thought contains many "green" elements, it also contains a number of beliefs that challenge some contemporary environmental values.

The key to the Jewish contribution to environmental ethics lies in the concept of balance—balance between the values and needs of humans and the claims of nature, and between viewing nature as a source of life and moral values and as a threat to human life and social values. On the one hand, the teachings of Judaism challenge attitudes toward the environment that place too much value on nature, thereby neglecting the fact that nature can be a hostile place for people. On the other hand, Judaism also challenges those perspectives that place too little value on nature, thereby neglecting the fact that nature is ultimately our one and only home.

Over the last decade there have been a growing number of efforts to reconcile religious teachings with the values of environmentalism.[1] These writings, in part, represent a response to Lynn White and others who claim that our present environmental predicament is rooted in "orthodox Christian arrogance toward nature"[2] or more generally in the Judeo-Christian legitimization of man's "domination" over nature as expressed in Gen. 1:26. A major theme of much contemporary literature on religion and the environment is to demonstrate the relevance of the principles and precepts of both Christianity and Judaism to contemporary environmental concerns.[3]

This article draws on the extensive contemporary literature on Judaism and the environment. This literature includes more than a score of scholarly and popular essays and articles as well as two volumes of essays.[4] In addition, the Jewish environmental organization Shomrei Adamah: Keepers of the Earth has published two volumes: *A Garden of Choice Fruit*, a collection of two hundred classic Jewish quotes on human beings and the environment, and *Let the Earth Teach You Torah*, a guidebook for teaching Jewish perspectives on the environment.[5] The Coalition on the Environment and Jewish Life represents a large number of Jewish organizations and engages in environmental advocacy and education in both the United States and Israel. The Jewish-oriented left-of-center monthly *Tikkun* has periodically published articles that present Jewish perspectives on biodiversity as well as on other current environmental issues.[6]

As this large body of writing suggests, classical Jewish texts have much to say about the relationship of man to nature. Whatever the merits of White's argument about the environmental implications of the Christian tradition, his criticisms do not apply to either the Torah or the teachings of Rabbinic Judaism.[7] Ancient and medieval Jewish texts both express and are consistent with a strong environmental ethic. Far from providing a blanket endorsement to man's domination of nature for his own benefit, Judaism imposes numerous restrictions on how, when, and to what extent people can use the natural environment. Rather than simply expressing anthropocentric values, many of its ideas and principles either explicitly or implicitly evoke themes that are consistent with ecocentric or biocentric understandings of the relationship between people and nature.[8] Indeed, the latter ethos, rather than representing a major new departure in or challenge to Western religious thought, is actually prefigured in both ancient and medieval Jewish religious texts.

But while Judaism may be consistent with many contemporary environmental values and doctrines, its teachings are not identical to them. Specifically, Judaism does not regard the preservation or protection of nature as the most important societal value; it holds that humans are not just a part of nature but have privileged and distinctive moral claims; it believes that nature can threaten humans as well as the obverse; it argues that nature should be used and enjoyed as well as protected. In short, Judaism contains both "green" and "nongreen" elements. It is inappropriate to overemphasize either the former, as have some Jewish environmentalists, or the latter, as have some environmental critics of Western religion.

In the Jewish tradition, humans have moral claims on nature and nature has moral claims on humans. But neither claim is absolute: Nature exists both for the sake of humans and for its own stake. While the natural world must be respected and admired, its challenge to human interests and values must also be recognized. The key contribution of ancient and medieval Jewish texts to contemporary environmental discourse lies in the concept of balance—balance between the values and needs of humans and the claims of nature, and between viewing nature as a source of life and moral values and as a threat to human life and social values. The teachings of Judaism challenge both those who would place too low a value on nature as well as those who would place too high a value on it.

ANTHROPOCENTRISM AND ECOCENTRISM

> When you besiege a town for many days, waging war against it, to seize it: you are not to bring ruin upon its trees, by swinging away (with) an ax against them, for from them you eat, them you are not to cut down—for are the trees of the field human beings, (able) to come against you in a siege? Only those trees of which you know that they are not trees for eating, them you may bring to ruin and cut down, that you may build siege-works against the town that is making war against you, until its downfall. (Deut. 20:19–20)[9]

This is perhaps the most frequently cited passage in contemporary writings on Jewish environmental ethics and is often invoked as a textual basis for Jewish environmental ethics. Yet it contains an important ambiguity. Put simply: Why should one not destroy the fruit trees?

One interpretation of this passage, expressed by the medieval Jewish commentator Ibn Ezra (1089–1164), is that we should not destroy the fruit trees because our lives are dependent on them and the food they produce. Thus destroying the fruit trees is forbidden because it is not in the long-term interest of humans. However, the medieval Jewish scholar Rashi (1040–1105) offers a rather different interpretation. He asks rhetorically: "Are trees like people that they can run away from an advancing army and take refuge in the town? Of course not—they are innocent bystanders. Therefore don't involve them in your conflicts, and don't cut them down."[10] In short, the trees have a life of their own: They don't just exist to serve human needs.

The former interpretation is anthropocentric. It evokes the concept of sustainable development: We are permitted to pick the fruit, but not destroy the fruit tree because the fruit is a renewable resource while the tree presumably is not. The latter interpretation is ecocentric or biocentric—it makes no reference to human needs. It posits that trees have an intrinsic value that is independent of human welfare or concerns.

Not only can one locate both perspectives within the Jewish tradition, but the very ambiguity of Deut. 20:19–20 contains an important key to understanding the Jewish approach to environmental ethics. The diverse interpretations of this passage suggest that Jewish environmental ethics incorporates both anthropocentrism and biocentrism. To argue that nature exists only for the benefit of humans is to refuse to acknowledge all nature as God's creation. But it would be equally misguided to claim that humans ought not use nature for their own benefit.

Thus, even if one were to agree with the ecocentric interpretation of the prohibition against destroying fruit trees, that is, that they are to be valued for their own sake, the fact remains is that is permissible to cut down the nonfruit-bearing trees for the purposes of waging war. But these trees are no less a part of nature than fruit-bearing trees. Neither is able to run away. Why are we then permitted to destroy them? Are they not equally innocent? Why are they not also valued for their own sake?

Clearly God does not want us to live in a world in which we are forbidden to chop down all trees, since such a prohibition would make the preservation and sustaining of human life impossible. At the same time, neither does God want us to assume that the entire natural world exists to satisfy our material needs, for as Ps. 24 reminds us: "The earth is the Lord's and all that is in it." The Torah's distinction between fruit-bearing and nonfruit-bearing trees seems to suggest both ideas: Nature both exists for the benefit of humans and has a value that is independent of human needs.

Both interpretations also inform the exegesis of Deut. 22:6–7, another biblical text frequently cited in contemporary discussions of Jewish views on ecology:

> When you encounter the nest of a bird before you in the way, in any tree or on the ground, (whether) fledglings or eggs, with the mother crouching upon the fledging or upon the eggs, you are not to take away the mother along with the children. Send free, send free the mother, but the children you may take for yourself, in order it may go well with you and you may prolong (your) life.

Once again: Why should one take the young but let the mother go?

According to Don Isaac Abravanel (1437–1508), "God has commanded us not to destroy that which generates progeny," adding that "this commandment is given not for the sake of the animal world but rather so that it shall be good for humankind when Creation is perpetuated so that one will be able to partake of it again in the future."[11] To translate this interpretation into a modern idiom, Abravanel has invoked the concept of sustainable development. Yet Nahmanides (1194–1270), another medieval commentator, views this commandment in terms of an ecocentric understanding of the value of species preservation. According to his interpretation of this passage, "Scripture will not permit a destructive act that will bring about the extinction of a species, even though it has permitted the ritual slaughtering of that species for food. He who kills the mother and offspring on one day is considered as if he destroyed the species."[12] Thus, according to Nahmanides, species extinction is intrinsically wrong—regardless of how or whether it affects humans.

THE RELATIONSHIP OF HUMANS TO NATURE

A similar ambiguity informs various interpretations of the creation story. Specifically, what is the significance of the fact that man was created on the sixth day—after the creation of the entire natural world? According to the Talmudic tractate Sanhedrin, "Our masters taught: Man was created on the eve of the Sabbath—and for what reason? So that in case his heart grew proud, one might say to him: Even the gnat was in creation before you were there."[13] Yet a midrash (a tale created for interpretative or pedagogical purposes) compiled in the early Middle Ages offers an anthropocentric perspective. It has God showing the Garden of Eden to Adam and saying to him: "All I have created, I created for you." Why did God create man at the end of the work of creation? "So that he may directly come to the banquet. One can compare it to a king who constructed palaces and embellished them and prepared a banquet and only then did he invite his guests."[14]

Indeed, both relationships of man to nature are expressed at the very beginning of the Pentateuch: "Let them (humankind) have dominion over the fish of the sea, the fowl of the heavens, animals, all the earth, and all crawling things that crawl upon the earth!" (Gen. 1:26). This passage has been frequently cited as the basis for the claim that the Bible legitimates, even commands, the exploitation of nature by humans. However, a classic rabbinical midrash on this passage suggests a more nuanced interpretation: "When God created Adam he led him past all the trees in the Garden of Eden and told him, 'See how beautiful and excellent are all My works. Beware lest you spoil and ruin My world. For if you spoil it there is nobody to repair it after you.'"[15] Moreover, it is followed in verse 30 by a clear restriction on man's domination of nature: People are permitted to eat only plants. And in the second creation story in Gen. 2:15, God places man in the Garden of Eden and instructs him "to work it and watch it"—which explicitly invokes the principle of stewardship.

The same complex relationship of people to nature also informs the environmental ethic implicit in the laws of the *kashrut*, which distinguish between foods that are permissible and prohibited to eat and sacrifice. Just as

Deut. 20:19–20 distinguishes which trees one can and cannot cut down while waging war, so Jewish dietary laws distinguish between which animals Jews can and cannot consume. The restrictions on fish and animal consumption specified in the laws of the *kashrut* are not anthropocentric in the sense that only a few of the forbidden animals pose a threat to human health and obviously there would be no health hazard in sacrificing them. It is noteworthy that a significant number of the animals currently protected by either American or international environmental law and whose endangerment has become a focus of considerable public concern are also forbidden to be eaten or sacrificed by Jews. These include lions, tigers, and the other animals of the cat family, elephants, bears, rhinoceros, dolphins (mammals), whales, eagles, alligators, and turtles.

This is obviously coincidental since the origin of the *kashrut* laws has nothing to do with animal protection; rather, they stem from the divine compromise with Noah, which permitted humans to eat meat, but only under certain conditions. But what is not coincidental is that both the ancient Jews and contemporary environmentalists believe that many of God's creatures do not exist for the sake of humans. The fact that much of the animal world was not created for man's use is further made clear in Job, when God points with pride to the various magnificent creatures he has created, virtually all of whom are useless to people. This list includes the lion, the mountain goat, the wild ass, the buffalo, the ostrich, the wild horse, the eagle, the hippopotamus, and the crocodile.

Critical to the observance of the Sabbath is the prohibition against productive activity. Jews are enjoined from tinkering with or transforming the world, which of course also includes tinkering with or transforming nature. Indeed, the commandment to observe the Sabbath is the only commandment that applies to nature as well as people, or, more precisely, to the relationship of people to animals and the land. According to Exod. 20:10, "[Y]ou are not to make any kinds of work, (not) you, nor your son, nor your daughter, (not) your servant, nor your maid, *nor your beast*, nor your sojourner that is within your gates," (italics added)—a stipulation that is repeated in Exod. 23:12 and Deut. 5:12.

According to one contemporary scholar, "The essence of the prohibition against *melacha* (productive work) on Shabbat is to teach that the productive manipulation of the environment is not an absolute right."[16] Thus, on the Sabbath one cannot slaughter animals (though one can eat them if they are prepared earlier), work them in the field, hunt them, harvest crops, chop down trees, pick fruit, and so forth. In short, on the Sabbath nature also has a day of rest from human manipulation. This is also true of the observance of most holidays. As Schorsh notes,

[A]n unmistakable strain of self-denial runs through the Jewish calendar. From the sacrificial cult of the temple to the synagogue of rabbinic Judaism, it is the absolute cession of work that distinguishes the celebration of Jewish holy days. . . . [S]piritual renewal is effected through physical contraction. . . . To spend one-seventh of one's life in "unproductive rest" is scarcely a mark of absolute power.[17]

But it is equally important to note that the Sabbath takes place only one day of the week. The other 86 percent of the time (not counting various holidays) humans may not only tinker with and transform nature, but they are required to do so. Indeed, as the twentieth-century philosopher A. J. Heschel observes, "[T]he duty to work for six days is just as much a part of God's covenant with man as the duty to abstain from work on the seventh day."[18] During the former, nature can and should be used productively. Moreover, the Sabbath and the six working days are interdependent: Neither can exist without the other.

The same sense of temporal balance underlies the Sabbatical year, which is akin in some respects to a year-long celebration of the Sabbath. During this year, which occurs every seven years, sowing, harvesting, and the gathering of grapes and other crops are forbidden (Lev. 25). Thus, every seven years the land has a year of rest. This law may have an ecological dimension. "In the days before crop rotation or the availability of chemical nutrients for the soil, the practice of letting the land lie fallow enabled it to regain its fertility."[19] But the rabbinical commentary on the Sabbatical year does not refer to this instrumental explanation. Rather the exegesis on this commandment emphasizes that its central purpose is the reaffirmation of God's ownership of the land.[20] Thus, while Gen. 1, Deut. 20:19–20, Deut. 22:6–7, and the rules of the *kashrut* limit which parts of nature one can consume, the commandment to observe the Sabbath and observe the Sabbath year places limits on when this consumption can take place.

A similar principle underlies the various rules regulating the treatment of animals that appear sporadically in the Pentateuch and are echoed in the rabbinic tradition. On one hand, compassion for all of God's living creatures is required: Animals have feelings that man is obligated to respect. The principle in rabbinic literature relating to the treatment of animals is *zaar baalei hayim*, "the pain of living creatures."[21]

In addition to the fourth commandment's explicit requirement that all creatures, human as well as animal, have a day of rest, Deuteronomy forbids the farmer to plough with an ox and a donkey yoked together because, according to one interpretation, this would impose greater hardship on the weaker animal (Deut. 22:10). Likewise a farmer is not permitted to muzzle an ox during the threshing period to prevent his eating grain (Deut. 25:4).

Nor can an ox or a sheep be slaughtered on the same day as its offspring (Lev. 22:28). (See also Deut. 22:6–7, discussed above.) The Torah also explicitly instructs Jews not to extend their animosity to the animals of their enemy: "(And) when you see the donkey of one who hates you crouching under its burden, restrain from abandoning to him—unbind, yet unbind it together with him" (Exod. 23:5).

Not only do the laws of kosher slaughtering (*shehitah*) seek to minimize the pain of the animal being killed, but the biblical basis for the Talmudic separation of the consumption of meat and milk is based on a passage that speaks to compassion for animals, namely that a kid cannot be boiled in the milk of its mother. This passage is considered so important that it is repeated on three separate occasions.

But on the other hand, it is permitted to kill animals for food and other purposes, subject to the restrictions noted above. Rabbinic law also permits hunting for food, commerce, or the removal of animal pests. And of course it also permits the use of animals for farm labor and transportation. And even unclean animals can be killed for their skins or if they present a danger to humans, and so forth.

That human life can take precedence over animal life is explicitly illustrated in one of the most dramatic and important biblical stories, namely the binding of Isaac. God instructs Abraham to substitute a wild ram for his son Isaac on the makeshift altar Abraham has been commanded to build. This passage makes explicit the Jewish prohibition against human sacrifice, but its environmental context is equally significant: The life of an animal is sacrificed so that a human being—one whose survival is central to the future of the Jewish people—may live.

This principle is repeated in the story of the Exodus when the Israelites are instructed to slaughter lambs and place their blood on their doorposts so that the angel of death may pass over their homes and not kill their firstborn as well as those of the Egyptians. Moreover, animal sacrifices are commanded throughout the Pentateuch and are a major component of temple worship. Yet once again, limits apply: Only domesticated animals can be sacrificed, thus assuring species preservation.

In this context, it is useful to note the historical context of Deut. 20:19–20. Ancient practices of warfare knew no limits; nothing was allowed to interfere with the achievement of military objectives, specifically in this case the conquest of a city. Presumably the besieging force stood to benefit in some way from the destruction of the fruit trees in the vicinity of the city being attacked, otherwise there would be no reason for invoking the concept of *bal tashchit* (do not destroy) in this context in the first place. The *halachah* (Jewish law) subsequently extended the principle of *bal tashchit* to prohibit the diverting of the flow of a river to cause distress to a besieged city. Thus even in the extreme case of warfare, Jewish law imposes limits on man's use of nature.

PERCEPTIONS OF NATURE

A major difference between anthropocentric and ecocentric environmental ethics lies in their respective views of nature. The former ethic assumes the existence of a tension between the interests of humans and nature, while both radical ecology and ecofeminism tend to regard nature as benign or at least innocent.[22] Once again, the Jewish tradition incorporates both perspectives. It also views nature in both positive and negative terms.

One finds a postbiblical harbinger of the deep ecology or biocentric perspective that man does not enjoy a privileged place in the universe in the voice that (rhetorically) questions Job from the whirlwind: "Where were you when I laid the earth's foundation? Who set its cornerstone when the morning stars sang together and all the divine beings shouted for joy? (Job 38:4, 6–7). More than five centuries before the advent of radical ecology, the Jewish medieval philosopher Maimonides (1131–1205) wrote in the *Guide for the Perplexed*, "It should not be believed that all the beings exist for the sake of the existence of humanity. On the contrary, all the other beings too have been intended for their own sakes, and not for the sake of something else."[23]

The Jewish tradition is also both respectful and appreciative of nature. Thus "Rabbi Yohanan ben Zakkai . . . used to say: if you have a sapling in your hand, and someone should say to you that the Messiah has come, stay and complete the planting, and then go to greet the Messiah."[24] The philosopher Bakhya ibn Pekuda wrote that Jews should engage in "meditation upon creation" in order to sense God's majesty while a large number of Kabbalistic works considered "nature itself as a garment of the Shekkhina."[25] "Perek Shira," a mystical poem from 900, has verses from all kinds of creatures singing God's praises while one tradition of Jewish mysticism included outdoor meditation.[26]

At the same time, the Jewish tradition is by no means uncritical of nature. This criticism has a number of dimensions. First, for all its paeans and testimonies to nature's beauty and majesty, the Torah also depicts nature as a malevolent force, one capable of wreaking havoc, death, and destruction. Indeed nature's destructiveness plays a central role in a number of important biblical narratives. The first of these is the flood. God's injunction to Noah to take two of every species into the ark has been frequently cited as demonstrating a biblical commitment to species protection. This is certainly a plausible interpretation: Having created each of these species earlier in Genesis, God presumably did not want his efforts to be in vain.

But what is equally critical is that the flood also destroyed countless millions of animals and plants. (The latter, incidentally, were not brought into the ark.) The most apocryphal contemporary visions of ecological catastrophe do not even begin to approach the magnitude of the destruction of nature described in Gen. 7:21–23:

> Then expired all flesh that crawls about upon the earth—fowl, herd-animals, wildlife, and all swarming things that swarm upon the earth, and all humans: all that had the breadth of the rush of life in their nostrils, all that were on firm ground, died. He blotted out all existing things that were on the face of the soil, from man to beast, to crawling things and to fowl of the heavens, they were blotted out from the earth.

Indeed, so great was the terror caused by this extraordinary destructiveness that God created the rainbow in order to assure people that such a natural catastrophe would not recur.

Another example of nature's destructiveness occurs in the story of Joseph. For seven years, the entire region is made barren, causing untold misery not only for the Egyptians but for the Hebrews who are forced to leave their ancestral land in search of food. A third example of nature's destructiveness, which also forms a critical part of the Exodus narrative, is seen in the plagues that are visited upon the Egyptians. Half of the plagues, namely frogs, vermin, wild beasts, hail, and locusts, directly use natural forces to make the lives of the Egyptians miserable, though for the most serious plague, the killing of the firstborn, God intervenes more directly through the angel of death. The Egyptian army seeking to recapture the fleeing Israelites also succumbs to nature's destructiveness—it is drowned.

Other biblical narratives also show nature as a life-threatening force. The biblical woods are wild places filed with dangerous animals, while thirst and starvation routinely confront wanderers in the desert. Indeed, God explicitly acknowledges the former danger when he tells Moses, "I will not drive them (the Canaanites) out before you in one year, lest the land become desolate and the *wildlife of the field* become many against you" (Exod. 23:29; italics added). In Yom Kippur liturgy, God decides which Jews will be eaten by wild animals during the coming year. And in one of the most dramatic passages in the *Tenach*, God tells Moses in Deuteronomy that if the Jewish people do not follow his commandments, natural catastrophes will follow (Deut. 27:15–68).

Obviously, in the context of the Jewish tradition, these natural disasters are not "natural." They are created by God in order to achieve various divine purposes. But it is surely significant that God chooses to reveal himself through nature's malevolence as well as through its beneficence. Both sides of nature appear throughout the Torah.

Second, nature is not only a source of physical danger to human beings; it is also a source of moral danger. Recall that it is an animal, the serpent, that leads to the first sin. A more significant and subtle example is illustrated by the setting of the revelation at Sinai, the defining event in the history of the Jewish people. Why does God choose to make his covenant with the Jewish people in a place utterly devoid of the capacity for sustaining life? Sinai is among the most desolate and barren places on the face of the earth. Why did God not choose a more hospitable setting, one that would enable him to display the myriad wonders of the physical world that he so painstakingly created at the beginning of Genesis? In other words, why not choose a setting of natural abundance to make his covenant with the Jewish people?

My explanation is that God did not do so because seeing natural abundance around them would have distracted the people gathered at the foot of Mt. Sinai. It would have undermined God's central message, namely that what is critical to the survival of the Jewish people is their relationship to God, not the abundance of the natural world. Indeed, it is the physical setting of the revelation at Sinai that marks Judaism's decisive break with the pantheistic traditions of nature worship of other ancient religions. Because there is no natural abundance to worship or even admire at Sinai, there is no possibility of intermingling God with nature or of viewing nature as sacred. There is only God and the Jewish people; everything else, including nature, is secondary.

The plausibility of this interpretation is suggested by the murmurings of the Israelites as they wander in the desert for forty years. What do they complain about? What makes them long for life as slaves in Egypt? What, in short, threatens to distract them from their obligations under the covenant? It is their memory of the abundance of nature's bounty in Egypt—a land that at one point they ironically recall as one of milk and honey. The contrast is clear. In Egypt, a land in which nature's abundance is manifold—and not incidentally where nature is also worshiped—Jews are slaves, while in the desert, where nature produces nothing of value to humans, Jews are free. Not until the Israelites reach and conquer the Promised Land will they be able to enjoy both at the same time.

The notion of nature as a source of distraction is also echoed in this passage from the *Mishna* composed in the third century A.D.: "Whoever is walking along the road reciting [holy texts], and he stops his recitation and says, 'How beautiful is this tree! How beautiful is this field!' it is reckoned as if he had committed a mortal sin."[27] Thus while the Jewish tradition encourages the appreciation of nature, it also recognizes that there must be limits on this appreciation: Nature is not to be worshipped. Indeed, for many commentators, the substitution of God for nature or the natural world as an object of worship is precisely what distinguishes Judaism from the pagan or pantheistic religions of the ancient world out of which it emerged.

DO NOT DESTROY

The rabbis wrestled with the practical implications of Jewish environmental ethics in part through their exegesis on the principle of *bal tashit*, a variant of the biblical phrase in 20:19 translated as "you shall not destroy," or "don't destroy wantonly," which many rabbis consider one of the 613 commandments that Jews are commanded to observe. But what precisely does it mean to "destroy" or "waste"?

While originally interpreted to place limits on the waging of war, *bal tashit* came to have more far-reaching applications. The Talmud applies it to both products of nature and products of man: "Whoever breaks vessels, or tears garments, or destroys a building, or clogs up a fountain, or does away with foods in a destructive manner, violates the prohibition of *bal tashit*."[28] According to Maimonides, "[A]ll needless destruction is included in this prohibition; for instance, whoever burns a garment, or breaks a vessel needlessly, contravenes the command: 'you must not destroy.'" The *Gemara* (a codified commentary on Jewish law compiled in the fourth and fifth century A.D.) instructs: "One who tears cloths in anger, breaks objects in anger, or squanders money in anger, should be in your eyes like an idolater."[29] According to the Babylonian Talmud, "[A]nyone who does not properly adjust the air flow of a lamp, thereby causing unnecessary fuel consumption, has violated the *bal taschit* prohibition."[30] The general principle is expressed in the *Shulkhan Arukh*, a major codex of Jewish law compiled in the sixteenth century: "It is forbidden to destroy or injure anything capable of being useful to men."[31]

Since the concept of ownership is irrelevant to its application, this principle clearly limits private property rights; after all, everything belongs to God. Thus, one is equally enjoined from wantonly destroying one's own property as well as that of others. Not incidentally, one is also forbidden from destroying resources that belong to the commons, for instance, the fruit tree, the river in front of a besieged city.

However, in another sense the Talmudic texts interpreted *bal taschit* more narrowly. Thus, the *Gemara* in *Bava Kamma* suggests that even the protection of fruit trees may be overridden by economic need, while the *Gemara* in Shabbat not only claims that destruction for the protection of health is permissible, but goes so far as to suggest that both a personal aesthetic preference as well as the gratification of a psychological need constitute sufficient grounds to override the prohibition of *bal tashchit*.[32]

Moreover, the Jewish tradition does not regard the economically productive use of natural resources as wasteful. Thus, according to a contemporary interpretation of a Talmudic passage, "[I]f the transformative use of any raw materials, including fruit-bearing trees, will produce more profit than using it in its present form, its transformative use is permitted."[33] For Judaism, it is the wanton destructiveness of nature that is wrong. But by using nature productively, humans appropriately mix their efforts with God's creation. Thus the blessing recited before eating most meals—one of the most frequently recited Jewish prayers—thanks God for bringing forth bread, which exists due to the productive collaboration of humans and nature.

NONGREEN ELEMENTS

While there are important differences between many contemporary environmental challenges and those that faced the world in which ancient and medieval Jewish writers lived, the latter do prefigure and incorporate many "green" elements. But it is equally important not to ignore the important ways in which Jewish texts dissent from a number of contemporary green values, especially those associated with radical ecology.[34]

First, while Judaism clearly regards the preservation and protection of nature as an important value, it is certainly not the most important value. What is more important is performing *mitzvot* (commandments), all but a small portion of which deal with the relationship of people to God and to each other. Of the Ten Commandments, only one—the commandment to keep the Sabbath—has even a remote relevance to the relationship of people to nature. A similar ratio likely holds for the hundreds of other commandments Jews are commanded to observe. For Judaism, how people relate to their God and how they relate to each other are more important than how they treat nature. Treating nature with respect and reverence is not incompatible with the former, but neither can it be considered a substitute for revering God and respecting other human beings. In this important sense, Judaism may contain "green" elements, but it is not a "green" religion.

Second, the notion that humans are not just a part of nature, but have distinctive—and privileged—moral claims is an integral part of Jewish thought. Thus preserving and maintaining human life is more important than protecting or preserving nature. It is significant that none of the numerous restrictions on man's use of nature in Judaism endanger human life or society, though some, such as the restrictions on which animals can be eaten, may at times make its maintenance more difficult. But Jewish concern for nature stops where the preservation of human life begins. While numerous commandments speak to the compassion for animal life, God did not hesitate to command the sacrifice of a wild ram to save Isaac or numerous lambs to save the lives of the Israelites in Egypt.

Thus, the Jewish tradition holds that while humans do have responsibilities for animals, these responsibilities should not come at the expense of human welfare. As Berman notes, "It is not acceptable in Jewish law to make an assertion of the independent rights of nature. The rights of nature need to be carefully balanced, calibrated against human interests; and in that balancing, it will be the human interests which will have the priority."[35] In short, in Judaism, nature does not have rights; rather, humans have responsibilities for the natural world.

Third, while it is certainly true that a strain of self-denial runs through the observances of many Jewish holidays, including the Sabbath, it is equally true that Judaism regards nature as something to be used. Recall that the Promised Land is described as one of "milk and honey," and thus a place where nature is to be used and enjoyed by humans. Indeed, in Deut. 8:7–9, God waxes eloquent in describing its abundance: "YHWH your God brings you into a good land, a land of streams of water, springs and ocean flows, issuing from valleys and hills: a land of wheat and barley, (fruit of the) vine, fig, and pomegranate, a land of olives, oil and honey . . . a land whose stones are iron, and from whose hills you may hew copper." While man's use or taming of nature must not be "wasteful," the Jewish concept of waste does not preclude the economically productive use of nature's assets or even the use of them to derive psychological benefits. As one commentator observes, "[T]he biblical imperative requires finding a balance between transformation and preservation."[36]

In this context it is worth reexamining the criticisms made by Jews of the activities of Pacific Lumber Company. This firm is owned by Maxxam Corporation, whose major shareholder is a Jewish businessman, Charles Hurwitz. After Pacific Lumber began to increase the rate at which the ancient redwoods on its property were being logged following its takeover by Maxxam, a number of Jews, including several rabbis, publicly appealed to its CEO to make a *teshuvah sheleymah* (a genuine change of direction) and perform a great mitzvah by dedicating himself to the preservation of the Headwaters Forest. The company's critics attempted to bring "Jewish wisdom and ethics" to bear on this issue as a way of pressuring the firm's owner.[37]

Preserving the redwoods in the Headwaters Forest may be a good or wise idea. But it is unclear that it is either mandated or logically flows from the teachings of Judaism. According to Talmudic interpretations of *bal tashchit*, natural objects should not be wasted or needlessly destroyed. But using the lumber harvested from the Headwaters Forest for commercial purposes is not necessarily wasteful. Rather, it constitutes an alternative use—one that may be more or less important than letting the trees remain standing. While it is clear that the community does have a stake in what happens to the redwoods—after all, Hurwitz is a trustee for God's creation—this does not mean that none of these trees can be cut down for productive uses. What the Jewish tradition does require is that these trees be harvested in a sustainable, nonexploitative way—one that strikes an appropriate balance between the need to protect what God has created and the needs of humans to use nature to sustain life.

Finally, Judaism does not view nature as inherently benevolent. While recognizing the beauty and majesty of the natural world, it perceives that nature can also be terrifying and threatening. According to Jewish thought, human efforts to discipline or subdue nature do not, as many radical ecologists claim, stem from the urge to dominate nature but rather represent a response to the real challenges to human survival posed by the natural world.[38] Notwithstanding the achievements of modern science and technology, these challenges have by no means disappeared.

These four ideas—that protecting the natural world is not the highest imperative, that human life is more important than nonhuman life, that nature is to be used and enjoyed as well as preserved, and that nature can threaten humans just as humans can threaten nature—should not be viewed as the outdated legacies of a preindustrial religion. They represent an important contribution to contemporary efforts to define and redefine the appropriate ethical relationship between people and the physical world in which they live and which God created.

QUESTIONS FOR DISCUSSION

1. How does the passage forbidding the chopping down of trees during a military campaign demonstrate the ambiguity the author sees in the Jewish position on the environment? How can this passage be interpreted both anthropocentrically and ecocentrically?

2. How is this same ambiguity present in the creation story in Genesis, in the dietary laws found in Deuteronomy, and in the laws regarding work on the Sabbath?

3. What evidence does our author find in Jewish tradition for the deep ecological, or biocentric, perspective that humanity does not enjoy a privileged place in the universe?

4. What evidence does our author use to demonstrate that the Jewish tradition, at times, does affirm the unique and privileged role of humanity in the cosmos?

5. Does Jewish tradition consider the natural world as either unambiguously good or evil? What evidence does our author use to show how one can find both views?

6. How does the rabbinical principle of *bal tashit*, "don't destroy wantonly," factor into a Jewish environmental ethic? How does it serve to limit absolute conceptions of the right to private property?

7. How is a traditional Jewish ethic, which respects the natural world conditionally, different from the environmental ethics of more radical ecological movements?

NOTES

1. For a general discussion, see "Thou Shalt Not Covet the Earth," *Economist*, December 21, 1996, 108–10.

2. Lynn White Jr., "The Historical Roots of Our Ecologic Crisis," *Science*, March 10, 1976, 1207.

3. On Christianity, see for example, Roderick Nash, *The Rights of Nature: A History of Environmental Ethics* (Madison: University of Wisconsin Press, 1989), chap. 4, "The Greening of Religion"; and Robert Booth Fowler, *The Greening of Protestant Thought* (Chapel Hill: University of North Carolina Press, 1995).

4. Saul Berman, "Jewish Environmental Values: The Dynamic Tension between Nature and Human Needs," in *To Till and to Tend* (New York: Coalition on the Environment and Jewish Life, 1994); Jeremy Benstein, "Leave Nature Out of the War," *Jerusalem Report*, September 7, 1995, 32; Jeremy Benstein, "One, Walking and Studying . . . : Nature vs. Torah," *Judaism*, Spring 1995, 146–68; Mark Bleiweiss, "Jewish Waste Ethics," *Jewish Spectator*, Fall 1995, 17–19; Eliezer Diamond, "Jewish Perspectives on Limiting Consumption," in *Ecology and the Jewish Spirit: Where Nature and the Sacred Meet*, ed. Ellen Bernstein (Woodstock, VT: Jewish Lights Publishing, 1998), 80–89; David Ehrenfeld and Philip Bentley, "Judaism and the Practice of Stewardship," *Judaism* 34, Summer 1985, 301–11; Eliezer Finkelman, "Kee Tetze: Do Animals Have Full Moral Standing?" *Jewish Bulletin of Northern California*, August 23, 1996; Eric Freudenstein, "Ecology and the Jewish Tradition," *Judaism*, Fall 1970, 1–11; Everett Gendler, "The Earth's Covenant," *Reconstructionist*, November–December 1989, 28–31; Robert Gordis, "Ecology in the Jewish Tradition," *Midstream*, October 1995, 19–23; Robert Gordis, "The Earth Is the Lord's—Judaism and the Spoliation of Nature," *Keeping Posted*, December 1970, 5–9; Ismar Schorsch, "Learning to Live with Less—A Jewish Perspective," unpublished talk, September 14, 1990; Eilon Schwartz, "Judaism and Nature: Theological and Moral Issues to Consider While Renegotiating a Jewish Relationship to the Nature World," *Judaism*, Fall 1995, 437–47; Abraham Stahl, "Educating for Change in Attitudes toward Nature and Environment among Oriental Jews in Israel," *Environment and Behavior*, January 1993, 3–21; Daniel Swartz, "Jews, Jewish Texts, and Nature: A Brief History," in *To Till and to Tend*, 1–14; Samuel Weintraub, "The Spiritual Ecology of Kashrut," in *To Till and to Tend*, 21–24; Bernstein, ed., *Ecology and the Jewish Spirit*; Aubrey Rose, ed., *Judaism and Ecology* (London: Cassell, 1992).

5. Ellen Bernstein and Dan Fink, *Let the Earth Teach You Torah* (Philadelphia: Shomrei Adamah, 1992); David Stein, ed., *A Garden of Choice Fruit* (Wyncote, PA: Shomrei Adamah/Keepers of the Earth, 1991).

6. See, for example, Badley Shavit Artson, "A Jewish Celebration of Biodiversity," *Tikkun* 12, no. 5 (Sept./Oct. 1997): 43–45.

7. For critiques of White's arguments as they apply to Christianity, see for example, Mark Stoll, *Protestantism, Capitalism and Nature in America* (Albuquerque: University of New Mexico Press, 1997), and Clive Ponting, *A Green History of the World* (New York: St. Martin's Press, 1992), chap. 8.

8. For a discussion of these two perspectives, see Avner De-Shalit and Moti Talias, "Green or Blue and White? Environmental Controversies in Israel," *Environmental Politics*, Summer 1995, 273–94. For a discussion of deep ecology, see George Sessions, ed., *Deep Ecology for the 21st Century* (Boston: Shambhala, 1995).

9. Unless otherwise noted, all biblical quotations are from Everett Fox, *The Five Books of Moses: A New Translation with Introductions, Commentary, and Notes* (New York: Schocken Books, 1995).

10. Quoted in Bernstein, *Ecology and the Jewish Spirit* (New York: Pelican, 2000), 32.

11. Quoted in Diamond, "Jewish Perspectives on Limiting Consumption," 85.

12. Quoted in Gordis, "Ecology in the Jewish Tradition," 20.

13. Quoted in Ehrenfeld and Bentley, "Judaism and the Practice of Stewardship," 302.

14. Quoted in Stahl, "Educating for Change in Attitudes," 6.

15. Ibid., 6.

16. Quoted in Meir Tamari, *With All Your Possessions* (Jerusalem: Jason Aronson, 1998), 280.

17. Berman, "Jewish Environmental Values," 15.

18. Schorsch, "Learning to Live with Less," 6.

19. Quoted in Marc Swetlitz, "Living as If God Mattered: Heschel's View of Nature and Humanity," in *Ecology and the Jewish Spirit*, 247.

20. Gordis, "Ecology in the Jewish Tradition," 22.

21. Gordis, "Ecology in the Jewish Tradition," 8.

22. Gordis, "Ecology in the Jewish Tradition," 20.

23. See, for example, the various essays in Carolyn Merchant, ed. *Ecology: Key Concepts in Critical Theory* (Atlantic Highlands, NJ: Humanities Press, 1994).

24. Quoted in Swartz, "Jews, Jewish Texts, and Nature," 6.

25. Quoted in Swartz, "Jews, Jewish Texts, and Nature," 4.

26. Swartz, "Jews, Jewish Texts, and Nature," 5.

27. Swartz, "Jews, Jewish Texts, and Nature," 5.

28. Quoted in Stahl, "Educating for Change in Attitudes," 7.

29. For a detailed exegesis of this text, which appears to admit to a variety of interpretations, see Benstein, "One, Walking."

30. Quoted in Gordis, "Ecology in the Jewish Tradition," 22.

31. Quoted in Bleiwiss, 18.

32. Quoted in Diamond, "Jewish Perspectives," 87.

33. Quoted in Gordis, "Ecology in the Jewish Tradition," 22.

34. Berman, "Jewish Environmental Values," 16, 17.

35. Bernstein, *Ecology and the Jewish Spirit*, 87.

36. A number of writers have pointed to the danger of "study[ing] the Sources with an eye for those particular teachings that are inspirational for—or at least compatible with—one's own predetermined 'green' positions and thus avoiding challenging oneself with texts that don't fit current environmental wisdom." Benstein, "One, Walking," 147.

37. Berman, "Jewish Environmental Values," 17.

38. Diamond, "Jewish Perspectives," 82.

The Spirit of Place:
The Columbia River Watershed Letter and the Meaning of Community

Douglas Burton-Christie

One important and recurring complaint heard from social activists is their critique of the rhetoric used in mainstream discourse to describe and evaluate social, political, and economic realities. Many social activists claim that too often we speak in abstractions using terms like peace, love, and stewardship, about generalities like war, poverty, and the environment. This use of language distances the user from the lived realities to such a degree that it often short-circuits genuine concern, which could, in turn, lead to effective positive change. In this chapter, the author evaluates a document on environmental issues published by the U.S. and Canadian Catholic bishops that makes important strides toward using more localized and concrete references to illustrate the more abstract principles embodied in its social teaching.

This chapter examines the theological and ecological significance of the International Pastoral Letter on the Columbia River Watershed issued by the U.S. and Canadian bishops in 2001. It argues that through its inclusive, participatory process, its emphasis on the watershed as a significant locus for theological reflection, and its strong moral, spiritual vision regarding what a watershed is and can be, the letter makes a significant contribution to Catholic teaching on the environment. However, Douglas Burton-Christie also claims that due to its generalizing rhetorical style, its weak vision of spirituality, and its lack of a critical, prophetic edge, the letter fails to realize its full potential. Burton-Christie poses questions about the central meaning and purpose of such a pastoral and about what the Roman Catholic community can learn from the present letter that might strengthen future attempts to address environmental or other pressing concerns.

The sheer enormity of it staggered my ten-year-old imagination. I felt dwarfed by it, reduced to something small and fragile and insignificant. My stomach pitched and churned as I gazed out onto its immensity. I thought: If it wanted to, this thing could engulf me. It was my first encounter with the Grand Coulee Dam. It was 1964. I was ten years old and traveling through eastern Washington on vacation with my family. We made a detour on our journey back home to Seattle just to see the dam. It did not disappoint. I stood there a long time looking out onto that vast expanse of concrete (enough to bury the state of Texas a foot deep I was told), listening to the roar of the water as it tumbled down, down, down into the abyss. I thought about the turbines, hidden deep inside the dam. They were especially fascinating to me. I did not even understand altogether what they were, how they worked, only that by some strange alchemy involving water, gravity, and the churning of those turbines, a massive amount of energy came coursing out of that dam. Power. Electricity. Enough electricity to run everything—the lights in our home, my electric train, the entire city of Seattle where I lived. My father worked for a lighting company at the time; those were his light bulbs (I imagined) lighting up the skyscrapers in downtown Seattle. I had just done a third-grade report on light bulbs, tracing the intricate path of those frail filaments along which a vast, unseen source of energy coursed and emerged, eventually, as light. Standing there that day on the Grand Coulee Dam, it all came together for me: the wonderworld of technology, the seemingly infinite promise of the future, all that we, I, could do to change the world.

Another thing I realize as I reflect back on that day: I hardly noticed the river—the mighty Columbia—at all. It was an afterthought. So were the salmon. Nor did I think to ask who had lived there before the dam was constructed, or what had become of their home and their culture. No, I was mesmerized by this technological colossus, unable to see anything beyond its mass and weight. It had created a cosmos all its own and for the moment I stood within it.

It is troubling for me, more than thirty years later, to have to reckon with this experience. It so clearly expresses the character of my life in that place at the time—detachment and alienation from the natural world—and my own complicity in its impoverishment. Certainly, I had a strong sense of the beauty of the Pacific Northwest, something that lives deeply within me even now. But I had no particular sense that my relationship with the place had a moral character, that it involved reciprocity or responsibility. Nothing in my Catholic school education had led me to think in these terms. Nor had I been taught to think this way at home. I was in this respect typical of many of those living at the time in the state of Washington: appreciative of the physical beauty of our home, but unaware of and/or unprepared to take responsibility for the effects of our lives upon the world around us. The damming of the Columbia by then had already drastically depleted the salmon run. It had flooded sacred sites of the native peoples, helped accelerate their displacement from the shore of the Columbia to distant reservations. But there were formidable economic interests that ensured that the dams would be built, that the wild Columbia would be reduced to a cluster of lakes.

That all of this could have unfolded without serious resistance or even comment by the large majority of those living in the Pacific Northwest is astonishing and, to me at least, shameful. Seen from another perspective, however, the fate of the Columbia is hardly remarkable at all. Rather, it mirrors the fate of wild rivers all across the West. Its fate in turn reflects the widespread acceptance of the notion that rivers are to be thought of fundamentally as natural resources—that is, as things to be used, taken advantage of, elements within a complex socioeconomic calculus that determines how wealth is defined and understood in our society. Gradually, this sense of things is beginning to change, as more and more inhabitants of this region have begun to ask about the health and well-being of their rivers and of the possibility of reimagining and restoring impoverished, degraded watersheds.

One such effort, which I will examine here, is the International Pastoral Letter written by the Catholic bishops of the Pacific Northwest region, entitled "The Columbia River Watershed: Caring for Creation and the Common Good." I want to note and evaluate some of the distinctive contributions the letter makes to the current discussion about the fate of our rivers and about our moral and spiritual relationship to the Earth. But I also want to ask about what the letter does *not* do, or at least what it fails to do as well or as clearly as it might have done. The churches, it seems to me, have the potential to play a significant role in shaping attitudes toward and even policy decisions about the environment. But realizing that potential will require faith communities to examine even more carefully and critically than we have done up until now our theological and spiritual convictions and the application of those convictions to the challenges before us.

THE SIGNIFICANCE OF THE LOCAL

The Columbia River Watershed letter makes several significant contributions to the ongoing conversation about what it means to stand in a more ethical relationship to the places we live. I want to highlight three of these here: the process of dialogue and reflection through which the letter came into being, the emphasis on the significance of the local as a starting point for reflecting theologically on what it means to be a community of faith, and the distinctive moral-spiritual vision that grounds the bishops' understanding of how we are called to live in relationship to the natural world.

Process

The first significant contribution of the letter I want to note is the *process* through which it came into being. The final draft of the letter was published on the Feast of the Baptism of the Lord, January 8, 2001. Its publication brought to culmination a four-year process of study, reflection, and hearings, called "Readings of the Signs of the Times," held in Oregon, Washington, and British Columbia in which representatives of different constituencies—industry, agriculture, fishing, education, and native peoples—presented their distinct perspectives on the river. Further input was received from a range of consultants, including theologians, natural and social scientists, and church representatives. The letter thus benefits from the same participative, inclusive process that has shaped a number of important documents of Catholic social teaching in this country, including the U.S. Bishops' Letter on Economic Justice and the Appalachian Bishops' 1995 Pastoral Letter, "At Home in the Web of Life: A Pastoral Message on Sustainable Communities in Appalachia."

This process of listening to the voices of diverse groups, sometimes with sharply divergent views about the future of the river, has contributed in important ways to the increasingly lively conversation about the fate of the river currently taking hold in the Pacific Northwest. It has also given the letter a credibility it might otherwise have lacked had it been perceived as reflecting the ideological convictions of only one or another of the constituencies. Still, this evenhandedness has also come at a price. It means that on certain issues where one might have expected the bishops to speak out more strongly, such as the fate of the native peoples, or the future of the salmon and the dams, their voices have an irenic tone strangely out of keeping with the urgency of the issues.

The Significance of the Local

A second aspect of the letter, which I judge to be one of its most important achievements, is the bishops' decision to *locate* their moral and theological reflections within a particular watershed. It would be easy to miss the significance of this. After all, the term watershed has long been a staple of environmental discourse; biologists use it as the fundamental point of departure for understanding and interpreting the ecological complexity of a given region. Where the water flows when it rains, how much water flows in a particular place determines so much about that place, especially what plant and animal species can thrive there. The character of a watershed also affects the kind of human culture that can exist in a given place, the myths and stories that arise and take hold there. It is a fundamental ecological fact around which the entire life and history and culture of places take shape.[1] If it is taken seriously by a local community, knowledge of one's watershed can profoundly affect a community's very sense of itself, especially its sense of relationship to and responsibility for a particular place. In this sense, awareness of one's watershed becomes a crucial element in the moral, spiritual language of a community. Still, as far as I am aware, the idea of the watershed has never before been given such a prominent place in Catholic social teaching. Certainly such attention has not been given to a particular watershed such as the Columbia.

There are two things about the choice of this term that are particularly striking. One is the adoption of a widely accepted ecological term as a starting point for theological and ethical reflection. The other is the resulting emphasis on the particular and the local. The two issues are related. The bishops begin their letter this way: "The Columbia River Watershed stands as one of the most beautiful places on God's earth." They then proceed to describe the scope and range of this watershed, encompassing 259,000 square miles, and of the river itself, extending 1,200 miles from its source in British Columbia to its mouth on the Pacific Coast of Washington. This watershed, suggests the bishops, "is an extensive ecosystem that transcends national, state and provincial borders."[2] Everything that follows in the letter takes as its point of departure the fact of this watershed. Clearly, the bishops are not interested in biology and ecology for their own sakes. It is always the moral and religious significance of the watershed to which they give their attention. Thus, the bishops make it clear that faith is the key to seeing what the watershed truly is. It is "through the eyes of faith," they suggest, that the watershed can be "seen . . . [as] a revelation of God's presence, an occasion of grace and blessing." Still, it is remarkable that the river itself and the extensive and complex ecosystem created by the river occupy the very center of their theological and moral reflections. What an astonishing and suggestive juxtaposition of language this is: "watershed" and "God's presence." This demands of any sensitive reader a reorientation of perspective, a willingness to attribute value and meaning to this vibrant ecological entity. The watershed is seen as something sacred, something possessing inherent meaning and value, worthy of the most careful attention we can give to it.

This means that theological reflection, spiritual practice, and ethical commitment are inescapably local. Environmental activists have long been advocating the need for deeper local commitments as crucial to the cultivation of meaningful ethical relationships with the natural world. The idea of the bioregion—a region with its own distinctive biological characteristics and cultural values—has come to stand as a fundamental starting point for such work. To imagine oneself as part of a bioregion (as distinct from a political entity such as a state, whose boundaries often reflect poorly the underlying physical, biological, and cultural shape of a given place) can lead to a deeper sense of relationship with and responsibility for that place. Bioregions are often defined by characteristic flora or fauna. In his book *The Practice of the Wild*, poet Gary Snyder gives the example of the coastal Douglas fir, one of the definitive trees of the Pacific Northwest, whose presence as far north as the Skeena River in British Columbia, as far south as the Big Sur River, and as far east as the Pacific Crest, roughly describes the boundaries of a distinctive bioregion. What is the value of thinking in these terms? As Snyder notes: "It prepares us to begin to be at home in this landscape. There are tens of millions of people in North America who were physically born here but who are not actually living here intellectually, imaginatively, or morally." Learning to think and live bioregionally, then, implies a radical reordering of our imaginations, our moral sensibilities, our spiritual lives. Orienting yourself toward the presence of the Douglas fir and the bioregion in which it thrives will help alert you to certain things that you might otherwise miss—"a rainfall and a temperature range . . . [it] will indicate what your agriculture might be, how steep the pitch of your roof, what raincoats you'd need. You don't have to know such details to get by in the modern cities of Portland or Bellingham. But if you do know what is taught by plants and weather you are in on the gossip and can truly feel more at home."[3]

Home. This is the central spiritual and ethical challenge that bioregionalists have put before us, the need to learn how to be at home in the places where we dwell, to truly inhabit these places. Although the bishops' letter nowhere refers to bioregionalism directly, it refers often to the Pacific Northwest *region*, to the religious and moral significance of learning to understand oneself as part of this specific region. In this sense, it echoes and joins its voice to the growing chorus among the environmental and religious communities calling for a renewed attention to local and regional ecology.[4] The bishops of the Pacific Northwest are asking their community to pay attention to the local and the particular realities of *this* watershed, this bioregion. Begin here, they seem to be saying. Begin locally. Learn to pay attention to local landforms, plants, and animals, to the way water (especially the Columbia) moves across the landscape. Value and cherish them. Identify yourself with your watershed, your home. Let your spiritual, ecclesial identity take root here, flourish and grow in this place.

In one sense, the letter's insistence on the importance of the local is not really so surprising. It is completely consistent with Catholic teaching on the Incarnation and on the nature of sacramental reality, both of which contribute to the Catholic understanding of the revelatory power of particular, physical things and of the world as a whole. Still, while this emphasis on the theological significance of the particular and the local can be traced to the very roots of the Catholic tradition, the ecological significance of this idea has not yet been sufficiently articulated in our own time.[5] In bringing these classic dimensions of Catholic thought to bear upon the ecological challenges arising in the Pacific Northwest, the bishops contribute something new and important to our understanding of how to respond to these challenges. In doing so, they offer a necessary complement to some of the more general, global messages on the environment that have emerged from the Catholic community in recent years.[6] Still, as I shall argue below, they do not take this commitment as seriously as they should have.

A Moral-Spiritual Vision

A third and final issue I want to comment on regarding the letter's positive contributions is the strong moral-spiritual vision it expresses. The bishops describe their aspirations in these terms: "We hope that we might work together to develop and implement an integrated spiritual, social and ecological vision for our watershed home, a vision that promotes justice for people and stewardship of creation."[7] Three aspects of this vision are noteworthy.

The first is the letter's insistence on the connection between environmental degradation and racial and social injustice. In this, the letter echoes the concerns expressed in John Paul II's 1990 statement, "The Ecological Crisis: A Common Responsibility," that "the proper ecological balance will not be found without directly addressing the structural forms of poverty that exist,"[8] concerns that have become central to Catholic social teaching on the environment. These concerns have already had the effect of focusing renewed attention on the serious impact of the reduced salmon run on Native American communities and on the effects of toxic dumping on low-income minority communities in the Columbia River Basin. As I will note in more detail below, much more could have been done in the letter to articulate the particular character of the injustice that has been visited upon the Columbia River Watershed. Still, the bishops place justice at the very center of their concerns, making it utterly clear that from a Catholic perspective, concern for the environment can never be separated from the commitment to justice.

A second noteworthy aspect of the letter's moral-spiritual vision is its approach to the question of the "commons" and the "common good." In addressing the commons as a central feature of its vision for a new community, the bishops draw upon and integrate at least three distinct ideas: the commons, the common good, and the Catholic sacramental tradition. "The commons belongs to everyone and yet belongs to no one," the bishops claim.[9] In doing so, they give voice to the ancient and radical ideal of land held in common for the good of the entire community (and for the sake of the land itself), an ideal that subverts many of our contemporary ideas concerning the primacy of private property. In its traditional form, this ideal usually expressed itself as a *local* or regional practice, which means that it should not be thought of as identical with the contemporary understanding of "public domain," which is land held and managed by a central government.[10] In the Columbia River Basin, where federal agencies such as the Bureau of Reclamation (being the principal architects of the massive irrigation projects in the basin) have long determined the fate of the land and the river, the idea of reimagining the commons as a local, regional practice has particular appeal.

For the bishops, this tradition of the commons is closely connected to the idea of the "common good." They insist that what they are aiming for is a situation in which "every[one] acknowledges individual responsibility for the common good and the good of the commons."[11] By common good, they clearly have in mind a realignment of the prevailing North American understanding of private property. The bishops cite with approval the Second Vatican Council Document, "The Church in the Modern World," which argues: "The state has the duty to prevent anyone from abusing his private property to the detriment of the common good. By its nature private property has a social dimension."[12] The fact that such an attitude is reflected almost nowhere in contemporary Western society suggests just how radical and potentially unnerving the principle of the common good remains. It sits uneasily alongside cherished American assumptions regarding the seemingly limitless horizon of personal liberties and rights against which human beings live their lives. Indeed, it suggests a very different moral vision in which the good of the whole community determines and limits what rights individuals (and corporations) may claim for themselves. In this sense, the bishops' appeal to the common good contributes something important and distinctive to the contemporary debate over how to manage our natural resources: a moral discourse that places the rights (or the good) of the individual within the context of the good of the whole. Seen within the ecological context of this letter, the appeal to the common good takes on an even deeper resonance, opening up the possibility that we might come to understand community as comprising not only human beings, but also plants, animals, the entire created world. The letter only hints at this possibility. But in its careful attention to the moral demands the watershed places upon us, the letter seems to invite further consideration of this important question.

Finally, the bishops state clearly and unequivocally that "[t]he commons of a local place can be revelatory."[13] Here, sacramental language enfolds language of the commons to create a new focal point for spiritual awareness and experience. The conviction that particular places can be revelatory is itself grounded in belief in the revelatory power of the entire world, "a world that discloses the Creator's presence by visible and tangible signs."[14] It is this conviction that enables the bishops to affirm that the created world can and ought to be a focal point for the spiritual lives of human beings, including members of the Catholic community: "Creation provides the opportunity for spiritual contemplation because it is from God and reveals God."[15] This insistence that human beings are invited to encounter God in and through the natural world has the potential to transform not only spiritual awareness, but also spiritual practice. The letter is insistent that there should be an integral connection between spirituality and ethics.

They frame this connection in terms of two ideas—stewardship and conversion. Stewardship is an idea that has come to signify for Christians the particular responsibility of human beings to care for creation. It is a biblical idea rooted in a fundamental sense of reciprocity and relationship between human beings and the natural world, not domination or arrogance of human beings over the natural world. But the letter notes that the idea and practice of stewardship have been significantly eroded from the Christian imagination: "As people have become more absorbed by material things and less conscious of spiritual and social relationships, consumerism has replaced compassion, and exploitation of the earth has replaced stewardship." It is for this reason they argue that there is such a deep "need for spiritual conversion to a better and deeper sense of stewardship for God's creation and responsibility for our communities."[16] The call to conversion makes it clear that responsibility is more than an ideal; it is a truth that must be lived into, praticed, embodied by individual human beings and communities. And it suggests too how costly and difficult this shift of perspective and reorientation of practice will be. A viable earth ethic, if it is to last, will need to arise out of transformed lives and spirits. This call to conversion, to spiritual transformation, is central to the larger moral and social vision of the commons that the bishops invite all people of good will to embrace.

GOING DEEPER INTO THE WATERSHED: RHETORIC, SPIRITUALITY, PROPHECY

There is much more that could be said about the positive contributions this letter makes to our understanding of and commitment to ecological responsibility. But I also wish to consider some of the areas where I believe the letter falls short in realizing its full potential. I do so in the hopes of raising some larger questions about the purpose and viability of such pastoral letters and about the particular contributions faith communities can make to the healing of the earth. One question has to do with *rhetoric*, in particular whether the generalizing rhetorical strategies employed by official church documents can adequately address the urgent ecological-social-spiritual issues at the heart of the letter. A second question concerns *spirituality*, especially the issue of how best to articulate the rich spiritual experience of the natural world that must ground and inform any genuine ethical response. Finally, there is the question of *prophecy*, namely, whether a pastoral letter such as this one has an obligation to take a critical-prophetic stance toward the practices and attitudes that have given rise to the massive human and natural degradation we are currently witnessing.

Rhetoric

The Columbia Watershed letter speaks largely in generalizations, in broad moral imperatives, something that places it firmly within the rhetorical tradition of most official statements of Catholic social teaching. True, the letter addresses the Columbia River Watershed and the moral-spiritual-ecological issues arising directly from this distinct geographical region. But in doing so, it speaks only in the most general terms. Its descriptions of the physical landscape are typical of this habit of generalization. One hears of the beauty of mountains, forests, animals, rivers, sunsets. But one looks in vain for the mention of any *particular* mountain, or tree, or animal (except the salmon, though even the salmon is only mentioned in a generic way). The same is true regarding place names and stories and myths associated with particular places. The place itself, the Columbia River Watershed, is missing almost completely from the letter. This omission of the particular character of the place is more than merely ironic; it represents a significant failure of the imagination and a missed opportunity. The letter raises many important moral and spiritual and practical questions, but it does so with the workmanlike character of a "white paper."[17] This means that a document that ought to move and inspire and engage the imagination largely fails to do so.

Does it have to be this way? Must pastoral letters speak in such general terms, even when the subject matter cries out for sharp specificity, for narrative and poetry? One need only look at the pastoral letter published in 1995 by the bishops of Appalachia, "At Home in the Web of Life," to see that there is a real alternative. This letter names, with obvious affection, the trees that cover the hills: "oaks and hickories and maples, locusts and poplar and cherry, and once an abundance of chestnut. . . . Overall," the letter reminds us, "there dwell here more than one hundred species of trees." So too does the letter recognize that the "woods are full of food, medicinal plants and glorious flowers. We recall especially berries and nuts, mountain laurel and rhododendron, azaleas and mountain magnolias, blossoms on tulip poplars and black locusts, ginseng and yellow root."[18] The animals of the Appalachian region are named with a similar specificity. So also does the letter take care to name the human inhabitants of this place and the rich and varied cultural heritage of these peoples: First, the ancient peoples who inhabited this region as far back as ten thousand years ago; then the great tribes, the Cherokee, the Catawba, the Monacans and Manohoacs, the Delaware, the Shawnee, and the great Iroquois confederation; then the Scots-Irish, the freed African slaves—all of whom contributed to the deep and beautiful culture of the Appalachian mountains.

The rhetorical style of the Appalachian letter reflects a deep conviction about the importance of naming and describing particular things. It expresses a kind of ecological sensibility, an awareness of how the complex interrelationship of utterly particular and distinct organisms, all of which are adapted in distinctive ways to fit into the ecosystem as a whole. This helps explain why field guides and ecological histories figure as importantly into the work of this letter as biblical and theological resources do, why descriptions of particular places and place names, regional songs fill the pages of this letter. It also helps to account for the letter's attention to specific instances of ecological degradation and of economic and cultural impoverishment. One feels in the pages of this letter the particular texture of this place, the affection of long-time residents for their home place, the reality of the struggle to recover a sustainable life in this place. One senses too the depth of experience of those who live in this place, their spirituality.[19]

Spirituality

These two issues—rhetoric and spirituality—are intimately related to one another. A crucial question arises—how best to articulate a sacramental spirituality? Nearly every major statement from the Roman Catholic Church on the environment that has appeared in the last twenty years has referred to the notion of sacrament as a bedrock theological-spiritual principle. The earth itself is sacrament. Every living thing is sacrament.[20] God comes to us through the particulars. Our responsibility for the things of the earth arises, at least in part, from this reality. If sacrament is somehow at the heart of how we are to think of our relationship to the physical world, then shouldn't our language reflect this? Don't our habits of language affect our capacity to see and experience the world as sacramental? This, it seems to me, is something we need to take absolutely seriously if we are to hope to express what the wild world is for us and what it might be, if we are to have any hope of cultivating an ethic of responsibility toward the living beings of this world.

Take salmon for example. Returning salmon were once so plentiful in the Columbia that they scared horses along the banks of the river. Now, preserving these organisms at any reasonable population density is becoming enormously difficult, and their decline and looming loss has incredibly debilitating implications for every population in and around the river—animals, plants, forests, people, businesses, towns. The issue of salmon preservation—together with related issues of what to do about the dams along the Columbia and clear-cutting of forests—has become a highly charged topic in the Pacific Northwest. The bishops' letter mentions salmon in passing as a key issue of concern. But nowhere in the letter do we get a feeling of what a salmon is, of the mystery and intricacy of their annual migration, of the genetic information that determines that they will return to spawn in this place and no other. Nowhere, in other words, do we get a sense of the *life* of salmon and what their life means to the Columbia River Watershed. Nor do we get any feeling for what it is like to *experience* the presence of a salmon. For this we need the help of writers and poets, like Freeman House, whose book *Totem Salmon* invites the reader to consider in the most intimate terms possible the lives of these mysterious beings. What does it feel like to draw near a salmon?

> King salmon and I are together in the water. The basic bone-felt nature of this encounter never changes, even though I have spent parts of a lifetime seeking the meeting and puzzling over its meaning, trying to find for myself the right place in it. It is a *large* experience, and it has never failed to contain these elements, at once separate and combined: empty-minded awe; an uneasiness about my own active role both as a person and as a creature of my species; and a looming existential dread that sometimes attains the physicality of a lump in the throat, a knot in the abdomen, a constriction around the temples.[21]

A *large* experience, he says, one for which he struggles and fails to find adequate language. But the language he does find is revealing and is analogous to the language often used to describe religious experience. It is an "encounter," a "meeting." It evokes in him a deep sense of humility as he struggles to find the "right place in it." It pervades his entire being. Later, at some remove from the immediacy of this experience, he reflects on its meaning: "Each fish brought up from the deep carries with it implications of the Other, the great life of the sea that lies permanently beyond anyone's feeble strivings to control or understand it. . . . True immersion in a system larger than oneself carries with it exposure to a vast complexity wherein joy and terror are complementary parts."[22]

Who is this Other whom we meet in such moments? The "world" of these luminous beings ("a system larger than oneself . . . a vast complexity"—a world that will forever elude our understanding and because of this remains fundamentally mysterious and alluring)? The beings themselves? God? An encounter with salmon, or any living species, compels us to confront the mysterious Other with honesty and imagination and, perhaps, faith. It also calls us to reconsider the meaning of community and who is included within that community. The letter does not really consider this question in any depth. It does not ask how a different understanding of community, in which the human family is seen as part of a larger, more-than-human community—a multitude of other beings—might alter our perception and experience of the world. In its discussion of community, it is largely the *human* community the bishops have in mind. The letter makes it clear that the natural world has meaning and value; it is a gift from God and we are responsible for its care and preservation. But nowhere are we given a sense of being responsible *to* the natural world; nowhere do we get the sense that the vast array of beings who inhabit that world are capable of addressing us and calling forth from us a meaningful response.

For this more expansive sense of community we must look elsewhere. "What we must find a way to do, then, is incorporate the other people—what the Sioux Indians called the creeping people, and the standing people, and the flying people, and the swimming people—into the councils of government."[23] This delightful idiom arises out of an ancient and distinct cultural sensibility, born of relationship, reciprocity, and respect. It arises out of a long tradition of living in proximity with these other "people." It expresses a lived spirituality in which all living beings participate, in which all living beings have standing (including political standing). It suggests an encompassing vision of community in which responsiveness and responsibility extend to every member.

Is it unfair to suggest that the bishops' pastoral statement on the Columbia River should take seriously such an encompassing vision of community, should evoke the spiritual significance of salmon, or, for that matter, the river or the forests? I do not think that it is. Without such attention to the particular character of spiritual experience, including the experience of the sacred mediated by animals, plants, indeed the whole watershed, it seems doubtful whether the idea of ecological responsibility will ever touch the depths of our religious imaginations. Nor, in the absence of such experience, is it easy to imagine how we will ever be moved to alter our relationship to the natural world, to alter our behavior and actions.

Prophecy and Resistance

This leads to a last question, having to do with the place of prophetic, critical resistance within the larger project of reimagining the watershed. Do the bishops, speaking on behalf of the Catholic Christian community, have an obligation to speak in a prophetic voice about the moral and spiritual challenges facing the larger community? I raise this question because of the muted tone the letter adopts when addressing some of the more contentious issues, such as dams along the Columbia, the displacement of native peoples, and the depletion of the salmon. Here is a typical statement on the dams: "Some urge the breaching of the four dams on the lower Snake River in order to improve the water environment for fish. Others advocate keeping the dams for energy and agricultural uses, and suggest other means of assuring the survival of fish and fish-related industries. The situation is very complex and unilateral answers appear to be inadequate."[24] It would be difficult to imagine a more equivocal statement on the question of dams than this one. The bishops do make it plain that in considering the fate of the dams, we will need to give serious attention to the spiritual and ethical dimensions of the questions. But there is something unsatisfying about both the tone and substance of this statement. Part of this has to do with the lack of specificity. The letter addresses only in passing the complex and often corrupt history of the U.S. Bureau of Reclamation's role in damming the Snake and Columbia Rivers. Nor does it address the glaring failures of policy and engineering that have plagued the construction and administration of the dams, including the mind-boggling refusal to build a salmon ladder on the massive Grand Coulee Dam. And the Hanford Nuclear Facility, now renowned for its huge cost overruns, its toxic spills into the Columbia, and its ultimate failure, receives barely more than a mention in the letter.[25]

A pastoral letter must of course address all the people of a given region. In this case that means addressing environmentalists, native peoples, those working in the logging industry, the hydroelectric industry, farmers, everyone who has a stake in the life of the Pacific Northwest. Perhaps this helps to account for letter's muted tone. Still, one cannot help but feel that bishops missed an opportunity to sound a more forceful, prophetic note regarding some of the more urgent challenges facing those living in the Columbia River Watershed.

Attending more honestly to the particular biological, social, and cultural *losses* that have occurred within the Columbia River Watershed—and doing so with the same sharp specificity one brings to the awareness of sacramental reality—seems a necessary part of any healing process that might yet emerge. Such an accounting needs to begin with the Columbia River itself. Gone is the wild, powerful, unpredictable river that used to rise twenty feet at Vancouver and fifty feet at the Dalles (the river's flow and level is now carefully controlled by engineers). Gone are the deep canyons and enormous towers of basalt that once marked the Columbia's path to the ocean, "broad bars of flood-washed boulders, gray sand beaches lined with cedar canoes, bright white water rapids where waves mounded higher than a man." Gone are the rapids and waterfalls, Redgrave Canyon, Surprise Rapids, Kitchen Rapids, Kettle Falls, Gualquil Rapids, Priest Rapids, Celio Falls, the Dalles—over 109 all told as recently as 1921. Gone are the native grasses that once thrived in the Columbia Basin: bunch grass, wild rye, Idaho fescue, Sandberg blue grass, sand grass, needle grass, Indian millet, bearded wheat grass. Gone (almost completely) are the salmon that once choked the river, from bank to bank.[26] Gone—flooded by the construction of the Grand Coulee Dam—are twenty-one thousand acres of prime bottom land where Indians had been living for nearly ten thousand years, the best hunting, farming, and root-gathering places, most of the tribal burial grounds. Nearly gone is an entire indigenous culture oriented around the river and the salmon; around the Grand Coulee Dam it is the Colville Indians who have felt this loss most acutely.[27]

Naming such losses is important and necessary. It marks a place to begin remembering the actual life and history of this place. And it provides a means for initiating the work of reparation that must surely follow. But it is only a beginning. We need a deeper and clearer expression of repentance for the losses we have inflicted upon this place. We also need a stronger conceptual framework for analyzing and interpreting such loss. Many of the resources and principles for doing so are present within the Christian tradition, specifically in the tradition of Catholic social teaching. The letter draws upon these in articulating the broad moral principles that the bishops believe ought to undergird the Catholic community's response to the Columbia River Watershed. But it refrains from applying these principles directly and specifically to the actual life of the watershed. It refrains from looking too closely at or analyzing too deeply the long history of moral and spiritual indifference that has resulted in recurring violence against the land, the living beings of this place, and the peoples for whom it has always been home. This, it seems to me, is an insufficient response.

CONCLUSION

Still, the Columbia River Watershed letter does represent an important step forward in the Catholic community's efforts to address seriously and thoughtfully the growing environmental crisis affecting us all. The willingness of the bishops to engage in honest, open hearings with the diverse constituencies across the state, their insistence on locating their reflections on the environment within a particular watershed, and their articulation of an integrated moral-spiritual-ecological vision all represent real signs of creativity and hope that can help us as we face the challenges ahead. That the letter fails to realize its full potential, in terms of rhetoric, spirituality, and prophetic critique, is regrettable. Nor are these failures insignificant. Future efforts to express what it means to live in a sustainable relationship with our places will need to be stronger and clearer. We will need to risk investing more in the particular. The future of the places we love depends on it.

QUESTIONS FOR DISCUSSION

1. What is significant about naming this official document after the Columbia River Watershed? Why is knowledge about one's local watershed important for moral deliberation?

2. What sorts of things did the bishops do to prepare themselves to write this document? What significance does our author see in this extensive preparatory process?

3. Our author claims that "theological reflection, spiritual practice, and ethical commitment are inescapably local." What does he mean by this? Why is this "local" character significant?

4. How is the ecological crisis connected to other issues of justice in the bishops' letter?

5. What is "the commons" and what is its relationship to the common good? How is the concept of the commons significant for the letter on the Columbia River Watershed?

6. What weaknesses does our author identify in regard to the letter's use of rhetoric and spirituality?

NOTES

1. "Technically, a watershed is the divide separating one drainage area from another. The term 'watershed' is commonly used to refer to an area: specifically, the area in which all surface waters flow to a common point." Bruce P. McCammon, USDA—Forest Service, Pacific Northwest Region, "Recommended Watershed Terminology," Watershed Management Council, http://www.watershed.org/news/fall_94/terminology.html (accessed June 4, 2006).

2. "The Columbia River Watershed: Caring for Creation and the Common Good. An International Pastoral Letter by the Catholic Bishops of the Region," 1.

3. Gary Snyder, *The Practice of the Wild* (San Francisco, CA: North Point Press, 1990), 40, 38. For a classic articulation of the meaning of bioregionalism, see Kirkpatrick Sale: *Dwellers in the Land: The Bioregional Vision* (Athens: University of Georgia Press, 2000).

4. Important environmental documents have also been published by the World Council of Churches and by a variety of non-Catholic Christian denominations. For the purposes of the present essay, my focus is on the writings published within the Roman Catholic community. See e.g. "Renewing the Earth," published by the United States Catholic Conference; "Care for the Earth," published by the Indiana Catholic Conference; "Celebrate Life: Care for Creation," by the Bishops of Alberta, Canada; "At Home in the Web of Life: A Pastoral Message on Sustainable Communities in Appalachia

(1995)," and "This Land Is Home to Me (1975)," published by the Bishops of Appalachia. For a more international focus, see "Global Climate Change: A Plea for Dialogue, Prudence, and the Common Good," published by the U.S. Catholic Bishops and the "The Cry of the Land," the 1988 Pastoral Letter published by the Bishops of Guatemala.

5. For an important study that argues for the ancient, biblical devotion to place, see Theodore Hiebert, *The Yahwist's Landscape* (New York: Oxford University Press, 1996). For a thoughtful analysis of the significance of place within the history of Christian spirituality and theology, see Belden C. Lane, *Landscapes of the Sacred: Geography and Narrative in American Spirituality*, expanded edition (Baltimore, MD: Johns Hopkins University Press, 2001); and Philip Sheldrake, *Spaces for the Sacred: Place, Memory and Identity* (Baltimore, MD: Johns Hopkins University Press, 2001). For a Christian "Theopoetics" of place, see Douglas Burton-Christie, "Words Beneath the Water: Logos, Cosmos and the Spirit of Place," in *Christianity and Ecology: Seeking the Well-Being of Earth and Humans*, ed. Dieter T. Hessel and Rosemary Radford Ruether (Cambridge, MA: Harvard University Press, 2000), 317–36.

6. Pope John Paul II, "The Ecological Crisis: A Common Responsibility."

7. "Columbia River Watershed," 1.

8. Pope John Paul II, "The Ecological Crisis," 11.

9. "Columbia River Watershed," 2.

10. Snyder, *Practice of the Wild*, 29–37. See also Garrett Hardin and John Baden, *Managing the Commons* (San Francisco, CA: W. H. Freeman, 1977).

11. "Columbia River Watershed," 10.

12. "The Church in the Modern World,": 71, cited in "Columbia River Watershed," 8.

13. "Columbia River Watershed," 7.

14. "Renewing the Earth," United States Catholic Conference.

15. "Columbia River Watershed," 7.

16. "Columbia River Watershed," 9.

17. I owe this felicitous comparison to Brian Doyle of the University of Portland, who made this observation during a panel session on the "Columbia River Watershed" Letter at the College Theology Society meeting at the University of Portland in June 2001.

18. "At Home in the Web of Life: A Pastoral Message on Sustainable Communities in Appalachia Celebrating the 20th Anniversary of 'This Land Is Home to Me,'" 11.

19. It is important to note that "At Home in the Web of Life" is considerably longer than the "Columbia River Watershed," roughly twice as long in its present form. The penultimate draft of the "Columbia River Watershed" Letter was much longer than the final version turned out to be, longer also than the Appalachian Letter. Much of the life and texture that is present in the Appalachian Letter and that is so noticeably lacking in the "Columbia River Watershed" Letter was in fact present in that penultimate draft. For various reasons, not the least of which was the Pacific Northwest bishops' hope that the letter actually would be read, it was significantly shortened. One needs to ask at what cost?

20. The bishops appear to have been uncertain about how far to push their sacramental vision of reality. The phrase "sacramental commons," which figured importantly

in the penultimate draft of the letter, was dropped in the final draft. According to at least one observer, one of the principal authors of the letter, this shift came about because of an uneasiness among some bishops about the implications of attributing sacramental significance to the entire created world.

21. Freeman House, *Totem Salmon* (Boston: Beacon, 1999), 13.

22. House, *Totem Salmon*, 70

23. Gary Snyder, *Turtle Island* (New York: New Directions, 1974), 109.

24. "Columbia River Watershed," 13.

25. For a searching and disturbing examination of the complex history of the Columbia River in modern times, see Blaine Harden, *A River Lost: The Life and Death of the Columbia* (New York: Norton, 1996).

26. William Dietrich, *Northwest Passage: The Great Columbia River* (Seattle: University of Washington Press, 1995), 187–95. Dietrich cites an account of the English explorer Adolph Baillie-Groham, who at the end of the nineteenth century spoke with nostalgia for a world of abundant salmon runs that was already disappearing: "Forty years ago the number of fish who reached these beds was so great that the receding waters would leave millions of dead salmon strewn along the banks, emitting a stench that could be smelled miles off, and which never failed to attract a great number of bears. Though I have never performed the feat of walking across a stream on the backs of fish, which many an old timer will swear he has done, I have certainly seen fish so numerous near their spawning grounds that nowhere could you have thrown a stone into the water without hitting a salmon." Dietrich, *Northwest Passage*, 188.

27. Harden, *A River Lost*, 105–16. Harden documents the harsh treatment of the Colville Indians, especially in the aftermath of the construction of the Grand Coulee Dam. "None of the irrigation water diverted from the river by the Grand Coulee Dam has ever been made available to the Indians. . . . As the non-Indian side of the Columbia . . . attracted industry and farmers with its subsidized power and water, the economy of the reservation withered. Unemployment hovered around 50 percent for decades. A chart of income distribution on the reservation in the early 1990s showed no middle class. . . . Electricity generated by the Grand Coulee Dam earns the federal government more than four hundred million dollars a year. Since the dam went on line in 1942, it has earned the government more than five billion dollars. Although half of the dam sits on reservation property, none of the power earnings was allotted to the Colvilles."

· 16 ·

Bridge Discourse on Wage Justice: Roman Catholic and Feminist Perspectives on the Family Living Wage

Christine Firer-Hinze

> In this chapter, Christine Firer-Hinze sets up a bridge discourse between John A. Ryan and Catholic social thought on one side, and feminist social theorists on the other. The purpose of a bridge discourse is to identify commonalities in perspectives that are otherwise considered disparate or incompatible in order to forge alliances between parties to achieve common goals. In this case, our author is bringing together strands of Catholicism and feminism—two traditions that are often perceived as mutually dismissive—and attempting to establish some theoretical common ground in regard to the issue of a living wage, and in this case, a family living wage. Firer-Hinze uncovers a number of unexpected and thought-provoking relations between the beliefs and commitments of these two distinct perspectives.

*J*ustice for working people has been a persistent concern in modern Christian social ethics. A hallmark of the modern Roman Catholic approach to economic justice has been its advocacy of the worker's right to a family living wage. In the United States, the Catholic case for a living wage was impressively articulated and advanced by ethicist and reformer Monsignor John A. Ryan (1869–1945). Ryan's classic Catholic defense of a family living wage was inevitably shaped by the ideological and practical features of the work-home relation that formed the historical context for its development. Since Ryan's time, however, significant cultural and economic shifts affecting workers and families have occurred. In particular, changes pertaining to the roles and rights of women call into question the case for a family living wage as it has been structured in the century of Catholic social thought since *Rerum Novarum*. Social theorists and contemporary cultural critics—chiefly feminists—who have analyzed the "family wage system" set these changes and these questions in high relief.

The questions raised cut to the quick of the Catholic conception of the good society. To address them, Catholic ethicists must reconsider assumptions about gender, power, and social flourishing that have decisively influenced traditional thinking about wage justice. Such critical examination can, I believe, open the way for retrieving the normative concept of a family living wage as part of a vital, radically transformative approach to worker justice. If the norm is to be revitalized, distortions that have bedeviled past thinking about the "family," about "making a living," and about "work" and the "wage" due it, must be identified and exorcised. Intertwined in all these are apprehensions about women and their activity. Unraveling this knot of issues will require an ideological turn, coupled with the awareness that ideology critique carries its own occupational hazards.

This consideration of the family living wage draws upon two distinctive moral traditions: progressive strands of modern Catholic social thought and socially transformative stands of radical feminist theory.[1] Catholics and feminists often find themselves in intense and even fundamental dispute. Yet they share an ardent commitment to individual and social well-being and to the pursuit of economic justice. Both communities have given careful and extensive attention to matters of wage and justice. Engaging these two literatures will, I hope, not only shed light on the issue at hand, but contribute to the forging of what philosopher Nancy Fraser calls "bridge discourse." Bridge discourse can enhance analytic lucidity and transformative power by amalgamating disparate and sometimes isolated conversations and agendas into "hybrid publics."[2] Such forays, as Fraser observes, are risky; one takes the chance of offending everyone. Yet, given the pluralistic context in which Christian ethicists seek to comprehend and pursue social justice today, building bridges and cultivating hybrids seem timely, indeed indispensable, tasks.

ROMAN CATHOLIC ADVOCACY OF A FAMILY LIVING WAGE

From Leo XIII's 1891 encyclical *Rerum Novarum* forward, papal teaching on modern industrial society has made the just treatment of wage workers a central moral concern.[3] In line with the natural law approach favored by Catholic moralists—and in contrast to influential individualist and collectivist alternatives—work is interpreted through an anthropology that posits the dignity of each person, realized within three primary social relationships deemed natural to humans: the political, the economic, and the familial.

The political realm contributes to the common good by coordinating and protecting through law the well-being of groups and individuals. The economic sphere serves human flourishing by providing fair access to the goods of creation intended for all. In modern industrialized economies, the majority of persons are dependent for such access on wages attained through their labor. Human dignity is upheld in this setting only if workers are assured that, through honest labor, they can obtain the material conditions necessary for survival and a reasonable degree of security and material well-being. For Leo XIII and his successors, this translates into the worker's right to a "living wage." Important as the political and economic dimensions of social life are, this modern natural law tradition particularly cherishes the family, "the first, essential cell of human society."[4]

The family, as an intimate "community of love," "school for a deeper humanity," "nurse and mother" of a holistic attitude toward the nature and dignity of persons in society, and "school of work," is regarded as the primary milieu for personal, interpersonal, and intergenerational growth and sustenance. As a "domestic church," family is an essential locus for spiritual education and formation. Family contributes to the common good by nurturing the bonds and values necessary if civic and economic life is to subsist and prosper, yet in a real sense the civic and the economic spheres are there *for the sake of* family. Family, for instance, functions as a warrant for private ownership in the papal writings.[5] In *Gaudium et spes,* marriage and family are described as the foundation of political life, and the well-being of political society is presented as intimately linked to the well-being of the community founded by marriage. Family needs and is obligated to the polis, yet retains an integrity and freedom within its sphere that ought not be violated by state or economic interference. A priority of family over economy is asserted analogous to the priority of individual over state and labor over capital. Economic justice is therefore understood as necessarily including measures that promote and protect family life. A right to a *family* living wage—that is, a wage sufficient to assure a basic level of material security for both the adult household head, normally male, and his dependents, normally, wife and children—is implied in Leo XIII's *Rerum Novarum* and is explicitly articulated in Pius IX's *Quadragesimo Anno.*

The consistent concern in this literature with labor and with workers' rights reflects a traditional emphasis in Christian social thought upon the moral priority of the basic needs of those who are economically vulnerable, over against the protection of the superfluities of the economically advantaged. Set as it has been with a normative vision of society as a harmonious, hierarchically interdependent organism, the conflictual, even radical implications of this bias have frequently been muted. Yet official Catholic support for union organizing and strikes, and for state planning to ensure a decent livelihood for all, has been augmented over the years by a heightened recognition of the need to combat underlying institutional imbalances of power, the reality of the sinful systems and structures, and the necessity of struggle for social justice, becoming especially evident in the social

encyclicals of the present pope and the later writings of his predecessor, Paul
VI. Seen in light of these developing sensibilities, the living wage is a means of
empowering the poor to fulfill their material needs, to cultivate their abilities and
aspirations, and to participate in just, enlivening social relationships.

In developing his argument for a family living wage, John A. Ryan was
self-consciously faithful to the Catholic natural law tradition and the papal social teachings of his day. Simultaneously, he employed an inductive analysis and
evaluation of the specifics of the U.S. economy to fashion a moral and practical
environment that was distinctively American. As ethicist and social reformer,
Ryan contended with both the theoretical and practical aspects of the issue
of economic justice, and as a sophisticated and influential American Catholic
case for wage justice, his work remains unsurpassed.[6] Not surprisingly, his work
displays the tension, characteristic of the tradition, between a theological affirmation of equal rights and dignity for all and a hierarchical, organic picture
of social relations that legitimates differential access to institutional power,
burdens, and benefits according to one's function in the social organism. The
tension is most obvious in treatments of gender roles, but it also affects other
areas, such as models of social transformation and of class relations. We shall see
in Ryan's writings the difficulties that this uneasy marriage of egalitarian and
hierarchical models wrought.

JOHN A. RYAN'S CASE FOR A FAMILY LIVING WAGE

Ryan's 1906 treatise *A Living Wage* contends that "the workingman's right to
a decent livelihood is, in the present economic and political organization of a
society, the right to a Living Wage."[7] Ryan defines "workingman" as the "adult
male of average physical ability who is exclusively dependent upon the remuneration that he is paid in return for his labor." An individual living wage denotes
remuneration sufficient to provide the laborer with a decent livelihood (81–82).
What is meant by a decent livelihood? This is, Ryan explains, "that amount of
the necessities and comforts of life that is in keeping with the dignity of a human
being . . . that minimum of conditions which the average person of a given age
or sex must enjoy in order to live as a human being should live" (72–73).

Here is a first noteworthy feature of Ryan's understanding of a living
wage. On the one side, a *living* wage supersedes the bare minimum needed to
stave off hunger, disease, or exposure to the elements. The laborer who responsibly conforms with "nature's universal law of work" is entitled to at least the
minimum of the material conditions of "reasonable" living. "This implies the
power to exercise one's primary faculties, supply one's essential needs, and develop one's personality" (117). On the other side, the living wage, while more

ample than bare subsistence, reflects Ryan's support for the right to acquire moderate but not unlimited material security. To champion a living wage was by no means to underwrite an unbridled quest for acquisition or upward mobility for laborers any more than for capitalists.[8]

> A *living* wage, then, refers to an ample minimum, limited by norms prohibiting greed and obliging consideration of the grave needs of others. A living *wage* signifies the whole return due the laborer for his hire: "Food, clothing, shelter, insurance, and mental and spiritual culture—all in a reasonable degree—are, therefore, the essential conditions of a decent livelihood. *Remuneration inadequate to secure all of these things to the laborer and his family falls below the level of a Living Wage.* (136, emphasis added).

Ideally, the worker should be paid a money wage that would enable him or her to provide for all these needs directly, rather than through benefits such as social insurance.[9] But regardless of the mode of delivery, the test of a living wage, and of economic justice, is whether the worker and his family gain access to all of the benefits mentioned.

Ryan's references to "the worker and his family" directs us to a second pivotal feature of his moral argument: He presents a case not simply for a personal, but a *family* living wage. Several elements stand out in Ryan's defense of every adult male worker's right to a wage sufficient to support not only himself, but also (potentially or actually) his wife and children. First, Ryan argues not on the basis of the rights of the family or any of its members, but rather on the basis of the dignity and rights of the individual man. He claims that remuneration for work is a right derived from the worker's own essential and intrinsic worth, whose primary end is his own welfare. Ryan, consistently, now contends that the primary end for the right to a family living wage is also the welfare of the male worker. "The right to the means of maintaining a family . . . is not finally derived from the *duty* of maintaining it—from the needs of the family—but from the laborer's *dignity*, from *his* own essential needs" (119, emphasis original). Further, in founding the right to a family living wage in the dignity of the male worker, who is presumed to be the conduit through whom the material needs of wife and children are met, Ryan relies on a strictly defined sex-role script drawn from both his contemporary cultural context and from the traditional theological and natural law sources favoring a hierarchical/ organic picture of society.[10] The basic lineaments of the male role as household head are dictated by unchanging nature, and ultimately, God (118).

The subject of the right to a family wage is the adult male, and he is the subject of this right by virtue of this patriarchal destiny in the social and familial order. Ryan admits that "if the support of wife and children did not in the normal order of things fall upon the husband and father, he would not have a right to the additional remuneration required for this purpose." But the right of a male worker to the conditions of being the head of a family seems to Ryan to be obvious; and this right implies the right to a family living wage "because nature and reason have decreed that the family should be supported by its head" (119).

Nature and reason have also decreed a role for women, and it is not in the public workplace. Ryan's comments betray an image of woman as ordained for the domestic, nonwage-earning realm. Ryan supports an individual living wage for the growing numbers of women in the workforce in his own day, and he seems to favor some form of family allowances to assist women who become the sole economic support of their children due to widowhood, desertion, or other calamities. Nonetheless, he consistently depicts the "normal" flourishing of women—and the flourishing of family and society—in terms of the confinement of wives and mothers to domestic duties in the home. Normally, a single working man has the right to a family living wage for savings against the day when he will exercise his male family rights.[11]

Ryan's enduring concern with a living wage for working persons is in line with the moral priority the Christian moral tradition has accorded the less advantaged in the economic realm. As a right due every full-time adult worker, the living wage is deemed not a matter of charity to the poor but of justice. Ryan also expressly identifies the living wage as an effective instrument in a scheme of distributive justice that would widely disperse moderate economic power and security. As a distributive strategy, it reflects the canons Ryan elaborates in *Distributive Justice*, where he gives the canon of human needs a central role.[12] Ryan's defense of the family living wage was a focal point in his agenda for social reform guided by legislation. This plan does not reject American capitalism in favor of a socialist alternative, but rather opts for "the existing system, greatly, even radically amended."[13] Ryan is usually categorized as a progressive rather than a radical, a practical reformer rather than a revolutionary. Yet elements of his position entail changes more thoroughgoing than the term practical reform conveys. Advocating what John Coleman calls "a widespread people's capitalism embracing industrial democracy and consumer and productive cooperatives," Ryan's vision of change went further than that of many of his progressive and even socialist counterparts.[14]

Ryan models a strategy in U.S. Catholic social thought that is of potential significance to others who seek deeply reaching economic and social transformation, yet who, like Ryan, must judge when ameliorating reform is a useful or necessary step on the long road to more radical change. We can detect in Ryan's work hints of an approach that harbors a long-range vision of profound social transformation and begins to enact it by selecting short-range, reformist strategies. I call this a "radical transformationalist" stance.

Allegiance to larger normative goals in this kind of approach requires two things, both found in Ryan's writings. First, particular reformist moves must be seen not as ends but as beginnings and must be assessed in light of their success in advancing a larger vision of social renovation. Second, a radical transformationist approach recognizes that steps toward social and economic reconstruction remain superficial and short lived unless accompanied and energized by intellectual and moral conversion: education of the mind and change of heart on the part of large numbers of persons. One aspect of that conversion, mentioned but not developed by Ryan, involves embracing a simpler, less acquisitive lifestyle and rejecting what later popes would call consumerism and materialism. He writes, "For the adoption and pursuit of these ideals and the most necessary requisite is a revival of genuine religion."[15] Nevertheless, he clearly does not believe the problem of injustice will be rectified by personal conversion and individual conviction; conversion must lead people to organize together, for only combined power will effect larger social change:

> It is true that the efficiency of social effort is limited by the character of the individuals through whom the effort is made....But it is also true that organized effort will add very materially to the results that can be accomplished through moral suasion addressed to the individual. This very obvious truth is superlatively true in our time, when man's social relations have become so numerous and so complex. Both methods are necessary. There must be an appeal to the minds and hearts of individuals, and the fullest utilization of the latent power of organization and social institutions. (330–31)

THE FEMINIST CHALLENGE TO FAMILY WAGE IDEOLOGY AND PRACTICE

At the time of Ryan's death in 1945, cultural mores concerning family and work, legislative trends in the wake of the New Deal, and a thriving postwar economy provided a congenial environment for the family wage norm. A broad middle-class consensus linked maturity and happiness to the roles of father-husband-wage-earner for men and wife-mother-homemaker for women. The expectation that the male breadwinner ought to earn a family wage and that he would use it to support his spouse and children was essential to this mind-set. In the 1960s, however, this "family wage system" began a period of decline. Chief among the undermining forces were changing work and familial patterns and challenges to the system's supporting ideology. Some of the most trenchant and damaging critiques of the family wage arrangement, though by no means the only ones, have come from feminists.[16]

Feminists' indifference to or attacks upon the family living wage as the centerpiece of a program for securing wage justice must be understood against the background of their own perspective on economic injustice. Feminists have been concerned with (1) establishing the *economic* value of work performed in the home, and at the same time, (2) dismantling the system of practices built on the belief that work traditionally done in the home is uniquely women's calling and women's glory. While Catholic teaching has traditionally stressed the value of the activities of women in childbearing, child-rearing, and maintaining kinship relationships, Catholic thought has characteristically presented the domestic sphere as an alternative to economic life rather than as any kind of expression of it. Even more seriously, the traditional theoretical underpinning of the Catholic arguments in support of a family living wage advances with remarkable explicitness precisely the system of beliefs that these feminists condemn. Clare Fischer, for instance, identifies a complicitous alliance between the modern family wage system and the denial of socioeconomic value to traditional "women's work." This deeply rooted cultural denial has made the practice of underremunerating those who perform domestic labor seem legitimate, even natural. Fischer identifies three ideological structures that support the mistreatment of women and domestic work endemic to the family living wage system: the division of labor according to gender, the division of labor according to location, and the assumption that these divisions reflect some important intrinsic (natural) difference between women and men.[17]

The *sexual division of labor* separates body and mind according to gender and then perceives them as reconciled in the distinctive efforts of the two sexes. Associating the public world of men with "mind" reinforces the asymmetric value and power relations between the public sphere and the more "bodily" sphere of women. The *division of work according to location or space* "assumes the symbolic and real division and unification of the sexes by way of the woman as wife/mother in the home, and man as breadwinner in the marketplace." Late nineteenth-century developments in industry and middle-class values helped shape a split between work and hearth that idealized both the domestic realm and woman as wife and mother. The home, with woman at the heart, came to be seen as a blessed retreat for children and men from the polluting effects of the city. Woman's role as guardian of domesticity and morals made it unthinkable that she should abandon home for wage work. Women who sought paid employment were perceived as "either unfortunate or perverse." The gendered distinction of spheres was widely embraced as a virtuous arrangement that gave every family member a special destiny in the building of a strong nation.[18]

Unfortunately, by relegating the meaning of "work" to paid labor performed outside the home (as in the question asked of married women, "do you work?"), this division denies public acknowledgment and economic value to the wealth of socially contributive work performed in and around domestic space. The "home-work" thus belittled encompasses a rich constellation of tasks involved in homemaking and housekeeping. It also includes volunteer work, involuntary unpaid work in consumer-related activities, and the reproductive work of assuring social and economic continuity through the raising of children.[19]

The first two ideological patterns feed into the third, involving the assumption of distinctive personalities according to gender, and segregation of occupational aspirations and opportunities accordingly. The combination of these three ideological structures, charges Fischer, has nourished a gender-based occupational hierarchy that undervalues, underprivileges, underrewards, and disempowers women, both inside and outside the home.[20]

As I noted, Ryan and the Catholic social tradition are vulnerable to this feminist criticism. Popes and moral theologians have relied on authorities who assume that male-female biological differences form a natural basis for asymmetries in capacity, characteristics, and social roles.[21] Such assumptions detract from the force of claims about the value of domestic work also found in modern Catholic teaching. For example, Pope John Paul II's 1981 encyclical on human work, *Laborem Exercens*, reiterates Catholic support for a family living wage; it also offers a broad definition of work that underscores the right to remuneration attaching to *both* "economic" labor and the "social" labor associated with family life. The test of a just system is whether work, thus construed, receives a just wage, explicitly described as a family wage.

Just remuneration for the work of an adult who is responsible for a family means remuneration that will suffice for establishing and properly maintaining a family and for providing security for its future. Such remuneration can be given either through what is called a family wage—that is, a single salary given to the head of the family for this work, sufficient for the needs of the family without the spouse having to take up gainful employment outside the home—or through other social measures such as family allowances or grants to mothers devoting themselves exclusively to their families (19). These words avoid an exclusively masculine reading of the breadwinner role, yet the traditional view of the mother as primary guardian of children and the home remains. The pope continues:

> It will redound to the credit of society to make it possible for a mother
> . . . to devote herself to taking care of her children and educating them in
> accordance with their needs. . . . Having to abandon these tasks in order to
> take up paid work outside the home is wrong from the point of view of
> the good of society and of the family when it contradicts or hinders these
> primary goals of the mission of a mother. (19)

The pope's strong appeals for equal treatment of women and for work arrangements that support parental responsibilities are likewise hobbled by a perduring understanding of woman as mother, and mother as primary parent. "The true advancement of women requires that labor should be structured by abandoning what is specific to them and at the expense of the family, in which women as mothers have an irreplaceable role" (19).[22]

Is it disingenuous to anticipate the emergence of "bridge discourse" and "hybrid publics" in the context of such a seemingly intractable disagreement? There are promising signs. Within the Catholic community, some scholars and religious leaders are reexamining traditional Catholic interpretations of sex-difference and gender roles. A spectrum of Catholic moral thinkers continue to affirm that "the implications of sexual differentiation extend beyond the minimum requirements of species propagation," and warn against a dualist denial of any relation between sexual and human identity.[23] Yet these thinkers vigorously reject the thesis that biology dictates rigid distinctions in personality, social roles, or power. On the feminist side, even feminists who denounce the record of patriarchy in Roman Catholicism might find a point of agreement with Catholic writers who reject schemes that would simply "treat women like men" in an effort to achieve economic justice. Over the last decade, feminists have been reconsidering the implications of gender differences for their political and economic agendas. Debate has centered on the question of how to admit and respect differences—between or among men and women—while preventing unjustly differential access to resources, opportunities, and power.[24] This knotty issue is directly relevant to the project of conceiving a new, feminist-informed family living wage argument.

There are, then, tentative indications that the construction of bridges may already be underway. To this we might add that whatever their ideological differences, these representatives of Roman Catholic and feminist social thought share three important convictions: (1) The problem of wage justice represents a moral challenge and a public policy issue of commanding importance because the wage structure that currently characterizes the U.S. economy is manifestly unjust. (2) Wage justice cannot be achieved in a policy context that attends only to the situation of individual workers—family life and relations of support and dependency must be taken into account. (3) Labor within the confines of the household contributes in a major way to the common good and should be recognized and rewarded in conformity with its real value.

RENOVATING THE FAMILY LIVING WAGE

Critique of family wage ideology would doubtless have had little impact had it not been accompanied by dramatic changes over the last three decades in the practices and compositions of workplace and family. The trends are well known: the dramatic rise in participation of women, especially married women, in the paid work force; the continuing gap in pay between men and women, with women making on the average less than seventy cents to each dollar earned by men; the doubling of female-headed households over the last two decades; the persistently higher under- and unemployment rates for minority women; and the continuing clustering of the female labor force (80 percent) in low-paying occupational categories (clerical, sales, service, factory).[25] Ironically, as the numbers of women in the paid labor market swell, women as a group are getting poorer—the "feminization of poverty" noted by sociologist Diana Pearce. Barbara Ehrenreich points out that the fastest growing segment of America's female poor are single mothers. She quotes the findings of Caroline Bird who asserts that in the 1970s, the number of "ill paid, dead-end 'women's jobs' increased so much faster than better paid 'men's work' that by 1976 only 40 percent of the jobs in this country paid enough to support a family." Ehrenreich comments that in the economy of the 1980s the only way most households have been able to make a family wage is by adding up the wages of all individual family members.[26]

Both as ideal and as reality, the family-wage norm has waned. Is it a norm worth retrieving? I am convinced it is. The great numbers of households in which adults are unable to support their families with the wages they are able to attain for their work is just as morally intolerable today as it was in Ryan's time. Such families, so many of them headed by women, testify to the continued relevance of framing wage questions in terms of basic human rights and social morality. The injustice these families suffer is still usefully expressed as the denial of sufficient remuneration to ensure a decent livelihood for self and family—that is, as the denial of a family living wage.

If the family living wage is to recapture public attention as a compelling agenda, however, both its rationale and its description require revision. It plainly will not do to frame the moral agenda for a family living wage *in the form or with the justification* familiar to Ryan and much modern Catholic social teaching. That form and justification were bound to patriarchal presuppositions that have bred an overly individualistic construal of men's public economic rights, while socially and economically devaluing women and children, homemaking and parenting. Economic justice today will require a new, more equitable, marriage of home and workplace. A revitalized case for the family living wage must incorporate and advance three major changes in the context for its discussion: (1) work connected with home and family, and any work performed by women, must now be valued and remunerated in ways comparable to the valuing and remuneration of the economic contributions of men; (2) responsibility for the rearing of children is being socially reshaped and this transitional period demands creative policy initiatives; and (3) the global dimensions of the U.S. economy must be taken into account. Let me consider these each in turn.

The Catholic tradition's appreciation for the value and importance of homemaking and parenting can be fused with a feminist affirmation of the rights and dignity of women to produce an adequate valuation of women's traditional contribution without circumscribing opportunities for women in the workplace and professions. John Paul II states, "Experience confirms that there must be a social reevaluation of the mother's role, of the toil connected with it and of the need that children have for care, love and affection."[27] The pope mistakenly attributes domestic activity solely to mothers; yet he is right that home-work and parenting-work demand social reevaluation. An honest assessment of the effort and time required for reasonable degrees of housekeeping, homemaking, and child care brings to light a fact obvious to practitioners: Homemaking and parenting constitute, in themselves, at least the equivalent of one full-time job outside the home; the question is only whether the work relating home and children will be performed by those partners as a full-time "second shift" (with duties either shared between partners or resting, as most studies show, primarily on the working mother/wife), be turned over to paid or unpaid others, or not get done at all.[28]

Declaring homemaking and parenting bona fide, socially enriching, and publicly indispensable occupations whose responsibilities devolve in some way on every adult householder seems innocuous enough. That impression is deceiving. To think of domestic work in this way cuts directly across privatized and interest-maximizing cultural images of work and family. To accept home-work as real work is to acknowledge that the wage-worker, householder, or parent is reducible neither to an isolated individual nor to a social role, but is a person enmeshed in a complicated network of relations and obligations. To admit that familial relations and home-work at times can and should take precedence over conventionally wage-rewarded economic activities, not just for women but for all workers, also flies in the face of common perceptions of careers as linear paths to be plied with undistracted and single-minded concentration. A social and economic system that began to treat domestic work, and public occupations that carry out traditional domestic functions, as equitably valued, remunerable vocations, would surely augur the demise of the current gender-based occupational hierarchy. To call home-work real work, in short, is to foment radical change.

Secondly, we must think in fresh ways about the responsibilities of child-rearing in our socially altered world. I have already discussed the pervasive ways in which the unsustainable but still widely prevalent assumption that only women can and should parent has contributed to economic injustice. Changes in the public valuation of children will also be required. The flood of women into the workplace has forced some improvising on privatized parenting and child care, but the deficient response of U.S. social policy to the so-called child-care crisis (and the persistent framing of this crisis as a women's issue) attests to an alarming lack of common accountability for children. Provision for the care and nurturing of the rising generation is a public as well as a familial responsibility.[29]

The third point, supported in both Catholic and feminist literatures, is that wage-worker justice in one country can no longer be pursued in isolation from the global dimensions of the economy.[30] The trend toward moving domestic manufacturing jobs into countries that offer higher profits and a "cheaper, more docile" labor force is well known. Many of these situations replicate to a shocking degree the abuses of nineteenth-century laissez-faire industrial capitalism in the North Atlantic, especially the exploitation of the labor of poor women. The fact that 85 percent of assembly line workers in developing countries are women, preferred precisely because of their economic vulnerability, underscores on the international scene what is true domestically: Because women are disproportionately affected by wage injustice, they must take center stage in schemes for change.[31] These facts also highlight the need to set programs for worker justice within an inclusive, complex construal of the common good.

This is, then, a decisive moment, demanding creative, concrete response. The work of John Ryan provides strategic guidance in the politics of implementation as well as in the development of moral theory. One lesson bequeathed by Ryan is that ethicists can serve social transformation by helping convince relevant publics that the morally required course can also meet reasonable tests of practicality and expediency. Some regard Ryan's "principle of expediency"—that good ethics can also be good economics—as his most innovative contribution to U.S. Catholic economic ethics. Ryan recognizes that expediency would never do as an overarching principle for Christian economic ethics. Yet, as Charles Curran points out, to argue that the moral course and the economically expedient course may at least intersect squares with the Catholic natural law view that the goal of moral activity is genuine flourishing, in the context of a common good whose material conditions economic activity provides.

Ryan addressed the objection that requiring all employers to pay a family living wage would result in capital losses, inefficiency, bankruptcies, job flight, and general economic harm. His rebuttal attempts to give due weight to the legitimate concerns of business and industry, the social obligations attaching to property and capital, and the natural right of workers to a decent livelihood. In a similarly nuanced response, contemporary advocates of the family living wage will explicitly attend to the ramifications and responsibilities of what John Paul II calls the "indirect employer": those influences, persons, conditions, and institutions (chief among these the State) that affect the direct employer's ability or willingness to justly remunerate employees.[32] Feminist analysis brings to light the extent to which the society as bearer of ideology must be considered as a dimension of the indirect employer.

Ryan also teaches us how important it is to cherish and preserve an animated concern for assuring dignified access to basic levels of material well-being to those who currently lack them. Over the past three decades, critics have sounded the death knell for the traditional theory and practice of a family living wage. Simultaneously the ranks of working or underemployed poor have swelled with people, largely women, who are losing ground or are unable even to make the amount sufficient to be called minimally just under Ryan's definition. In the face of these realities, top priority must continue to be given to the struggle for *minimal* wage justice that preoccupied ethicists like Ryan.

RETHINKING THE TERMS: "FAMILY," "LIVING," "WAGE"

The pro–family wage turf of the 1970s and 1980s was dominated by the forces of religious and social traditionalism. In the future support for a family living wage flowing form the hybrid public joined by radical transformationist feminism and progressive social Catholicism could fuel a different and more powerful movement for change than that so far accomplished by conservatives.[33] The family living wage agenda this unlikely partnership might beget would be animated by a fresh understanding of each of its central terms.

Family and the roles of its members in relation to home and work would be newly considered from a nonsexist perspective. One feature of this vantage point would be its appreciation for the heterogeneity of forms family is actually taking today. The Catholic tradition holds out lifelong, monogamous, heterosexual marriage as the normative context for children and family. The encounter with feminist and pluralist values, and the experience of the persistence of variety, argue for elasticizing, without abandoning, the traditional Catholic norm.[34] Varied expressions of family would be not merely tolerated but actively supported. This is an admittedly difficult feat—to continue to affirm a norm without excoriating, marginalizing, or demanding those who by necessity or according to their best judgments take a different path. Steps toward this goal are taken when Catholics respectfully attend not only to the "traditional" family, but also to the heterogeneity of familial forms and styles that have historically existed outside the narrow confines of the dominant race, class, and culture.

In building its normative picture of family, a Catholic and feminist hybrid public could jointly affirm the dignity and worth of the intimate circle of family life in its various forms and stages; the need to realize in any form a genuine and equal partnership of men and women; the constitutive value that meaningful work holds for the flourishing of each family member and of the family unit itself; and the fact that labor must be set within a broader picture of family life that makes provision for, as Ryan would put it, the reasonable bodily, intellectual, moral, spiritual, and cultural development of all members. This means time and space for rest and celebration for civic participants, for work, for justice, for religion. Feminists and popes can both call the family "a school for deeper humanity," and both have a high stake in preserving this privileged locale for the care and nurture of persons.

This vision of family leads directly to new thinking about what the word *living* in "a living wage" entails. In a major poll conducted in 1989 by the *New York Times*, over 80 percent of working men and women with small children stated that they felt unable to devote proper time and energy to their children.[35] Making a living must surely imply having the sustenance, time, and energy to live with and in one's family; all this is included in the meaning that "a decent livelihood" held for John Ryan. By this yardstick, however, a great many jobs today, including some of the most cash-productive, fall far short. Workers today continue to deserve, and too many do not attain, access to these aspects of decent living. Redirecting policies and resources in order to assure those minimums will be aided by appeals to the moral limits on acquisition and ownership that the Catholic moral tradition has stressed.

The word *wage* in "family living wage" will also have a different meaning in the future. Progressive Catholics and radical feminists can agree that work has moral significance. This moral regard, bestowed equally upon work located in the home and outside the home, can ground claims about the right to a just return for one's domestic as well as one's nondomestic labor. Ryan implicitly admitted the right of the full-time homemaker to a living wage, but assumed that this right was normally honored by channeling wages through the male household head. Feminists debate whether work in the home should be subject to money payment, but, like mainstream writers, have developed no consensus as to whether home-work fits properly under the category of waged labor. The ideological and practical questions involved are many and are badly in need of critical scrutiny.

I support explicitly extending wage to mean the whole remuneration given the worker. Benefits, insurance, opportunities for time off, and other forms of payment, such as family allowances, may augment or substitute for cash wages to form a sum total that may be deemed a living wage. Again, Ryan's formulation can guide: The total remuneration must provide the minimum material conditions for a decent livelihood, empowerment for a reasonable degree of flourishing. While it will be difficult to specify this in dollar amounts for future families, quibbling over how to precisely define "just level of remuneration" will not excuse policymakers from recognizing and counteracting grossly unacceptable levels and conditions where they currently exist.

REFORMIST PROPOSALS; TRANSFORMATIVE PROSPECTS

If we can agree that childrearing and home-work should be regarded as a full-time occupation, *for which just remuneration in some form is due*, we then face difficult policy questions: How much remuneration? Delivered in what form? From whom? Under what system of accountability? Given that change starts from where we presently stand, what is the most promising path toward realizing the family living wage agenda sketched here? Let me propose for a debate a two-staged approach.

A first step, one that may already be gaining some implied consent in contemporary U.S. practice, is to press for full employment and for a "family living wage" (an amount sufficient to reasonably support self, spouse, and children) for every adult wage worker, male or female, regardless of marital or family status. This goal has the advantage of being simple and clear, and it avoids applying different wage scales to people in different life situations—an option that was rejected by Ryan for prudential reasons (though he accepted wage differential for single women and single men). Today the female employee is at least as likely as her male counterpart to be head or sole breadwinner of her household. Since at present, white women employed full time make, on the average, only two-thirds the salary of white men—black and Hispanic women only about one-half of white male salaries—the struggle to achieve comparable worth for female-concentrated occupations is of critical importance.[36] Such an approach can draw on many of the arguments advanced by Ryan, extending the designation of individual familial rights and duties to adult women as well as men. Choice and monetary freedom would be maximized for individual adults in this "liberal" expansion of Ryan's proposal.

If this level of remuneration were accorded all adult workers, dual-earner households could in theory afford for either worker to forego earnings during periods of high familial intensity, or to pay a fair rate to competent assistance in upholding domestic duties while both parents work outside the home. Single household heads could afford full-time domestic and child-care help[37] and could, at least theoretically, choose to work part time at different points in the family and child-rearing cycle. Lacking some family allowance system, single parents would not, however, have the option of caring for their own home and children full time. Nor, given present workplace practices, could dual-earner families expect to periodically switch to part-time status without paying penalties in salary scales, advancement, and job security.

These limitations return us to a central point. Short of qualitatively upgrading the social and economic value placed on the domestic activities of citizens, and adjusting the mutual expectations of employers and employees accordingly, simply upping the sense of "family living wage" introduced here, "living wage" must come increasingly to mean not just cash amounts, but hours and conditions of work, career tracks, benefits and leave policies, pension and insurance plans that conduce to the fulfillment of one's domestic, along with one's public vocation.[38]

To be complete, this program for workers and family economic justice will have to address two critically important sets of issues that I can only mention here. First, a thicket of specific economic and political questions concerning policy goals, strategies, and means of compliance and enforcement surround my reformist proposal that a family living wage must also analyze the relationship between higher wages and unemployment and must consider how a wage system that honors domestic rights will refract in reforms of the public welfare system.[39]

Behind these specific questions about reform are more foundational questions that also demand attention. The institutions and ideology of the capitalist, free-market economy that have underpinned the notion of a family living wage must be subjected to more thorough critique and reconsideration. If the logic of capitalism is to commodify work and reduce its value to the wage it commands, how can remunerating people for home-work avoid corrupting this sphere of human practice? Would extending a family wage to each individual adult decrease the incentive to marry, undermining traditional marriage as a social institution? Might this renovated approach call, finally, for reweaving the economic and cultural fabric out of which the family living wage was originally cut?

As strategic and foundational concerns of this sort are encountered, the initial, seemingly straightforward plan may begin to give way to pressure for more radical changes in the family-work relation. We may find ourselves called, at this second stage, to "utopian envisagement" of what ought to be and "anticipatory action" to bring the present order into better conformity with the normative vision.[40] A more deeply transformative goal can be advanced: a concrete historical ideal of a social order that balances and coordinates economic and domestic participation, in the context of a pluralistic common good. Of course, for the vast majority of workers today, even in elite professional settings, such an order is at best a dimly perceived hope. Yet such an orienting ideal is, I believe, entailed both in a Catholic vision of a family living wage liberated from oppressive distortions and in descriptions of the sought-for society proffered by feminists.[41] Such images are not in themselves policy answers. Yet they can serve as lodestars to those engaged in the tedious and messy labor of articulating middle axioms and executing courses of action that might move the present closer to God's future.

The feminist spirit we have tapped here presses toward radical change. But, in the spirit of Ryan—who also harbored some radical predilections—the work of transformation can begin, I think, with building consensus on particular reforms that ensure the minimum to those who lack it, simultaneously moving toward an enriched public understanding of what is minimally due. So refashioned, the family living wage can be a compelling norm that attracts the support of hybrid politics.

In the present domestic and international circumstances, pursuing such a full-fledged economic and social goal may seem quixotic. Yet a glance at the milieu of social and economic crisis in which Ryan developed his ethics, and at the great disparity that then existed between the norms he articulated and the actual situations of workers, reminds us that neither assurance of success nor certain economic prospects fed Ryan's dedication to the task. What impelled him forward was the need to alleviate the suffering of the economically vulnerable—and honor their God-given dignity and rights.

The difficulty of specifying a contemporary program for wage justice and the daunting problems facing its implementation should neither paralyze ethical analysis nor dissuade us from testing every promising means of instantiating in policy the norms we analyze in theory. Here again Ryan, theorist and reformer, remains a model. Ryan knew that every concrete initiative laid him open to being called either dogmatic or oversimplisitc. Yet, he insisted,

> neither honesty nor expediency is furthered by an attitude of intellectual helplessness, academic hyper-modesty, or practical agnosticism. If there exist moral rules and rational principles applicable to the problem of wage justice, it is our duty to state and apply them as fully as we can. Obviously, we shall make mistakes in the process, but until the attempt is made, and a certain (and very large) number of mistakes are made, there will be no progress. We have no right to expect that ready-made applications of the principles will drop from Heaven.[42]

Probing, articulating, and negotiating steps toward flourishing in that space between heaven and the ground we presently occupy—these are perduring tasks of a Christian ethic of wage justice.

QUESTIONS FOR DISCUSSION

1. Is it true, as our author claims, that to call home-work real work is to foment radical change? Why, or why not?

2. Do you agree with the author's claim that providing for the care and nurturing of the next generation is a public as well as familial responsibility? Why, or why not? To what extent does it "take a village" to nurture the rising generation? How can this social responsibility be institutionalized through government wage policies?

3. Is it true that wage-worker justice in one country can no longer be pursued in isolation from the global dimension of the economy? How has globalization affected the way we think about issues of just wage and the ways we pursue policies that promote a family living wage?

4. What is meant in Catholic social thought by "indirect employer"? How has feminism brought to light the extent to which social ideologies (especially those which define and value gender roles) must be considered as a dimension of the indirect employer?

5. In what ways might our notions of the "family" and the roles of its members in relations to home and work be newly considered from a nonsexist perspective?

6. In what ways might the idea of "living" need to be reframed to include more than simply monetary rewards?

7. How might we redefine the term "wage" in order to encompass a more holistic rendition of worker remuneration?

NOTES

1. "Radical transformationist feminist" denotes a variegated group of writers who judge existing social structures to be radically diseased by patriarchy, yet who are committed to transformative struggle with and within those existing structures. Among Christian feminists, radical transformationists who often align themselves with liberation theology include Rosemary Radford Ruether, Beverly Wildung Harrison, and Dorothy Solle.

2. Nancy Fraser, *Unruly Practices: Power, Discourse, and Gender in Contemporary Social Theory* (Minneapolis: University of Minnesota Press, 1989), 11–13, 174.

3. For a comprehensive study, see Donal Dorr, *Options for the Poor: A Hundred Years of Vatican Social Teaching* (Maryknoll, NY: Orbis, 1983). On the question of the coherence of modern papal social teaching, see Michael Schuck, *That They Be One: The Social Teaching of the Papal Encyclicals* (Washington, DC: Georgetown University Press, 1991).

4. *Gaudium et spes*, in *Vatican Council II: The Conciliar and Post Conciliar Documents*, ed. Austin Flannery, O.P. (Northport, NY: Costello Publishing, 1977), 52.

5. *Rerum Novarum,* 9; *Quadragesimo anno,* 45; *Mater et magistra,* 45, 112.

6. For a balanced appreciation and critique of Ryan, see Charles E. Curran, *American Catholic Social Ethics* (Notre Dame, IN: University of Notre Dame Press, 1982), 84–91.

7. John A. Ryan, *A Living Wage: Its Ethical and Economic Aspects* (London: Macmillan, 1906), 81. Further references to *A Living Wage* noted parenthetically in text.

8. Ryan distinguishes three separate levels of wealth: (1) wealth sufficient to provide the necessities of life; (2) wealth sufficient to provide the conventional necessities and comforts of one's own social plane or station in life; and (3) wealth that is superfluous to maintaining the standards of decent livelihood or one's station in life. Everyone has a natural right to the first level, which determines the basic living wage. Ryan attempts to enumerate the specifics included in this frugal, yet more-than-basic, level of material comfort and security (and to estimate the dollar amounts needed to acquire them at various times and in various geographical regions). He includes a moderate amount for amusement and recreation, clothing that will allow one dignity in the society of one's peers (for example, one good set of dress clothing and several changes of underclothes), organizational memberships, some periodicals and other literature, and money for charity and religion. In addition to *Living Wage,* 117, see John A. Ryan, *Distributive Justice: The Right and Wrong of Our Present Distribution of Wealth,* new revised edition (New York: Macmillan, 1927), chap. 21, esp. 273. John Coleman observes that Ryan seemed to regard upper-middle-class wealth (or the lower reaches of it) as the utmost moral limit to material possessions—this would refer to the second level. Anyone attaining wealth at the third level would morally have it entirely subject to the call of grave necessity. John A. Coleman, *An American Strategic Theology* (New York: Paulist Press, 1982), 94–95.

9. Ryan recognizes that in the American legislative and business milieu, some of this remuneration takes the form of benefits such as social insurance. He places the main responsibility for social insurance on the business sector. The principle of subsidiarity and the rightful autonomy of the worker and family dictate that state-legislated insurance be avoided when possible; if deemed necessary, such public insurance plans should be supported by a levy on business. Ryan, *Distributive Justice,* 380–81. For a different contemporaneous view, see Barbara Nachtrieb Armstrong, *Insuring the Minimum: Minimum Wage Plus Social Insurance Equals a Living Wage Program* (New York: Macmillan, 1932).

10. Hierarchical and organic images of society have a long lineage in Western Christian thought. The importance of social hierarchy in the thought of Thomas Aquinas, for instance, is treated by Katherine Archibald, "The Concept of Social Hierarchy in the Writings of St. Thomas Aquinas," *Historian* 12 (1949–1950): 28–54; reprinted in *St. Thomas Aquinas on Politics and Ethics,* ed. and trans. Paul E. Sigmund (New York: W. W. Norton, 1988), 136–41.

11. For Ryan's argument that unmarried working women ought to be paid a personal living wage equivalent to that paid unmarried men doing the same job, see *Living Wage,* 107–9, and *Distributive Justice,* 333–35. For his argument that, nonetheless, even single adult male workers have a right to the higher, family living wage, see *Distributive Justice,* 395; *Living Wage,* 109 n. 1. For his belief that women should not, except in

the case of calamity, work outside the home, see *Living Wage*, 133. For his discussion of what is due in the "abnormal" situation of a single female household head who is a wage earner, see *Distributive Justice*, 335. Note that for Catholic natural law theory, the "normal" serves as a powerful moral guide both in judging men's and women's nature and roles, and in determining the substantive meaning of the standard of a decent livelihood. A similar appeal to "normal standards" occurs when Ryan specifies a minimum living wage as one which renders access to "that quantity of goods and opportunities which fair-minded men would regard as indispensable to humane, efficient, and reasonable life" (*Distributive Justice*, 321). Such appeals reflect confidence that close observation of human nature and experience can yield trustworthy moral insight. Yet, when uncritically employed, this method can assume and reinforce existing power relations and their ideological supports, as when Ryan writes, "The welfare of the whole family, and that of society likewise, renders it imperative that the wife and mother should not engage in any labor except that of the household. When she works for hire she can neither care properly for her own health, rear her children aright, nor make her home what it should be for her husband, her children and herself. . . . The wife become a wage worker is no longer a wife" (*Living Wage*, 133). Definitions of what is normatively normal may unwittingly be controlled by the class, gender, and ethnic biases of their formulators. Even feminist sensitivities do not guarantee escape from the blinding power of the "normal"; the tendency of U.S. social reformers to judge what is normal and beneficial for poor women from the vantage point of their own middle-class mores and assumptions is documented in Sheila Rothman, *Woman's Proper Place: A History of Changing Ideals and Practices, 1870 to the Present* (New York: Basic Books, 1978).

12. Ryan, *Distributive Justice*, chap. 16. The prominence of the criterion of actual human need is also illustrated when Ryan discusses what is due in the "abnormal" situation of the single female household head who is a wage earner. "In view of the large number of women wage earners who have to support dependents, they ought to be included in any family allowance system. The objections drawn from the integrity of the family, the normal place of the mother, and the responsibility of the father, seem insufficient to outweigh the actual human needs of so many thousands of working women and their children" (*Distributive Justice*, 335).

13. Morris Hillquit and John H. Ryan, *Socialism: Promise or Menace* (New York: Macmillian, 1914), 13.

14. Coleman, *American Strategic Theology*, 88. See also Curran's helpful discussion of Ryan's program for social transformation in *American Catholic Social Ethics*, 51–58. In pressing the radical import of Ryan's long-range vision I differ with commentators, among them Curran, who stress Ryan the progressive reformer and who judge that Ryan's realism and practicality limited him to ameliorative programs. Ryan's advocacy of economic democracy suggests something more. Ryan's vision of industrial democracy was a radical proposal, more so than perhaps Ryan at the time perceived. The tumult caused by the use of the term "economic democracy" in early drafts of the recent U.S. bishops' pastoral letter on the economy (*Economic Justice for All* [Washington, DC: National Conference of Catholic Bishops, 1986]) supports this claim.

15. Ryan, *Distributive Justice*, 397. Though Ryan employs the phrase "revival of genuine religion" with some regularity, he neither makes clear what such a revival would

entail nor elaborates religion's specific place in his moral vision, which relies heavily on natural law philosophy.

16. For works that trace the development of the assumption of the worker's right to a family living wage from the late nineteenth through the middle twentieth century under the aegis of the "family wage system," see, e.g., Barbara Ehrenreich, *The Hearts of Men: American Dreams and the Flight from Commitment* (Garden City, NY: Anchor Books, 1983), esp. chap. 1; Mark Line Taylor, *Remembering Esperanza: A Cultural-Political Theology for North America Praxis* (Maryknoll, NY: Orlus, 1990), 87–97; and Arthur Brittan, *Masculinity and Power* (Oxford: Basil Blackwell, 1989), 113–18. For a discussion of "the aberrant 1950s" as a period of unprecedented and atypical cultivation of the family wage system and the gender prescriptions attached to it, see Sylvia Ann Hewlett, *A Lesser Life: The Myth of Women's Liberation in America* (New York: William Morrow, 1986), chaps. 10 and 11. For feminist criticism of the family wage system, see Eleanor Rathbone, *The Disinherited Family: A Plea for the Endowment of the Family* (London: Edward Arnold, 1924), esp. chaps. 2–4; Jean Bethke Elshtain, "The Family Crisis, the Family Wage, and Feminism," in Jean Bethke Elshtain, *Power Trips and Other Journeys: Essays in Feminism as Civic Discourse* (Madison: University of Wisconsin Press, 1990), 61–72. Ehrenreich and others also document revolts by some men against the theory and practice of male-as-breadwinner. See *Hearts of Men,* chaps. 4–8; Hewlett, *A Lesser Life,* chap. 13.

17. Clare B. Fisher, "Liberating Work," in *Christian Feminism: Visions of a New Humanity,* ed. Judith L. Weidman (San Francisco: Harper & Row, 1984), 123–24. "Each of these represents an ideological structure that generates and sustains difference and hierarchy in the work world [and home]. Each possesses a nuanced value-orientation that promotes and legitimates the devaluation of and discrimination against women in their daily activity of earning a wage, [and] of securing an adequate environment for the family. All three structures are intertwined in the fundamental assumption about the naturalness of differentiated labor [and remuneration] according to gender."

18. Fisher, "Liberating Work," 133–36. An insightful analysis of the cult of motherhood is found in Sara Ruddick, "Maternal Thinking," in *Rethinking the Family: Some Feminist Questions,* ed. Barrie Thorne with Marilyn Yalom (New York: Longman, 1982), 76–94.

19. Fischer cited Nona Y. Glazer, *The Invisible Intersection: Involuntary Unpaid Labor outside the Household and Women Workers* (Berkley, CA: Center for the Study, Education, and Advancement of Women, University of California, 1982). See also Elshtain, *Power Trips*; and Arlie Hothschild with Anne Machung, *The Second Shift: Working Parents and the Revolution at Home* (New York: Viking, 1989).

20. Fischer, "Liberating Work," 135–39.

21. One might begin with Thomas Aquinas, *Summa Theologica* I-I, Q. 92, but a locus classicus is Pope Pius XI's critique of female emancipation in the 1930 encyclical *Casti connubu*: "[T]his false liberty and unnatural equality with the husband is the detriment of the woman herself, for if the woman descends from her truly regal throne to which she has been raised within the walls of the home by means of the Gospel, she will soon be reduced to the old state of slavery (if not in appearance, certainly in reality) and become as amongst the pagans the mere instrument of man" (in *Seven Great Encyclicals,* 75).

22. The pope does not envision a similarly irreplaceable domestic and parental role for the father. The implication remains: The male is indispensable in the breadwinner role and is allowed and appreciated in—but not fundamentally meant for—the domestic role. For the female, the reverse is assumed. John Paul II's stance on the quality and public role of women is far more positive than that of some of his predecessors, and more is said about the role of the father in other documents. See, e.g., John Paul II, *Familiaris consortio: Apostolic Exhortation on the Family* (Washington, DC: U.S.C.C., 1982), 22–25. Yet the problems noted here are never fully overcome.

23. Lisa Sowle Chaill, *Between the Sexes* (Philidelphia: Fortress Press, 1985), 96, 98. See also U.S. Catholic Bishops, "One in Christ Jesus, A Pastoral Response to the Concerns of Women for Church and Society," *Origins* 19, no. 44 (April 5, 1990): paras. 23–26.

24. For a theologically informed treatment of the implications of difference for feminists, see Susan Brooks Thistlewaite, *Sex, Race, and God: Christian Feminism in Black and White* (New York: Crossroad, 1989). For the vigorous debate over heterogeneity among feminist philosophers and social theorists, see the thematic issue "Reason, Rationality, and Gender" (ed. Nancy Tuana) of the *Newsletter on Feminism and Philosophy* [of the American Philosophical Association] 88 (June 1989). One crucial practical arena for this debate is the current struggle over "comparable worth." The comparable worth principle, which has gained legislative and judicial acceptance in a number of states, beginning in Minnesota in 1984, holds that "jobs dissimilar in nature can be compared in terms of knowledge, skill, effort, responsibility, and working conditions, and that jobs equivalent in value in these terms should be paid equally." Sara M. Evans and Barbara J. Nelson, *Wage Justice: Comparable Worth and the Paradox of Technocratic Reform* (Chicago: University of Chicago Press, 1989), 11.

25. These trends are documented in Fischer, "Liberating Work," 122, and are discussed in Evans and Nelson, *Wage Justice*, chaps. 2 and 3; and Hewlett, *A Lesser Life*, esp. chaps. 4, 15.

26. Ehrenreich, *Hearts of Men*, 172–73. For the quotation of Caroline Bird, see 173; exactly seven decades before the period studied by Bird, John A. Ryan decried as morally unconscionable the fact that only about 40 percent of American workers were paid a decent living wage. Ryan, *Living Wage*, chap. 8.

27. John Paul II, *Laborem Exercens*, 19.

28. Hochschild, *Second Shift*, 2–4, inter alia.

29. Studies of family policies in various countries highlight the atypically individualistic and privatized approach toward the care of children taken in the United States. These findings are summarized in Hewlett, *A Lesser Life*, 127–29.

30. Pope John Paul II underscores this point in his most recent social encyclical, declaring that in third-world contexts, the objective of a decent family living wage is still a far distant goal. *Centesimus Annus*, in *Origins* 21, no. 1 (May 16, 1991): 34.

31. For revealing studies of the situation of women in global industry, see Rachel Grossman, "Women's Place in the Integrated Circuit," *Radical America* 14, no. 2 (January/February 1980): 29–49; and Naomi Katz and D. S. Kemnitzer, "Fast Forward: The Internationalization of Silicon Valley," in *Women, Men, and the International Division of Labor*, ed. J. Nash and P. Fernandez (New York: SUNY Press, 1983).

32. John Paul II, *Laborem Exercens*, 17. See also Gregory Baum, *The Priority of Labor* (New York: Paulist Press, 1982), 53–54.

33. Some conservation pro-family organizations favor a family wage system that would support an at-home wife and be increased according to the number of children involved. Like Connaught Marshner, chair if the Pro-Family Coalition interviewed by Ehrenreich, these "New Right" leaders do not seem to recognize that implementing such a plan might involve a massive, even revolutionary downward redistribution if wealth. Ehrenreich, *Hearts of Men*, 174–75.

34. See Lisa Cahill's similar suggestion in *Between the Sexes*, chap. 8.

35. *New York Times*, August 21, 1989, 1.

36. U.S. Bureau of the Census, 1986 figures quoted in Evans and Nelsons, *Wage Injustice*, 43.

37. This would be practically true only if the amount of money paid the household head actually included the wherewithal for a just wage for domestic work.

38. See Barbara Hilkert Andolsen, "A Woman's Work Is Never Done," in *Women's Consciousness, Women's Conscience*, ed. Barbara Andolsen, Christine Gudorf, and Mary Pellaue (Minneapolis, MN: Winston, 1985), 15–16. "Enormous changes will be required in order to integrate family and work in a structure humane to all parties." Such seemingly disparate issues as land-use patterns that segregate businesses from residential housing; inflexible hours of work or mandatory overtime for service and factory workers; and career tracks for many professional careers which demand work hours that preclude domestic participation during the very years when parenting and household responsibilities are greatest, all need to be challenged in the quest for a more genuinely equitable relation between home and work.

39. Ryan questioned the assumption that higher wages, widely distributed, would be detrimental to employment rates. See "Higher Wages and Unemployment" (1931) in John A. Ryan, *Seven Troubled Years: 1930–1936* (Ann Arbor, MI: Edwards Brothers, 1937), 19–22. For a judicious treatment of the welfare issue that also contends that a family living wage should be attainable by one full-time adult worker per family, see David Ellwood, *Poor Support: Poverty in the American Family* (New York: Basic Books, 1988).

40. I am borrowing the language used by Letty M. Russell in *Household of Freedom: Authority in Feminist Theology* (Philadelphia: Westminster Press, 1987), chap. 1. Russell and others propose that eschatology, with its envisagement of God's intended future, be adopted as a starting point for feminist and liberationist ethics. The difficulties involved in applying the vocabulary of eschatology to public policy issues have yet to be addressed.

41. See Rosemary Radford Ruether, "Spirit and Matter, Public and Private: The Challenge of Feminism to Traditional Dualisms," in *Embodied Love: Sensuality and Relationship as Feminist Values*, ed. Paula M. Cooey, Sharon A. Farmer, and Mary Ellen Ross (San Francisco, CA: Harper & Row, 1987), 75. Describing a Christian feminist vision of society, Ruether writes, "we seek a society built on organic community, where the processes of child raising, of education, or work, or culture have integrated in such a way as to allow both men and women to share child nurturing and homemaking on the one hand, and creative activity and decision making in the larger society, on the other hand."

42. Ryan, *Distributive Justice*, 355–56.

· 17 ·

Sneakers and Sweatshops: Holding Corporations Accountable

David M. Schilling

There was a mistaken assumption in the West in the late twentieth century that the draconian working conditions and the below-subsistence wages in what came to be known as "sweatshops" were a reality that we all could safely assume had been relegated to a sad footnote in our history. Tragically, this belief proved to be mythmaking at its worst as major U.S. companies were shipping work out to subcontractors around the world that relied on sweatshop conditions and paltry wages in order to be the lowest bidder for these big production jobs. In this chapter, David Schilling chronicles some of these abusive circumstances and identifies some of the religious organizations that are at the forefront of the battle against sweatshop conditions in Mexico and around the world. Religiously based organizations like the Interfaith Coalition on Corporate Responsibility (ICCR) and the Coalition for Justice in the *Maquiladoras* (CJM) were the first to identify and respond to the horrendous conditions and pitiful wages that are the hallmark of the sweatshops of the twenty-first century in the underdeveloped world.

A twelve-year-old worker in Pakistan earns 60 cents per day stitching soccer balls that are sold for more than $10 in the United States; an Indonesian worker needs over a month's pay to purchase a pair of shoes she makes for Nike; Mexicans employed by Alcoa must choose between buying food and paying rent.

Although sweatshop conditions in factories throughout the world are not new, they became headline news when the public learned that clothes made under Kathie Lee Gifford's label were sewn by children at Global Fashions, a *maquiladora* factory (where products are made for export) in Honduras. Gifford, a television talk-show celebrity and children's advocate, was appalled when the National Labor Committee announced that clothes bearing her

319

name were made by girls ages twelve to fourteen who were forced to work thirteen-hour shifts under armed guard for 31 cents an hour. When she found that the charges were true, she convinced Wal-Mart to withdraw its contract from Global Fashions.

It would have been easy for Kathie Lee Gifford to end her involvement there. But she met with Secretary of Labor Robert Reich, who urged her to join the Department of Labor in its effort to end sweatshop conditions in the United States and abroad. Since that meeting, Gifford has recruited other celebrities in that effort.

On July 16, 1996, the Department of Labor sponsored the Fashion Industry Forum at Marymount University in Virginia. Retailers, buyers, designers, manufacturers, endorsers, contractors, consumers, unions, and social responsibility groups gathered to discuss strategies for eradicating sweatshops in the garment industry. As Gifford observed, "The problems are not simple, but insidious and pervasive."

Nancy Penaloza, a sewing machine operator in New York City, described the sweatshop conditions under which she has worked for nine years:

> I sew high-quality women's suits priced at $120 or more. I get paid $6 per suit. I work at least 56 hours a week, Monday through Saturday, and get paid $207 a week ($3.75 an hour), off the books. If there are deadlines, we work till the job is done. My boss screams at me all the time to work faster. There is only one bathroom for one hundred people. We do not have a union. If you complain, you get fired and someone else takes your job.

When Reich asked her, "What if you want to work forty hours a week, can you?" Penaloza answered, "I have to work the number of hours my boss tells me."

Who is responsible for these substandard labor conditions? Corporate giants in the U.S. apparel industry rarely own the factories that produce their goods. As part of a globalized economy, companies like Levi Strauss, Nike, and Reebok contract with suppliers who produce their goods. The working conditions of many suppliers fall far below the most basic standards of fair and humane treatment. Companies typically distance themselves from responsibility for workplace conditions and low wages by contending they do not own or operate these facilities. Yet their orders enable these facilities to operate.

In an interconnected world, both consumers and investors are hearing about child and exploited labor conditions via the evening news or the Internet. Most Americans do not want to purchase a soccer ball made by a Pakistani child who is paid 6 cents an hour. As both consumers and investors, Americans are pressing U.S. companies and their suppliers to address exploitative work conditions. According to a survey released by Marymount University, more than three-fourths of Americans would avoid shopping at stores if they were aware that the stores sold goods made in sweatshops. The challenge is to make companies enforce their codes of conduct and use their economic power to see that their suppliers observe basic standards of human and labor rights.

The Interfaith Center on Corporate Responsibility (ICCR) has been working with labor groups, companies in the apparel industry, the Department of Labor, and the newly formed presidential advisory committee to explore strategies to eradicate sweatshops. ICCR is not new to this work. For twenty-five years it has been challenging corporations to pay a living wage, provide safe working conditions, and contribute to the communities where they operate. ICCR members have raised their voices in corporate boardrooms and shareholder annual meetings since 1971, when the Episcopal Church filed the first religious shareholder resolution calling on General Motors to divest of its operations in apartheid South Africa. Currently, ICCR has 275 Catholic, Protestant, and Jewish institutional investors, including denominations, religious communities, pension funds, dioceses, and health-care corporations with combined portfolios worth over $50 billion.

ICCR members combine a principled and pragmatic approach. As religious shareholders, they are "in" but not "of" the corporation—insiders because they are part owners of the company, outsiders because they believe the exclusive focus on bottom-line profits is idolatry. As board member Sister Barbara Aires, S.C., explains,

> Economic decisions have profound human and moral consequences. Faith communities measure corporate performance not only by what a corporation produces and its profitability, but also by how it impacts the environment, touches human life and whether it protects or undermines the dignity of the human person. Protection of human rights—civil, political, social and economic—is a minimum standard for corporations seeking to act responsibly.

ICCR, along with two religious counterparts in Great Britain and Canada, has released a draft document titled "Principles for Global Corporate Responsibility: Benchmarks for Measuring Business Performance." This is the first time that religious groups have developed comprehensive global standards for responsible corporate citizenship. The principles urge companies to envision themselves as one of many stakeholders in the global community and to set high standards for how they treat their employees, the environment, and the communities where they operate.

ICCR's approach to corporations involves talking with company officials, filing shareholder resolutions that address changes in policies and practices, running public campaigns focusing on media and public education, and screening out investments in companies whose actions violate members' principles. In many instances, ICCR uses all these tools at once. Sometimes it takes a public campaign for a company to agree to dialogue. In other cases the filing of a shareholder resolution gets a company's attention and leads to constructive dialogue and change. In 1996 ICCR members filed 172 shareholder resolutions with 118 companies.

Like many U.S. corporations, Alcoa operates manufacturing plants in Mexico's *maquiladora* sector, where goods are assembled for export. In 1965 the Mexican government set up the Border Industrialization Program, creating low-tariff, low-wage export platforms for U.S. companies on favorable terms—long before NAFTA was instituted and made all of Mexico an export platform. U.S. companies shift work to Mexico to cut labor costs. The rapid expansion of this sector has created jobs, but jobs at poverty-wage levels.

ICCR members, along with the Coalition for Justice in the *Maquiladoras* (CJM)—a broad-based coalition of labor, environmental, and religious groups from Mexico, the United States, and Canada—were concerned about Alcoa. Among the concerns were low wages and poor health and safety conditions, including the gas poisonings of Alcoa workers in 1994. In 1995 the Benedictine Sisters of Boerne, Texas, filed a shareholder resolution calling on Alcoa to initiate a review of its *maquiladora* operations and to recommend changes. Alcoa was urged to participate in a survey to determine the purchasing power of the wages of its Mexican workers. A similar resolution was filed with ten other U.S. companies, including General Electric, Johnson & Johnson, and Zenith.

Alcoa and other U.S. companies rationalize paying poverty-level wages in two ways. They point out that wages paid to workers are competitive with what other companies are paying in a specific area and that the wages paid to workers are above the minimum wage set by governments. But workers in Mexico and elsewhere can be paid a competitive wage well above the minimum required by law and still not be able to feed themselves and their families.

Before the 1994 Mexican economic crisis, the average pay of a *maquiladora* worker was $30 to $50 for a forty-eight-hour week, or barely a subsistence wage. As a result of the peso devaluation and the inflation of over 50 percent that accompanied it, the purchasing power of *maquiladora* wages plunged below subsistence level. In January 1996 a group of Alcoa workers in Ciudad Acuna did an informal market study which revealed that basic food items (not including meat, milk, vegetables, or cereal) cost $26.87 per week while wages averaged between $21.44 and $24.60 per week.

How can companies like Alcoa determine what a sustainable wage is, particularly in countries where standardized wage data are difficult to obtain and legal minimum wage levels are so low as to be meaningless? Sister Ruth

Rosenbaum, T.C., cochair of ICCR's Global Corporate Accountability Issue Group and director of the Center for Reflection, Education, and Action, has devised an innovative method to determine wage levels. Rosenbaum has developed the Purchasing Power Index (PPI) study, which is based on the standard "market basket" survey similar to the Consumer Price Index done by the U.S. Department of Labor.

The PPI takes the market basket survey an important step further by calculating the intersection of wages and prices documented in the survey. Rosenbaum writes:

> Based on wages paid, calculations are performed to determine the number of work minutes required in order to purchase any given item. Since each week contains a limited number of minutes, the calculations reveal how many items the worker can possibly purchase. The purchasing power of the wages is made evident, and the effect of the wage scale upon the life of the worker and the community is clarified in an objective way.[1]

A sustainable wage is defined by religious shareholders as one that allows a worker to meet basic needs, set aside money for future purchases, and earn enough discretionary income to support the development of small business in the community.

How has Alcoa responded to religious shareholders? In January 1996 the company agreed to come to the U.S.-Mexico border for a meeting with *maquiladora* workers. But at the same time the Securities and Exchange Commission ruled in the company's favor that the Benedictine sisters' resolution would be kept off the proxy statement and would not be brought up for a vote at Alcoa's shareholder meeting. Susan Mika, primary filer of the resolution; Martha Ojeda, executive director of CJM; and two Alcoa workers from Mexican plants traveled to Alcoa's annual shareholders' meeting. Workers Juan Tovar and Irma Valadez described the starvation wages, the lack of protective equipment and sanitary conditions, and the lack of toilet paper in the workers' bathrooms. The Pittsburgh Labor Action Network on the Americas and the United Steelworkers of America helped draw press attention to the workers' concerns by distributing leaflets outside the meeting.

Mika called on Alcoa CEO Paul O'Neill to meet with the delegation after the annual meeting. O'Neill agreed and promised to review the wages and working conditions in Alcoa's Mexican plants. The combined pressure of religious shareholders, key labor groups, religious investors, and *maquiladora* workers had an impact. In July 1996, Alcoa announced that its workers in Ciudad Acuna would receive a raise of 40 pesos per week (about $5.25). Said Mika: "This small wage increase, as applied to the reported 5,600 workers in Acuna, would nonetheless represent an additional investment of $30,000 per week in salaries received by workers." O'Neill visited the plants, checked out workers' allegations, fired a human resources person for not reporting health and safety violations, put soap and toilet paper in plant bathrooms, and raised wages.

The next step is to secure Alcoa's participation in a PPI study that could lead to a systematic wage increase for all of Alcoa's Mexican workers. Two U.S. companies that operate *maquiladora* plants in Mexico—Baxter International and W. R. Grace—have already agreed to participate. If ICCR can persuade a few key companies to raise wages, they can put pressure on all companies to pay a sustainable wage, whether the workers are in Michigan or Mexico, Indiana or Indonesia.

Sometimes work with a corporation produces results in one area but not in another. For example, two years ago General Motors endorsed the CERES principles on the environment, a major mutual victory for environmental responsibility. In regard to its *maquiladora* operations in Mexico, however, GM has demonstrated little interest in participating in a study or in raising the wages of its sixty-two thousand workers.

GM executives from Detroit and local GM managers did agree to visit GM workers at their homes in Reynosa, Mexico, which are made from corrugated metal and have no running water or electricity. At the time these workers were making 180 pesos (less than $26) per week in take-home pay. As a result of this trip, GM pledged to raise its workers' standard of living. CEO John Smith announced a housing initiative that "would make affordable housing a reality for thousands of its workers." ICCR supported the initiative but argued for more. "The housing program is a generous and compassionate response to the deplorable living conditions of some of GM's Mexican workers," said Barbara Glendon, O.S.U., of Mercy Consolidated Asset Management Program, for years a key sponsor of GM resolutions. "But compassion without justice is not enough to fulfill the obligations of our company to its employees. We are morally and ethically responsible to provide a sustainable wage to the people whose daily labor benefits us who are GM shareholders." A shift in wage policy from a competitive to a sustainable wage would improve the lives of over seven hundred thousand GM workers worldwide and set a standard for other corporations to meet.

A public campaign over working conditions at a supplier in El Salvador turned into a collaborative relationship between ICCR and The Gap, a San Francisco-based clothing chain. The National Labor Committee Education Fund in Support of Worker and Human Rights in Central America (NLC) had found violations of The Gap's "Sourcing Principles and Guidelines" at Mandarin International, a shop in San Salvador owned by a Taiwanese firm. Workers had complained to the NLC about the use of child labor, forced overtime, unsafe working conditions, threats to prevent workers from organizing, and firing of union leaders. After six months of leafleting at stores, letter writing by religious and community groups, and face-to-face discussions, The Gap agreed to explore independent monitoring at Mandarin International and to urge Mandarin to rehire union leaders who had been fired.

Four widely respected Salvadoran institutions agreed to form the Independence Monitoring Group: the secretariat of the Archdiocese of San Salvador, Tutela Legal (the human rights office of the archdiocese), the Human Rights Institute of University of Central America, and CENTRA (a labor research organization). These institutions now monitor Mandarin on a regular basis for worker abuses. In addition, when Mandarin receives enough work orders to restore the workforce to former levels, union leaders will be rehired.

This development is historic. The Gap is the first company to agree to develop an independent monitoring mechanism for its contract suppliers. Other companies have hired third-party consultants (like Ernst and Young, the accounting firm hired by Nike to do social audits of their contractors), but their reports are not independently generated nor publicly disclosed. There are signs that independent monitors, made up of respected local institutions committed to human rights, will play a crucial role in ensuring that worker rights are respected, company codes of conduct upheld, and sweatshop conditions eliminated.

Individuals and congregations can make a difference by refusing to purchase products made under sweatshop conditions, by writing to companies to inquire about their code of conduct and how it is enforced, by getting the directors of denominational pension funds involved in sweatshop issues, and by voting for socially responsible resolutions.

There are companies that are willing to look for ways of doing business responsibly in the global economy; others are reluctant to enter the unknown territory where business operations and human rights intersect. But consumers' growing concern about conditions under which products are made will not go away. As corporations struggle to do the right thing, we must hold them accountable and support those organizations that are helping to find principled and practical solutions to the challenges posed by the new global economy.

QUESTIONS FOR DISCUSSION

1. When we hear of the low wages and terrible work conditions at the sweatshops, our first reaction is to be indignant and condemn the corporations involved. But corporations have a responsibility to their shareholders to reduce costs and maximize profits. In a globalized economy where labor is treated like one among other commodities, why is it wrong for companies to use sweatshops?

2. There are those who will ask: If sweatshops are so awful, why do people choose to work there? No one is forcing people to take these jobs, so they obviously represent an opportunity for the people of these under-developed nations. What is this perspective overlooking? (Hint: think of the history of the West—especially the nineteenth century). Why might people work in these conditions in spite of the fact that they know these jobs will consign them to lifestyles that few people in North America would choose?

3. Do the desperate circumstances within which subcontracted workers live have an impact on their willingness to take sweatshop jobs? Do corporations need to take into consideration more than simply the willingness of people to work under these conditions for the lowest wages?

4. What kinds of strategies are religious organizations like the ICCR and the CJM using in order to raise awareness in corporate boardrooms about the conditions among laborers who make their products? How would you evaluate the ethical value of these strategies beyond their obvious effectiveness?

NOTE

1. See Ruth Rosenbaum, "In Whose Interest?" Unpublished diss. (Boston, MA: Boston College, January 1996).

• *18* •

Global Capitalism:
The New Context of Christian Social Ethics

M. D. Litonjua

Globalization represents one of the great transitions in the practice of business in the past century. The ability to move goods,
services, and information quickly around the globe has revolu-
tionized many dimensions of the capitalist economic system. In
this essay, M. D. Litonjua analyzes the phenomenon of globalization from the perspective of Christian social ethics. He considers
the effects of globalization, specifically its impact on economic
inquality, its effects on democratic social structures, and its ero-
sion of the natural environment, as serious problems that need
to be addressed by ethical inquiry. He concludes by bringing the
work of Pope John Paul II and others in defense of the creation
of sustainable communities.

*S*ince the Second Vatican Council, there has been a significant shift in the
approach of Catholic documents and theology to social issues. This method-
ological shift has been away from a deductive, natural law approach in dealing
with questions of social ethics to an inductive approach of social analysis and
scriptural-theological reflection. Vatican II's *Gaudium et Spes* exhorts Christians,
first, to scrutinize the signs of the times, to decipher the human meanings and
aspirations underlying events and happenings in the world, and then to respond
to them in the light of the gospel. Latin American liberation theology is em-
phatic that theology is a second step. Theological reflection comes only after a
prior commitment to the emancipation of the oppressed and a sociopolitical
analysis of their situation has been made.

Thus, without reducing theological reflection to a mere reflection determined by context, an understanding of context is a necessary requirement in
shaping theological reflection and ethical response. Context, in the first place,
in which individuals and communities are rooted, forms and gives meaning to

their lives; influences their hearts, minds, and aspirations; and sets limits to their horizons. This chapter contends that it is this context that is dramatically changing before our eyes, a context that is no longer local and national, but is fast becoming global. The purpose is to draw the lineaments of this global context, the implications and consequences of which must be taken into account by Christian social ethics. While these reflections arise from a specifically Catholic context, global capitalism is just as much a challenge to Protestant traditions, to Christian social ethics as a whole, and even to social ethics in general.

However, as the sociology of knowledge teaches, there is no neutral vantage point from which to view the global context, to watch the globalization process that is fast eliminating economic and cultural boundaries between nations. The contours of the one world coming into being will be defined according to one's interests and expectations, according to whether one benefits and wins from the globalizing process or one falls victim to and loses in the structural transformation. In this chapter, the preferential option of the poor is adopted. Its hermeneutical aspect demands that we study social reality and social structures from the point of view of the poor, that we analyze events and happenings in society and in the world in terms of how they impact the lives of the disadvantaged and marginalized. The contours of global capitalism will be defined, therefore, from the perspective of the poor and downtrodden. The new context of Christian social ethics is primarily one that affects the victims and casualties of global capitalism. What does the global economy do for people, especially the poor? What does global capitalism do to people, particularly the poor?

THIRD GREAT TRANSFORMATION

Human society is presently undergoing a third dramatic and wrenching structural transformation. If anatomically correct human beings like you and me appeared on Earth some fifty thousand years ago, the first great structural transformation happened some ten thousand years ago when small, nomadic tribes settled down in permanent villages and later in towns and cities. Whereas animal and vegetable sources of food were hunted down and gathered in nomadic life, life in settlements was based on agriculture made possible by the invention of the plow and the domestication of animals. The agricultural revolution resulted in economic surplus that, in turn, led to the erection of cities, the establishment of full-time service workers, the beginnings of what we now call civilization.

Some two hundred years ago, a second great structural transformation occurred with the industrial revolution. Human and animal sources of energy were replaced by nonanimal and nonhuman sources of energy. The results were hitherto unimaginable increases in efficiency and productivity. The industrial revolution was actually composed of several distinct but interrelated phases of technological breakthroughs. The first phase was the application of steam power to textiles, mining, manufacturing, and transportation. The second phase involved the use of oil and electricity, the invention of the telephone and the telegraph, of the automobile and the airplane. The third phase was marked by the technologies of atomic fission and fusion, supersonic aircraft and missiles, television and computers.[1] This third phase of the industrial revolution is still in process and is giving way to a third great structural transformation.

The agricultural revolution took almost ten thousand years to run its course, and the industrial revolution lasted but two hundred years. The third great structural transformation has given rise to what has been variously referred to as an information/knowledge/postindustrial society. Whereas the agricultural evolution was ushered in by the plow and the industrial revolution by the use of steam power, the technological tool of the postindustrial age is the silicon microchip that has been ranked just behind the wheel and equal to the steam engine among history's technological thresholds. All three mark fundamental turning points in human history, which have brought, and are bringing, fundamental changes to economies and societies, to the relationship of people and work, to family and other organizations, to nature and the environment, and to planet Earth itself. The changes were, and are, wrenching, leaving in their wake human winners and losers.

GLOBAL CAPITALISM

The most dramatic manifestation of this third fundamental transformation of human society is the globalization of the economy. Because of the microelectronic revolution, the economy has become global, not merely international. An international economy is characterized by a division of labor between the extraction of raw materials in third-world countries and the manufacture of finished goods in first-world countries. A global economy is one single market for capital, commodities, skilled labor, and technical knowledge, all of them easily crisscrossing boundaries through worldwide communications and transportation systems in search for the highest returns on investments or profits for products. One result is that first-world economies have undergone deindustrialization and are now dominated by their service sectors, whereas some third-world countries are registering higher rates of industrialization than first-world countries. William Greider has written a compelling narrative of this one world fast coming into existence, whether we are ready or not.[2] Whereas the agricultural and industrial transformations were gradual enough to allow for adaptation, the rate of change today is so phenomenal and unprecedented that there are marked discontinuities. It is a veritable global revolution. Greider compares it to a huge machine that is reaping tremendous benefits for a few, but wreaking enormous havoc in the lives of the many. It is a wondrous machine whose efficiency churns out excess supplies of goods and services, which exert downward pressures on prices and wages, and which, in turn, reap enormous wealth for its beneficiaries. Thus, the dynamics of the global economy play out as a human struggle in which peoples and nations, rich and poor alike, face a multiplicity of opportunities and dangers. Some win; more lose.

The manic of global capitalism is especially evident in finance capital, which Greider calls "the Robespierre of this revolution."[3] Finance capital is the driving force of expansionary capitalism. It fuels increasing production, starts new ventures and new enterprises, and enables the creation of multiplying new wealth. In the global economy, finance capital has become totally unfettered and completely mobile, beating the best efforts of governments to contain or regulate it. But the most alarming aspect of globalized capital is not its speed or its volume, but its price.[4] It has become detached from real economic activity, and thrives on debt and speculation. Fortunes are made and lost in financial markets without much reference to productive activities. They have become casino economies. The divergence has become pathological, so much so that when there is good news in the real economy, such as low unemployment, the financial markets are bearish for fear of inflation and higher taxes to cool the inflation down, whereas when the unemployment rate goes up, the financial markets are bullish because there is neither the threat of inflation nor of higher taxes. Greider points out that "finance capital's capacity to become deranged in search of higher returns has played out again and again in different forms of manias and crashes," which disorders, history also informs us, have been corrected in grim and violent ways: economic depressions and great wars.[5]

One reality that became evident with the disappearance of its archenemy, communism, is that there are many kinds of capitalism, different ways of organizing a market economy. East Asia has state capitalism: the alliance of big business and government. Western Europe has social or social democratic capitalism, which provides a generous social safety net of welfare. The United States has liberal capitalism, the most laissez-faire of the three, where the market is the freest. In the global economy, however, as Lester Thurow puts it, "the market, and the market alone, rules. . . . 'Survival of the fittest' capitalism stands alone."[6] It has destroyed the implicit post–World War II social contract in the United States, has started to undermine the welfare state in Western Europe, and will make untenable East Asian state capitalism.

Global capitalism marks the third stage in the worldwide development of capitalism. First, there was competitive capitalism in which relatively small businesses competed on the basis of price. Then came monopoly capitalism, which saw large corporations trying to get oligopolistic holds on market share. Now we have global capitalism whose main characteristic is the mobility and volatility of capital on a global scale.[7] It is primarily this "new leviathan" of global finance that is currently devastating the economies and societies of Asia. Once foreign capital takes flight and financial panic starts, the value of local currencies takes a precipitous fall despite the sound "fundamentals" of their economies. Thus, globalization significantly augments and spreads the inherent instability of capitalism. The International Monetary Fund, the surrogate government in global financial matters, neither acts to contain its volatility nor cushions the effects of its instability because it has become the main proponent of an unfettered global economy.[8]

The unfettered market ideology is the new fundamentalism sweeping across the one world in the making, commodifying and commercializing human life and everything it touches—without moral moorings, without human values and considerations, without humane intentions and aspirations.[9] The banner program of this revived social Darwinism is the Republican Party's Contract with America.[10] "In fact," E. J. Dionne Jr. adds, "the new Republican philosophy looks backward to the late nineteenth century, seeking to revive the radical, unregulated capitalism of the Gilded Age and that era's belief that material progress depends on the fiercest forms of unchecked competition."[11]

TRANSNATIONAL CORPORATIONS

Multinational corporations (MNCs), or, as the United Nations prefers, transnational corporations (TNCs), have become the main actors in the global economy. The term "multinational" strictly denotes ownership by several nationalities and implies equality between and identity with the different nations in which the corporations operate. The adjective "transnational" is more descriptive of a parent firm in one (home) country with a number of operating branches in other (host) countries, and is more reflective of the characteristic of domination inherent in parent-subsidiary relationships and in home-host country interactions.

As the economy globalizes, even the notion of a home base has become obsolete because these giant corporations have become, in reach and power, "supranational." In the words of the president of NCR (National Cash Register) corporation: "I was asked the other day about U.S. competitiveness and I replied that I don't think about it at all. We at NCR think of ourselves as a globally competitive company that happens to be headquartered in the United States."[12]

TNCs roam the global economy in the race to the top for profits and in a race to the bottom for wages. Through global commodity chains in which they contract out production, TNCs move capital and production in and out of national boundaries in search of the cheapest labor without regard to the devastation of human lives and the disintegration of human communities they create in their wake.[13] It is disconcerting to read of armed groups in the U.S. hinterland venting their anger at and blaming the government and the United Nations for the wrenching and calamitous changes that have happened to their lives and communities when the real culprits are transnational corporations.

William Greider is very instructive in his dissection of General Electric as an example of a powerful American transnational corporation.[14] General Electric has violated numerous laws and federal regulations, has committed fraud, has been found guilty of criminal conduct, and has been penalized to the tune of millions. Yet it has been the beneficiary of tax laws, of tax exemptions, deductions, and loopholes in a perverted form of corporate socialism. In spite of all these—and this is the most disturbing aspect—unlike individual criminals who are banned from the political process, GE remains Good Citizen GE, it pours money into think tanks, disseminating the ideology of laissez-faire capitalism, lobbying Congress, influencing not only elections but public policy. "The modern corporation," points out Greider, "presumes to act like a mediating institution—speaking on behalf of others and for the larger public good."[15] It has taken the place of mediating institutions, such as political parties, labor unions, and voluntary organizations, which constituted the vitality of American democracy, to form a more perverted form of corporate politics. For all these, GE's and the modern corporation's "most impressive political achievement is the debate that never occurs on the nature of the multinational corporations."[16]

In the 1970s, when TNCs made their not-too-benevolent presence palpably felt on the world scene, commissions were formed and hearings were held to investigate corruption and wrongdoing by TNCs; there were books and articles analyzing and criticizing their behavior and operations;[17] there were calls for codes of conduct to regulate their illegal and immoral practices.[18] It is certainly a measure of their hegemonic power that there is nary a whisper of criticism and complaint lodged against them today. Even the United Nations has dismantled its Center of Transnational Corporations, its code of conduct, begun in 1972, left unfinished. Yet these imperial corporations are the drivers of the juggernaut that is globalization, amassing fortunes for their few beneficiaries, flattening cultures that lie in their path, leaving human wreckage in their wake, and despoiling the land and the environment.

TNCs, in the imagery of two early titles in the 1970s, attained such a "global reach"[19] that they held national "sovereignty at bay."[20] They have only grown more powerful and expansive. In fact, Barnet and Cavanagh argue that TNCs are becoming "the world empires of the twenty-first century," free of all political control, unencumbered by geographical boundaries, with veto power over national policies. They owe no loyalty to their laborers, their consumers, their countries, except to the almighty bottom line, as they promise and sell "global dreams" of a new economic and cultural world order.[21] They rule the world.[22]

GROWING INEQUALITY

The worst effect of globalization is the growing inequality that cuts across both developed and developing countries. There are now 170 billionaires in the United States compared with 13 in 1982, but there is also a new category of the working poor. There are about 14 billionaires in Mexico and 2 in the Philippines, and they are neither drug lords nor the Marcoses, but the plight of the majorities in both countries has grown more miserable. In 1992, the United Nations Development Program dramatized the inequality by representing the world's income distribution in the shape of a champagne glass, in which the richest fifth receives 82.7 percent of total world income, while the poorest fifth of the world's population receives 1.4 percent. This will only grow dramatically worse in the future. For example, after a decade of popular patience, a fury against the social and economic costs of neoliberal economic reforms, as they are called, or of structural adjustment programs, with unemployment as the most compelling issue, is brewing throughout Latin America.[23] There are a number of factors involved in the growing gap between rich and poor. Robert Reich argues that a country's standard of living no longer depends on the competitiveness of its corporations or its industries, but on the competitiveness of its labor force. Economic well-being rests on the value that one adds to the global economy through one's skills. Put simply, your real competitive position in the world economy depends on the job you perform in it. "The widening gap between rich and poor seems to be related to a growing divergence in how much money people receive for the work they do. And that divergence, in turn, appears to have something to do with the level of education."[24] One consequence of this in the United States is that "no longer are Americans rising or falling together, as if in one large national boat. We are, increasingly, in different, smaller boats."[25] It is the same all around the globe.

Reich elaborates his argument by pointing out that there are three broad categories of work emerging in the global economy. They are "routine production services," which entail repetitive tasks, like the traditional blue-collar jobs and routine supervisory jobs; "in-person services," which also entail simple and repetitive tasks, but are provided person-to-person, like the traditional service jobs of retail sales workers, hospital attendants, taxi drivers, and security guards; and "symbolic-analytic services," which involve problem-identifying, problem-solving, and strategic-brokering activities, like software engineers, biotechnology scientists, design engineers, and investment bankers. "In this new world economy, symbolic analysts hold a dominant position. American scientists are especially advantaged. . . . For the other two major categories of workers, however, the law of supply and demand does not bode well. . . . [They] are losing ground in the global economy."[26]

Put differently, it is the classic clash between capital and labor, now situated in a new global economy in which capital has the unquestioned dominance of the globe, decisively shifting therefore the balance of power against all who make their living from work. To succeed in the global economy, you need capital to invest in financial markets, capital that Reich's "overclass" of symbolic analysts have in great amounts. On the other hand, because of a vastly expanded global labor pool, ordinary workers have no recourse from reengineering, downsizing, and other management fads they are subjected to. In fact, the *Economist* points out that "in many cases, the rich have got richer by doing rather little. An American who had $500,000 in shares and a $500,000 New York apartment fifteen years ago, and has merely held on to them, is now $5 million better off."[27] Thus, a chief economist and a former staff writer at *Business Week* rightly calls it "the Judas economy," in which capital has triumphed and labor has been betrayed.[28]

The most troubling aspect, however, is the nature of this new class of capitalist symbolic analysts. There has been, and will always be, an elite in society. The question is, Thurow asks, whether the elite is an establishment or an oligarchy.[29] The key difference is that an establishment's central goal is to ensure that the system works so that the country will in the long run be successful, whereas an oligarchy is a group of insecure individuals who are always on the lookout for their own immediate self-interest and are not interested in investing either their time or their effort in improving their country's long-run prospects. Without doubt, the new privileged class is acting like an oligarchy.

Robert Bellah and company, in an update of their classic work on individualism and commitment in American life, discern two characteristics of the members of this new knowledge/power elite.[30] First, they are deracinated: They are located less securely in their communities than in the networks linking them, flexibly and transiently, to others like themselves who are scattered all over the world. They live in guarded, gated enclaves. They work in ultramodern offices and research centers. They fly from airport to airport in search of profit and pleasure. They are what Jacques Attali has named the modern "nomads," who travel light with regard to family, church, locality, and even nation. But they will be increasingly surrounded by a sea of other nomads, impoverished nomads—boat people on a planetary scale—condemned to ply the planet in search of sustenance and shelter.[31]

Secondly, they are predatory. More disturbing than its secession from the common good is the new oligarchy's manipulation of the system and its exploitation of society. Not only does it pursue its narrow and selfish interests without regard to the welfare of the less fortunate in society, but also at their expense. Two examples from the American scene will suffice. The first example is taxation. Bellah and company argue that one other principal difference between an establishment and an oligarchy is that an establishment taxes itself most, while an oligarchy taxes itself least.[32] The oligarchical class, in connivance with their fellow members in the political system, has made the American tax code a gold mine of loopholes and giveaways. More, they have enacted law after law to create two separate and distinct tax systems and, therefore, a two-class society, in which the tax burden is transferred from people who can most afford to pay to those less able to pay, and from corporations to individuals.[33]

The second example concerns the American corporation. Daniel Bell considers Bryan Burrough and John Helyar's *Barbarians at the Gate* the most "subversive" book about American corporate capitalism. It is "the story of the battle for RJR Nabisco, which at $25 billion, was the largest corporate take-over in American economic history, and a fitting symbol of the Reagan era."[34] The deal was made at the expense of shareholders and of managers and workers who may have spent most of their lives in the company. Banks, brokerage houses, and lawyers—all symbolic analysts who managed the leveraged buy-out—received $1 billion in fees. For the small inner-circle group of principals, the deal "had nothing to do with shareholder values or fiduciary duties. It was all a test of wills among an intensely competitive clique of macho, Park Avenue bullies in pinstripes. . . . Each was determined to be King of the Sandbox."[35] No wonder that the American Dream has ended for the majority of Americans. In the past two decades, the top 5 percent of the American population has gained the most, the middle class continues to shrink, the working poor cannot make both ends meet, and the underclass are left to fend for themselves in drugs and crime. It was limited to the fields of athletics and entertainment before, but now "the winner-take-all society" is spreading across American society.[36] And it is recurring all over the world as well.

What needs to be pointed out, according to Dani Rodrik, is that the postwar period was marked by

> two apparently contradictory trends: the growth of trade and the growth of government. . . . It is not a coincidence that social spending increased alongside international trade. . . . The [data] reveals an unmistakably positive correlation between a nation's openness to trade and the amount of

its spending on social programs. . . . All the available evidence points to the same, unavoidable conclusion: The welfare state has been the flip side of the open economy.[37]

Herein precisely lies the problem:

Today, however, the process of international economic integration is taking place against the backdrop of retreating governments and diminished social obligations. Yet the need for social insurance for the vast majority of the population that lacks international mobility has not diminished. If anything, this need has grown. [38]

What the new knowledge/power oligarchical class of market ideologues does not realize out of enlightened self-interest is that they are creating a basic contradiction in global capitalism that can only implode. In their race to the top for profits, they are expanding capitalism's productive capacities and creating a greater and greater supply of goods and services. But in their race to the bottom for wages, they are slashing the buying power of consumers and constricting the demand for those self-same goods and services. Something has to give.[39] England's most staunch proponent of the market, the *Economist*, is concerned enough to point out the eerie similarities between the beginning and the end of the twentieth century, the 1900s and the coming 2000s, to warn of a likely backlash and to point out the dangerous notion that "America's rich owe their wealth entirely to their own brilliance, when in fact they also owe much of it to the system that allows and encourages great wealth to be created."[40] What a world of difference from that of Henry Ford who increased the daily pay of his laborers to five dollars, an unprecedented sum at that time, so that they could afford to buy the products they themselves were making. Who else would?

THREATS TO DEMOCRATIC POLITICS

It is often forgotten that Adam Smith penned *Theory of Moral Sentiments* before he wrote *The Wealth of Nations*, because capitalism requires a moral order to prevent it from descending to predation and chaos. From the time of Franklin Delano Roosevelt and his New Deal, government has acted as the counter-vailing power to capitalism's nature and logic at accumulation, mitigating the cruelty and inexorabilities of the market and providing a social safety net for those who are disadvantaged and marginalized. However, a basic disparity now exists between a global economy and a politics that is still confined within the nation-state. Government has become powerless before the onslaught of global capital. Worse, governments have turned subservient to the demands of global corporations because national economic performance has become the ultimate legitimation of governance.

In fact, the new economic fundamentalist ideology of an unfettered market would reduce the role of government to the libertarian role of a night watchman. Two theoretical movements, Law and Economics, and Public Choice, would make law facilitate the natural logic of markets and would subject all political decisions to the economic criteria of costs and benefits. In an examination of the virtues and limits of markets, Robert Kuttner has demonstrated that no society can be a grand auction block where everything is for sale.[41] The economic misery and political chaos in Russia, the spread of criminal organizations and unregulated sales of nuclear weapons show that well-being and liberty itself need an affirmative and efficacious government. "Ironically, Russians today have more reason to worry about the debility of the state than about its power. . . . Just as you cannot have capitalism where everything is planned, so you cannot have capitalism where everything is for sale."[42] Even Jeffrey Sachs, a veritable Lenin of neoliberalism, it seems, has become bitter after his failed stint as a shock therapist in Moscow.[43]

Today, especially with the disappearance of the iron curtain in Eastern Europe, much is being made of the compatibility of democracy in politics and capitalism in economics in that both require and promote the freedom of the individual. But there is a deeper underlying incompatibility in that democracy is built on the equality of persons, whereas capitalism is predicated on the inequality of resources. The hope is that the equality of democratic politics will curb and mitigate the economic inequality of capitalism. This is the benign version of the classic case against democracy, that the many would use their democratic control of government to violate the property rights of the few. The fear, on the other hand, is that the economic inequality generated by capitalism would subvert the democratic foundations of equality.

The reality is for all to see in the "most democratic" of all countries, the United States of America. American democracy, Greider has documented, is now a "democracy for hire."[44] It is held captive by money and, more insidiously, by the ideas that money can buy. Information has become the driving force of the political and the governing process. Information is supposed to lead to rational analysis, rational decision making, and rational policies. The trouble is that the information—the data and research, the policy studies, the position papers—that gets a hearing in the echelons of power is being cranked up by the think tanks, now dominated by the extreme right wing, into which money is poured. The ideas they promote are not only the efficiency and productivity of the market mechanism, but the ideologies of libertarianism in politics and of an unfettered market in the economy, ideas that are congenial, to say the least, to the interests of their sponsors. There are even think-tank theological justifications of the moral superiority of the economic system of capitalism that ignore its inequalities and indignities. The ideologues of laissez-faire capitalism have learned well the importance of cultural hegemony propounded by the Italian Marxist Antonio Gramsci that, to put it colloquially, if you own the vocabulary, you control the agenda. But the result is that American democracy has become a "mock democracy . . . that guarantees the exclusion of most Americans from the debate—the expensive politics of facts and information."[45]

If that is not enough, consider David Stockman's *The Triumph of Politics*, which Bell considers "the most subversive book on American politics and the myths about policy making."[46] Stockman was the director of the Office of Budget Management in the first Reagan administration. What struck Stockman most, he writes, was the economic illiteracy of Reagan's top advisers, including the president himself. His book is a detailed account of his efforts to hide the rising budget deficits that were to quadruple under Reagan; "the massive fiscal policy error that had been unleashed on the national and world economy was beyond recall. . . . I out-and-out cooked the books, inventing $15 billion per year of utterly phony cuts in order to get Ronald Reagan's first full budget below the $100 billion deficit level."[47] That is outright criminal fraud perpetrated on the American people and their future. Yet, when conservative ideologues decry the role of government as fostering moral decay, as creating dependency on the part of the poor, they never say a word about the crimes in the high levels of government in which they reside. If Americans want democracy, therefore, they will not find it in Washington—in fact, they have given up on democracy in Washington—they have to look for it elsewhere. Nor can it be found in the capitals of other leading democratic nations. National democracies are being dismantled by the dynamics of global economics. Worse, "the market economy and democracy combined cannot provide a sound basis for a lasting civilization," a warning about the dictatorship of the market that surprisingly comes from the former president of the European Bank for Reconstruction and Development.[48]

CULTURAL HOMOGENIZATION

Like modernization, globalization is not only a material process, but involves a transformation of ideas, values, attitudes, and aspirations. It is a package that has economic aspects, but also contains cultural consequences. In modernization, a distinction is usually made between "modern" and "modernist." The former refers to the material, economic, scientific, and technological aspects of the process of modernization, while the latter refers to the transformation of ideas, values, mentalities, and orientations that usually accompanies modernity. Modernization and globalization involve dramatic changes, but the changes in cultural values are more wrenching, questioning as they do traditional identities, undermining social cohesion, and destroying traditional cultures. The global expansion of modernism is a steamroller that culturally flattens everything in its path. It is against this background that the rise of religious fundamentalism and the emergence of ethnic nationalism have to be understood. Religious fundamentalism, exemplified in Islamic revivalism, is a reaction not against modernity, but against modernism. In a world that is fast becoming "McWorld," the only weapon that threatened groups can wield is "jihad."[49] For cultures that are experiencing their dissolution, the last resort is to reassert their distinctive identity, which sadly and tragically descends to tribal hatreds and conflicts. Even in the United States, multiculturalism first arose to protest the hegemony of reason, the exclusive reliance on science, the universalizing tendencies based on white male domination, which became the cultural hallmarks of modernity, inherited from the Enlightenment. In its extreme forms, multiculturalism has since descended into a narrow, sectarian, and divisive "political correctness."

Modern culture did not begin in the United States, but its individualism and consumerism have their most unfettered expression—and now their global center—in the United States. Joe Holland points out both the good and the bad in the global spread of modern American culture:

> The positive side of American culture, I propose, is that through its innovative spirit, expressed through the English language, the American cultural drive has shown a remarkable openness to enrichment from other cultures. What is distinct about the United States is that it is a continuing creation of all the world's cultures, and increasingly so. Thus late modern American culture may be gaining such global cultural power precisely because, despite its economic exploitation and political domination, it remains culturally open to the gifts of the many peoples of the earth. English as a world language is mediated through American culture, but in a deeper sense the English language is a global creation, again the first truly global language.
>
> The negative side, however, as so many commentators have warned (myself included), is that modern American culture—with its powerful technoscientific commitment to autonomous definitions of freedom and progress may also be destroying the ecological, social, and religious foundations of the life system on planet earth. Modern American freedom and progress may be producing their dialectical opposites. The global culture may be emerging only to face the death of all life at every level from the womb to the planet. In the meantime, American culture seems to be propagandizing the world with a trivialized definition of sexuality and massive celebration of violence.[50]

But as globalization proceeds at an increasingly faster pace, the individualistic and consumeristic aspects of modern American culture are gaining the upper hand in the global traffic of information, ideas, and values. American music, American movies, American television, and American software are so dominant, so sought after, so visible, that they influence the tastes, lives, and aspirations of virtually every person on the globe. The emphasis on sex and violence, the exclusively individualistic focus, the consumerist ethos, the ultimate criterion of money, and the commodification of life itself are corrupting. Even the Wall Street financier George Soros has called attention to the threat that the values propagated by global laissez-faire capitalism pose to the very values on which open and democratic societies depend.[51] With the destruction of nonmarket value systems, societies lose their social anchor. Without social justice as the guiding principle of civilized life, life becomes a social Darwinian survival of the fittest. Unless nonmarket institutions and mechanisms are put into place, the open global society that prevails at present is likely to prove a temporary but disastrous phenomenon.

These are the contradictions of capitalism that conservatives find themselves playing out. Economic conservatives have no use for the state, but desire an unfettered market to work its magic in more and more areas of life, including the law and polity. Cultural conservatives decry moral decay, the decline of the family, and violence and pornography in the media, and want the government to rectify matters, to impose standards, and to penalize violators. But what cultural conservatives crusade against results from what economic conservatives crusade for. Bell has reaffirmed what he had written twenty years ago about the cultural contradictions of capitalism, that the instant gratification promoted by capitalism has undermined the work ethic that brought it about, that the tension between bourgeois society and modernism has been overtaken by the vulgarity of postmodernism, and that the separation of law from morality has been completed with the market becoming the arbiter of all economic and social relations.[52]

But the cultural contradictions of capitalism continue to be ignored. One example will suffice. David Blankenhorn is to be commended for publicizing the epidemic of fatherlessness that has swept the country and that has become our most urgent social problem.[53] But because the analysis of the culture of fatherlessness is completely detached from the wrenching changes in the economy and in society in which at the very least it must be situated, it ends up blaming the victims and flagellating deadbeat dads. "Family values," if it is not a cynical political ploy, must be discussed in the context of what is happening culturally in society and the world, increasingly being dominated and devastated by the values of a global market.

What is more worrisome, however, is how global, for-profit culture industries are affecting religious traditions and communities to the extent that the prospects of Christianity maintaining an independent, critical voice in world affairs are not encouraging. Michael Budde specifically addresses himself to the Catholic Church, whose influence as the transnational movement par excellence flows from its cultural (not economic, military, or political) power.[54] The church's capacity to continue to do so cannot remain unchanged by the unprecedented commercial and symbolic saturation of life in contemporary capitalism. This is especially so since the church has less and less access to the traditional processes of inculcating the symbol systems, the narratives of Jesus and Israel, of the prophets and the saints, and of other stories of the faith through which people make the priorities, dispositions, and practices of Jesus their own.

What may be worse is that "the Church may well respond by reconfiguring itself into something of a knockoff of the culture industries,"[55] by embracing the advertising and marketing strategies of Madison Avenue in hyping the gospel. The pope has already entered the ranks of big-advance authors in the employ of global publishers and has become the pitchman of a multimedia package for the rosary (video and compact disc) in television, radio, and print ads. The danger is the "Disneyfication of Catholicism," the promised kingdom of God blending into Disney's Magic Kingdom—"a promise fulfilled in the here and now, and one with abundant merchandising and shopping opportunities."[56]

SUSTAINABLE COMMUNITIES

In the last two hundred years of the industrial period, we have done more damage to the environment than in the previous ages when we lived as hunting, gathering and fishing, and agricultural societies. The controlling image of industrial society is the machine. You use a machine, even misuse and abuse it, and then you discard and replace it. But planet Earth is not a machine, and there is only one planet Earth. With all the environmental problems we have today, our attitude toward planet Earth must be one toward a living organism. You protect, nurture, and cherish a living organism. But "the culture of capitalism," Robert Heilbroner has written, "expresses a voracious, even rapacious, attitude toward the material world—a point of view that would be impossible if that world were portrayed as 'mother' Nature."[57]

Continued economic growth on a global scale, however, cannot but aggravate further environmental problems. It cannot be achieved without further degrading the environment's capacity as a source of resources and as a sink for wastes. Consider briefly the case of China if and when it attains first-world status, which it is now relentlessly pursuing: the number of cars emitting carbon dioxide, the agricultural land diverted for industrial construction and uses, the amount of food needed to satisfy its population. And if creating a global culture means generalizing the Western lifestyle, it simply is not possible without destroying the environment's ability to function and renew itself. On the other hand, globalization has had a positive effect in that it has created consciousness of the global dimensions of environmental problems. They cannot be solved to any significant degree without an unprecedented level of global effort and cooperation. That, however, has remained mostly on the level of rhetoric and promise.

Ever since the Brundtland Commission (The United Nations' Commission on Environment and Development, headed by Mrs. Gro Harlem Brundtland) issued its report, "Our Common Future," in 1987, it has become fashionable to speak and write of "sustainable development," which enjoins us to bring about development in such a manner that we hand over to the next generation the environment in no worse shape that when we received it from our forebears. The idea sounds so wholesome that everybody endorses it: governments that do nothing about it, corporations that grossly violate it. The problem is that "sustainable development" remains on the level of idea; it does not pinpoint the moral agent responsible for carrying out a sustainable ethics.

Larry Rasmussen prefers to speak of "sustainable communities" that have accepted the specific responsibility of embodying a "sustainable ethics."[58] In fact, it is environmentally conscious and environmentally committed grassroots communities—oftentimes referred to as nongovernmental organizations (NGOs) and popular organizations (POs) proliferating all over the globe that are fighting poverty and environmental degradation.[59] Moreover, they are creating a people-centered model of development that is equitable, sustainable, and participatory.[60] It is a model that is in striking contrast to the Washington neoliberal consensus of structural adjustment imposed from above by the World Bank–International Monetary Fund consortium. Far ahead of labor unions, these environmental groups are forging ties across national boundaries, coordinating priorities and programs, and holding alternate world forums. They constitute an emerging global civil society that is already exerting countervailing power to the global market and subservient nation-states.[61]

CENTESIMUS ANNUS

The end of the Soviet Union brought about the end of "really existing socialism," though certainly not the end of ideology, nor the end of history. The attitude of official Catholic social thought on the economic systems of capitalism and socialism has always been one of "a pox on both your houses." However, it is accurate to say that the value of equality for the sake of fraternity that socialism promoted, at least theoretically, resonated more with the values that

Catholic social thought stood for than with the liberty of acquisitiveness and competition that underlies capitalism.

In this connection, Robert Schreiter believes that "what the collapse of socialism has meant for liberation theology has been the loss of a horizon of utopia and prophecy. . . . The apparent conquest by capitalism to the point that the only hope is exclusion from hope altogether has more than anything else prompted the crisis in liberation theology."[62] Prior to this was the Vatican's repression, which now appears all the more ill-advised and ill-founded. Instead of supporting and promoting the prophetic values and utopian ideals of liberation theology and the basic Christian communities that tried to embody them as countervailing civic values and civil societies, the Vatican's institutional fears blocked them, thus helping to leave open Latin America and third-world countries to the neoliberal assaults of "really existing capitalism."

To celebrate the hundredth anniversary of *Rerum Novarum* in 1991, John Paul II issued *Centesimus Annus*, which American neoconservatives tried to preempt in owning. It could not but refer to the events that began to unravel in 1989: the liberation of Eastern Europe, the fall of the Berlin Wall, the disintegration of the Soviet Union, and the end of communism. Accordingly, it asks: Has capitalism triumphed?

The answer is obviously complex. If by capitalism is meant an economic system that recognizes the fundamental and positive role of business, the market, private property, and the resulting responsibility for the means of production, as well as free human creativity in the economic sector, then the answer is certainly in the affirmative, even though it would perhaps be more appropriate to speak of a business economy, market economy, or simply free economy. But if by capitalism is meant a system in which freedom in the economic sector is not circumscribed within a strong juridical framework which places it at the service of human freedom in its totality, and which sees it as a particular aspect of that freedom, the core of which is ethical and religious, then the reply is certainly negative.[63]

In an earlier section, the encyclical provides the grounding for its affirmative answer.

> The state, however, has the task of determining the juridical framework within which economic activities are to be conducted, and thus of safeguarding the prerequisites of a free economy, which presumes a certain equality between the parties, such that one party would not be so powerful as practically to reduce the other to subservience. . . .
>
> The state must contribute to the achievement of these goals both directly and indirectly. Indirectly and according to the principle of subsidiarity by creating favorable conditions for the free exercise of economic activity, which will lead to abundant opportunities for employment and sources of wealth.

Directly and according to the principle of solidarity, by defending the weakest, by placing certain limits on the autonomy of the parties who determine working conditions, and by ensuring in every case the necessary minimum support for the unemployed worker.[64]

John Paul II, therefore, recognizes that there are different kinds of capitalism, different ways in which the market economy is organized, different combinations in which the principle of subsidiarity that reaffirms the market economy and the principle of solidarity that justifies the welfare state are worked out in practice. But *Centesimus Annus* does not evince a full realization that the "really existing capitalism" is a global capitalism and that this global capitalism is predominantly a laissez-faire capitalism. What has happened to the principle of subsidiarity in global capitalism, ruled as it is by the ideology of an unfettered market? What would the principle of solidarity mean in a global economy that is still circumscribed politically by individual nation-states? Ten years after the American bishops' *Economic Justice for All*, Archbishop Rembert Weakland agrees that "the globalization of the economy would be the lens" under which an updating of the pastoral letter would be made.[65] This is especially an urgent responsibility for American Christians since the United States is the center of the market ideology and the market values sweeping across the globe.

This chapter has been written from a specifically Roman Catholic point of view because that is the religious tradition to which I hold and with which I am most familiar. But the challenge and the task that the process of globalization and the state of globality pose face all religions and confront all social ethics. Daniel Bell ended the 1978 foreword and the 1996 afterword to his now-classic book with a final note on religion, which he understands as "the sense, a necessary one, of the sacred, of what is beyond us and cannot be transgressed."[66] His central charge is that for capitalism there is nothing sacred, there are no boundaries of transgression. For example, religion upholds the dignity of the human person, whereas the market treats the individual as a commodity. The ideology of the market knows no values except efficiency, productivity, and profitability. "But the deeper question remains: If one loses the anchorages of tradition and religion, what will be left of economic power . . . if not some further contradictions of capitalism?"[67]

Religion has resources to answer the questions posed by Ronald Preston: What sort of global society do we want? What sort of people do we need to be in order to achieve it? What sort of social structures do we need to help the formation of people to be what we need them to? But religion can answer only after it understands and has analyzed the context in which those ethical questions are asked and must be answered: the new context of global capitalism.[68]

QUESTIONS FOR DISCUSSION

1. What are the great transformations in economic life described by Litonjua? What is the hallmark of the transformation through which we are now living? What kinds of changes have resulted from this transformation?

2. What is the distinction between an "international" economy on the one hand and a "global" economy on the other?

3. What are some moral issues raised by the prominence of transnational corporations in the global economy? How does the case of General Electric illustrate some of these issues?

4. How does the global economy increase inequality, according to Litonjua? What role does the rise of "symbolic-analytic" services play in this? What are some of the characteristics of the members of the new "elite" according to Robert Bellah's analysis? Is this an accurate reflection of American society today? Why or why not?

5. How does Litonjua argue globalization is a threat to democracy? How do market forces affect this?

6. What effect does globalization have on cultural diversity? How is this related to the opposition of "jihad" to "McWorld"?

7. How does Litonjua argue in favor of the creation of "sustainable communities"? What is the role of Catholic social teaching in this project? How would you evaluate his proposals? What are some advantages and disadvantages to this approach?

NOTES

1. D. Stanley Eitzen and Maxine Baca Zinn, "The Forces Reshaping America," in *The Reshaping of America: Social Consequences of the Changing Economy*, ed. D. Stanley Eitzen and Maxine Baca Zirn (Englewood Cliffs, NJ: Prentice Hall, 1989), 1–2.

2. William Griedler, *One World, Ready or Not: The Manic Logic of Global Capitalism* (New York: Simon and Schuster, 1997).

3. Griedler, *One World*, 250.

4. Griedler, *One World*, 234.

5. Griedler, *One World*, 227.

6. Lester Thurow, *The Future of Capitalism: How Today's Economic Forces Shape Tomorrow's World* (New York: Penguin, 1996), 1–5.

7. Robert J. S. Ross and Kent C. Trachte, *Global Capitalism: The New Leviathan* (Albany: State University of New York Press, 1990).

8. See, e.g., Lester Thurow, "Asia: The Collapse and the Cure," *New York Review of Books* 45, no. 2 (February 5, 1998): 22–26; Jeffrey Sachs, "The IMF and the Asia

Flu," *American Prospect* 37 (March–April 1998): 16–21; Martin Feldstein, "Refocusing the IMF," *Foreign Affairs* 77, no. 2 (March–April 1998): 20–33; Jagdish Bhagwati, "The Capital Myth," *Foreign Affairs* 77, no. 3 (May–June 1998): 7–12.

9. The sweeping story of the pendulum swing from the state to the market in economic affairs is masterfully told by Daniel Yergin and Joseph Stanislaw, *The Commanding Heights: The Battle between Government and the Marketplace that Is Remaking the Modern World* (New York: Simon and Schuster, 1998), but even they pose five critical tests that will determine if the move is permanent or if there will be a shift back: delivering the goods, ensuring fairness, upholding national identity, securing the environment, and coping with demographics.

10. Thurow, *Future of Capitalism*, 249.

11. E. J. Dionne, *They Only Look Dead: Why Progressives Will Dominate the Next Political Era* (New York: Simon and Schuster, 1996), 12.

12. Quoted by Robert B. Reich, *The Work of Nations: Preparing Ourselves for the 21st-Century Capitalism* (New York: Alfred A. Knopf, 1991), 119.

13. See Gary Gereffi, "The Elusive Last Lap in the Quest for Developed-Country Status," in *Globalization: Critical Reflections*, ed. James H. Mittelman (Boulder, CO: Lynne Rienner, 1996), 53–81.

14. William Greider, *Who Will Tell the People: The Betrayal of American Democracy* (New York: Simon and Schuster, 1992).

15. Greider, *Who Will Tell the People*, 331.

16. Greider, *Who Will Tell the People*, 346.

17. M. D. Litonjua, "Multinational Corporations: Critical Views from the Perspective of Developing Countries," unpublished paper.

18. M. D. Litonjua, "Codes of Conduct for Multinational Corporations," unpublished paper.

19. Richard J. Barnet and Ronald E. Miller, *Global Reach: The Power of Multinational Corporations* (New York: Simon and Schuster, 1974).

20. Raymond Vernon, *Sovereignty at Bay: The Multinational Spread of U.S. Enterprises* (New York: Basic Books, 1971).

21. Richard J. Barnet and John Cavanagh, *Global Dreams: Imperial Corporations and the New World Order* (New York: Simon and Schuster, 1994).

22. David C. Korten, *When Corporations Rule the World* (West Hartford, CT: Kumarian, 1995).

23. David Scrieberg, "Dateline Latin America: The Growing Fury," *Foreign Policy* 106 (Spring 1997): 161–76.

24. Reich, *Work of Nations*, 207.

25. Reich, *Work of Nations*, 173.

26. Reich, *Work of Nations*, 144–45.

27. "The Challenge for America's Rich," *Economist* (May 30, 1998), 15.

28. William Wolman and Anne Colamosca, *The Judas Economy: The Triumph of Capital and the Betrayal of Work* (Reading, MA: Addison-Wesley, 1997).

29. Lester Thurow, *Head to Head: The Coming Economic Battle among Japan, Europe, and America* (New York: William Morrow, 1992).

30. Robert Bellah, *Habits of the Heart: Individualism and Commitment in American*

Life, updated edition with a new introduction (Berkeley: University of California Press, 1996).

31. Jacques Attali, *Millenium: Winners and Losers in the Coming World Order* (New York: Times Books, 1991).

32. Bellah, *Habits of the Heart*, xiii.

33. Donald L. Barlett and James B. Steele, *America: Who Really Pays the Taxes?* (New York: Touchstone, 1994).

34. Daniel Bell, *The Cultural Contradictions of Capitalism*, twentieth anniversary edition with a new afterword (New York: Basic Books, 1996), 324.

35. Quoted by Bell, *Cultural Contradictions*, 326.

36. Robert H. Frank and Philip J. Cook, *The Winner-Take-All Society: Why Few at the Top Get So Much More than the Rest of Us* (New York: Penguin, 1995).

37. Dani Rodrik, "Sense and Nonsense in the Globalization Debate," *Foreign Policy* 107 (Summer 1997): 25–26; see also his *Has Globalization Gone Too Far?* (Washington, DC: Institute for International Economics, 1997).

38. Rodrik, "Sense and Nonsense," 27.

39. See the interesting colloquy between William Greider, Jeffrey E. Garten, and Ted C. Fishman, "Global Roulette: In a Volatile World Economy, Can Everyone Lose?" *Harper's Magazine,* June 1998, 39–50.

40. "Challenge for America's Rich"; see also "The Gospel of Wealth," 19–21.

41. Robert Kuttner, *Everything for Sale: The Virtues and Limits of Markets* (New York: Alfred A. Knopf, 1997).

42. Stephen Holmes, "What Russia Teaches Us: How Weak States Threaten Freedom," *American Prospect* 33 (July-August 1997): 31, 35.

43. James Surowiecki, "Dr. Shock," *Lingua Franca* 7, no. 5 (June-July 1997): 62.

44. Greider, *Who Will Tell the People?*

45. Greider, *Who Will Tell the People?*, 35.

46. Bell, *Cultural Contradictions*, 326.

47. Cited in Bell, *Cultural Contradictions*, 327.

48. Jacques Attali, "The Crash of Western Civilization: The Limits of the Market and Democracy," *Foreign Policy* 107 (Summer 1997): 59.

49. Benjamin R. Barber, *Jihad vs. McWorld: How Globalism and Tribalism Are Reshaping the World* (New York: Ballantine, 1996).

50. Joe Holland, "Faith and Culture: An Historic Moment for the American Catholic Laity?" in *American and Catholic: The New Debate*, ed. Joe Holland and Anne Barsanti (South Orange, NJ: Pillar, 1988), 27.

51. George Soros, "The Capitalist Threat," *Atlantic Monthly* 279, no. 2 (February 1997): 45–58.

52. Bell, *Cultural Contradictions*, 283–85.

53. David Blankenhorn, *Fatherless America: Confronting Our Most Urgent Social Problem* (New York: Basic Books, 1995).

54. Michael Budde, "Embracing Pop Culture: The Catholic Church in the World Market," *World Policy Journal* 15, no. 1 (Spring 1998): 77–87; a longer treatment is found in his *The (Magic) Kingdom of God: Christianity and Global Culture Industries* (Boulder, CO: Westview, 1997).

55. Budde, "Embracing Pop Culture," 83.

56. Budde, "Embracing Pop Culture," 86.

57. Robert Heilbroner, *The Nature and Logic of Capitalism* (New York: W. W. Norton, 1985), 135.

58. Larry Rasmussen, *Earth Community, Earth Ethics* (Maryknoll, NY: Orbis, 1996).

59. Alan Durning, "People Power and Development," *Foreign Affairs* 76 (Fall 1989): 66–82; "Groundswell at the Grass Roots," *World Watch* 2, no. 6 (November-December 1989): 16–23.

60. Robin Broad and John Cavanagh, *Plundering Paradise: The Struggle for the Environment in the Philippines* (Berkeley: University of California Press, 1993).

61. Central to the global civil society will be a global ethic of responsibility. Of all world-renowned theologians, Hans Küng has lately devoted himself to calling for a global ethic in the face of a global economy and politics; see his *Global Responsibility: In Search of a New World Ethic* (New York: Crossroad, 1991); *A Global Ethic for Global Politics and Economics* (New York: Oxford University Press, 1998); but he has not pointed out specific problems of globalism that need to be critically reflected upon and responded to by a global ethics. In contrast, see, e.g., Jerry Mander and Edward Goldsmith, ed., *The Case against the Global Economy: And for a Turn toward the Local* (San Francisco: Sierra Club, 1996).

62. William Schreiter, *The New Catholicity: Theology between the Global and the Local* (Maryknoll, NY: Orbis, 1997), 103; see also Peter Burns, S. J., "The Problem of Socialism in Liberation Theology," *Theological Studies* 53 (September 1992): 493–516; David Hollenbach, S. J., "Christian Social Ethics after the Cold War," *Theological Studies* 53 (March 1992): 75–95.

63. *Centesimus Annus*, no. 42.

64. *Centesimus Annus*, no. 15.

65. "'Economic Justice for All' 10 Years Later," *America* 176, no. 9 (March 22, 1997): 22.

66. Bell, *Cultural Contradictions*, 338.

67. Bell, *Cultural Contradictions*, 339.

68. Ronald Preston, *Religion and the Ambiguities of Capitalism* (Cleveland, OH: Pilgrim, 1993), 79.

Index

About the Editors and Contributors

Paul J. Borowski, C.Ss.R., is currently the director of formation for the Baltimore Province of the Redemptorist Order. He has taught business ethics at St. John's University.

M. L. Brownsberger is an ordained Presbyterian minister and has served as a financial executive at a pharmaceutical manufacturing company in Chicago for many years.

Douglas Burton-Christie is professor of theological studies and the graduate director for the Department of Theological Studies at Loyola Marymount University. He teaches in the area of Christian spirituality. He earned his Ph.D. in Christian spirituality from the Graduate Theological Union in 1988 and his M.A. in theology from Oxford University in 1980. His primary research interests are in the areas of ancient Christian monasticism, the relationship between spirituality and the natural world, and spiritual writing.

Martin Calkins is assistant professor in the College of Management at the University of Massachusetts Boston. He earned a Ph.D. in management from the University of Virginia, M.Div. and Th.M. degrees in theology from the Weston School of Theology, and an M.I.M. in international management from the American Graduate School of International Management. His academic interests include moral theory (in particular, casuistry and virtue theory) as well as contemporary international business issues such as international codes, whistleblowing, sweatshop, and the impact of computer and Internet technologies on societies.

Paul F. Camensich, professor of religious studies, emeritus, taught at DePaul University for thirty-seven years, where he served as chair of the Religious

Studies Department and held other college and university positions. Working primarily in the areas of business, medical and other professional ethics, he authored one volume on professional ethics, numerous academic articles, book chapters and shorter items. He also edited two other volumes. He holds degrees from Centre College of Kentucky, Yale University Divinity School, and Princeton University.

Ronald Duska, Ph.D., has held the Charles Lamont Post Chair of Ethics and the Professions at the American College since 1996. The post chair supports research and studies of the social responsibilities and ethical challenges facing business. He also is the director of the Center for Ethics in Financial Services at the college. Professor Duska has recently authored two books, *The Ethics of Accounting* and *Ethics for the Financial Services Professional*.

Christine Firer-Hinze received her Ph.D. from the University of Chicago. Following fifteen years at Marquette University, she is currently on the faculty in the Department of Theology at Fordham University. She specializes in theological ethics with a focus upon foundational questions in Christian social ethics, Catholic social thought, and political and economic ethics.

Kenneth E. Goodpaster has taught philosophy at the University of Notre Dame and business administration at Harvard University. He currently teaches at the University of St. Thomas in Minnesota where he holds the Koch Endowed Chair in Business Ethics.

Christopher Gryzen was a student of Dr. Robin Klay at the time of the publication of the article, "Six Economic Myths Heard from the Pulpit."

Stewart W. Herman received his Ph.D. from the University of Chicago Divinity School and teaches in the religion department at Concordia College. Books related to business ethics include *Durable Goods: A Covenantal Ethic for Management and Employees*; *Spiritual Goods: Faith Traditions and the Practice of Business* (edited with Arthur Gross Schaefer) and *International Businesses and the Challenges of Poverty in the Developing World: Case Studies on Global Responsibilities and Practices* (edited with Frederick Bird).

Harvey S. James is currently an assistant professor in the Department of Agricultural Economics at the University of Missouri–Columbia, where he is affiliated with the Agribusiness Research Institute. He is also a senior fellow at the Contracting and Organizations Research Institute.

Robin Klay graduated from Whitman College with a major in economics, after which she completed a Ph.D. at Princeton. She spent three years teaching and doing research in Cameroon. Klay's principle area of research and publication regards the connections between Christian faith and practice and economic theory and policy. Her book, *Counting the Cost: The Economics of Christian Stewardship*, has been used in many colleges as a supplement to standard introductory economics textbooks. Klay has published articles in *The Christian Century*, *Perspectives*, *Faith and Economics*, and *Markets and Morality*. She is especially interested in issues involving international trade and economic development, and is engaged in efforts to communicate with lay audiences about the benefits of markets and trade—for reasons of both efficiency and Christian values.

Daryl Koehn holds the Cullen Chair of Business Ethics at the University of St. Thomas in Houston, Texas. She has a Ph.D. in ethics (University of Chicago), an MBA in finance (Northwestern University), and a BA in philosophy (University of Chicago) and in philosophy, politics, and economics (Oxford University). She has written many articles on ethics and six books—*Trust in Business: Barriers and Bridges*; *The Ground of Professional Ethics*; *Corporate Governance: Ethics across the Board*; *Rethinking Feminist Ethics*; *Local Insights, Global Ethics for Business*; and *The Nature of Evil*.

M. D. Litonjua is professor of sociology at the College of St. Joseph in Cincinnati, Ohio. He holds licentiates in philosophy and theology from the University of Santo Tomas (Manila), a Ph.D. in sociology from Brown University, and an MBA from the University of Missouri at St. Louis. Professor Litonjua has published two books: *Liberation Theology: The Paradigm Shift, and Structures of Sin* and *Cultures of Meaning: Social Science and Theology*.

Dennis McCann is the Wallace M. Alston Professor of Bible and Religion at Agnes Scott College in Atlanta/Decatur, Georgia, where he teaches in the fields of religious social ethics, comparative religious ethics, philosophy of religion, and Catholic studies. McCann received his STL in theology from the Gregorian University in Rome in 1971 and a Ph.D. in theology from the University of Chicago Divinity School in 1976. McCann has had extensive academic experience in Hong Kong, China, and other countries in East Asia. In 1998, McCann was the Au Yeung King Fong University Fellow at the Centre for Applied Ethics at Hong Kong Baptist University, where he did research on East Asian business ethics within the framework of comparative religious ethics. Currently, Dr. McCann is the Fulbright Scholar in Residence at the Hong Kong America Center (2005–2006), and Visiting Professor in the Department of Management at Chinese University of Hong Kong.

Laura L. Nash, Ph.D., is senior lecturer on the faculty of Harvard Business School specializing in values and ethical influences on business leadership, corporate culture, and fundamental notions of success. A member of the Entrepreneurial Management unit, she teaches in the executive and MBA programs at HBS on critical dimensions of lasting success, personal values, and work/life choices.

Farhad Rassekh is a professor of economics in the Barney School of Business of the University of Hartford. He holds a Ph.D. in economics from the University of Houston, Houston and an M.A. in economics from the University of North Texas.

David M. Schilling is program director for the Interfaith Center on Corporate Responsibility, a coalition of 275 Catholic, Jewish, and Protestant organizations. For ten years, David has worked with ICCR members and associates on a range of global corporate accountability issues including human rights and labor rights in the contract supplier system. David, a United Methodist minister, has participated in delegations to Mexico, El Salvador, Honduras, Indonesia, Thailand, Turkey, Vietnam, and China visiting factories and meeting with workers and nongovernmental organizations. He currently is a member of the Coalition for Justice in the Maquiladoras; the International Advisory Network of the Business and Human Rights Resource Centre, chaired by Mary Robinson, former United Nations High Commissioner for Human Rights; and the Global Reporting Initiative's Advisory Group on Human Rights. David was a member of the Independent Monitoring Working Group for six years, which supported independent monitors at Gap supplier factories in El Salvador, Honduras, and Guatemala and was a member of President Clinton's Anti-Sweatshop Task Force. Rev. Schilling graduated from Carroll College, Union Theological Seminary, Columbia University (International Fellows Program) and received an advanced professional studies degree from Pacific School of Religion in Berkeley, California.

Gerry Shishin Wick Roshi is president and spiritual leader of Great Mountain Zen Center in Lafayette, Colorado. He is a Dharma Successor of Taizan Maezumi Roshi in both major lineages of Zen, having received transmission from Maezumi Roshi in 1990 after twenty-four years of Zen training under Maezumi, Shunryu Suzuki Roshi, and Sochu Suzuki Roshi. He administered the Zen Center of Los Angeles and the Kuroda Institute for the Study of Buddhism and Human Values for eight years, from 1978 to 1986. He has also been a technical manager in the software industry. He founded the Great Mountain Zen Center in 1996.

Robert C. Solomon is a specialist in the philosophy of emotions, business ethics, and post-Kantian continental philosophy, he has also published extensively on ethics and the history of philosophy. His more than forty books include *The Passions; In the Spirit of Hegel; From Hegel to Existentialism; Continental Philosophy Since 1750; Ethics and Excellence; The Joy of Philosophy; A Better Way to Think about Business; Living with Nietzsche; Spirituality for the Skeptic; Not Passion's Slave;* and *In Defense of Sentimentality.* He regularly consults and provides programs in business ethics for corporations and organizations around the world.

David Vogel received his Ph.D. from Princeton University in politics and is currently the Solomon Lee Professor of Business Ethics at the Haas School of Business and professor of political science at the University of California, Berkeley. He also is the editor of the *California Management Review.*